THE EVOLVING SCIENCE OF MANAGEMENT

Edited by Melvin Zimet and Ronald G. Greenwood

THE
EVOLVING
SCIENCE OF
MANAGEMENT

*The Collected Papers of Harold Smiddy
and Papers by Others in His Honor*

*A Publication of
The Manhattan College School of Business*

 A Division of
AMERICAN MANAGEMENT ASSOCIATIONS

Library of Congress Cataloging in Publication Data
Main entry under title:

The Evolving science of management.

    Includes index.
    1. Management—Addresses, essays, lectures.
2. Smiddy, Harold F. I. Smiddy, Harold F. II. Zimet,
Melvin. III. Greenwood, Ronald G.
HD31.E86   658.4   79-15784
ISBN 0-8144-5552-2

First Printing

In Commemoration
of the
Fiftieth Anniversary

School of Business
Manhattan College
1978

Foreword

Who builds a church to God and not to fame,
will never mark the marble with his name.
                                    Alexander Pope

Harold Smiddy has never "marked" the title page of a book with his name, yet he has truly "built" a philosophy of management that has been profound in its impact on management thought and practice. More interested in "building" than in developing his own fame, Harold Smiddy has nonetheless been prolific in his thinking, his unpublished writings, his professional activities, and his public speaking. It is only fitting, therefore, in order to mark the fiftieth anniversary of the School of Business of Manhattan College, that we serve the world of management by collecting the unpublished works of this man of managerial genius, who has served the school so well for many of its 50 years. It is also appropriate that we call on the leading management thinkers of our day, giants in their own right, and all friends and colleagues of Harold Smiddy, to contribute original essays on some aspect of management theory.

The purpose of this book, then, is twofold: to assemble the works of Harold Smiddy and other luminaries on the forefront of management thought into a compendium on the general theme of "The Evolving Science of Management," and to pay tribute to the man who has inspired and helped so many. It is in Harold Smiddy's honor, therefore, that this book was compiled.

As the general chairman of the Advisory Council of the School of

Business, Harold used his interest, support, wisdom, and untiring efforts to make major contributions to the progress of the school. It was a professional privilege and personal pleasure to be one of his colleagues and friends. Never did I turn to him for help, either as dean or as friend, and not received that help in abundance. Harold was a guiding light in assembling this book, making suggestions, reviewing ideas, offering names of potential authors, working on the format and structure. All this he graciously did despite the grave illness and frustrating blindness that he bore with saintlike patience. It is our hope that this work provided a life-prolonging interest for him; it is our regret that he died before "seeing" the finished book.

Acknowledgments for an undertaking of this magnitude are extensive and include but are not limited to the co-editors of this work, Dr. Melvin Zimet and Dr. Ronald Greenwood, for their professionalism and enormous efforts in making the book a reality; to the colleagues of Harold Smiddy for their contributions of original articles; to the administration of Manhattan College for its support of the project; to the General Electric Foundation for its generous funding for the project; to the American Management Associations for its publishing involvement; to Lois Smiddy, Harold's wife, for her assistance, interest, support, and, above all, her graciousness; and, of course, ultimately, to the man who provided the raison d'être for this book, Harold Smiddy.

ROBERT F. VIZZA
Dean, School of Business
Manhattan College
Riverdale, N.Y.

Preface

As the nation emerged from World War II, one aspect of its surging vitality was a widening interest in the theory and practice of management.

We can remember that it was a period of conversion from war production; of pent-up demand for civilian goods and services; of limitless frontiers to technological advances; of an unstable world order where opportunities were matched in amplitude only by their risks; of people readjusting the order of their personal lives. In a word, an exciting world.

To no less an extent all organizations, both large and small, were subject to that same current of excitement, in anticipation of a new era. They needed to examine how they managed themselves; how they prepared to define and meet the challenges of their future; and how to understand and apply the best in theory, concepts, and practice to their own strategy structure and operating effectiveness.

One of the organizations that stepped up to that challenge was the General Electric Company. For some years Ralph J. Cordiner had been quietly examining the whole area, under the direction of the then chief executive officer, Charles E. ("Electric Charlie") Wilson. The company had become very large and had diversified into many industries and markets; it was foreseen that it could soon become unmanageable in its centralized form.

When Cordiner moved into the CEO post in 1950, he instituted the process of decentralizing ("divisionalizing") the corporation; and Harold Smiddy was the indefatigable formulator and spokesman for the underlying concepts of management that would be necessary to the conversion of the monolithic corporate structure and to the growth in sales that the marketing-oriented Ralph Cordiner envisioned for its many businesses.

A central theme to those concepts—one that Smiddy kept hammering home throughout the ensuing years—was this: the work of managing is a distinct and professional kind of work; and the role of the professional manager is one of leading by persuasion rather than by command, blending thought and action through planning, organizing, integrating, and measuring.

Harold Smiddy published little in his own name. He employed three other primary means of communication of his essentially prescriptive approach.

The first means was the formulation and publishing by the company of a series of volumes (the "Blue Books," so-named after the color of the GE monogram) on company history, company organization, the work of the professional manager, and the work of the functional individual contributor. These volumes embodied much of his thinking and insights and those of others who worked with him throughout the late forties and the fifties.*

A second means of communication and education was the establishment in 1956 of the General Electric Management Institute at Croton-on-Hudson, New York—widely known as Crotonville. This adjunct to the whole decentralization program was regarded as essential to its ultimate success. Thirteen-week in-resident executive education programs were conducted almost year-round. Between 1956 and 1961 practically every senior person in the company had attended its Advanced Management Course. Not only did it promulgate company doctrine, but many renowned outside speakers were brought in to help foster small group discussions around major societal issues. In addition, a research arm continuously explored frontier ideas in management.

Harold Smiddy's third means of communication were the many talks he gave both within the company and to many professional societies and special conferences. He was widely read, and personally in touch with a limitless number of thinkers in the field of management and organization philosophy. His special talent in his talks was in drawing these strands of thinking together, not hesitating to quote where a quote helped to enrich an idea.

---

* The original editions have long been out of print. However, special-order reprints are available from the Hive Press, Eaton, Pennsylvania.

This volume for the first time pulls together in one place selections from many of Harold Smiddy's talks—his "remarks," as he liked to call them—that were hitherto available only in unpublished form. The flavor of the man comes through. Those who have heard him, recall his racing mind—the words tumbling out, a table beside him loaded with books to which he referred constantly during the talk and in the following discussion.

Here you can see one of those epochal thinker–practitioners who were setting the stage in the 1950s for the burgeoning of managerial literature and development of thought that have taken place since then. Yet with all the new insights and new ways of expressing them, one can sense an unbroken thread of thought back to many of the precepts that Smiddy expressed. Perhaps, these days, we have become cleverer. I don't think we are any wiser.

ARTHUR A. FICKEL *

* Before his retirement in 1976, Arthur Fickel was manager of the Executive Education Operation, Management Development Institute, General Electric Company, Croton-on-Hudson, New York.

Contents

Part II
THE EVOLVING SCIENCE OF MANAGEMENT

Part I

THE SEARCH FOR A SCIENCE OF MANAGEMENT

The Collected Papers of Harold Smiddy

Ronald G. Greenwood

1
Introduction

Very few men of his generation have had greater impact on management than Harold F. Smiddy. Although Harold Smiddy was a scholar and philosopher, he was first and foremost a manager. His individual concept of management is legendary at the General Electric Company. He was best known by his peers and co-workers (he detested the word subordinates) for his sincerity, dedication, unlimited drive, comprehension, vision, and especially for his ability to develop the potentialities of others. He spent countless hours with many young managers and provided those who were willing to pay the demanding price for success with opportunity. He never failed to sense the need to give a challenging idea or assurance to someone who was not quite aware of the need himself.

Harold F. Smiddy demanded total dedication to meeting deadlines. During his days at General Electric's 570 Lexington Avenue "Ivory Tower" his emphasis was heaviest on managerial research and organization structuring. Yet all his managers and consultants knew that no excuse was acceptable for failing to meet the due date for any report or project. Those who worked with him during that period still recall some of his verbal urging.

"The time for laboratory testing is over. I enjoy study, research, and testing as much as anyone, but if you wait for all the questions to be answered the project will never get out of the lab." "The best testing ground for lab work is at the customer level." "I never met a researcher who was willing to let a study go. He will always find a

3

reason to keep on researching." "There comes a time when the research, to date, should be tested in operational practice. If you can't be practical, *I* can't use *you*."

Harold never had to remind anyone of a target date. No one dared not meet it and Smiddy knew it. To illustrate the point: One of his managers has a vivid recollection of receiving instructions from Harold late one Friday night to provide a cleanly typed, hardcover preliminary draft of Book I of the *Professional Management* series by Monday at 1:00 P.M. so that he could hand it to Ralph Cordiner.

Harold's penmanship was never a strong point and he handed me several hundred of his handwritten pages, all of which were further covered by his own marginal notations. It looked like a well-used scratch pad.

At exactly 1:00 P.M. Monday I delivered my finished work to him. He was on the elevator on his way up to Mr. Cordiner's office. Remember, I had not seen or communicated with Harold since Friday evening, and I still feel certain that he never had a doubt but that he would have the report on time. I had been so busy that the thought never entered my mind until after the work was completed that there had been a possibility that he wouldn't have it on time.

Harold was a compulsive reader. With his enormous retentive powers he was able to absorb up to several hundreds of pages of information each and every day. Yet his mind was so active, so completely filled with diverse ideas gleaned from a combination of his reading and his very creative, analytical mind that he really could not listen without taking over the conversation. He would then literally express, with machine-gun rapidity, a library of knowledge on the subject. If you wanted him to "listen," your safest recourse was the written word. Every man has a weakness and overlong listening was not his forte.

Charles Agemain, at one time executive vice-president of Chase Manhattan Bank, had heard of Harold Smiddy's mind, which some people even thought of as equivalent to one of General Electric's original computers. He decided to put that concept to the test by directing a luncheon conversation with Harold into a field that he suspected would force Harold into the role of listener.

Charlie, as he was called by close associates, was one of Chase's most articulate and knowledgeable bankers. He relates that Harold took that conversation concerning the financial condition of Brazil and its long-range future down avenues that caused him to feel that Harold Smiddy either had the greatest mind in the world or had spent a lifetime in the field of international money management.

Harold was a tough-minded executive. Unwittingly, he sometimes instilled unwarranted fear among his peers and, unfortunately, in many who worked for him. A former Smiddy employee recalls,

Early in my relationship with Harold I knew that there were few men who deserved this criticism less. I recall telling him about a young man whom he hardly knew who was stricken with leukemia. Harold personally obtained and paid for medical specialists and private room facilities for this young man, who had worked in General Electric's Management Consultation Services for only a very short time. No one knew that Harold had done this but I did, because I was in his office when he made the telephone burn. His request to me was, "Let's not talk about this." He didn't want people to know that he was a concerned, warmhearted man who took on nasty problems.

Harold's perfectionist ideals caused some to conclude—wrongly—that he was unreasonable and intolerant. If unwavering convictions and constancy in his beliefs made him "intolerant," it was because of his devotion to a philosophy and its inherent concepts that he did not want endangered or misrepresented. He was tough and firm, but fair and loyal to his beliefs and to those who worked with him to present convincing results.

What Harold could tolerate is not really known, of course. He was severely critical of mistakes. He expected order and neatness in those who worked with him, and in their office environments. Their personal appearance and all work that resulted from being a part of his organization had to meet these criteria.

Harold was work-oriented and demanded that those working with him devote full time and energy to their jobs. He believed in the doctrine of completed work. He always gave his people all the tools needed to do a job, including full authority to make decisions commensurate with their responsibility, but he accepted no excuse for anything short of the best they were capable of giving. If it did not represent a person's very best effort, he didn't want the report. He felt that reports should be attractively completed—perfect in form and arrangement. "The man who can write clearly and logically must present those matters of substance in the same way—without errors."

Harold disapproved of decisionmaking committees. He was responsible for Cordiner's decision to discontinue them. He was adamant against "assistants" and "assistants to" with similar results. Other words deleted from General Electric's definition of a manager were "coordinate," "coordinators," and "liaison." "A liaison man is one who is placed between two men who are paid to work together." Harold would have none of that idea.

The respect he received from fellow managers was great, but even those who did not know of his managerial ability were drawn to him, albeit for other reasons. Although he and his wife, Lois, did not have children of their own, Harold could and would adopt any and all. He was never too busy to fix the boy's bicycle next door or help build a "camp" in the outer garden or explain a problem in a textbook. He was a born teacher, so gifted at it that children—and adults, for that matter—didn't realize they were being taught. He was "Smiddy" to his neighbors in Frankfort, in upstate New York, where he frequently spent his summers. Harold Smiddy was always besieged with requests for favors because people felt, quite correctly, that he could do anything. He would usually accept any request, promise twice as much as requested, and deliver twice again that amount.

Peter F. Drucker claimed that the godfather to his now-classic *The Practice of Management* was Harold F. Smiddy. There are no books extant with Smiddy's name listed as author. Still, a number of books were produced under his leadership. The four-volume set of *Professional Management in General Electric* was mostly penned under his direction. Every word in those books was either written by Harold Smiddy or approved by him, and the books have the stamp of his philosophy. Although they were technically team-produced the concepts in them are a thinking through of what can be called the Smiddy philosophy of management.

Smiddy also edited the three-volume set of Harry Hopf's work, entitled *Some Classic Contributions to Professional Managing*. In addition, he wrote countless articles and speeches for the president of General Electric. These are still quoted often as outstanding contributions to the work of managing.

The reputation that the General Electric Company enjoys today in the field of manager development stems back to the many volumes Harold Smiddy produced. These books served as the very foundation for the Crotonville Management Institute. Prior to Smiddy's contributions in this field General Electric had no component working on research and development in manager development. Today it leads the field.

In *Professional Management in General Electric* (four published volumes and one unpublished), Harold Smiddy developed the philosophy of management for the General Electric Company. It is the first well-documented philosophy for any corporate structure.

The series was meant not only to set the corporate philosophy down on paper but also to be used as a guide on how to manage, to help further the study of management, and to help organize the investigation of the practice so as to upgrade understanding through greater in-depth reasoning. The *Professional Management* series forced a logical analysis/thinking through of both the work of a manager and that of an "individual contributor." This thinking through led to the conclusion that management is leadership through inspiration and persuasion.

Harold Smiddy's biography is an example of success achieved by natural brilliance, hard work, and pragmatist vision, of a rare combination of philosopher and practitioner. Harold Francis Smiddy was born on June 3, 1900, in Southborough, Mass., and lived there during his youth. He entered the Massachusetts Institute of Technology when he was sixteen and received his bachelor's degree eight days after his twentieth birthday.

After graduation Smiddy joined the Public Service Electric Company of Newark, New Jersey, as a cadet engineer and a year later he became service engineer for the West Penn Power Company of Pittsburgh. He advanced rapidly, and was made assistant to the vice-president in 1927 and operating manager in 1928. In 1930 he transferred to Electric Bond and Share Company of New York, first as assistant to the vice-president of the operating department and later as assistant to the executive vice-president.

In 1935 Smiddy became head of the sales department for Ebasco Services, operating sponsor for the South Central region, and a director of the parent organization, Electric Bond and Share Company. Shortly before World War II he joined the consulting firm of Booz, Allen and Hamilton and in 1944 he was made a general partner. Smiddy opened both its New York and San Francisco offices.

It was through his work at Booz, Allen and Hamilton that Smiddy's ability was recognized by Charles Wilson, president of the General Electric Company, and by Ralph Cordiner in particular. Cordiner was about to begin a reorganization study for the company, a truly awesome undertaking, and he perceived clearly the need for acquiring the services of Harold Smiddy to manage its research, development, and implementation at an early date.

Wilson and Cordiner persuaded Smiddy to join GE as a consultant on President Wilson's staff in 1948. He became a vice-president in 1948, heading both the chemical department in Pittsfield, Massachusetts, and the air conditioning department in Bloomfield, New

Jersey. Ralph Cordiner at that time became Wilson's assistant and heir apparent to the president, scheduled to succeed him in 1951. One of his first appointments after Cordiner became president of General Electric was to make Harold vice-president of the management consultation services division, a position he held until his retirement in 1961. It was in this post that his true genius was to surface, as the architect of the decentralization plan, philosophy, and ultimate structure General Electric adopted and uses today.

As vice-president of management consultation services, Smiddy organized the first operations research and synthesis department known in private industry and the first major formal executive development training center still continuing outside of academia, the Crotonville Human Resources Training Center (originally called The Management Research and Development Institute).

Harold Smiddy always felt close to young people and spent many hours each year speaking to college students here and abroad. One trip to England included talks to over 20 business schools and college groups. He served as a trustee to Ithaca College, as general chairman of the Council of Advisors at Manhattan College for 25 years, and as honorary professor of management at Columbia in his retired years.

Smiddy was also a long-time member of the International Academy of Management; a fellow of the American Academy of Management, serving as president in 1963; and director of the Council for International Progress in Management; and he was active in numerous other organizations. Among the many distinguished awards he received, perhaps three management honors should be mentioned—The Taylor Key (Society for the Advancement of Management, 1953), Gantt Medal (American Society of Mechanical Engineers, 1957), and Wallace Clark Medal (Comité Internationale de l'Organization Scientifique, 1957). He was given honorary degrees, as well, from Manhattan and Ithaca colleges.

After his retirement from the General Electric Company, Harold continued to carry a Herculean workload, being in great demand as a management consultant. He was elected president of the American Academy of Management for 1963, which is especially noteworthy because of the recognition this predominantly academic body was bestowing.

As a thinker and a doer, Smiddy had a profound influence on management theory and practice. This is an editing of the collected thoughts of a very important person of our time.

2
The Search
for a "Science
of Managing"

The story of the search for a "science of managing" can be traced through modern industrial history much like stories of exploits in the world of physical adventure. Both show very similar characteristics when divorced from the actions required by the context or nature of the objective. Planning, organizing, integrating, measuring, exercising judgment, decisionmaking in the face of risk—risk itself—all are part of both the intellectual and the physical search of men for something new.

Yet there is a significant difference in what men do in their attempts to create new vision; and that lies in the purposes for which the exploration is undertaken. But, to make the prize worthy of the winning, there must, for men willing to accept perils and defeats, be reason and purposes in the ultimate objective of the search, which go deeper even than the search itself. There has been this kind of dedicated and intensive search for understanding of the principles and precepts of scientific managing.

Originally titled "Present Status of the Work of Managing." Presented at the second annual convention of the Institute of Management Sciences, October 20, 1955, New York.

9

This chapter will establish the basic meaning of a science of management; and thereby reveal the intent that has guided the steps of many who have chosen to search through the complex of social, political, and economic variables that both describe the direction in which understanding may be found and inhibit the progress toward it.

Principle of Organization

At the root of the intense activity of management scientists there has been a search for order. It has been unnamed until recent years, and yet, viewing the clearly marked paths along which the science has developed, we can be sure it has been the invisible and often unrecognized guide that has brought us to our present level of understanding.

The principles of effective and productive managing as we understand them today are basically the outgrowth of our historical attempts to sense the patterns and structures by which the complexities of modern social relationships can be viewed rationally. The conflict of incompatible drives which Bolitho described concerns man himself, and yet suggests that there is no real choice—that men must continue to choose adventure—because society presents a conflict which challenges survival itself.

In his ably written book, *The Biology of the Spirit*, Edmund W. Sinnott, dean of Yale's Graduate School, defines this challenge as the search for the principle of organization. He writes, of course, of the biological order of the world, and yet there is a meaning which penetrates into every kind of social and physical complex when he says:

There seem to be in nature two opposing streams—the tendency toward organization and goal-seeking, and the tendency toward chance and randomness. The upward purposeful thrust of life, which continually opposes the downward drag of matter, is evidence, I think, that in nature there is something that we may call—to name what never can be put in words—a Principle of Organization.

Not only does it lift man ever higher but it provides three great essentials for his religion—it brings order out of randomness, spirit out of matter, and personality out of neutral and impersonal stuff.

As significant, perhaps, as these words themselves is the implied rejection that would flow from such views of the traditional hypothesis of physical scientists that the evolution of plant and animal life from single cell to complex organism has been a matter solely of chance situations and random development. Otherwise, acceptance of a theory of organization and progress by accident could only lead into an endless jungle of increasing intellectual disorder and rapidly attenuating understanding.

The history of social philosophy, with its emphasis on the spiritual and intellectual concept of man as a being in search of some sort of rational foundation for his presence, has been directed toward discerning and interpreting those patterns of order, which are believed to exist necessarily beneath the superficial layer of normally experienced turmoil.

As the physical sciences probe deeper into the visible, sensible, and demonstrable characteristics of the world, they are being brought—sometimes literally dragged by their heels—into a recognition of an encompassing, universal direction which, beyond explanation itself, yet is necessary to explain the endless interlocking and correlation of the endless variety of phenomena observed.

It is, I suggest, this mating of the physical sciences with those kinds of speculation, which attempt to sense causes beyond pragmatic physical data, that reveals the true search of people for patterns of order by which they may govern their lives and in which they may find personal peace and security of deeper than merely economic significance.

MANAGING THROUGH PATTERNS OF ORDER

"Managing," in such a world, needs to be the kind of science that is dedicated to bring into being in the affairs of men the kind of order that nature exhibits all about us.

The basic problem in lifting a science of managing to its highest value as a contributive social philosophy lies within the unchanging nature of man in a rapidly changing world. It is satisfying to think of ourselves as advancing on the evolutionary ladder, yet whatever advances we have made in intellectual capacity or emotional stability, we have been repeatedly outstripped by the even faster multiplication of the complexities of civilization.

Each new bit of understanding about our physical world—each technological discovery—is immediately ramified into an endless series of possibilities that have first to be searched out and then to be integrated both into the thread of individual life and into the fabric of living together as people.

The science of managing, therefore, needs to deal primarily in the systems of a countervailing *pattern of simplicity;* that is, the systems of bringing rational order into the organizations by which men accomplish work. Managers are the scientists of managing; they must know, communicate, and gain acceptance of the need for, and validity of, such simplifications by the men whose work they are managing.

The processes of simplification need to be kept in pace and in balance with complicating developments, for it is in this way that, as Zay Jeffries put it, "individuals with essentially fixed ability can expect to go forward indefinitely without becoming casualties of their own complexity."

The Basis for an Acceptable Science of Managing

An acceptable science of managing thus must have roots far deeper than those needed simply to manipulate the day-to-day processes of society or of business to achieve apparently favorable results. Good and evil are intransient values, unchanging in their essence with the changing times, and that which is created by men to be lasting needs always to be measured against this permanent scale.

The science of managing must be based upon, and adhere to, those conceptual patterns which—like those of the great religions of the world—have the power to arouse the faith and win and hold the vital support of individual men and women throughout the ages.

It needs, therefore, to rise above the sources of its principles, above the "social matrix" that otherwise would determine and circumscribe its opportunity to observe, to analyze, and to act upon the needs created by the matrix. Without doubt, methods that seem practical and that seem to cope with the problems of the day often develop well without reference to philosophical considerations. And yet there are within them the seeds of disaster, for they are, at their best, curative without being preventative in nature.

"Does it work?" consequently falls short of the question men need to ask about the processes they apply to living. Indeed, it can only be answered with, "It *seems* to." The science of managing, if it is to rise above the level of a repetitive art, must seek more basic answers. It needs to ask, and to reply with confidence to, those questions that strike to the very core of valid action and consequent progress. Not, I suggest, "Does it work?" but rather, "*Why* does it work?"; and "What far-reaching value is there in its working?" or "Is it right?"

THE NEED FOR ACTION

We live in a coursing and sometimes seemingly erratic world. Yet we know that the changes once characterized by Fenton Turek as the "American Explosion" are necessarily the result of social, political, economic, or technological advances that we can learn to recognize, and whose effects we can anticipate with increasing skill.

In order for the science of management to move out of the bower of academic speculation and into a position in which its principles can be brought more effectively to bear in the structuring of our social organizations—including, by the way, the business or industrial enterprise—I would suggest that it must meet two general conditions.

First, it needs to evolve from the basic concept of man as an individual who gathers with his fellow men for accomplishment and for economic profit and security, but at the same time also for the satisfaction of intellectual and spiritual hungers, without losing his individual identity.

Second, it needs to present a set of principles and a method that are directed toward the establishment and maintenance of social order, and yet stimulate the society to grow and to progress.

The problem in the first instance is to develop an understanding of managing as a science of universal applicability that can ultimately be related to every kind of work in every area of collective effort. It is unnecessary to couch our terms within the particular limits of the business world itself, for managing is a science that needs to be applied wherever work is to be done, and wherever men value their independence and freedom.

In the second instance, the science of management needs to deal with the world as it is, and to measure its accomplishments in terms of the changes it is able to effect in the face of those developments that constantly re-form the foundations upon which progress can be built. Above all, it needs to develop insight into its own processes and modify them as the changing structure of society creates requirements for different emphasis and action. I have quoted these words of Ortega y Gasset many times, and yet I think they are worth repeating many times more:

Life cannot wait until the sciences may have explained the universe scientifically. We cannot put off living until we are ready. The most salient characteristic of life is its coerciveness; it is always urgent, "here and now," without any possible postponement.

In sum, the science of management has to be a practical as well as a valid discipline. That is, it must be one dealing with situations as they are found by applying known principles based on the inferences of experience and observation to the very limit of our ability to understand and interpret them.

Now, before turning to some specific ideas on the science of management, I would like to review the current status of the work of managing in America. Here again, we are faced with the need to summarize in a very brief fashion a set of conditions and relationships that are worth an entire book in their own right.

I will touch upon what I see in the status of managerial work with regard to only three, but a significant three, of its characteristic aspects today; namely, objectives, organization, and manpower planning.

Business and Its Objectives

With regard to the setting of business objectives by its managers, business—as it has passed from the proprietor to the corporate stage as the major vehicle for its operations—has made significant and accelerating progress. Managers have learned to do a better balanced job in selecting both fair, economic profit objectives and, at the same time, collateral objectives reflecting the overall social relationships and responsibilities of business so that it may make the soundest contributions in the interest of customers and the public, as well as of investors, employees, and suppliers.

They have similarly learned to achieve better balance between short-range objectives and long-range objectives; giving due regard to the continuity of tenure of the corporate business beyond the life of particular generations of managers, employees, customers, or investors.

Progress in such respects was both stimulated and achieved because of unusually severe economic conditions in the thirties and of global war pressures for production and for public-spirited goals in

the forties. It is pertinent that such progress has been most outstanding in the United States where competitive enterprise has been the order of the day and where research and technological innovations have been most widely sought and accepted.

It is noteworthy also that, in such progress, leaders in large and small enterprises alike have moved in parallel with each other in pursuit of both broader and more comprehensive business objectives. The ever-widening interest in manager education and the multiplying participation in greatly expanded management and professional society activities and programs have given visible evidence of such fundamentally satisfying trends.

Coupled with such strides, and overshadowing slowness to adopt such kinds of goals and viewpoints by some current managers, has been the steadily mounting number of business leaders and organizers who have recognized—and publicly professed—that, as Norbert Wiener put it, in the face of today's radical changes "the statesmanship of management cannot stop at the edge of the individual firm."

The strength, the continued growth, and the profitable operation of a single business is now a matter that typically concerns a wider field than that business alone. The broad base of public share-owner participation that constitutes the ownership of the characteristic major modern business, the growth of investment per unit of output that distinguishes this era of increasing mechanization and automation, and the need to link many kinds of processes, steady jobs, and operations together smoothly for the profitable, yet stable and continuing, production of products and services call for objectives set in the light of voluntarily accepted public responsibility and designed to fulfill complex social obligations.

And it is in precisely these directions and these respects that leading American business managers are constantly strengthening their planning and their pursuit of broader, longer-range business objectives to achieve soundest continuing balance among customer, investor, employee, supplier, and public interests.

BUSINESS AND ITS ORGANIZATION

The status of management thinking and action with regard to the problems of organization is, I think, even brighter. Perhaps the pressures are more immediate than in the case of planning of objectives;

or perhaps it is simply that courses of action are more easily derived from obvious situations.

Whatever the causes, however, it is certain that great progress has been made in the design, staffing, and constant dynamic improvement of organizational structures that answer simultaneously the needs of the individual for recognition and for clear assignment of authority, and of the enterprise for productive and profitable operation.

The growing pattern of product diversification makes it important for alert managers to continue so to review the structure of their businesses, to look hard at the work to be done and the resources available, and to rearrange and restate the relationships needed to keep the growing business flexible and dynamic, especially as to decisionmaking authority at the point where actions actually take place.

It is most important to approach such work in a creative and imaginative way, for particular tables and charts of organization, like family traditions, tend to be preserved too long after their usefulness is gone. The elements of the organization need to be related and combined both to support the present requirements of the business and also to be adaptable to progressive and constructive changes to meet future needs and demands. Because the organization structure is, in a very real sense, a model of the business itself, it is the continuing responsibility of the manager to maintain its validity.

Business and Its Manpower

We seem also to have made notably great advances recently in solving the problems of manpower planning. Studies of organizational theory have brought to light the total dependence of all projections with regard to business upon the assumption of both more, and more competent, managers on the one hand, and of more able, skilled, and resourceful individual workers on the other hand.

Our graduate schools working in the field of management or business administration are crowded, and an increasing number of industries are doing more practical thinking and taking more specific steps toward intensive, on-the-job education. There is an ever-growing number of full-dress adult educational programs within industry at the present time. There may very well be as many different approaches, too. However, to paraphrase George Orwell, they are all probably equally right, but some are just more equally right than others!

All of them, I'm sure, are based on essentially the same alternate concepts—that managing is both a distinct and a professional kind of work, that it is founded on principles that can be taught and can be learned, and that the needs of the enterprise can best be met by the most widespread extension of opportunity to individuals, whether they elect either of the "parallel paths" of working as managers or of working as individual contributors.

Differences or conflicts in the areas of manager education seem increasingly to be primarily those of method rather than of goals. Time, in its way, will blend the best of each into an ever more useful pattern for each.

In his book, *The Practice of Management,* Peter Drucker points out that:

The modern business enterprise for its survival needs to be able to recruit the ablest, best educated and most dedicated of young men into its service. To attract and to hold such men, a promise of a career, of a living, or of economic success is not enough. The enterprise must be able to give such men a vision and a sense of mission.

Surely our progress in this most essential field can be measured in terms of the vision that is imparted to men. For it is that, basically, which, freely and voluntarily shared today, will shape the designs of the future.

True Status Is Measured in Philosophical Concepts

These three elements—the objectives, the organization, and the man-power planning of business—strike me as typical of the many parts of the total picture of modern managerial work. If we can look at them together, and estimate their worth for good or bad, I think we should have a fair idea of the status of professional management.

On balance it is good, and the performance of recent years gives excellent reason to believe that we will progress with increasing speed and certainty in the years ahead. Yet, unless we are able to understand the ideas that nourish the roots of the work of managing, our assessment must remain directed primarily to method and to technique.

As indicated earlier, we need to look behind the simple processes of merely "efficient" managing and to ask ourselves, "Is it right, is it good, is it ethical, is it moral?" We, after all, are part of a social and a human organization that has, by its very nature, become more than a simple supplier of goods and services for profit alone, even though making a profit continues to be an essential mainspring of such an organization.

The influences of industry reach into the deepest foundations of our political and social, as well as of our economic, environment; and all are influenced at once by our ramifying and multiplying technology.

The questions that need to be answered include both whether there is a science of managing that is successful in the day-to-day operation of an organization and, simultaneously, whether there is one acceptable to people as a whole and contributive to their well-being both as customers and as citizen members of the overall public.

Many of us believe there is such a science, and, indeed, we find measurable added pleasure in our work just because we do so hold. Let me then, in much oversimplified form, mention ten points that I think are the essence of this faith and the reason for our support.* They will, perhaps, suggest an outline for a science of managing.

CONCEPTS OF MANAGEMENT

The Invariate Foundation

I spoke briefly before of the need for the science of managing to rise above its sources within the current social matrix. The *first* fundamental concept of this science is that it needs to be invariate—unchanged by either the area of its application or the climate in which it operates. It is, I think, clear that its values need to be established from and measured against some system of principles that, in themselves, are stable beyond the best transient status local society has achieved at any current moment.

This need is, after all, characteristic of all sciences, for they—each of them—need a recourse to primary standards. To be a science, rather than an art, managing needs to be developed in terms that can be stated, verified, taught, learned, and used with unvarying reliability, despite and in the face of impinging social pressures. It needs to be rooted in principles that themselves can be used both to test the

---

* These ten points are abbreviated here from a talk by the author on "The Changing Structure of Management," given at the December 1952 conference of the Management Division of the American Society of Mechanical Engineers.

validity of objectives and to mold the results of managerial work to approach these objectives fairly, efficiently, and profitably under whatever pressures are impinging.

Basic Principles

Second, a true science of managing, and the work of a professional manager that derives from it, will have to grow from seeds planted in:

The principles of liberty, rather than those of compulsion.
Of reason, rather than of force.
Of leadership by integration and by persuasion, rather than those of leadership by command, control, or dictation.

And yet, these principles are derivatives, and there is an even more fundamental kind of understanding that is needed to sustain the difficult work of professional managing. Really at the heart of it all, the science of managing needs to seek its strength from:

◇ The principles of morality, not the principles of materialism.
◇ The principles of religion, not the principles of atheism.
◇ The deep belief that the natural rights of the individual as a person—including the right to acquire and hold property—are of a different order of priority from all other rights and cannot be subverted or destroyed by the increasing complexity of the social relationships that involve those people and their natural rights.

Indeed, it is clear that the rights of society can only be created, and stably held, by the voluntary modification of individual liberties by the individuals themselves in recognition of a mutual need for security or benefit that can only be obtained by collective action rooted in such personal free will and choice.

The Principles of Relationship

The *third* point in the outline grows naturally out of a recognition of such need of individuals to establish collective institutions and relationships to achieve commonly held purposes and objectives.

Personal liberty can only be maintained when the permissive quality of such types of organizations is clearly recognized as resulting from such voluntary modification and interchange of personal rights. The science of managing, therefore, in order to deal effectively with structures so founded, necessarily needs to derive and to be developed from a correct understanding of these fundamental relationships.

The Right of Self-Determination

The *fourth* point is equally clear in its derivation from the basic principles of point two. When we acknowledge that the right to own—and hence to buy and sell—property is a natural right that cannot be abrogated, we then can come to understand the principle of free choice that is exercised by the customers in the marketplace.

The nature of our society, and of our business economy and its processes, is such as to offer only a choice of such rights of self-determination or the alternative of force and dictatorship. The ultimate question is still, as Bishop Fulton J. Sheen has put it, "whether man shall exist for the state or the state for man, and whether freedom is of the spirit or a concession of a materialized society."

The Common Interest

The *fifth* fundamental concept in the science of managing is established by a focal point of common interest among all members of society that arises from their common status as individual customers in the marketplace. Whether they are managers, engineers, employees, share owners, vendors, educators, clergymen, legislators, government officials—no matter what they are or what their separate place in society may be—this fact of being customers in common affords a focal point of common interest among them, about which a practical integration of their otherwise highly diverse capacities, interests, individual aspirations, and needs can be developed into a pattern of order designed for mutual progress, satisfaction, and security.

We tend, I think, too much to mistake "economic security" as the object of their search whereas, in truth, if such is to be achieved at all, it can only come from, and as the result of, an understanding and application of principles of order upon which it must depend for any permanence and that are, in fact, the true goal of the deepest individual yearnings.

The Legitimacy of Purpose and Authority

Certainly a true science of managing needs to be based on legitimate purpose and on legitimate authority. The *sixth* point for our consideration, therefore, is the relationship of such a science to its purposes and the legitimacy of managerial authority under such concepts.

The growth and strength of the economy as a result of the rightness of the objectives, policies, plans, and schedules of its institutions and enterprises constitute an acceptable purpose for the work of professional managers when—but probably only when—such an economy and the aims of its enterprises are built on the customer, and hence on the free market. In turn, building the economy, and its enterprises, on the customer, and hence on the free market, gives the managers of such enterprises, whatever their size or corporate form, that genuine legitimacy that flows from the common purposes of the leaders and the followers.

This is, at the same time, the true starting point from which managers may *plan* the operation of their enterprise or component of a business. Indeed, I suggest to you that it is the only point from which the processes of managing and the basic constituent elements of professional managerial work can begin to coalesce into patterns that have a validity, and a legitimacy of authority, as unvarying as the principles they serve.

The Work of a Professional Manager

These first six points have been presented to provide a foundation upon which the process of professional managing can be described and made rational. The *seventh* point deals then with the nature of the work of a professional manager, as a specific, distinctive occupation that flows from the need for leadership, based on blending thought and action in decisionmaking and on leading by persuasion rather than command, which is inherent in all kinds of social organizations.

There are four functional elements in the work of a professional manager. They are distinct in concept and yet the successful doing of each is intimately dependent upon the degree of perfection achieved simultaneously in the others. These work elements are planning, organizing, integrating, and measuring. Let's take just a moment to look at them more closely.

Planning, the united task just described in point six, needs to be done to set objectives and to outline plans and schedules, as well as policies or guides and canons, within which such objectives can be attained.

Organizing describes the total work needed to be done to achieve the designated objectives; to classify that work into a pattern or structure or orderly components, tasks, jobs, relationships, and structures; to assign men to such jobs, relationships, and structures in the most advantageous manner; and, finally, to make known and to have understood the authority, functional (work) relationship (teamwork) responsibilities and the accountabilities of all who will do the work.

Integrating is done to show the common purposes around which the efforts of individuals and components may be blended into a visible pattern of the total work. It is, in its effect, the creation of a climate in which both work and teamwork are accepted as voluntary personal responsibilities; and out of which an optimum flow, pace, and synchronism of effort results on the part of each individual and the group as a whole, and, finally, at every stage of the managing process.

Measuring gets, analyzes, and uses facts to devise and establish standards and systems of evaluating performance. Through this element of the work of a professional manager, a voluntary flow of two-way communication is facilitated so that, as a result, decisions may be made on the "authority of knowledge" rather than on that of rank or force.

And as facts flow from the measuring element of managerial work, they are in turn used to close the loop of the managing process by feeding back information to modify the continuing parallel elements of planning, organizing, and integrating, to modify and reaffirm or reform the assumptions and premises of these functions. And, indeed, measuring is also applied to itself to refine the techniques and standards of the measuring element of such managerial work.

The total work of a professional manager is, therefore, a closed-loop process that is capable of selective regeneration and continuing improvement. It thus results in an optimum approach to, and use of, the available human and material resources of the enterprise to attain its designated objectives economically, profitably, competitively, and on sound time schedules.

The Distinct Nature of Professional Managing

The *eighth* point is rather simple. We have come to a stage of understanding that allows us to talk beyond the general concepts of scientific management as such, and to describe with considerable detail the actual work of the scientific and professional manager. We have moved from viewing the container, in a sense, and are able to study and assess the things contained.

I believe it is clear that managing is a distinct kind of work. It is distinct not only in what it involves in comparison with other recognized functional kinds of work in a business, but also in the purposes and methods of its doing. Yet it is integrated with them to the twin ends of blending the efforts of all individuals in the enterprise smoothly with each other, and of fitting the enterprise itself harmoniously into the larger society of which it is a part.

The Span of Manageable Situations

Particularly notable, as the *ninth* point, is that such a science of managing incorporates inherently the seeds of solution of other types—possibly of all types—of troublesome problems that are part and parcel of the operation of a business enterprise.

Certainly within its framework, for example, there is the best opportunity to meet the challenges of problems imposed by the need to blend the efforts of both engineers and managers, of both "white collar" and manual workers, and, more fundamentally, of both leaders and followers.

The Principle of Self-Regeneration

And so we come finally to the *tenth* point in this suggested outline of a science of managing. It is the principle of self-regeneration, which we saw evidenced within the managing process itself, applied more broadly now to the total science in order that it may offer us a teachable "theory of managing" that has within itself great resources for absorption into itself of the best grist from the field of daily practice.

Managing necessarily has to be a dynamic activity related to the organic needs of the enterprise within the changing climate of social perceptions and anticipations. The principles of the science have been held to be invariate, and so, once discovered and defined, to be repetitively applicable.

What needs to be done is to measure that statement in terms of successive applications; and to feed back the resulting increase of understanding into the strengthening of the patterns of order and organization and ultimately to communicate such patterns with new clarity and persuasiveness into every part of the business enterprise.

It is doubly significant that, in the burgeoning fields of cybernetics and of operations research and synthesis, skillfully used together, we can cross new thresholds in measuring the elements of managerial work.

And it will be an era in which new data, new data-using techniques, and new electronic data-handling machines can progressively overcome past managerial limitations due to the inability to get and use, adequately and promptly, the facts genuinely needed to make sound managerial decisions.

THE PATH AHEAD

I suggest you think of these words by Dr. Alfred North Whitehead:

Animals wander into new conditions. They have to adapt themselves or die. Mankind has wandered from the trees to the plains, from the plains to the seacoast, from climate to climate, from continent to continent, and from habit of life to habit of life. When man ceases to wander he will cease to ascend in the scale of being.

Physical wandering is still important, but greater still is the power of man's spiritual adventures—adventures of thought, adventures of passionate feeling, adventures of aesthetic experience.

The environment in which this challenge, to managers and their co-workers alike, so plainly exists is sweepingly sketched for us by Peter Drucker in these ringing phrases:

Because the enterprise is the basic economic institution of the modern economy, profit has acquired an entirely new meaning. The question whether profit can be justified, and how, no longer makes any sense; the question is rather how much profitability an economic system and an enterprise need to discharge their now-basic duties to society. . . .

The limiting factor in a modern industrial economy—that is, the factor which decides how much wealth can be produced—is not raw materials or machines but the supply of human, *especially managerial,* knowledge and understanding. . . .

Management is the new socially leading group in industrial society. . . .

No modern society can exist in which the basic self-interest of the enterprise and the interest of society are in conflict. . . . An industrial society can be organized in such a way that the self-interest of an independent, autonomous, privately managed enterprise is best satisfied if it satisfies and serves the social good. In this possibility of establishing harmony lies the best chance for the survival of Western society as a free, strong, and prosperous society.

The science of managing—the search for the principle of order—is all of these adventures in one. It is thought, it is feeling, and it is spiritual as well as aesthetic experience.

3
Principles of Organization

"Principles" is a word of many meanings, but the meanings fall into two main classes: "principles" as settled rules or laws of action and "principles" as essential characteristics or propositions inherent in the nature of the field covered. The first category is conceptually mechanical, routine focused, and often most apparent in connection with bureaucratic organization. The second is also fundamentally causative, but in the sense of affording a source from which thoughtful and imaginative action can evolve, though not in precise or predetermined form. The word "principles" is used here in this second context.

"Organization" is used fundamentally to connote the act of organizing, as distinct from the work structure or the personnel so established in a pattern of ordered—and, hopefully, orderly—relationships.

THE BASIC NATURE OF ORGANIZATION

Organization always faces the historic dilemma of conflict between the freedom of the individual working alone and the restraints

Handbook of Business Administration, H. B. Maynard, Ed. (New York: McGraw-Hill, 1967), pp. 2-3 through 2-17.

on that freedom that flow automatically when it is brought into systematic, continuing interlock with the corresponding personal freedoms of all the other individuals in the organized entity or working team.

The principles of organization that apply to a given situation are a function of the philosophy of organization—or, more broadly, of human relationships—that is to govern the design and operation of the organized entity, as expressed through the personalities of both the managers and nonmanagers, or functional individual contributors, of which it is composed.

Choice of Organizational Philosophy. The available philosophies from which to choose are of innumerable variety in detailed differentiation. In practice, they classify more simply into two basically contrasting systems of leader–follower relationships.

The first is that of "command and obey," in which "organization" becomes primarily the definition and ordering of authority. The alternative is that of leadership of voluntary followers by inspiration and persuasion. Here, "organization" focuses primarily on identification, classification, and division of the work to be performed and of the responsibilities and accountabilities for that work in terms of personal work assignments and of teamwork or relationships, duties, and obligations, so that overall performance and individual contributions will be optimized.

From the followership vantage point, the opposing philosophies, as determinant of the purpose of organization, are similarly clear. In the first, obedience to authority is assumed as a specific or implied contractual obligation of the employee–employer relationship, and fundamentally tends to be limited to areas—of both work and teamwork—specifically spelled out by the employer.

In the second, responsibility and accountability—again for both work and teamwork—are voluntarily accepted on the premise that the interests and purposes of both employer and employee have persuasive elements of commonality, with a consequent tendency toward flexibility rather than rigidity, or mere conformance to employer design, in scope of responsibility assumed.

Freedom and Teamwork. In either case, the mutual give-and-take required to adapt individual freedoms to team performance may be achieved. In the first approach, the employee in effect contractually limits his freedom to the prescribed degree. In the second, the concept of "freedom" is in terms of the old expression, "Freedom is the right to discipline myself so I don't have to be disciplined by others."

The key word is "discipline," used in the sense of education to effectiveness, rather than of punishment or chastisement.

PURPOSE AS BASE OF PRINCIPLES OF ORGANIZATION

Recognition that the purpose of organization, and hence of choice of philosophies of relationships on which to base organization, is the primary factor fixing applicability of principles of organization is, perhaps, itself the first such principle.

This is because this deeply fundamental choice, whether to organize essentially in terms of division of authority or of specification of responsibility and accountability for voluntary personal contribution and performance, closely governs the selection and phrasing of the other principles needed and applicable.

Subgroupings of Principles. Further categorization of principles of organization, once the basic choice is clearly faced and taken, in turn falls into three broad groups.

The first deals with factors influencing organization that arise essentially out of its external relationships. An organized entity does not function in a vacuum, but is an element of wider systems, industries, or communities within which its own operations necessarily have either orderly and "organized" or only casual, fortuitous, and too often chaotic relationships.

The second and third categories deal with organizational factors internal to the organized entity. One comprises the principles dealing with identification, classification, and division of the work to be performed; that is, with the nature and structure of the pattern of organization of the work.

The other class takes in those principles that apply to the doing of personal work within the organized pattern or framework and the defined objectives, and hence apply to team, or relationships, as well as purely individual work responsibilities. They deal, that is, with the progress and dynamics of personal work performance within the voluntarily assumed restraints inherent in the organizing process, to facilitate joint as well as individual performance and results.

The compensation for such voluntary limitation of personal freedoms goes beyond the monetary consideration that is, in fact, the major exchange measure under the command philosophy. It includes this monetary return but also added satisfaction from the opportunity to contribute and to share in accomplishments beyond those feasible if working entirely alone.

Again, the element of imaginative and creative flexibility is characteristic in such context; whereas bureaucratic rigidity and rather limited conformance to arbitrary routine is the normally predominant aspect in the "command" environment.

HISTORICAL ROOTS OF ORGANIZATION

Historically, organization applied in communities in which direction came from a rather small elite. Followership was the role of a lesser educated and motivated but much larger workforce. It also applied when the work being organized required predominantly physical energy and skills.

It was probably natural, under such circumstances, that "authority" was the chief organizing factor, because capacity to carry more than limited, or even minimal, individual responsibility was considered relatively scarce for the work required, and was normally rather restricted for the relationships, and therefore for the teamwork, needed for organizational progress and success. "Principles of organization," as found in the managerial literature, accordingly tend to reflect—in both number and content—the predominance of these historic circumstances as to the actual or assumed capacity of the employees entrusted with work.

The applicability and usefulness of many of these principles—especially those in the first and third categories, where teamwork or relationships, rather than direct personal work responsibilities constitute identifying elements—seem open to increasing question in today's and tomorrow's organized entities.

THE IMPACT OF CHANGE ON MODERN SOCIETY

The prevalence of change, indeed of accelerating change, in all phases of our society and economy is even more widely sensed. Changes impinge in the technological sphere, as is dramatically evident to all. But parallel changes in the economic, social, and political aspects of our overall culture and civilization are probably of even greater organizational significance, although often less clearly visible.

The historic family, tribal, pastoral, and agricultural dominance in the local and national community give way progressively to a prevalence of organizational elements that recognize increasingly technological, industrial, urban, and international characteristics.

A corollary distinguishing factor is the higher level of education—and so of knowledge and capacity to use it—of more and more individual members of the modern work community.

The instinctive will to human freedom and to creative application of personal mental and physical talents is presumably present before education, as such, takes place. But education, itself the systematic development and cultivation of natural powers, normally brings a progressive increase in awareness of such instincts, talents, and potentials for their imaginative use in daily work and relationships.

A further corollary factor of modern change, and its impacts on all aspects of current and evolving culture, is a direct product of the greater ease of communication and transportation, and the automation of both physical and mental work, that have flowed from such change.

Teamwork in Complex Organizations. This latter factor takes form in the greater diversity, the more specialized content, and the more intricate interrelationships of resultant larger and more complex organizational entities.

A clear by-product is the progressive emergence of more, and of more complex, teamwork or relationship responsibilities in the combination of work and teamwork duties of individual jobs—both managerial and other, and both professional and nonprofessional.

Indeed, the day when the luxury of allowing dichotomies, or splits, to dictate job content—either "this" or "that," or, as often put, "this versus that"—could be indulged has already passed in modern sizable and industrial organized entities, which function in urban rather than rural environments. It has to be "both," not "either–or."

The "no place to hide" aspect of modern living is visible in the shadow of globally destructive weapons. If perhaps less visible, it is no less dominant for most individuals today with respect to the social and political—the organizational as distinct from the individual—aspects of their lives both at home and at work. Community is a fact of modern life and community requires a choice, sooner or later, between anarchy (or chaos) and organization for mutual, but no less for personal, freedom.

The suggestion is pertinent here, therefore, that in judging or choosing between the essentially contrasting philosophies of organization—on the basis of authority or of responsibility and accountability, respectively—in today's real-life world, the historic prevalence of principles of organization geared primarily to the command-and-control approach is already undermined and is prospectively subject to progressive attrition and collapse. Education always has multiple consequences.

Organizing Educated Work Contributors. With increasingly educated, knowledgeable, and free individuals at all echelons of organized activities, the possibility that "command" can be imposed, or even that it will be contracted for, shrinks proportionately. The desire for "freedom" in organized efforts grows globally, whether in a follower or a leader post. It grows faster than understanding of its impacts and its implications for wisest choice of "principles of organization" on the part of leaders and followers simultaneously.

The preservation of "freedom" in the work community requires, as it did earlier in the civil or political community, the clearest of thought. Here, the historic examples of dictatorship, and its ultimate unacceptable human consequences and resultant practical unworkability, become as pertinent for the governing and the organizing of the new types of sizable complex work communities as for the older civil organizational units.

The Basic Conflict of Freedom and Organization

Indeed, the first category of principles of organization dealing with external factors, including political as well as customer and other private relationships, only emphasizes the manager's mounting need to understand the essential conflict of freedom and organization and to develop competence to maximize personal freedoms in even the most complex organizational relationships. To do so calls for acute judgment in basing selection and use of "principles of organization" on the realities of today's and tomorrow's individuals and communities.

Thus the most basic nature of "organization," in the sense here used, is that it necessarily differentiates men working together to accomplish targeted common objectives from individuals working each for himself. The inevitable implications of such differentiation apply as much to the skilled "professional" worker, bringing chiefly mental skills to bear, as to the uneducated worker doing mainly manual work.

Human beings having the nature they do, this is a profound distinction. It is in the nature of a man to be interested in himself to a high degree, to want and cherish the freedom to do things his own way, to try out his own ideas, and even to make—and hopefully to learn from—his own mistakes.

When that man is working entirely on his own, using his own time and capital and inner resources to satisfy his own purposes, the freedom to do so may be in proportion, limited only by the general statutory and community restrictions applicable and by the golden rule to do unto others as you would have them do unto you.

But when a man agrees, for compensation and/or for the greater opportunity opened up, to work within an organized entity or group, although his desire for a similar measure of freedom may be unchanged, it clearly runs into new restraints required so that the parallel quests for personal freedom and creativity of all the others on the team may receive properly parallel recognition.

Restraints Inherent in Organization. The first and deepest nature of organization is thus that it brings restraints on individuals at the same time that it makes possible personal opportunities, challenges, and means for fulfilling them with personal satisfactions greater than those feasible or available when working alone. The identification and response to such restraints, on the part of leader and of follower alike, is a primary field for selection and application of principles of organization in the modern enterprise and community.

The root of most organizational problems, however unclear or difficult they later seem to get, is in this simple condition: namely, that organization for joint effort necessarily introduces restraints on purely personal freedom. And it also introduces, therefore, the basic issue of how best to sense, handle, and, if necessary, enforce these essential restraints—and of how to do so in ways humanly acceptable, on the one hand, and benign for greatest personal contributions and satisfactions, on the other hand.

The dilemma of organizational restrictions is, of course, inevitably personal to every individual in the organized enterprise. The more people in a particular entity, the greater the need is to face it in terms of mutually acceptable philosophy and principles—and acceptable to those specific persons and personalities—expressed and made known to all, rather than only by intuitive incident-by-incident approaches. Managerial second-guessing is properly cramped in such circumstances.

Managing as Leadership of Free Followers. A modern solution to the classic dilemma may be sought by defining "managing"—especially for organizing purposes—in the following terms:

Managing, as a distinct and professional kind of work, is *leading*, by inspiration and persuasion rather than by command . . . to secure balanced best results through the specific work of other people, who themselves are also acting with initiative, self-development, self-discipline, and competence in both their personal work and their voluntary teamwork and two-way communication.

Plainly, that definition is a broad philosophic base for preserving maximum personal freedom and yet achieving successful, timely, and profitable joint results. Because managing is practiced in a real-world organization of practical operating managers and other competent people, a "footnote" such as the following is perhaps also in order.

It is recognized that there may be emergency conditions or situations in which persuasion has failed, and results of continued efforts at persuasion—in the judgment of the manager—would be worse than temporary use of a command to get on with the job. In so doing, the manager is acknowledging temporary failure as a professional manager, and hence resorts to this course as an expedient only and takes requisite steps to identify and correct the root causes of the failure in order to prevent subsequent similar failures.

Voluntary Rather Than Imposed Discipline. The above approach represents obviously strong dedication to the principle of organization that discipline should normally be voluntary rather than imposed. This concept is at odds with the principles of organization predominant in the past and most familiar to a great many pragmatic managers.

In essence, the root idea is that the degree to which managers are likely—in organizations of educated, reliant, thinking persons—to be continuingly successful and productive as leaders of fellow men is a fairly direct function of the attitudes and the values, no less than the managerial knowledge and skills they bring to their work. In the long run, it takes more than technical competence to lay out work for others and to lead and train them to get effective, economical, and enthusiastic continuity of performance in its doing. It takes ability to motivate so they will make the organizational goal their own and will voluntarily want to accomplish the tasks and timetables for which they are personally responsible, and in the context of the jobs and relationships of the others on the team.

In the United States, at least, taking and holding a job in an organized entity is voluntary. Anyone who does not care to discipline himself to adopt the organization's objectives, in addition to and in synchronism with his personal, professional, or other work aims—and thus to live harmoniously so that normal organizational restraints are most mutually effective and least chafing—can, and in due course he normally should, switch jobs to be able to operate in the context he most prefers.

The Rights of the Majority. A parallel principle of organization should be that any employee who is not of such mind, after due discussion and trial, should be removed. The organizational structure should not be unduly warped and varied to adapt to the idiosyncrasies of jobholders whose incumbency is transient relative to the really long-run continuity of the organization and its dynamic teamwork requirements.

It is vital for the legitimacy of authority—and authority, in this sense, of both leaders and followers—to be clear, to be mutually recognized, and to be consistently exercised.

AUTHORITY OF KNOWLEDGE, NOT JUST COMMAND

Organized business and other efforts are carried on by increasingly educated people, many of them genuine professionals in their own work calling. In such an organizational world, a man's authority is really legitimatized, and accepted in the organization, by his authority of knowledge versus only of rank; by personal, visible competence in the specific situation; and, only as a last resort, by power to "boss" someone on the simple "do as I say" principle.

This does not mean that a manager, as such, should not have the power to decide and act, or that he should be a namby-pamby about using this power as good sense and good economics require and on time. It does not mean that, in trying fretfully to keep everybody happy, he should overlook personal failures or incompetence when, and for whatever reasons, the course of one threatens the aims and progress of all. The rights of the majority are not to be ignored, nor is the cooperation of the majority to be demotivated by tolerating non-cooperative attitudes by the few.

Circuits of Authority. With highly skilled specialists, and even professionals, in nearly all functional work areas, it does mean that today's manager follows the principle of organization that he needs to acquire the skill to operate and perform effectively in what Richard Armand has called "circuits of authority"—not just "lines of authority" in the old-fashioned sense.

"Circuits" indicate flow, and the modern dynamics involved as the site of authority of knowledge for a particular situation shifts in real-life operations. "Lines" tend to imply the more static, and perhaps bureaucratic, aspects of the organization structure.

Channels of Contact. As a related principle of organization, the operational concept of "channels of contact" is similarly to the point. This is the modern organizational practice that any two persons in an organization who have pertinent mutual, responsible interest in a situation or development should get in direct contact for information or ideas. The simple action of "go see the guy" will often save a bale of increasingly costly and delaying memoranda.

There are limits, of course, and times to get back into formal organizational lines. This is specifically so when two persons in contact cannot agree, and therefore should refer the issue to their respective managers; when third parties are also involved; when the action considered would run counter to, or require amendment or waiver of, established policy; and when the direct responsibility of an upper-echelon manager is at stake. But by and large, one phone call will often save 10,000 words later.

Effective Use of Managerial Authority. The manager does have to exercise his authority, as a basic managerial skill, to move boldly from thought to action when the time is ripe. But throwing his weight around is more likely to develop experts in sidestepping its impact than in taking it on the chin.

Fundamentally, in the modern enterprise, what is structured and organized is really responsibility, which then carries with it the appropriate authority to function, so as to be fairly accountable on a measurable basis. This inherent authority needs to be full and undiminished in each job so the individual incumbent can cope with its defined, and assigned, duties except only as most sparingly reserved, in writing and in advance, for particular kinds of organizational interests or recognizable operating situations.

Wise Delegation of Decision Responsibilities. Wise delegation to make a responsible organization workable involves more than decentralizing geographically or by readily identifiable products. Rather, it gets into delegating responsibility to make and to be accountable for particular kinds of purposefully riskful decisions. The aim of this decentralization is that resultant decentralized decisions will be made promptly and right the first time at the scene of the work and the job. In an internationally competitive world, it is not sensible, as an organizational alternative, to have the costs to do the work of deciding in duplicate or triplicate at two or three successive organizational levels, if only because these added costs would have to come out of hard-won net profits and could not be passed along in added prices to the customers.

Duplication of costs by excessive cushions of staff, audit, or so-called coordinating or control personnel—at any organizational echelon—causes competitively unfeasible delays, places emphasis on cure rather than prevention, and represents organizational clutter where streamlining is essential.

The attitude and skill of wise delegation are at the heart of profitability—that is, of the measure of value to customers above costs incurred—of the organized enterprise. They call for delegating, really, to every human being in the enterprise the responsibility for making the timely decisions involved in carrying out his personal assigned work and teamwork duties within the established organization pattern. The aim is to maximize the creative contribution of each individual in both his functional work and in the way he voluntarily gears that work in with the work of the others whom it affects.

Separation of Ineffective Workers. A collateral requirement is that an employee who cannot or will not carry realistic responsibility needs either clarification or retraining on his job duties, or finally removal if, after fair trial, his continuing failures of either commission or omission threaten the effectiveness of the others and the profitability without which the jobs of all are at risk.

As the latter conclusion impinges, it is a basic organizational duty of the manager to see individual situations whole, to see individual men whole, and so to aid all concerned to develop the best pace, synchronized flow, timing, and turnover throughout all of the operations of the organized enterprise.

SPECIALIZATION IN THE ORGANIZED WORK COMMUNITY

Concentration on itsy-bitsy specialties alone is not enough. If the cost of their performance is part of the costs of an organized entity, they have to be carried out responsibly and realistically in that context. This is one price—but a fair one—for the privilege of functioning in the organization, with resources greater than the individual (even the highly dedicated professional) can have working by himself.

"Business" is truly an amalgam of economics and politics in the finest sense of both words: "economics" in the sense of being the base of the daily work satisfactions of most of our associates and fellow workers; "politics" in the sense of being the base of principles for the governing or managing of human affairs that truly rests on the consent of the governed, and with such consent by increasingly educated, creative, and reliant associates—volunteered and exercised with demanding self-discipline and personalized responsibility.

Organizing the Manager's Own Work. As an organizational principle of sharp pertinence, only if the manager does seek, find, appoint, and wisely delegate responsibility to such associates is he safe to concentrate more of his own work in truly strategic fields.

He needs to do the latter so that he may better see and define overall goals, purposes, policies, and programs for attaining them—or alter their course in time as they advance or retard or shift. But he does not need to spell out end elements or steps for accomplishing those goals, for he can be confident that his associates will do this better than he as their reciprocity for his confidence and motivation.

Unique Elements of the Organizing Process. Viewed from this stance, the organizing process—for which persistent principles of organization are needed—comprises the following five unique components, here stated sequentially but carried on simultaneously and continuously in the dynamic real world.

1. *Determining and classifying work required* to accomplish plans and programs within the framework of designated objectives and policies; and dividing that total work into manageable components and jobs, in due combination with the facilities necessary for work performance, to provide best channels for coordinated application of available effort.

2. *Grouping components and jobs into an orderly organization structure;* grouping like and related work together in proper and most natural relationships to other work, to achieve best application of the combined human and material resources of the enterprise, with appropriate parallel incentive and compensation for the organization structure so designed.

3. *Selecting individuals for designated positions and jobs,* with needed personal characteristics, skills, and knowledge and with personal values and character to perform the work of each job competently and in voluntarily integrated relationships to other jobs in the overall structure. The aim here is to man the organization structure to use the talents of each individual logically and effectively; finding and using what a man does well rather than what he does badly, to fit round pegs in round holes with sympathy and understanding—in turn re-

moving, after fair appraisal against performance standards and after proper discussion with the man, any individual who is consistently inadequate either in performance or in compatibility.

4. *Formulating and defining methods and procedures for performing work to be done*, by seeking and describing the best and simplest way to do each task or kind of work, especially if repetitive, so that the aggregate work may be accomplished most imaginatively, quickly, easily, economically, systematically, understandably, and in good fit with perceived, or creatable, patterns of order in work and relationships that will facilitate understanding, communication, and economy of money and energy in performing all necessary work (and no more) with greatest productivity rather than with greatest intensity of labor.

5. *Organizing the manager's own work and time* to allow focus on his specifically managerial responsibilities—especially to plan, organize, integrate, and measure to accomplish desired performance and results of the job, the component, and the enterprise as a whole.

Collateral Steps in Organizing. Pursuing most effectively the unique organizing work, composed of the above five chief elements, calls also—as for other fundamental elements of managerial work—for three collateral steps on the part of the manager.

1. Making the designated organizational pattern, structure, and methods and procedures known to those in the organization, so that they and he can all perform as an effective, cooperative team.

2. Using results of regular and continuing measuring of all the work of organizing so as to facilitate its constant improvement, upgrading, expediting, and readjustment as practical experience and progressive observation and planning make possible.

3. Exercising judgment and making reasoned, objective, and timely decisions to effectuate the organizing work and progress; taking reasonable risks confidently, competitively, courageously, and on his own responsibility, on the basis of facts and lore presently available; and choosing wisely from among possible alternatives as opportunity, responsibility, and need for each particular decision arise.

THREE CATEGORIES OF ORGANIZATIONAL PRINCIPLES

As indicated earlier, principles of organization within chosen organizational philosophy and structure fall into three broad categories: those dealing with relationships external to the particular organization, those internal to it, and those embracing the structuring of the work itself as distinct from elements or relationships arising out of its performance rather than its nature.

External Organizational Relationships. If the classic textbooks on organizing principles offer progressive weakness as aids in modern organizing efforts, a major reason is the multiplying complexity and impact of external relationships in today's world of work.

The classic categories of external groups whose interests have to be considered and balanced in organizing an enterprise are usually cited as customers, share owners, suppliers, and the public, including government as the public's specific representative.

The complexity of relationships with all four of these groups (or five, looking on government in its own growing dimensions) grows apace, and this factor itself demands meticulous and progressive consideration of their respective, but also interlaced, interests in keeping the organization currently workable.

Before considering the four separately, a relatively new development of late years, with still undetermined consequences in impacts on organizing a competitive enterprise, deserves note.

External Aspects of Employee Relationships. Relationships with and among employees—managers included (even when they also have some proprietary interests)—have long been classified as essentially internal to the organization. For three major parallel reasons, employee relationships now, and on a forward-looking basis, have to be thought through as also having significant external aspects bearing on the corporate organizing process.

1. All employees to some degree have multiple interests and live multiple roles. Work relationships are rarely even approximately coterminous with individual personal interests.

2. Unions, or organized bodies to represent groups of employees who make up their memberships, have growing practical and legal status in industrial nations. In many vital operational areas, they actually supplant the individual employee to a high degree as a determining factor in managerial organizing potentials and processes.

3. Professional societies, or voluntary membership societies for individuals pursuing professional callings, make pertinent claims on the work choices and decision parameters of individual members even when the members are working as employees in organized enterprises rather than solely as personal professional practitioners.

As these combined internal–external relationship factors emerge and call for innovative managerial thought in keeping organization effective for future progress, the need for new research for identification, restatement, and new or revised application of pertinent principles of organization mounts proportionately. Nor do principles for external relationships with the older recognized categories—customers, share owners, suppliers, and the public (and its representative, government)—escape need for similar innovative research.

Customer Relationships. Customers, in particular, are more affluent, more mobile, more educated, and more likely to have new wants (and the income to satisfy them) than ever before in history.

Competition consequently takes on bewildering new dimensions, with specific impacts on organizational principles.

The customer has new kinds of alternative wants beyond historic needs and also has available, from the fruits of technology, diverse avenues of fulfillment of particular wants. Competition, which once was generally recognizably on a product-for-product basis, now takes in choices among greatly dissimilar devices for achieving a particular customer satisfaction.

Multiplicity of choices as a variable in customer decisions, and naturally in competitive thinking too, sets new norms. They in turn hold stable for shorter time cycles. Organizational principles and practices require anticipatory, or at least parallel, change and updating.

Share Owner Relationships. Among share owners, a striking characteristic of modern society is that the proprietors or owners of the larger, usually pacesetting, enterprise and its managers or entrepreneurial decisionmakers increasingly are separate individuals.

As more businesses are conducted in the government-ownership sector of more nations, this dichotomy becomes even more striking. At the same time, managerial risks mount, and "professional" interests may seem to diverge substantially from those of management.

The legitimacy of managerial authority, divorced in a personal sense from that of proprietorship, calls for new foundations—hard to define and harder to communicate—so that public acceptance, with parallel scrapping of superseded traditions, keeps abreast of actual operational functioning. Here too, new "research" to discover, refine, and apply pertinent new or old organizational principles becomes ever more essential.

With people all over the world clamoring for improved local living standards, the business environment becomes more and more that of a savings-short, capital-short, and credit-short economy. Demands for venture, or share owner, capital become cumulatively more intense. At the same time, political nationalism raises new barriers to free flow and supply of capital both at home and abroad. Resultant strains introduce wholly new aspects and factors in share owner relationships, again with organizational as well as directly financial consequences.

Supplier Relationships. Suppliers of both materials and services also change in availability, scope, and interests, and external relationships of an organization are affected accordingly.

As technology and automation supplant variable direct labor or clerical costs with more fixed-capital costs, with markets and customers still staying highly variable and dynamic, the enterprise moves toward rigor mortis unless old organizational principles are reappraised, reformulated, and remixed.

New kinds of make-or-buy decisions, especially on services rather than materials or product components, are called for. This is because specialized new kinds of vendors arise, and also because they may afford the only practical relief for painful or disruptive organizational cramps. Once more, "research" for continual modification and enhancement of useful principles of organization is demanded.

Public and Government Relationships. Public and government relations—because these groupings embrace the people in all the others—have, in a sense, multiple impacts on the organization, directly and indirectly through the others. With the public sector of the economy broadening at national and local levels, changes here have a heavy influence on corporate operations and organization.

New uncertainties are created as governments tend to function in this period of rapid changes by having statutory law and regulations precede and form, rather than follow and codify, cultural customs in the business community.

Changes in all external relationships of organizations thus become constantly more intricate, uncertain, and bewildering. The general effect is to make anticipation of long-range organizational requirements more difficult and riskier, yet more necessary precisely due to the likelihood that past and current trends cannot be extrapolated safely far into the future years.

A peculiarly new and still unclear result is to create urgent needs for longer-range decisions. But these longer time cycles of decision responsibility increasingly tend to become shorter than those of the normal tenure of an executive who has to make specific decisions currently. Normal present-day executive and managerial turnover consequently creates new needs for discriminating thought in measuring organizational performance against personal decision responsibilities. Inadequate, out-of-phase, or inapplicable managerial information has to be guarded against, lest it precipitate organizational changes of the wrong nature at the wrong time.

BUSINESS SYSTEMS RESEARCH

Under rapidly changing circumstances, from the standpoint of principles of organization, one new common denominator begins to appear widely as a current factor in corporate organization. However disguised in evolving nomenclature—often misguidedly clouded by thinking of "planning" as something of an end in itself—this new factor may be identified more sharply as the developing realization of, and recognition for, an additional primary work function in the organized enterprise, in parallel with such old standbys as research and engineering, manufacturing, marketing, financial and accounting, legal, and human relations work, and managerial work as such.

In its intrinsic aspects and characteristics, the new and evolving function perhaps may best be deemed "business systems research." Its work and purpose, broadly sensed, is to discover the patterns and relationships in the total situation of the organized enterprise, as well as of its responsible workers, whether as leaders or as followers in particular respects, in order to facilitate the wisest choices and risks in setting the enterprise's scope, goals, timetables, and overall operating efforts to reach optimum objectives successfully, profitably, and on time, both long and short range.

Organization Principles in Business Literature. Modern business literature comprises many thousands of volumes and articles on "principles of organization" applicable either for designing an organization structure or for staffing and operating an organization for effective human functioning. A competent business librarian can provide any interested manager with a reference list of such material of any desired scope, length, and depth.

But a warning and an indication of typical trends is in order to alert today's manager to the fact that organizational literature is still in the making. Indiscriminate application of so-called classic principles may fall far short of already foreseeable managerial needs.

INTERNAL ORGANIZATIONAL RELATIONSHIPS

In the sphere of internal relationships—the dynamics of operational human teamwork in the going concern—still-evolving factors have to be considered, such as the following:

1. Research into flow patterns or systems in operations, not alone into functioning in individual jobs or single organization components.

2. The concept of "circuits of authority" earlier cited; perceiving the dynamics involved, or desirable, as the site of the "authority of knowledge" for a particular decision shifts in real-life situations, often at a pace making the conventional "lines of authority" concept economically hazardous.

3. Perception and definition of the practical as well as the legalistic legitimacy of corporate managerial authority, with recognition that such legitimacy has to be humanly and practically acceptable in the organization, rather than only as statutorily applicable, where individual proprietary and organizational authority continue to diverge.

4. Staffing to accommodate to multiplying needs to use specifically allotted work-time hours for long-range reeducation and retraining of all workers (managerial, professional, and others), to anticipate early obsolescence of current work skills and greater mobility in specific jobs for both personal and work-connected reasons.

5. Need for earliest feasible development of indigenous local work leadership, of requisite technical and cultural competence and responsibility, as decision responsibilities are progressively decentralized, not only within an organization but even internationally on an ever-faster scale.

6. Realization and understanding that the advent of multiplying technology—especially by way of more rapid communication and transportation—creates human conditions under which new organizational norms apply; under which, on the one hand, change itself is a normal rather than a rare aspect of organizing, and, on the other hand, multiple rather than narrowly channeled personal interests are the normal dimension of human participation in organized work.

7. Organizing functionally around continuing career work classifications, for synthesis and continuity of the output of individual people as current problems and tasks or projects come and go.

8. Helping present personnel and organization structure or relationships to develop and perform effectively, rather than impulsively trying needless changes that sacrifice critical competitive time, when a

little more persistence and skill to get workers doing their best in relationships they already know can often get quicker results in work output and in satisfactions for all concerned.

The above partial list of changing factors affecting internal relationships in the organization process is suggestive only of the scope of new concepts, varying emotional responses, diversifying interests, shifting motivations, evolving new man–machine interfaces, and reactions that call for the manager's attention and research to develop, define, and apply the currently most useful principles of organization for the changing work and people under his leadership, guidance, and inspiration.

Organization Structuring

In the area of organization structuring as such, new factors also arise or take on a different emphasis almost continually as an aspect of normal operations. Again for example only, the sorts of new aspects impinging now embrace such items as:

1. Balancing the components of the organization structure so that due place is accorded for relatively stable and continuing functional work and also for essentially short-lived programs, projects, task forces, study teams, and so on; appreciating the high desirability of keeping the latter type of activities organized on essentially an incremental basis, so that upsets to established and familiar work contacts and relationships as projects rise and fade are effectively minimized.

2. Achieving genuine decentralization and sincere acceptance of decision responsibilities and accountabilities.

3. Putting long-range organizational emphasis on purposes and objectives rather than on detailed means and methods of subsequent individual performance.

4. Making long-range plans for organizing in terms of the essential structures of the organization that are most subject to anticipatory guidance, such as the structures of the

    a. Product and market scopes
    b. Corporate financing
    c. Information and report system
    d. Facilities and material resources
    e. Human resources and their managerial leadership

f. Overall enterprise within the structure of the larger environment, industry, and communities of which it is but a component part.

5. Minimizing so-called staff personnel external to the basic operating work functions and flow, with particular avoidance of duplication of staffs at each echelon of the organizational hierarchy so they become blockages rather than channels for decision flows and competitive, profitable work progress.

6. Also minimizing the number of echelons of the organization structure, so that two-way interlevel communication is simplified and so that individual manager jobs have sufficient spans of responsibility to require full time on truly managerial work and to inhibit either kibitzing or, worse yet, second-guessing of the manager's own follower or leader associates.

7. Understanding that conventional past accounting and report measurement periods increasingly may fail to give suitable information for measuring decision accountabilities of current incumbents of jobs with long-cycle decision requirements.

8. Generally, re-researching accounting concepts and their operational applicability as the mix, in accounting statements, of ascertained current facts and of estimates (or guesses) for uncertain future impacts becomes evermore unstable and variable.

9. Keeping operational information systems attuned to changes in the operating characteristics of the organization and its people and also to presently revolutionary changes in available computer-communication hardware and peripheral software for use in such systems.

10. Sensing always that the imagination, the courage, and the ethical and spiritual values and beliefs of individuals will be the continuing basic source of creativity, change, and progress, with the technology of the physical sciences usefully employed but as tool, not master, for the men and women of the organization.

Broadly, the need for enough stability of organization structure, and hence of attendant working relationships, to optimize individual creative performance and workable team results has progressively to be kept in good operational balance—both long and short range—with all the changing circumstances and interests that are normal in the ever-varying operating environment.

Keeping the basic organization structure workably and recognizably steady and humanly comfortable, while still free of bureaucratic rigidities that cause opportunities to take advantage of new developments to be missed, taxes managerial skills and organizational principles heavily and constantly.

The Manager's Search for Principles of Organization

Faced with both the opportunities and the challenges of today's technological, industrial, heavily urbanized, international competitive trends, the modern manager's search for helpful and useful "principles of organization" has to center no less in his own head and heart than in his organization's library, or. even in new managerial and organizational handbooks. Wisdom beyond mere knowledge, and beliefs beyond mere facts, are deeply essential for leadership.

Also essential is the ability to motivate increasingly educated followers by inspiration and persuasion beyond that of mere command authority. The continuity of the organized enterprise has to be apprehended, and comprehended, as an aim and purpose beyond current "problem solving" or projects.

The traditions and basic objectives of the organization, and its policies as their by-products, have to be made as clear and contributory as transient current work assignments or interests. Individuals oriented to the continuing work of the enterprise and willing and able to think and act to contribute to its effective performance for successful organizational continuity are always needed.

Imagination and continuing learning have to be consciously asked of all employees. Participation on their part as their personal work and teamwork responsibilities continue to become more complex and sophisticated has to extend to the organizational impacts no less than to the technological nature of the results of each man's thoughts and actions.

The manager's job, in turn, calls for an ever-clear sensing that a fundamental purpose of formal organization is to fit the needed work and work relationships in the organization structure to patterns and trends that normally are longest lasting, change most slowly, facilitate continuing personal career development, permit confinement of temporary project organizations to incremental functional activities, and offer a framework for teamwork least likely to require frequent upsets in working contacts, and in personal give-and-take, that at best take time to get flowing in a smooth groove with least friction.

The responsibility to integrate as a specific personal commitment of work in organized enterprises is common and reciprocal to both the functional individual contributors (each reasoning and applying to contribute through his own work and teamwork) and the manager (planning and organizing to provide demanding yet inspiring leadership for such individuals).

The obligation and willingness to bring the combined power of wisdom and of empirical knowledge and skills to organized work is at once the governor and the flywheel for converting accelerating technological change into beneficial human progress.

Principles of organization are required that place that fundamental duty on both managers and their co-workers in good partnership in the modern work community.

4
Notes on
the Nature of
Organizations

I have back home a personal library with, literally, several hundred full-length books and quite a spate of shorter articles on "management theories." Space forbids trying to categorize such "theories" here. Any good business librarian can give you a reading course of any desired length if you wish to get into deeper personal study in this field.

In an admittedly oversimplified, but correspondingly graphic, approach for practical and pragmatic progress here and now, I'll merely suggest that the core issue here is whether "management"—and in terms of the specific managers who comprise its personnel—is something that can be defined, planned, developed in a more or less orderly and systematic way in a tough, real-world competitive business organization, or whether, in contrast, when practical men work together—in greater or lesser restraint and control—the day-to-day operations add up to the leadership needed to keep the ship afloat and headed for its chosen port.

Again in oversimplified fashion, many devotees of the latter viewpoint want no part, anyhow, of formal organization, of organization charts, of defined responsibilities and authorities for either

From previously unpublished notes written in 1965. These notes in part overlap (with additional insight) the preceding chapter, "Principles of Organization." They also summarize much of the material in following chapters.

organizational components or individual jobs, or of systematic planning and development of the manager corps for designed future growth and progress.

The history of business, paradoxically, is stuffed with examples of companies that—for considerable periods, at least—grew profitably and successfully along this latter line of thinking.

My own observation is that sheer successful size and growth themselves cross a line at which key decisions have to be made in many heads rather than one, and that formal "management theories" and formal "organization" (charts, job descriptions, and all) do become essential as this line is crossed.

And I believe this is why both a whole vast literature and an enormous complex of management education activities have developed in this country, and why, also, many thousands of companies have grown, and continue to grow, beyond the capacity and indeed the working lifetimes of their founders and pioneers, however able.

If you want to read a single fascinating book that depicts how such progress—such successive crossing of lines demarking increasingly organized stages of management and corporate growth—can be tackled positively, and with great personal challenges and satisfactions, rather than only negatively or grudgingly, let me urge that you pick up a copy of Alfred Sloan's story—*My Years with General Motors.* There are few comparable expositions of management theories for a tough, growing, profitable, and complex outfit that combine its clarity of presentation, its deep understanding of the nature and importance of management theories, and its tightly interwoven record of testing such theories in the hot fires of practice in one of the most competitive of all management fields.

Management Knowledge and Skills

What does a manager in a profit-and-loss business need to *know?* Basically he needs to have three parallel kinds of mental knowledge. I will merely list them briefly at this point.

1. Knowledge of the *specific business*—of its salable products (or services), of its markets and customers, and of its competitors in kind or otherwise; that is, knowledge of the "something to sell" and of the "someone to buy it," which are the ultimate indispensable ingredients of a profit-and-loss business.

2. Knowledge of the major *functional kinds of work* needed to

carry on such a business, normally classifiable as research and engineering, manufacturing (including purchasing), marketing (including promotion and advertising, physical distribution, and specific selling and service after sale), financ, and accounting, employee and public relations, legal, and, increasingly, research into the system of the business as a whole. The manager's knowledge should embrace at least one of these key functional disciplines in depth, and a sufficiently clear understanding of the others to respect their fields, to know what to expect from them, and to be able to staff them with requisitely competent key personnel in each case.

3. Knowledge about *managing*—as a distinct and identifiable kind of work in itself, distinguished by personal responsibility to function, chiefly by integrating the work of others rather than by purely personal functional contribution and teamwork.

In addition to such kinds of knowledge, a manager has also to have various skills to put his knowledge to fruitful and productive work. For example, but only for example and by no means to exhaust the list, such important managerial skills as:

1. *Seeing the dynamics*—the ongoing nature—of business work; a moving picture, not just a bunch of stills, or problems.

2. *Making present structure and staff function*—and at optimum effectiveness, economy, and satisfaction—rather than just cutting and trying, making changes just to change something, often unwittingly going back to an approach earlier abandoned for cause.

It takes time for men to form the habit of working together in *any* organizational structure, so unwise or needless changes cause sacrifice of competitively needed time when just a little more skill to get them doing their best in relationships they already know and fit could get quicker results both in work progress and in inner satisfaction for all concerned.

3. *Starting "development" from where you are*—and going forward together without losing the momentum you already have—in both structure and personnel, with new personal development programs, for both managers and nonmanagers, then folded in smoothly to accelerate rather than eddy up the pace of the business.

4. *Learning to think conceptually*—seeing patterns as well as continuity in events, not just itemized happenings. The manager here shows his capacity to multiply himself not by sheer intensification of personal ideas and efforts, but by ability to give all his associates a moving "theory of the situation"—a pattern of common interests that all will feel inclined to help attain.

In decentralized operations particularly, mistakes that the manager may feel he shouldn't have made are highly visible to him. Less visible often are the different—and good—ideas he probably would not have had at all. If the key men in place have been reasonably well chosen, the bulk of these will considerably outweigh the costs of some mistakes he would not have ventured. Of course, if someone makes a career of making mistakes, the remedy is to change the man rather than let him delegate his responsibility for judgment upstairs to his boss.

5. *Being careful about role and game playing*—popular approaches, and of some usefulness if discriminatingly used, in much current management theory. But business in competitive fields is "for real" and the able manager has the knack of getting inside the struggle and the fury of the real-life, real-time, real-scale action of the organized enterprise. Models, images, and so on need—if used—to be seen for what they are, means and not ends. You can't get your whiskers off your face by scraping your razor over your image in the mirror.

6. *Seeing and metering all human and material resources available prudently into the operations,* and only at times when they are needed and productive.

To "measure" what he does, and what his associates are doing, is a mark of the cost-and-profit-center manager. And it aids him to facilitate getting, using, and dispersing the right information for the right people at the right time so that all can make their *own* work and teamwork decisions sensibly and on their own initiative.

7. *Understanding the legitimacy of authority*—recognizing that in organized business efforts today, carried on largely by increasingly educated people, a man's authority is legitimatized by the authority of knowledge, not that of rank; by personal, visible competence in the specific situation and only as a last resort of power to "boss" someone on the "do as I say" principle.

8. *Delegating wisely*—duplication of costs by provision of excessive cushion of staff, audit, or so-called control personnel, at any echelon of the organization, is likely to be curative rather than preventive—to put the emphasis on postmortem autopsies rather than on keeping alive and well.

A lot of current banalities and nonsense—like the miscalled Parkinson's Law that men will expand work to fill their time—can be wiped off the slate by applying the managerial skill of wise delegation in designing and staffing the organization structure in the first place.

9. *Seeing situations whole*—this is the skill to see individual situa-

tions whole, to see individual men whole, to see both in continuing dynamic balance, and so to aid all concerned to develop the best pace, synchronized flow, timing, and turnover throughout all operations of the enterprise. Years ago Rudyard Kipling wrote:

> They copied all they could follow
> But they couldn't copy our minds
> And we left 'em sweating and stealing
> A year and a half behind.

The manager's skill in applying his mind, his vision, if you will, is thus one of the highest evidences of professionally competent managerial workmanship—as a foundation of leadership that inspires all his associates to seek the same kind of personal dedication. It calls for ability:

◇ To seek facts patiently but persistently and promptly.
◇ To pull principles, not merely procedures, from such facts.
◇ To integrate and synthesize principles into primary patterns for the planning, organizing, integrating, and measuring of complex operating enterprises.
◇ To present such principles and patterns so that other managers and other associate workers may have at their command bases of personal decisions rooted in firmer ground than purely personal experiences, or, worse yet, than purely personal whims.

In some ways this may be the most controversial of the several brash suggestions I have put before you. It comes right out and says bluntly that the old saying that "the way to learn is by doing" may not tell the whole story. It is another old saying in business that the other fellow's mistakes and experiences are the cheapest way to learn if you only take advantage of them, rather than insist on always rolling your own. As one of my former associates, Lem Boulware, said, "It is not necessary for us all to start in the Garden of Eden."

With managerial knowledge and managerial skills of such dimensions, it might seem that a man has all the ingredients for managerial success. Many textbooks in the field of managerial competence might lend weight to such an assumption. And in the days when only the manager and a few key aides brought educated minds to the operation, there was at least some ground for their thinking so.

In today's economy, managerial capacity in the "know what" and "know how" areas is no longer enough. The educated and highly trained personnel who exist pretty much throughout today's technical manufacturing complex look for still a third basic dimension—namely, "know why"—in the manager they are prepared to respect and "put out" for.

If such employees are to consider it their jobs, no less than the manager's, to stick their necks out, to take risks on purpose, they want to be sure of the manager's attitudes or values, as well as of his knowledge and skills.

So behind the "know what" and "know how" of successful managing lurks the less clear, less logical area of its "why"—of its *purpose,* not just its nature, as revealed by the human values the manager holds, applies, and is able to make plain, persuasive, and inspiring to all associates in the organization or component managed, but also to his contemporaries in the industry, community, and society in which he and they perform.

A burgeoning new management literature shows cognizance of such realities in modern organized affairs. The necessity of the manager to consider the personal views and interests of the men in the organization, along with those of the customers and of the owners, is being sensed, documented, and applied in practice as well as discussed in theory.

An authentic businessman–philosopher, the late Thomas F. Woodlock of *The Wall Street Journal,* put it this way:

There are three fundamental things which have always been man's concern. The *first* of these is his concept of his own nature, his idea of *what* he *is* and all that implies. The *second* is his concept of the world in which he lives, its meaning. The *third* is his concept of the *purpose* of his own life, and what he *ought* to do about it. The character and the significance of a civilization are determined by his *attitude* toward these things.

In my judgment—after both past and recent opportunity to observe how organizations perform under widely different cultures and economic and political philosophies, on all continents of the globe—the degree to which managers are continuingly successful and productive as leaders of their fellow men is a pretty direct function of the attitudes and the values, no less than the knowledge and the skills, they bring to their work.

In the long run it takes more than technical competence to lay out work for others and to train them in how it may be performed well, to get effective, economical, and enthusiastic continuity of performance from them in its doing. It takes, in short, ability to motivate so they will make the goal their own, and will voluntarily want to accomplish the task in the appropriate time frame and in the context of the jobs and relationships of the others on the team.

This is basically the "integrating" aim of the manager, and it calls for more than a tough taskmaster, or even some all-seeing "leader," to win such motivation; certainly also for more than open or instinctive fear of the boss as its basis.

In Helsinki a while back, a knowledgeable Finnish executive expressed it to me in these words:

Soviet machinery when delivered has competent design and manufacturing and can function well. But if I were to show you the "penalty clauses" against late delivery which we are forced to write in our purchase contracts, you would just not believe them possible. . . .

The troubles they have getting all the necessary components for an order from different bureaus, each operating under its own yearly plan to meet what it considers firm and unchangeable requirements from "on high" to follow priorities laid down in its own central plan, make it unbelievably difficult to meet contracted delivery dates for end products. Hence the purchasing customer's own plans are upset, and costs are caused and continued due to resultant delays that are economically impossible to accept. Higher "costs" for Free World—especially for United States—equipment, which, however, can be counted on for scheduled delivery, are highly acceptable in contrast, even when they look high in comparing competitive quotations.

In moving to a discussion of the pros and cons of centralization versus decentralization in industrial organizations today let me point out that there is no magic in either. My own philosophy, after long years of combined thought and practice in the managerial meadows, is to set up any organization to get both authority and incentive to decide, to risk, and to act as closely as possible to the work affected by the decision.

There are plainly two hedges here. One is in the phrase "as closely as possible," and the other in the words "affected by" the decision. As the latter words imply indirectly, the work of any man—manager or nonmanager, professional or nonprofessional—functioning in organized activity affects and is affected by the efforts and decisions of his co-workers as well as those he makes himself, and vice versa. Very few of his own decisions are free of side effects, currently or subsequently, on the work of others.

This is why any charter for a decentralized business division, or for some functional component or some project, and similarly any job guide for a particular position, is inadequate unless it visualizes both the work and the teamwork responsibilities (or relationships)—and their corollary and matching accountabilities.

A derivative idea here is that in any sizable, complex, and dynamic organization—of dimensions and continuity to outlast present position incumbents—such identifications of responsibilities need to be in writing, and need to be made known generally to all whose decisions interlock, rather than only narrowly.

Inherent managerial discipline is required here so that the opportunity to second-guess a man by giving him only a vague indication of the responsibilities for which he will be held accountable and then judging him by the power of hindsight rather than foresight is correspondingly cramped. This is tough on a top man who likes to keep his own responsibility hard to define, but it's good for him and for his co-workers, too, in the long run. As President Truman once put it, "If you can't stand the heat, stay out of the kitchen." The top man's work is not easy, but it's better done if the rules of fair play apply to it, too.

A little later, I want to mention the key role that information, and its thoughtful communication, plays in facing questions of centralization and decentralization, especially because the crash landing in our midst of the modern computer (particularly the new time-sharing breed) is often now said to offer a way to pull many presently decentralized decisions back to the "front office."

My other hedge, in preferring highly decentralized decision-making authority, was in the phrase "as closely as possible" to the work affected. This raises many neat questions in the real, workaday operational world—doubly so because so many decisions are better made in timely fashion with incomplete information and only partial rationalization than put off unduly so that the pace, rhythm, and flow of the organization is slowed down, its costs strung out and raised, and its competitive sharpness blunted.

There is—as any veteran operator instinctively realizes—a deep sense in such timely decisionmaking "to get on with the job" because so few of our many daily operational decisions are really or seriously irreversible, if ongoing experience indicates they should be reversed. Of course, those that are irreversible plainly should be made more carefully unless in fields of truly little, and only transient, consequences.

To the extent that a manager or other worker may fear to lose face if he backs off a decision he has made, the facts of the situation have priority over his pride. Once more, if he makes a career of making mistakes, change the man. But otherwise, since the facts will out, the best mistakes are those soonest corrected and with the least fuss and feathers. Nobody bats a thousand in this operational decision league and nobody should be expected to.

As regards my two hedges, the suggested organizational approach to decentralized decisionmaking is worth two added comments.

Fundamentally, the philosophy I have sketched so briefly itself implies a basic concept of organizational decisionmaking that needs to be absolutely clear. It is that decentralization, in such a view, goes beyond mere separation of operations according to readily identifiable factors like physical location and product line differentiation—whether vertically between a transmission and the vehicle in which it goes (that is, between component and end product or between element and system or subsystem) or horizontally as between a trailer and a refrigeration display case.

The heart of decentralization is rather that it involves planned and deliberate, but measured and watched, dispersion to many people of both responsibility and authority, and also of accountability, to make decisions on their own with respect to both the work and the teamwork of their assigned positions.

Once this mental bridge is crossed, many arguments about control become visible in their true dimensions, and have to stand up for observation and rational thought, stripped of concealment in such semantic Mother Hubbard petticoats as mere phraseology about "line versus staff" or "centralization versus decentralization."

The true issue, as performance falters or gaps in any specific situation, is essentially twofold: *First,* do the facts, including those dealing with the timetable, truly indicate that performance is inadequate? *Second,* do you correct it at the source—that is, at the point of the man specifically failing his assigned accountability—or do you avoid facing it and try to correct the performance by incurring additional costs, having someone else take a second look (or a third, or a fourth) before a decision is made.

If a man *can* pleasantly delegate his true decision responsibility upstairs to his manager—or to some "they" in a distant front office—it makes, at least temporarily, for a kind of personal "social security." But if enough people do it, it also makes for a wildly harassed "front office," a bureaucratic organization, and costs in inaction, delays, and buck-passing that easily produce poorer competitive steam and profits than normal errors of operational judgment directly at the work place.

Although the personal job insurance may seem to go up, the company-continuity insurance tends to lapse as the top managers get mired in short-range operational decisions with necessarily inadequate hours for the longer-range strategic decisions that are most unlikely to be made at all unless ample hours are saved and used to make them.

In today's fast-paced economy the cycle for such strategic decisions gets shorter, compounding the bad results. The growth of a company, and of its major product divisions, has no mortgage on permanency in the fluid scene in which all in business have to swim. Organizational changes, in time, may be needed due to such impinging strategic items as new technology, new acquisitions (or dispositions), new competitive developments, new international trends or relationships, new situations just due to attained size or diversity, new legal imposition, new possibilities for simplifying or consolidating product components, new markets in new systems or components, new processing or distribution potentials, new financial practices, and so on.

Perhaps you have spotted that this list of factors, which may justify new organizational forms, omits any foregone conclusions that mere changes in executive personnel are basic reasons for major organizational shifts to accommodate to such new personalities. The omission was intentional. I would be last to deny that a strong leader does, and should, put his own mark on the organization he leads. But the question is whether he should do so primarily by altering organization structure and personnel all over the map because his personal experience, or habits or attitudes, naturally vary from those of his predecessor.

A fundamental purpose of formal organization is to fit the needed work relationships, and hence the basic structure of organization, to patterns and trends in the operations that normally are longest lasting, change most slowly, and hence offer a framework for teamwork least likely to require frequent upsets in working contacts and personal give-and-take, which at best take time to get in a smooth groove.

A useful organizational approach, therefore, is to give a real try to "make it work" before rather than after experimental changes. The old carpenter's maxim is worth recall—"Measure twice and then cut once."

This is no plea to suffer on with inefficient or unproductive setups; only to discern the root causes before barging in with changes for their own sake. A well-designed organization structure, evolved in the fires of experience over years of practice, with known contacts (and even frictions), is to be prized in being. Upsets—even when necessary and, in time, productive of substantial improvement in operations—are bound to bring time delays before the parts are running smoothly together once more so that the teamwork as well as the functional work may proceed with minimum attention to their mechanics and maximum attention to their creative betterment in costs, timing, and results. Allowing for time to make these beneficial, innovative changes brings the real balance, and offsets the restraints on personal initiative that go with organized activity.

In decentralized operations—especially as heavy responsibilities are delegated to aggressive younger personnel—mistakes inevitably will be made that the top echelon would have encountered before and avoided. But, if personnel have been well chosen, trained, and tested for competence and growth potential, a vast number of nonmistakes, of genuine advances and favorable steps, will also result. These, also, would *not* have been made by the top echelon.

Here, indeed, is the major reason responsible decentralization— responsibly delegated and responsibly accepted—is likely, in the long run, to produce innovations, progress, and profits not likely to the same extent in highly centralized operations once overall corporate size grows out of the one-man range. The old pilots flew with goggles in a seat out in the wind, but a trained crew watching hundreds of instruments is needed for the big jets now.

An important principle of organization structuring is to get the organizational spans long enough so a resultant minimum number of managers each has a full-time managerial job. The manager should not have any hours left over to mess into work presumptively delegated to those individuals for whose *overall* results he carries basic accountability. Thus, concurrently, the layers, levels, or echelons of management should also be kept to a minimum, facilitating the deep organizational requirement to keep communication channels short and flowing freely both up and down.

Such organization structuring more or less naturally enhances sound decentralization and cuts out work not needed at all. It does this particularly by reducing the dampening effects, and the easy resultant tendency to add multiple-layer staff personnel as a countermeasure when organizational levels are too many and "repeater stations" in the vertical communication flow are more likely to add "noise" than amplify the basic messages carried.

By designing for both minimum levels and a minimum number of organizational components, you reduce the dangers of overorganization, with its excessive costs and delays, proportionately. As one wise manager, Russell Robb, said over half a century ago,

There is such a thing as overorganization, excess of systematization, excess of division of specialization. Dividing out a function that is independent of other activities simplifies, gives definiteness to the plan, places responsibility more accurately, and increases the product of effort through specialization; but, when we attempt divisions that are too fine, when we get to dividing functions that are not naturally independent, we weaken the connection of the activities with the nerve center which coordinates, and we greatly increase the difficulty of cooperation. . . .

Organization is but a means to an end; it provides a method. It can never take the place of business judgment or initiative sense of what it is wise to do, or vigorous initiative that sets things in motion. . . .

One cliché frequently heard is that a division manager in a decentralized division has essentially the same job as the president of an independent company carrying on similar or competitive activities. There's just enough truth to this to make it dangerous.

The two kinds of jobs *are* similar in having general managerial responsibilities to complete, and to do so profitably and accountably in both the short and the long range, with parallel authority for such purposes as required to get results. But they are sharply dissimilar in that the owner interests in whose ultimate behalf such responsibility and authority are exercised, and from which they flow and are delegated in the first place, are distinctly different.

In the independent company, they are concentrated and unique; in the decentralized division, they are common across the several divisional businesses, and need, therefore, to be recognized and heeded accordingly. Hence, at the division level, just as at the individual worker level, functioning in the organized context introduces the added capacity of the joint and multiplying efforts. At the same time, however, it also introduces the restraints on full and separate freedom that are inevitably the concomitant of heeding freedoms for connected components or people just because they are connected. The ties may not be as visible as in Siamese twins but they are just about as binding.

In this country, at least, taking a job in an organized entity is voluntary. Anyone who doesn't care to discipline himself to live harmoniously with such restraints so that they are most mutually effective and least chafing can—and, in due course, should—switch jobs to be able to operate in the context he most prefers.

Earlier I stressed the vital role of information in both the design and the functioning of a complex industrial organization. I also noted that the crashing advent of today's computers is bringing quite a welter of reexamination of the feasibility and desirability of greater degrees of recentralization within widening potentials for getting, using, and dispersing business information.

Having personally been interested in and enthusiastic about developing and introducing computers from their earliest days, my own considered judgment is that they do bring a wholly new dimension to managerial potentials. They definitely can make available information of a scope and timelessness about the work and the teamwork, plans, possibilities, and performance in a complex organization that was never available before. This is a striking current fact of managerial and organizational work.

Easy mental extrapolation might postulate that such availability makes it possible for centralized managers to make decisions simply not feasible for them before, and so, in turn, to downgrade materially the decision responsibilities, and even the organizational existence in heretofore normal proportions, of middle- and lower-echelon managers. New theories have evolved, and new books in profusion, to advance this managerial and organizational concept.

Yet, somehow, I still wonder if we have among us any really universal geniuses—people who marshal in one body and mind the energy, knowledge, skills, and values to make decisions (even with the new breadth and timeliness of factual, recordable data at hand) across all the areas of products and markets; of business, technological, functional, and managerial lore and resources; and of diverse human emotions and values. Can they match what the responsible managers and employees in a sizable show cumulatively can bring to bear on the ever-shifting, highly interlocked, innumerable daily operational situations that are the very body and blood of any dynamic, successful business?

So, with glad recognition that the computer is here to stay and opens up new potentials for effective human organization, I still believe that such potentials will be best and earliest attained when we realize that the same computer-communication system that brings current information to central computer equipment at the speed of light can and should be used to bring the computer's output back to the people at the actual work points with equal speed.

These people would then have fuller and more timely information on the progress of both their work and their teamwork responsibilities. Their response should be better, faster decisions, of a scope and impact not previously feasible at such individual work stations. Thus, if they are competent, they can relieve the upper and corporate echelon executives to devote more of their limited time and wisdom to those corporately significant policies and decisions that are unlikely to be made well, or at all, unless they make them their high-priority personal responsibilities.

This introduces the concept of *policies*, but time permits only briefest coverage of their place and usefulness in corporate organization.

Sometimes a decentralized manager gets results that displease those in higher corporate echelons. When this happens, experience too frequently reveals that the differences are at least as likely to come from failure of the latter to make clear to the former either what is expected from him or in what precise respects he is not coming up to expectations in actual divisional performance as they are to come from either willful concentration on different objectives or basic incompetence.

The inherent restraints of organization on full initiative were stressed earlier. What remains to be said is that, to the maximum reasonable degree, where specific restraints, especially of corporate policy significance, are imposed on particular components or people, they should be expressed clearly in known policies, in writing, and in advance, before performance is measured.

The main thrust is that corporate officers, and the executives of substantial decentralized profit-and-loss operations, should first try to minimize the restraints they feel essential. They should also put those restraints sifting through this judgment screen in writing as defined business policies that have to be accepted in taking, and keeping, any job they affect.

Even then, skillful executive thought will result in policies expressed to define the common interests involved, which emphasize what *can* be done and *why* it is mutually desirable as well as essential. It will not merely result in irritating "thou shalt nots," all too often tempting sinful evasions as diverse as those prevalent in those side-stepping the Ten Commandments.

It is human nature to need and enjoy freedom and to balk at curbs on its scope or exercise. Good managerial values, then, no less than good organizational techniques, call for organization structural design, and for minimum but clear company policies. These policies must maximize freedom and personal initiative and simultaneously minimize restraints and rationalize those required so as to inspire the highest voluntary, and need the lowest imposed, compliance or control.

A wise and very successful general manager friend of mine once explained his concept of the way to the fastest and most profitable growth by saying, "Try to grow with a developing market rather than into an existing and occupied market."

Substitute human nature, with its great potentials all geared in with its historical limitations, and the same principle can be a wise guide for the successful, profitable organization and management of today's large, diversified, technological, industrial enterprises.

5
The
Managerial Functions

The primary elements of the work of a professional manager are planning, organizing, integrating, and measuring as he leads the other employees in their component and in the business as a whole.

You are undoubtedly all deeply familiar with two of these four managing work elements—planning and organizing.

The third element in the managing work of leading, which we can now only examine briefly, is called integrating. Integrating, so conceived, stems specifically from the fundamental managerial philosophy that true managerial leadership is found in accomplishing the common aims of the business and of all employees in the business by example, by participation, by self-discipline, and by persuasion and the logic of the situation, rather than by a command or directive approach.

Integrating thus springs from a clearly understood necessity to bring seemingly divergent strengths into a harmonious direction—a "stronger-bundle-of-sticks" approach. Its value, as a managerial approach and as a primary element of professional managerial work, is that it totals the strengths of an enterprise rather than eliminating those that seem, at the moment, to be pulling in the wrong direction or diluting them by mere compromises that needlessly give up rather than blend in some of the total strengths available.

Integrating is, then, the active creation by the joint efforts of the managerial leader of an enterprise, or of any component in an enterprise, and of the employees themselves, in a climate in which a coalescence of individual and personal intents, desires, skills, and energies

63

and of corporate and component objectives is encouraged to take place voluntarily in order to attain chosen, broad, overall objectives.

We believe that the proper climate for productive unity of purpose cannot be achieved by executive order or command or controls, since such compulsions destroy or dilute understanding by their very nature. And it is understanding, "one for the other" at all levels and throughout all levels of a business, that is the simple result of such integrating activity.

It thus preserves by exercise of self-discipline the essential freedom of the individual in what characteristically and necessarily is a collectivist organization. We should also note here that it preserves both the opportunity and the requirement to base measuring on the work of each such individual—directly and as a part of that work in which the individual is directly interested, and for which he is responsible and accountable.

I think it may be clear, then, that we do "measuring," the fourth element of the managerial work of leadership, as part and parcel of every activity that contributes to our business effectiveness, including especially our managerial effectiveness, and not—instead—as an isolated function; though it is still a discrete work element, harmoniously geared to the rest of the work of each job.

It is difficult to analyze the complex amalgam of activities that constitute the work of successful and professional managing, just as it is to do so for successful accounting, engineering, marketing, or manufacturing. In attempting such analyses, we are forced to try mentally to "stop" an apparently continuous process energized by many diverse drives in an effort to see and understand the parts that constitute its dynamic whole.

So, in these instants of observation, it is necessary to draw heavily upon our experience, in order to give meaningful classification to what we see, and in order to integrate it into our whole system of thought meaningfully.

Command as a Natural Concept of Early Organizations

In earliest days the major, really large organizations requiring management were usually states, armies, churches, and similar noncommercial or nonprofit institutions. In these the task of the leader was fundamentally authoritative. He did command, or govern, or even define doctrine or dogma in an authoritative manner.

Business organizations were generally of lesser scope; and they were chiefly proprietorships, where the functions of owner, with its unique authority, and of manager were commingled in the same individual.

The Technological and Social Inadequacy of Command

Hence, the leader, in fact, possessed authority to lead authoritatively. And, therefore, historically he also commanded.

However, as business or commercial organizations expanded in size, in diversity, in technological complexity, and in dispersion of ownership in the hundred years following the industrial revolution, with their attendant great growth of technology, new basic conditions became controlling.

Even in the history of states, however, the classic evolution has been that of people resisting dictatorial leadership, demanding personal participation, with personal liberty and freedom, in the governing of their lives and affairs.

The two contrasting philosophies of leadership—by command and by persuasion—have evolved accordingly. And out of the perpetual struggle between them has also developed a widening conviction that these are truly not supplemental but contrasting or opposing philosophical concepts; that they are specifically *different* mental approaches to the governing of the affairs of men.

The essence of the difference has also been concentrated in the recognition that, under the one system, motivation is by the leader, imposed on the followers; while under the other approach, the motivation is mutual, is characterized by voluntary participation and joint efforts of followers and leaders, focused by their joint acknowledgment and acceptance of common purposes as definitive of the results and ends they jointly strive to attain.

There are, of course, in our modern business organizations many, many examples of the "proprietor–manager" who serves the objectives of the enterprise in both these roles. In this situation the psychology of proprietorship, essentially and naturally authoritative, needs to be separated from the work of professional managing because different—but not opposing—standards are necessary for the conduct of each function.

The Search for a Properly Descriptive Word

Hence, the element of "command" in the work of managerial leadership early began to be supplemented by various parallel or modifying ideas. Some of these, to cite but a few, were expressed by words like govern, rule, control, and direct. Later modifications—and even, finally, alternatives—included instruct, motivate, administer, guide, counsel, coach, and teach.

The resultant observation and classification process with respect to clearer definition of the work of a manager went on for many years, and the writings between 1910 and 1930 were threaded with efforts to describe the substance of the work.

Dr. Harry Arthur Hopf summarized the advances to which he contributed heavily when, in 1933, he proposed the recognition of four primary elements in the body of the work of a manager, dropping the word "command" entirely in favor of the two words "coordinate" and "control." The work of the manager, then, as he conceived it, consisted of planning, organizing, coordinating, and controlling.

Dr. Hopf thus sensed that managing—especially in the modern business world—had become definitely different from the command concepts that dominated the leadership function in earlier institutions.

With his many contemporaries in the generation following Taylor, the Gilbreths, Fayol, Gantt, Emerson, and other pioneers of Scientific Management, he gave positive and creative thought to the point that the human urge that has inevitably sought liberty and resisted dictatorship in the governing of men had the same validity in diversified business and industrial organizations as in the earlier forms of human association.

Along with Hopf, such gifted contemporary and following practitioners and writers in the field of management as Mrs. Gilbreth, Metcalf, Dennison, Filene, Cottingham, Wallace Clark, Walter D. Scott, Cooke, Persons, Alford, Tead, Donald, Gulick, Lewisohn, Hoover, Alfred Sloan, Spriegel, Mayo, McKinsey, Mooney and Reiley, Hook, Francis, Kimball, Barnard, Schell, Appley, Cordiner, and Drucker all progressively coped with this problem of defining the dynamic, or motivation, phases of the work of a manager more clearly.

Their observations, research, practice, and writing were both aided and complicated by parallel developments in the business institution itself, especially as the modern industrial corporation became the characteristic form of competitive business enterprise.

Such developments were, in turn, also paralleled by the emergence of corporate bodies of increasing size and scope in the fields of government, education, charity, welfare, and, finally, organized labor.

In all of these ran the common thread that the work of the manager, as such, was steadily disassociated from authority rooted in either personal proprietorship or sovereignty. Thus, the quality of managerial leadership needed ever more cogently to find its roots in the ancient principles of liberty, freedom, and human dignity, rather than in any meaningful right to demand obedience from fellow workers in the enterprise or activity being managed.

6
Planning as a Fundamental Component of Managing

Planning as a fundamental component of managing is of such scope that voluntary restraint is pertinent. As Bennett Cerf once wrote, "They should have given an 'A' to the resourceful student who, asked for a principal use of cowhide, hazarded, 'to hold the cow together'!"

Realistically, the manager is the "cowhide" of the complex organization, responsible for holding the cow together—especially by planning it that way as a basic component of his specifically managerial work.

In practice, professional training and education is producing too many analysts, too few synthesizers and integrators.

Despite the assumption in academic literature that management is just problem-solving for rational technologists to exploit and enjoy for their personal satisfaction, real-life management is a dynamic, continuing, and complex human process.

Managing is that process which calls for anticipating, and for avoiding or minimizing, problems through effective leadership of highly motivated fellow workers—both professionals and others—so

Remarks at the eleventh annual symposium of the Institute of Management Sciences College of Planning, Century Plaza Hotel, Los Angeles, November 12, 1968.

the contributions of all cumulate into output performance for which customer value exceeds production cost. If that cycle stops, the economy and the whole society in which it operates are in trouble.

Planning has such a part in business managing that in the United States historically it has helped build an economy surpassing the trillion-dollar mark in gross national product and throwing off a tax stream in proportion. But government planning has sponged up that whole swollen tax flow and still run up debts of astronomical proportions—for the young to pay in tribute to their parents' fling. Might some perceptive realization of its prospective inheritance explain some of youth's tremors today? And will they save to pay the debts or let them sink in mounting inflation?

The background of planning as a component of managerial work lies deep in early management practice and literature. Parallel components have also long included organizing, and then several others.

Earlier, the others were usually called directing or commanding. Thus, in 1925 Henri Fayol wrote on "the reasons for a long-term plan":

In an undertaking with any complexity at all it is necessary to have well-thought-out directives, which indicate anticipated progress for a period of time.

These directives must be based on an understanding of the undertaking, its present position, and the reasons for this and external circumstances. . . . The act of forecasting is of great benefit to all who take part in the process, and is the best means of ensuring adaptability to changing circumstances.

Today many experts name the other components of managerial work coordinating and controlling, but different practitioners call them integrating and measuring.

The latter philosophy and concept connote leadership by inspiration and persuasion of self-disciplined co-workers offering creativity, initiative, and teamwork to attain common goals for the enterprise. The former view and terms connote instead the leader who exercises authority over others, who uses them to work out his ideas rather than to get performance and innovations from their aggregate brains beyond his personal resources.

Making a clear personal choice between the two contrasting concepts is a rough but necessary commitment that every practicing manager ought to make and profess.

The contrast pictures the broader strife in today's real world.

From Mexico to Czechoslovakia to Peking to Paris to Berkeley or the Columbia campus, the cry is strident for greater personal participation by all in the organization in making decisions that affect their lives and interests.

This is a human cry. It is the real world cry. It is not going away. It has to be the base of assumptions by today's and tomorrow's planners. And it *can* be. That's the great live fruit of the technology now so questioned; and it had better be, so anarchy does not become the too-prevalent alternative.

Against that backdrop, what *is* planning as a basic component of distinctly managerial work?

Essentially, for a manager at *any* organizational echelon, his planning task for the particular component managed is to set objectives and to outline policies, plans, programs, timetables, and performance standards, and to get them realized. These fundamentals apply alike to long- and short-range plans, and to top managers and managers of functional, departmental, product, or project components of the organization.

The concept so stated is not to be skipped over lightly. Bluntly, it is that all managers should participate in the planning process of the enterprise of institution. An elite group of planners should not plan for the others, whose chore is then to execute plans handed to them.

In other words, planning is a basic part of the work of every manager, in the context of his respective component and its relationships within the total organization and in its total external environment.

If a need exists, especially in large complex enterprises, for a specific planning group at the corporate level, consideration should be given to focusing the work of its members heavily in three limited fields.

1. To act as experts in the planning process available as counsellors to all managers, so all may understand how to plan as part of their own generic managerial work.

2. To help shape the planning policies and standards of the institution.

3. To do wise corporate planning and to look into unclear areas that may have new significance in the future of the enterprise but do not fall plainly within the responsibility scope of particular functional, operating, or project components.

In long-range planning, the primary contribution can often be from imaginative rethinking of scopes and aims, rather than from usually futile exercises to predict or prescribe far into the future the detailed methodology or programs to attain new or revised objectives. The real goal is to help develop challenging common purposes that all can make their own; and so have a voluntary incentive to program the work, the teamwork, the costs, and the schedules to reach chosen objectives competitively, early, and profitably.

In determining objectives, the manager analyzes old trends yet thinks open-mindedly ahead, anticipating future choices with perception, imagination, courage, and faith. He looks toward the future hopefully, constructively, and creatively to combine originality and boldness with a capacity to think straight under pressure, to take advantage of all opportunities, while at the same time avoiding costly mistakes, confusion, rigidity, and stagnation. Goals so shaped can win powerful organization acceptance and implementation in detail in myriad ways never visible in advance but strangely contributive to continuing competitive growth.

Another subelement of managerial planning is establishing policies. Sound policies—not to be confused with methodology— reflect broad human values and maintain a balance between long- and short-range goals and between all jobs or components of the entire enterprise. Properly prepared, they are positive statements of common interests in defined types of situations. Properly conceived, they rarely consist of only negative rules, except in some very few areas, where some potent restriction—as of law, finances, or public good— clearly has to apply for all in the organization.

Well-drawn and communicated policies, used as aids to wise planning, also facilitate picking sound priorities and keeping a realistic balance among specific objectives in the face of the normal conflicts that arise among them from time to time. Such policies invite loyal employee understanding and public acceptance. They anticipate difficulties to be met, allow for persistent and confident steps to surmount same, and expect high performance standards from all involved.

The third phase in planning work is to formulate chosen courses into well-designed plans, schedules, and performance standards. This calls for grubby detail to research orderly paths to progress, to analyze alternatives resourcefully, to see opportunities beyond problems, and to assemble and make adequate facts available in advance to all concerned as a basis for reasoned, cool, and impersonal decisions. This process culminates in selecting and stating tasks to gain objectives and in determining programs and timetables clear enough to facilitate accurate visualization and participation by all involved.

Such plans are usually expressed as budgets—both long- and short-range—for (1) manpower–managerial, other professional, and other; (2) facilities and equipment, especially if they are to be capitalized, not expensed; (3) operations; that is, sales and income, expenses and outgo, net profit and return on investment; and (4) cash and financing. The latter includes any new money required and a balanced use of cash for planned needs rather than in gear with its origin in the organization. This calls for tough managerial decisions, for building strengths as well as eliminating weaknesses, for seeing the picture as a whole as well as in detail. As Ralph Cordiner so sharply summed it up:

The manager who merely tries to keep his plans and policies up-to-date is already out-of-date. He must keep them up-to-the-future where the objectives of the business will be achieved.

That is a good note on which to shift from "background" to "perspective." The perspective offered you is personal, conjectural, and surely controversial, but it aims to outline some areas in which conventional long-range planning—in both business and government—may need a crisply fresh look.

In the business domain two comments may suffice to light up the potentials—and the pitfalls. First, the desirability of deliberately decentralizing planning as the work of all managers, not of an elite few, and of focusing on long-range objectives but short-range operational plans, has already been stated plainly. This decentralization will be more, not less, necessary in the future.

Such decisions are part of the pressing requirement for each top and other manager to make and proclaim the philosophy—the theory, if you please—of his managerial approach. He can lead by command, limit scope to what he can see, and get others, by actual or implied contact relationship, to implement on agreed terms rather than by deep personal commitment. Or he can lead by inspiration, persuasion, and integration of voluntary followers whose aggregate contributions can well exceed what he can think up.

In perspective—with ever more alert, informed, and educated co-workers—signs of the times say the second alternative can be more common, necessary, and productive. The choice here is focused on the manager's planning work, but it has to apply also to the totality of his generically managerial function. His associates are saying that he has to make and proclaim his choice. This choice will not go away in days ahead.

For many bold commanders, for many who aspire to the elite role, the second alternative is unwelcome. It can raise fears of giving up familiar powers and roles with no certainty of quick competence in the new role. Overdramatized, it may even seem to risk switching the unemployment threat to the executive ranks. What will *they* do, if many decisions they formerly made can now be decentralized?

Well, just don't worry too much over that one, because many factors are converging to give the so-called "top managers" unique responsibilities and ever greater work opportunities to "risk" in the best competitive economic sense, on the one hand, and to play the game so that they will receive adequately motivating rewards and satisfactions for competent professional performance, on the other. They include:

◇ The increasing size of their overall organizations.
◇ The multiplying intricacies of internal and external relationships.
◇ The growing need for clearer, yet more involved, goals and policies.
◇ The ever-growing size, futurity, and risks of resource-commitment decisions.
◇ The intensifying need, as risks widen and extend, to make the essential profits—representing customer-voted values in the marketplace in substantial excess of mounting costs.
◇ The constantly penetrating, and proper, customer and public scrutiny of both goals and results.
◇ The shocking failures of performance, productivity, and publicly acceptable deployment of human talent and of substantial but still scarce physical and financial resources in more and more nonbusiness institutions.
◇ The steadily growing requirement to manage with ethical and professional personal dedication, no less than technical competence.

For every historic skill, thrill, and decision—especially in planning—now delegated confidently to others in the organization, whether managers or functional individual contributors, greater new "top" responsibilities will continue to arise.

The human factors involved are likely to change, but slowly. The men and women in the Bible, in your ancient history book, or in your foreign geography for that matter, always seem uncannily familiar to us. The situations in which they involved themselves, the idioms they developed in the language, the garments in which they garbed themselves, the worldly focus to which they applied their thoughts and emotions, the tools and machines they devised to lighten the manual or the mental toll of their work, all these have shifted, evolved, and changed; yet the people themselves still seem brothers under the skin. And, in perspective, it is highly questionable if even the "new biology" is going to change that very fast.

In 1937, facing a similar world crisis, Anne O'Hare McCormick, returning from Europe just before World War II, phrased the human perspective in these thoughtful words:

The capacity of ordinary people to adapt themselves to the whims of their masters is much more remarkable than the capacity exhibited by any government.

The resilience of the human species, the immortal quality of mortals, is the first wonder of the world; never more wonderful than now. Under the pressure of dictatorships or the uncertainties of democracy, populations everywhere go quietly about their daily business, scheming for profit, seeking for pleasure, eluding, evading or humoring their masters, by their normal habits preserving the effect of normal life in abnormal times. . . . There is more light and cheer in the encircling gloom than you'd expect.

So much for the first "perspective" comment in the business field. The second is that, by any fair judgment, the business planning process has worked, and marvelously well, in the United States. The trillion-dollar economy, even carrying the huge government tax load piggyback, is the reality of these days and times. The fundamental legitimacy of this decision process flows from the impersonal, multiple-risk realities of the marketplace; positively not from some overriding master plan.

In fact, the swelling pressures of attempts to supersede the marketplace with more master planning are at the root of a great deal of the unrest that today's vocal, educated, and even violent majorities are expressing to a degree beyond that seen by Miss McCormick in 1937.

So, to repeat, the second "perspective" comment is that the business planning process—highly diversified, decentralized, and exposed to the hard economic test of the marketplace—does work even in the complex seventies and, prospectively, will still do so in the even more complex eighties.

The conclusion should be—and this opens up parallel "perspective" comments on government planning—that the business planning concept should be extended to a greater segment of the nation's overall operations. Very precisely, as a first of two "perspectives" on government long-range planning, this calls for a corresponding narrowing, in an orderly programmed way, of the activities that have developed in the governmental sector; and doing so with "all deliberate speed" to heed the expressed views of the clear majority of American voters, customers, and employees.

Consideration is clearly appropriate here of why narrowing the field of government planning is worthy of the best thought, imagination, and constructive speculation we can give it, and of how such a fundamental rearrangement of national efforts can be approached in nondestructive ways. But let's come back to that after a second basic "perspective" comment on the government planning situation today.

The second "perspective" is that the external, or international, dimensions of government planning have reached an historic crossroads—with old trends exhausted and new approaches crying to be devised. The background of popular unrest and of failures of big government planning is as visible abroad as at home. The situation is well stated in the commonsense words of the editor of a small, upstate New York daily paper:

A kind of addiction to violence is becoming increasingly noticeable everywhere, reflected in the rising crime rate, the outbreak of minor clashes and uprisings all over the world, the unwillingness of more and more people to accept even minimal restraints on their activities. Yet the very fact that the population is rising and we are living closer together makes it more important than ever to get along peaceably with each other.

The trend is worldwide. From personal observation on successive visits to a wide, around-the-world sampling of nations, eight outstanding realities impressed on my mind are, in brief:

1. Power greater than understanding of its use.
2. Nationalism on the rise; old alliances slipping.
3. Communication outstripping comprehension, with personal fears greater than understanding.
4. Revolution on the increase; but a nasty business.
5. People surprisingly ahead of their leaders; a great vacuum for the future-oriented and youth-oriented leaders today.
6. The nonprofit economics of socialism spreading; but failing.
7. A leadership vacuum as a world problem; conditions in the

new nations deteriorating fast, with colonial-trained bureaucrats dying off or retiring, and essential indigenous leadership out of the new generation simply not visible in even minimum required quantity or quality.

8. Military dictatorships insidiously dominating, of apparent necessity, the ruling party bureaucrats in the Communist world; but with focus on foreign expansion both to fill the colonial gap and to use the "foreign devil" to rally home populations increasingly unsatisfied with home situations and trends.

These, I believe, are realistic dimensions of the international political economy in which a younger generation now has to take up the leadership (and the planning) torch. To me they add up to still more reasons for decentralizing U.S. domestic governmental activities, following the lead of business organizations to a major new degree. For one thing, the military share of the total U.S. economy—with at least much of it necessarily governmental—is not going to shrink much in this sort of itchy world. Next, top government leaders need the time for new planning, policymaking, alliance building, and trade development at the level of international government affairs and relationships.

To gain this time, those leaders must demand the maximum feasible reduction of the present scope of government and the decentralization of resources, costs, and personnel into nongovernment institutions. This is essential both to avoid public revolt against the government's costs and pressures and to be able to competently manage the still necessarily huge government sector with available leadership, especially since rotating, short-tenured elected top leaders have to be more responsive to short- than to long-range requirements. Like it or not, future government planning will not be workable unless conceived in such dimensions.

Like the top managers in business, the top leaders in government need to delegate more old, familiar decisions; and to confront—however ill-prepared they are psychologically—the new and different decision scopes they alone can, and should, take on and risk.

Let us go back now to why fundamental government planning should consciously shrink the scope of domestic government and how—with new imaginative thinking—orderly progress in that groove may be made. The "why" has many dimensions, but the overshadowing fix is in the threatening confrontation of the coming generations with the inflationary pressures bequeathed to them so far.

In a powerful book called *The Promises Men Live By* (back in 1938), Harry Scherman pointed out that whereas, historically, promises in the economic area are largely kept, if only because they are so heavily interdependent, those in the government area

. . . may almost infallibly be expected—if we allow sufficient time to elapse—to be broken. That is the hard fact. . . . The capstone of the arch, the governmental promise, proves never to be anything but clay.

Scientists generally—and perhaps management scientists particularly—characteristically disregard the practical old adage that "the other fellow's experience is the cheapest" and want deeply to roll their own, to experiment individually. But when their field—planners included—is that of the human sciences rather than only the material sciences, more caution seems in order than many presently display.

The key thought here involves the new scope, in all kinds of institutions, of managing "professionals," with a lot of education and with natural loyalties to their own intellect and profession rather than to organization goals. As a 1966 report to the Pentagon by the Aerospace Industries Association said:

In as complex a business as ours, there is almost no end to the areas of specialization in being or coming. This in itself presents a difficult management task; keeping cultists from becoming the tail that wags the dog.

We have always managed "specialists," but without confusing the specialization of their work with their being "special" people. The new dimension of today's specialist is the high degree to which he may be educated in his specialty, coupled too often with inadequate education (or inclination) to function in his specialty in the real world with equally self-important co-workers. As one nonspecialist so aptly said, "He has to put his pants on one leg at a time, same as I do."

Of all the calamitous possibilities today, possibly that of disastrous inflation—even ultimate repudiation of the enormous government debt on a violent rather than an evolutionary scale—could well be the "perspective" most challenging for government planners. With such a specter peeping over the planning horizon, any casual convergence or conjuncture of present trends in government and business planning needs real reflection.

However, a parallel fact of life also needs appreciation. The constructive possibilities of government—and government planning—have shone in the white light of the real world in the critical decades since the worldwide depression of the thirties, which exposed the limitations of unscrutinized business planning and performance insofar as paying full attention to the overall public interest goes. This lesson is still not to be forgotten.

Science and technology have produced vast new potentials, however untidily. They conjure up potential new citizen wants and needs, on a continuing basis, that surpass readily available resources. Hence, planning for optimum resource allocations, and creation, will get tougher. One survey of customer wants came up with the pragmatic, but probably realistic, finding that at any given time they are "about 110 to 115 percent of current personal income." Word does get around; and the economic motive is still human and potent.

Many technological potentials, of great human interest, are clear enough to be visible and discussed, yet not clear enough to be planned and achieved within normally tolerable risk patterns of even large private enterprises. Sometimes the potential—whether of an atomic bomb or a nuclear power plant, whether of elimination of pollution or provision of new housing on an all-city scale—seems broadly desirable to the citizenry at large and increasingly possible. In those cases, constructive experience in both democratic and socialistic economies shows rising demands for government to pioneer, to take such high risks on a communitywide basis, to bring the potential to reality in the public good earlier than otherwise practicable. This too is today's reality.

Hence the mess in which our inflation-ridden polity and economy now founders. The great hope for planners with modern technology and new computer-based information systems as tools is to find out how to continue to make progress without bringing down the governmental roof and destroying everything in the process.

To review, planning decisions legitimatized by the open-market process generally have worked, but those based only on the sovereign power of government increasingly seem to be forced to choose between loss of freedom in the "order" of military dictatorship and loss of freedom by inflationary collapse into economic chaos.

An apparently obvious way stands out to have your cake and eat it too. Use the government process for things only government presently can do—the public defense for overall peace, as distinct from the provision of identifiable services to particular voters, pioneering in unclear and still highly risky areas, and so on. But limit it to just such areas, where public support is not likely to wane. At the same time, by orderly and progressive planning, using all the possibilities of modern information systems as major, expensive fields are entered, take positive steps to switch out of those in which there is enough experience for business to step in without incurring unreasonable risks.

Fortunately, examples already are being visualized and exploited. The COMSAT-type of corporate organization holds such a promise. The use of some similar institution to get the post office out of politics would help. As experience from such orderly experimentation unfolds, imaginative possibilities develop.

Huge as governmental debt obligations now are, and threatening as their future repudiation by progressively destructive inflation now seems, there are overbalancing government assets and operations that could be used to offset and retire such debts and, simultaneously, to shrink the government sector of the total economy accordingly.

The kind of thinking required demands the best possible contributions from both business and government planners. The practical goal should be to work out publicly acceptable plans and feasible timetables, from both economic and political standpoints, to increase the segment of the national economy in which the market test legitimatizes the decision process. These plans should also aim to reduce the huge government sector to a still acceptable and nondisastrous scope. Even in that sector, planning should seek to decentralize from federal to state to local levels, where public observation and judgment of both plans and results can be maximized.

At the same time, the positive lessons of recent decades for the business sector manager need to be heeded. For example, the whole concept of the corporate "plowing back" of earnings in excess of fair current dividend payments has had a constructive part in developing large, successful private corporations today. However, it does shortcut the test of the open capital market in a direct sense, and it does bring more and more public questions on the size, scope, and disclosed visibility of very large operations with correspondingly broad public impacts.

Business planners would be wise to reexamine such matters constantly, to make, rather than obstruct, maximum disclosure of their diversified operations, to submit many major and fairly conventional capital programs to the test of the public market for new money, where all claimants can compete, rather than proceed only internally because cash is so available.

Such tests to keep business planning both successful and publicly acceptable, coupled with parallel experiments to apply a rough "one out for one in" principle in government planning, might well show areas in which the two might come to closer convergence by integrating their respective unique strengths rather than compounding their weaknesses.

In 1952, in response to Professor Livingston's ASME "Ten-Year Progress Report," I set forth some potentials for a science of management. They seem pertinent here:

A true science of management will have to be rooted in:

The principles of liberty, not the principles of compulsion;

The principles of reason, not the principles of force;

The principles of leadership by integration of voluntary individual efforts in cooperative teamwork, not the principles of leadership by command, control, or dictation; and, therefore, in

The principles of morality, not the principles of materialism;

The principles of religion, not the principles of atheism; and, finally, in

The deep belief that, however complex society and its social interrelationships may ever become, the natural rights of the individual as a person, including the right to hold and acquire property, are of a different order of priority than all the other rights in the so-called social matrix; and

In recognition that if such other rights are to have validity and permanency, they must themselves flow from initial, voluntary agreement of the *individuals* concerned to modify their full personal liberties mutually for their mutual, or collective, security or benefit.

So, in closing—and on no little evidence of a tendency of too many academic and professional specialists today, again with planners included, to put themselves in a class apart—I suggest that we all be skeptical of the abstract ideas of specialists that, they claim, can't be expressed in simple, normal language. And let us also watch that evasive substitute for thinking, "You have to experience this to appreciate it."

Some make a career of defining problems by taking normal work situations out of context and then, by jargon and repetition, building a generally unnecessary, overriding activity (at times even called a planning component) that, like a barnacle on the hull of a ship, distorts the normal flow, requires excess energy and money, and in time, if left alone, multiplies both in size and in distortion. Instead, we should reserve faith approaches for faith areas, like religion.

Each of us, singly, has the power to seize the opportunities still before us to keep our free society and its diverse institutions both progressive and manageable. We can do so by taking on a fair share of the personal research, the development, the application, and the responsibility and teamwork to make that goal come true.

7
Long-Range Planning

The choices men in an organization—and also out of the organization—are making today are shaping the organization and the choices of the men who will work in it in its future years in some measure and degree; just as such current choices are themselves influenced by those of predecessors in years gone by.

Whether the current choices are being made in conscious anticipation—even in planned causative anticipation—of the "shape of things to come" or only being made regardless of subsequent events and consequences, the fundamental principle inexorably applies.

Dr. Jay W. Forrester of the Massachusetts Institute of Technology, in his book on *Industrial Dynamics* (1961), put it this way,

Past decisions on new product research, development of personnel, choice of products and markets, and construction of manufacturing facilities have already determined the essential characteristics of the corporation. The challenge lies in how today's decisions will affect the time between five and twenty-five years hence.

The principle of managerial responsibility thus indicated is of long standing. The dangers of not understanding and following it

Unpublished speech, 1962.

81

were cogently stated by Henri Fayol nearly half a century ago, in 1916,

Lack of sequence in activity and unwarranted changes in course are dangers constantly threatening a business without a plan. The slightest contrary wind can turn from its course a boat that is unfitted to resist.

When serious happenings occur, regrettable changes of course may be decided upon under the influence of profound but transitory disturbance. Only a program, carefully pondered at an undisturbed time, permits of maintaining a clear view of the future and of concentrating maximum possible intellectual ability and material resources on the danger.

The significance of the "time" dimension in business thinking, decision, and action has always been critical to managerial and other business planning. The "new" elements are the accelerated rate of changes in contemporary knowledge and society, compounded by the greater length—and the attendant increased uncertainties involved—of the time period that is pertinent.

"Long-range planning" now means, for more and more businessmen—and no less for leaders in other organized institutions, both private and governmental—the necessity to look from five to twenty-five years forward. An earlier generation could settle, with a fair balance of safety and risks, for, say, five to twenty-five months. The new period is thus of the order of twelve times longer—a difference distinctly in order of magnitude, not simply in degree. The words "long range" in the title of this dissertation take on meaning in these terms as a result.

An equal clarity of conceptual thought is appropriate here with respect to the word "planning" in that same title. It is important to be as precise as feasible; both as to what the word does, or should, or can, imply and as to what it doesn't, or shouldn't, or can't, embrace.

First and foremost, for long-range business planning, planning is probably a questionable word to begin with. This is because—especially in political circles in this day and age—it is so commonly used to cover a deterministic or positivistic approach.

No matter how effective such an approach may be in scientific planning in purely physical or closed systems, it is of limited and even dangerous appropriateness for application in the open, biologically human-type systems with which the "planner" in business has to deal. This chapter, to keep it within feasible bounds, will focus heavily on long-range planning in *business* organizations, especially as performed by managers in business; although the majority of the points made will probably be as appropriate for planning in other kinds of institutions.

The systems of which human beings—with their emotions, imagination, and beliefs as well as logical reasonings and thoughtful rationalizations—are internally constituent elements are intrinsically "open" systems, even by definition. Any attempt—by direct approach or by default—to consider them otherwise can, at best, be but an approximation of some of their more obviously stable current patterns, and, at worst, a dangerous delusion or a vicious perversion of their human aspects.

Perhaps the best recourse would be to throw the title away and to substitute some such caption as "Causative Anticipation as a Factor Affecting Future Decades in the Course of an Organization's Development, Progress, and Growth." But even if that is better, it's just too long and cumbersome to keep repeating. So, for current purposes, this paper will continue to use "Long-Range Planning" and to have these words carry the general connotations of the longer and less cryptic caption.

With terms so defined, therefore, it is worthwhile next to consider such aspects of long-range planning as the what, why, when, how, where, and who—the "six honest serving men" Kipling found so useful some six decades ago.

WHAT TO PLAN

In long-range planning, two principles stand out to help choose what to plan. First, plan the objectives and results sought over the planning period, rather than the comparatively detailed operations through which such performance will be attained. Second, plan in terms of the essential structures of the organization that are most likely to hold relatively stable, or at least to be subject to optimum anticipatory guidance as the course of events develops, rather than just in terms of current but more transient specific tasks, projects, or activity campaigns.

The necessity for heeding the first of these two principles is multiplied as new knowledge flows from widening research in innumerable fields of speculation and inquiry and as modern technology progressively facilitates the almost worldwide spread, understanding, and use of such new knowledge. As a result, familiar work habits, methods, equipment, and relationships are constantly changing, and at accelerating rates of change, defying precise long-range visualization many years in advance.

Speaking on the complexity of economic problems, John F. Kennedy gave this graphic description of the situation:

I would like to say a word about the difference between myth and reality. . . . The fact of the matter is that most of the problems, or at least many of them, that we now face are technical problems, are administrative problems. They are very sophisticated judgments which do not lend themselves to the great sort of passionate movements which stirred this country so often in the past.

Now they deal with questions that are beyond the comprehension of most men, most governmental administrators, over which experts may differ. . . . The sophisticated technical questions which affect our economy cannot be solved without the wholehearted cooperation of all groups.

These remarks illuminate two vital aspects of today's world for the long-range planner. It is a world of highly complex activities and relationships; and it is a world in which no planner, even with all the resources of huge governments to call on, can "plan" realistically except in terms of the working fit of his policies and programs with other policies and programs planned by other men, whose decisions thus are as vital to fulfillment of his plan as his decisions are.

The long-range plan, therefore, can pick and delineate aims, ends, or objectives to be sought by men under such complex realities. It neither can nor should try to fix the ever-changing operational activities to be devised to carry on the detailed work required for such purposes. And in deliberately avoiding doing so, the planner gains the great opportunity to be able to take advantage of, and to benefit from, countless subsequent operational ideas of others, germane to the progress of the enterprise, that it is not at all in his human power to anticipate to any great degree.

On the other hand, in order "to get there from here," a useful long-range plan clearly has to comprehend more than objectives alone. Its content as to interim periods covered needs to be a nice blend of perception of structures and patterns, underlying the detailed activities, that can be expected to change at least comparatively slowly, and relatively more predictably or determinably than their ramified operational manifestations.

Such more plannable structures vary from enterprise to enterprise. The more usual and more basic among them include the fundamental product or service charter and market or customer scopes that are to be the basis of the "buy and sell" business; the corporate and financial structures required; the informational and report structure; the general organization structure to be able to plan the human resources essential and the managerial and other professional leaders they will need, in time, for their efforts to be effective; the basic structure of facilities and material resources called for; the primary distribution and marketing structure; and the structural aspects of the overall enterprise as itself a component in the larger industry, community, nation, and international structures, within which its managers will either function on a voluntarily cooperative basis or find either failure or imposed gearing of relationships by external authorities as an obviously undesirable alternative.

Within the two broad principles outlined, the "what" to plan can then embrace such main constituent steps as:

1. Determining objectives.
2. Establishing policies.
3. Formulating plans (including schedules) and standards of performance.
4. Making known the objectives, policies, plans, and standards.
5. Using the results of measuring to readjust continually the work of planning.
6. Exercising judgment and making reasoned, objective, and timely decisions to effectuate the planning work and progress.

A special word is pertinent about Step 2. The concept of "policy" is deliberately used here in the sense of the result of identifying common interests—and hence areas of common purposes individually and voluntarily sought in daily work. It is *not* used in the sense of a centrally promulgated order resting solely on top-down authority.

There is a deep philosophical contrast. The policymaking approach urged here is a system of leadership in which both managers (or governors) and their professional and other worker associates define common interests; translate these into common purposes, objectives, or goals; and then initially and voluntarily accept individual responsibility and commensurate authority to make their personal decisions, at whatever level of the organizational hierarchy, in the interest of the overall enterprise and not merely in the interests of their individual selves, or jobs, or organization components.

Modern technology, for the first time in history, makes it possible to acquire and distribute the needed information on both work and relationships (or teamwork) so that individual workers, informed enough to be pursuing the same goals as their managerial and other colleagues, can make personal decisions on such a basis.

Long-range planning for tomorrow's decades plainly should be such as to plan for successful future employment of such thrilling new organizational potentials; and not be mere extrapolation, or defensive preservation, of past conditions, past practices, past relationships, or past planning failures.

Why to Plan

The interests of managers in business in why to plan can be constructively differentiated from those of many others who also have occasion or desire to think about the future. The planning responsibility of managers is that of men deliberately carrying the responsibilities of leadership in key institutions in tomorrow's complex society and economy and exercising them increasingly in the public interest; not merely looking irresponsibly for crisis in human events as an opportunity for seizing power over the lives of other, more confused, and more uncertain people.

As indicated in a paper of July 1960, by the author and Edward D. Kemble of General Electric Company, on "The Future of Managing and Organizing for Managers in Business,"

The point of differentiation—that of viewpoint on crisis—probably is most helpful in swinging the focus on the future to a direction that is businesslike for managers. The work of managers is to achieve manageability in human courses of action, and so their businesslike viewpoint of a crisis is merely of a situation that is in need of being manageable.

Probably the essence of what is businesslike in this viewpoint is that there is little of the exhilaration of excitement, drama, or heady power in the approach to crises. Rather it is conceived of as a situation calling for hard work, cool and collected action, and a systematic, piecemeal reduction of what is a roadblock to manageable courses of action.

Crises are thus routine matters of business. In the development of courses of action, managers in business attempt to anticipate situations that have a crisis potential and to provide routine, rather than crisislike, methods of handling them. When uncontrollable circumstances, or their own errors of judgment, nevertheless produce a crisis, managers expect to use their managerial abilities to reduce it, as a part of the regular routine business of the day.

This is not to say that managerial ability is capable of quick and smooth elimination of troublesome challenges. Rather, the point is one of attitude, manner, and expectancy in the approach to a crisis. It is one of employing workmanship, innovation, and evolution, rather than one of explosive force, unrestrained power, or revolution. It is one of weighing many courses of action in judgment, rather than the unrealistic "black" or "white." And it is one of employing the means available to competitive enterprise . . . in a "free civilization."

From such a stance, the planning—and, more particularly, the long-range planning—work of managers in business is a basic constituent of appropriate, legitimate, and responsible leadership on their part; both in the organization managed and in the larger communities in which such an organization functions and serves.

Such a vision of managerial responsibility contrasts markedly with one of merely applying administrative skills in adapting to the current environment (and particularly to take selfish advantage) and in passively accepting a future as if already determined by the current frame of reference. As the Smiddy–Kemble paper mentioned above also stated,

Although rigorous observation does indeed indicate that today's events are at least a partial causative factor in determining tomorrow's situations, there is the eternal possibility that human events consist of something more than a mere interaction of blind forces and that faith to that end is a normal human characteristic. The human mind has the gift of creative imagination. The mind can imagine a situation that has not yet occurred, and such imagined situations can be more than a mere consequence of prior conditioning—that is, an inevitable outcome of prior events. They can be creatively fashioned to fit a purpose, to satisfy objectives, to fulfill desired ends.

Thinking backwards from such imagined situations, individuals can frequently conceive of a series of events by which the present situation might and can be converted into the desired future situation. When this has occurred, the conscious purpose, objective, or desired end of a human being has become an additional causative factor in the events that unfold. Individuals, managers, and others can thus do more than plan for a future. They can follow courses of action, each one of which makes a change in the current environment according to the preconceived series of events, until the desired situation finally is a reality. . . . There are, of course, limitations on such human action. One of them pertains to the idea of human fallibility . . .

fallibility in scope and rigor of imagination and no less in rigor of intended action.

Another limitation occurs when—as is mostly the case in the modern industrial (and governmental) complex—*concerted* action is required of many people. In such cases leadership is frequently required. Some of the leadership is that of people with the most advanced specialized competences, so that the most feasible means of achievement will be obtained in the many involved courses of action.

In view of the constantly expanding knowledge, however, there is increasingly needed a specialized competence in leadership itself. This is a competence in understanding the *purposes* of the concerted action and in understanding the ways in which people work together and recognize their common interests in voluntary concerted action. The work involved in *this* competence is indeed the work of managing. This is the professional managerial contribution to the achievement of manageability.

Leadership in long-range planning, visualized in such a context, contemplates planning that will serve as a solid basis for leadership through inspiration and by persuasion of fact and logic, rather than by command—recognizing always that the resultant required work is performed largely by other individuals who themselves, like the manager, are also acting with initiation, self-development, self-discipline, and competence in both their personal work and their voluntary teamwork and two-way communication.

As the general responsible for the planning that resulted in the 1962 realignment of the organization structure of the large and far-flung U.S. Army aptly said, "Planning is for the future; and the future is for those who think about it—whose skills are fortified by values and attitudes causing them to *prepare* to meet challenges as they arise."

Such planning has its roots in research, in informed thought, in effective communication—in advance; or, as Fayol said, in terms of "a program carefully pondered at an undisturbed time."

Today's economy, with all its new industrial and technological characteristics, is still a human economy—and so still a political economy. The old economic content of managerial planning consequently has to be enhanced to take in such new public and social responsibilities. The need and goal were crisply condensed in Pope John XXIII's encyclical "Mother and Teacher," under the heading "Respect for the Hierarchy of Values," in these cogent comments:

Scientific and technical progress, economic development, the betterment of living conditions are certainly positive elements in a civilization. But we must remember that they are not, nor can they be, considered the supreme values, in comparison with which values they are seen as essentially *instrumental* in character.

In this modern working climate—or culture or environment— quite different from that of the old-time proprietor-capitalist and entrepreneur, there is a corresponding imperative need for future-oriented managerial leadership, and planning, founded on:

◇ A positive, not a negative, mental approach.
◇ A will to sense opportunities, and to risk to win them; not merely to solve problems or to concentrate on fire fighting rather than on fire prevention.
◇ A competence to see the enterprise, the community, and the nation as a whole; not merely to focus on one's own job, own projects, or own gains, irrespective of the methods used to attain them.
◇ A capacity to plan for dynamic continuity and progress and growth; not just for coping with crises as they crop up.
◇ A vision of long-range planning to anticipate and help create and shape change; not just resignedly to adapt or yield to pressures from without.

The "why" of imaginative and dedicated long-range planning for such purposes and causes is in seeing its use as a bridge from present to future to keep above interim crises, rather than to be submerged and strangled in them.

A most curious facet of modern progress is that in this day of research as itself a major industry, with innovations and new knowledge spilling forth at a geometrically progressive pace, the normal industrial time cycle, from conceptual innovation of a new product or service through its financing, working design, production, and distribution to the stage of satisfied customer acceptance and use, is typically little or no shorter than in earlier periods.

Perhaps there is no more expediently compelling "why" for more competent and effective long-range planning than the opportunity it offers to shorten, by an order of magnitude—say from about twenty years to perhaps five—that dreadfully overlong cycle. To do so, the "why" will have to be so perceptively and imaginatively understood as to overcome two conditions that are much too prevalent currently, and probably responsible directly for the unconscionably long span of the typical innovation cycle.

The first condition arises from overconcentration on research for progress in the physical sciences as such, failing to realize that advances in knowledge in those areas cannot be translated into practical gains in human progress until implemented in the disorderly workaday world, so different from the detached, analytical context of the experimental laboratory as such.

Innovation in fact—as distinct from only in mind—has to come about in the real-life world of people, working both individually and in pluralistic complex and confusing social and economic and political collectives, more or less loosely organized and interrelated. Traditions, beliefs, emotions, habits, cultural lags, and even downright cussedness or positive opposition to change itself are as much factors to be dealt with in a real-world long-range plan as are scientific discoveries, rational programs, and systematic procedures or techniques.

So first, therefore, there is as much reason to concentrate on such factors as on the more popular, perhaps even more logical, elements of the kind of still quite theoretical long-range planning that has not as yet made badly needed progress in drastically shortening the innovation cycle.

The second condition is characterized by an understandable but inexcusable maldistribution in organizational location and use of available creative and innovative talented individuals across the normal organization structure of the total business work field.

The Ph.D's are highly overconcentrated in the physical versus the so-called social science fields of thought; and in the research function as distinct from the engineering, manufacturing, marketing, financial and accounting, human relations, and legal functional fields of work of the usual business organization structure. Hence, excellent and imaginative conceptual ideas, dropped too casually into the boiling pot of expedient working routines and techniques, either are dissolved and lost so that they never emerge or too often are steam-stewed to sogginess before they finally make it.

In fact, the opportunities for creative innovation are greater, and the competition to evolve them is less, in all these other functional work fields than in the more glamorous domain of the typical scientific research laboratory.

A prediction seems fairly safe that the managers of the first firms to attack and correct this obvious maldistribution of human talent in their evolving long-range planning will reap startling rewards from gratified public and customer recipients of the benefits of new discoveries, say, a *decade* earlier than they now get them. To win such public esteem on the one hand, to be first to gain the new profits that such new values can earn on the other hand, are alone powerful reasons to plan.

WHEN TO PLAN

Planning is never perfect, but it can grow better with practice. The sooner it is started, therefore, the earlier the march of improvement can begin; and the sooner the effectiveness achieved can be brought to competitively acceptable standards and levels.

It is a peculiarly important aspect of long-range planning that, while it seems easier to tackle more pressing short-range affairs, there are few elements of managerial work where the old copybook maxim is so potent—"Never put off 'til tomorrow what you can do today!" Conversely, it is not feasible or sensible in a going concern to shut up shop, or to delay reasonable short-range decisions, to wait for the perfect long-range plan to be created.

Hence, if such a long-range plan is to offer, as one of its most useful contributions, a carefully thought-through long-range course and objective, the practical usefulness of such a plan as a plotted course against which to test the deeper suitability of alternative current actions simply cannot be achieved until a first working draft of that plan, at least, is in being, in mind, and in use.

Another powerful reason to plan now for the longer cycle is that having a comprehensive long-range plan for the overall enterprise is by far the best way to ensure that a long-range plan of inferior quality does not simply ooze into being. In reality, you do not want a long-range plan that is nothing more than an unconscious aggregate of unbalanced, unintegrated, and often only loosely appraised plans of various organizational components, task forces, individuals, and outside pressure groups.

The normal human tendency in organized institutional bureaucracies is to add more tasks and projects—and costs, but not necessarily values or profits—far more easily and naturally than to purge, alertly and consistently, existing operations that have either served their purpose or perhaps never been successful in terms of the hopes that inspired their initial introduction.

Particularly as research, new knowledge, and today's climate of ceaseless change constantly produce new opportunities for undertaking new ventures, new projects, and new purposes, does the manager's long-range planning responsibility call for deliberate, selective anticipation of which added activities—and costs—are most likely to produce the most progress in the fastest way.

The objectivity made possible, in consideration of individual new potentials, is obviously greater when each can be appraised in advance against a solid long-range plan in existence, rather than solely against the enthusiasms, and effectiveness of presentation, of its sponsor. The sponsor is often more entranced with, and more knowledgeable about, his pat idea than about how it may or may not stack up comparatively against other possible uses of the available, and necessarily finite, financial and human resources of the total enterprise.

One tested, pragmatic, but also profoundly sensible, guide for consideration of the desirability of taking some particular new operation into the working long-range plan is to ask, "Just what *current* activity should now be dropped, or phased out, to make way for this stranger in our midst?"

Such a question has twin advantages. It affords a practical comparative yardstick for a relatively objective evaluation of the new proposal. At the same time, it produces a currently compelling incentive to reexamine, and cull out, work and costs that are not fully profitable or productive; or that, if only incrementally or marginally so, are draining off resources and talent from potential new activities with promise of full profit contributions and strengths.

From the long-range viewpoint, it is sound to get the promising new venture off the ground before competitors take the lead. It is equally sound to face up to getting rid of the less productive old operations early rather than too late. Peter Drucker succinctly said, "To abandon rather than merely postpone, or worse yet just make more studies, is often the course of wisdom in such circumstances."

The principle of planning in point is that it is better to focus available resources on enhancing strengths than on nursing weaknesses—especially when future time cycles need to be collapsed sharply in the impinging period of accelerating change. The "when" of long-range planning can be well summed up in the old entrepreneurial habit to do it now. It remains as true as ever that "Procrastination is the thief of time."

And time, in a world of fast communication and perception of new knowledge, may well be the prime competitive resource for market and profit leadership; especially if use of it is boldly and imaginatively planned—and on as long a time cycle as able managers can envision and contrive.

HOW TO PLAN

Since this particular dissertation on long-range planning is so very broad in its chosen scope, its coverage of how to plan has to be confined chiefly to the general *process* of planning, rather than to a detailed review of planning methods and techniques—on which, fortunately, there is a large, growing current literature available for those whose interests focus there.

If, as urged earlier, a sound long-range plan starts with a discriminating choice of major organization objectives, emphasis is again in order to root it fundamentally in those structures of the business that lend themselves sensibly to such careful, anticipatory long-range thought. In an article on "Organizational Planning" at Du Pont, a consistently successful and profitable firm, Robert L. Hershey said,

. . . if organizational planning is an activity having as its purpose the preparation for those changes which will be necessary to keep the organization at top efficiency, it . . . must concern itself always with the problems of people, perhaps much of the time with organizational structure, and perhaps even now and then with a reexamination of broad objectives. . . .

The present general structure of the Du Pont company has been in existence for just over 40 years. . . . When responsibility for *achieving a result* is handed over there must go with it fully commensurate authority to do those things necessary for the desired accomplishment, and he who delegates cannot properly interfere with the exercise of that authority so long as the responsibility remains delegated. This principle does not deny, on the contrary it positively affirms that the recipient of the authority must be held accountable for results and not the details of every tactic employed in their production for which he must be held to an accounting.

The lesson of such success, and of such principles, for the purposes of this paper, is that the principle of delegation and accountability is as applicable to the work of planning itself as it is to the other phases of an enterprise's operations.

Much is being published presently about a method of planning called Program Evaluation and Review Technique, or PERT, for short. Examination of this process suggests two points. First, it seems to be really but a modernization of the classic Gantt chart principle, applied, however, to the work of planning itself, rather than to that of factory production. Second, it seems to suggest that the underlying principles involved can also be useful if applied imaginatively for long-range planning, as they have been in the areas of project planning in which it has been most customarily and spectacularly used to date.

Perhaps a further pertinent key principle for how to do long-range planning is that a theory of the case for doing such difficult thinking understandingly and systematically is doubly essential when the planning deals with such necessarily vague fields as those of the highly unpredictable future, some five to twenty-five years ahead.

While many references are now available, allusion is sufficient here to one well-conceived and carefully executed book in this subject area; namely, *Planning Theory* by Preston P. Le Breton and Dale A. Henning. Its scope is suggested by the subtopics on the book's jacket—need determination, choice data collection, testing, communication, and persuasion, all in a theory of planning.

As a review in *The Wall Street Journal* noted,

Business planning can be as immediate as deciding on a plant fire-drill tomorrow or as futuristic as *anticipating* the sales volume for 1980. . . . Whatever the area the *planning process* generally goes through several stages or steps [which are then cited]. . . . Will the planning work? Well, no one knows. But it seeks to insert some certainty in an uncertain future.

Attention is called to the characterization as "anticipating" rather than predicting or forecasting, and to the phrase "planning process," as ideas significant for the "how" of long-range planning.

Special mention is also warranted in this condensed discussion of the how of long-range planning of an increasingly perceptible realization that the information system of a business is itself a most productive field for ever more original and competent work. Probably in the future it will be done more and more at the primary functional level in the basic organization structure of a business—in the field of what may be called most descriptively "business systems research." Other names used as the function has been evolving include "operations research," "operations analysis," and "operations research and synthesis."

Such efforts have been partly instigated and vastly stimulated by the realization that evolution of the modern high-speed computer and of far-flung geographical data communication linkages has opened wholly new vistas and potentials. Since many computer installations were economically justified chiefly to reduce office labor costs—such as for repetitive accounting, statistical work, or detailed engineering design alternatives—there was a natural tendency in some firms to associate responsibility at first with the accounting function.

Experience over the last ten years, however, has progressively indicated that the specialized, classic accounting information structure is but one rather limited model of the complex operations of a business, heavily past-oriented; and that new potentials go far beyond such scope and envision master information systems, dealing with all the real-life aspects of operations and not just their dollar equivalents.

Since these embrace information on the work both within separate functional areas and on that growing area concerned with viewing the business as a dynamic entity, and as itself a component requiring rational integration in the larger industry and community systems in which it has to function in practice, there is a widening consensus that the business systems research function concerned is likely to evolve as a primary-level functional effort.

A suggestion is accordingly in order at this point that the most fruitful future benefit to man from new technology may well be anticipated in this field of information systems, rather than merely in computer hardware or other new physical products. The author expressed the potential in a lecture in 1962, at Notre Dame University, in these words,

You are as familiar as I with the fruits of technology in the form of new products and new physical services—which you properly present as "material benefits."

The point I want to make is that—at least, looking now to the second half of our current century—I believe an ever-deeper kind of "fruit" of technological research, discovery, and advances will flow from the fact that they make possible and available *information;* and information of the new dimensions and kind essential for truly responsible, voluntary participation and initiative, even in very large collective enterprises (whether governmental or industrial), so that they may combine the opportunities and benefits of the collective organization and still preserve the freedom of the individual participant (whether manager or other individual contributor worker, professional or otherwise).

To emphasize, therefore, I suggest that it is this existing and potential "information and communication revolution" that is the sharply and distinctly different aspect of the (future) phase of the Industrial Revolution—which is probably essentially still ahead of us, but certainly is clearly in sight for the informed observer and increasingly is in place in a growing number of applications and areas of enterprise.

Looked at from this independently fundamental viewpoint, the *new* worker understanding is, therefore, to be not simply in the operation of more intricate or powerful machines, with greater skill and training requirements in proportion.

In contrast, the real new understanding possible and usable by the ordinary individual—with reasonably developable training requirements and skills—is in understanding of the economic, as well as the technological, process involved in collective enterprises, and hence, in similarly and progressively understanding the social and political process, as well as the technological and economic processes.

Perhaps this is a more optimistic foresight than that which inspired President Kennedy to despair somewhat that "the sophisticated judgments of our times do not lend themselves to the great sort of passionate movements which stirred this country so often in the past." Maybe they *will*.

The bearing of such possibilities on the "how" of long-range planning is clear. The lesson is to give play in planning for the future for success in new directions, not merely to extrapolate the past, even exponentially.

The greatest asset of a human organization is the diversity of initiative and imagination latent in *all* the human minds in the enterprise at all hierarchical levels. The managerial opportunity—in long-range planning as in other scopes—is simultaneously to release and to integrate the experience, the lore, the observations, the experience, the intelligence, the constructive emotions, and the divinely granted wisdom waiting to flow from all those minds.

What a travesty on progress if new technology, or new hardware even in such complex tools as modern computers, should be used to swap such a tremendous available aggregate asset, in those human resources, for the limited wisdom of either an individual top manager or an individual central planner, just because such an individual can now be deluged with enormously more so-called "factual" information than any single mind can truly absorb or apply with genuine understanding and wisdom.

A parallel pitfall, to be equally shunned, is a growing and too-apparent tendency of high-level managers—in governments, labor, educational, and other circles no less than in business—to think carelessly that models, patterns, images of a complex human system can be used as if they were its reality. The six-foot fisherman can drown as dead as the four-footer in a stream of "average depth of five feet" if it has a ten-foot pocket in the real topography of its bed.

Calling complex things simple does not make them so. Misusing useful statistics, indices, and tools—valuable for the specific technical purposes for which they were skillfully designed—as if they gave a usable view of the real world and of the complexity they condense, is perhaps the easiest way to turn the future "how" of long-range planning into a menace to the public instead of a booster for future success of the enterprise.

Too often today statistics are misconceived so they hide reality rather than illuminate it. They are then taken as the vehicle for super-layers of human action in the organization, whose payroll costs are considerable but whose most damaging financial potentials are more likely to be in manipulating the business plan as if it were itself a workable substitute for the real complexities and the dispersed human resources of the organization.

In the long run, even more than transiently, individual imagination, effort, dedication, and voluntary teamwork will always matter. The essence of the "how" of long-range planning is to seek to recognize, anticipate, identify, preserve, motivate, and reward the individuals who do the real work of the organization. As M. Predseil of France wrote,

Business management must be a teaching that uncovers to industrial leaders everything that there is in man, and not only how he can be manipulated. It must open a door upon the ideal for them, and offer them a powerful motive for action—simply by showing the exceptional task that has befallen our generation, a generation more burdened by *responsibility* than all those forming the long history of man.

Virgil Jordan, as president of the National Industrial Conference Board in 1941, accurately summarized the underlying thought:

The fundamental principle which the enterprise organization must seek to follow, and the imperative responsibility which rests upon it, are summed up in the ancient adage: "Discover how and do it yourself." . . .

In the enterprise principle not merely independence, self-discipline, and voluntary cooperation but responsibility and capacity are inherent and inescapable. The most important of these is responsibility. There can be no limit to its scope except that of capacity, and capacity depends mainly upon a willingness and determination to discharge responsibility which has been deliberately assumed.

The future of the Free World—and ultimately of the Communist world too—is heavily tied into long-range planning whose "how" is wrapped in frank recognition of such principles. The alternative in all its ugly mien was equally frankly published in the 20-year plan published in Moscow in the fall of 1961. For example:

Communist construction presupposes . . . a strengthening and improvement of centralized economic management by the state. . . . The Party calls for the education of the population as a whole in the spirit of scientific communism. . . . The Party considers it an integral part of its Communist education work to combat manifestation of bourgeois ideology and mentality, and the remnants of private-owner psychology, superstitions [meaning, of course, religion], and prejudices.

In commenting on why such emphasis is still made, the Research Institute of America, Inc., pointedly noted that "What worries the Kremlin is not that some people still want to buy and sell for a living, but that they want to think for themselves."

The "how" of long-range planning for nontotalitarian approaches can be shortly stated. Let it encourage and require people to think for themselves.

Where to Plan

As preceding sections make clear, decentralization of planning—fortified by new potentials to supply men on all organizational work fronts, on a liberal need-to-know policy basis, with adequate information to plan both their personal work and their teamwork intelligently—is offered in this paper as the very foundation for successful future long-range planning.

The philosophy was set forth in the same Notre Dame lecture already mentioned, under the heading, "The True Nature and Consequences of Genuine Decentralization."

I am afraid that, to many people yet, the concept of "decentralization" merely means the classic type of centralized governing authority—or in industry, managerial authority—with its inherent top-down approach, applied to smaller and dispersed components of people, rather than to very large, collective organizations, either states or corporate, industrial enterprises. This is, I grant, one tenable concept of decentralization. On the other hand, this merely represents the centralist—or authoritarian—philosophy, as I see it—unchanged in nature and restrained only by limiting the scope of its application; especially as to the number of people or areas so governed.

This in itself would, of course, result in dispersion and balance of power, and presumably in resultant limitation and avoidance of the potential bad consequences of overextended and centralized powers. Hence, it is essentially desirable, rather than the contrary, considered only by itself. What troubles me, however, is that if this were all that we were aiming at, I do not see at all that it represents any change in the philosophy of relationships among men involved. It merely represents application of the authoritarian philosophy on a controlled, limited basis. . . . The limited area of impact would, in no fundamental sense, under this organizational approach mean abandonment of rule by command or dictation from the top, rather than inspiration and persuasion to get voluntary initiative and participation from the followers, no less than the leaders, to progress toward jointly held common interests and common purposes.

It is in this latter direction that I would seek *real* decentralization in the sense that decentralization would thus mean a sincere change in the philosophy involved, from one kind of a philosophy to another, rather than application of a given kind only on a limited scope.

To put it positively, I would say, therefore, that the real basic point of genuine decentralization—as a philosophy—would be a system of leadership in which both managers (or governors) and their professional and other worker associates define common interests; translate these into common purposes, objectives, or goals; and then, initially and voluntarily, accept initial responsibility and commensurate authority to make their personal decisions, at whatever level of the organizational hierarchy, in the interests of the overall enterprise and not merely in the interests of their individual selves, individual jobs, or individual organization components.

This would involve a genuinely different philosophy; namely, that of accepting responsibility to act and to do things right, in the first place, and on one's own initiative. It is only from this philosophical foundation, as I try to reason all this out, that you can truly get the corresponding effects we all desire in the way of creative productivity, low-cost operations (whether of business or government or labor union, or church, or university, or what-have-you), and of deeply personal satisfactions.

The aim in planning, under such a philosophy, would be to get as much of the planning done as close to the actual work and operations planned as an executive desire to do so, backed by the new information potentials of modern technology, could make possible in the future.

The challenge here is precisely the kind of challenge so frequently dodged in so-called "long range plans" that blandly open with the assumption that no change is allowed for in the most complex, uncontrollable, and unpredictable forces likely to have the most effect and cause the most changes in the business as the real future unfolds.

This latter type of planning seems more like a futile exercise in figure manipulation, and in a wishful hope that the familiar ways of past and present can somehow be preserved by ignoring the factors surest to make them obsolete.

In contrast, the *greatest* need for doing real long-range planning at all is to come more surely and systematically to grips, and earlier, with just such basic uncertainties, so that they may be in at least some measure anticipated and prepared for. The essence in doing so is to think realistically about them; to understand that you must think realistically about them; to understand that they will require important changes from familiar ways; and to plan competitively to act in directions needed in advance, not merely to adapt to crises and pressures after they have impinged.

The sheer scope of such basic uncertainties, far from being a reason for only a few planners to look to them deliberately, is the compelling reason to call them to the attention of all the available minds and to get the ideas of all as early as possible.

The "where" to plan thinking on long-range planning should consequently explore potentials of genuine decentralization—sooner rather than later—of such planning itself, no less than of the other critical work of the overall enterprise.

Who to Plan

As always, the opportunities—like the problems—of the enterprise come down to the actions of the individual persons in its organization. Attention has been called to the danger of mistaking images or models for reality; of falsely equating their apparent simplicity with the greater complexity they only approximate.

An equally cogent warning is in order—never to be misled by that false simplicity that seems to come by considering either (a) inanimate objects or (b) collective social groups of individuals as if either could itself be considered to have the intrinsically peculiar attributes of the individual human being.

Decisions are made finally within the bounds of separate individual heads. Communication and integration between and among individuals in an organization faces more than merely semantic or time-lag difficulties.

Any organization, or system, of separate individuals differs from the closed systems of the physical sciences simply because human beings—each with his own will and power to reason, based on his beliefs and emotions and values no less than on his knowledge and skills—are *inside* the system; and are free to alter all its carefully stated a priori assumptions whenever their will so prompts them, whether rationally or purely capriciously.

The analogy often seen of so-called "social science" approaches to the tested ways of the physical sciences breaks down if its real limitations are ignored and its bounds of usefulness overstepped.

Human beings are not sticks and stones; and mobs are different from separate individuals. Clearheaded long-range planning never skips over these fundamentals. Attempts to depersonalize people are futile except as sheer force gives them apparent short-range usability.

Individuals may not be able to understand all the technical aspects of the work of their leading managerial and other professional associates. But they are surprisingly able to judge even those elite associates as fellow human beings. The "who" of wise long-range planning will anticipate such capacities, and their applications in practice, at all organizational levels.

FUTURE OF LONG-RANGE PLANNING

So much for the what, why, when, how, where, and who of long-range planning. They illustrate its inspiring potentials. They highlight its impressive weaknesses and pitfalls. They leave to the individual manager the decision of how much and what kind of long-range planning to undertake in the particular organization.

In spite of the apparently attractive features of pragmatism in today's disturbingly complex societies, the public press reflects growing a public awareness that *values* still count; and attitudes stemming from values deeply held gain great confidence for inspired leaders.

No elite, even in the hard-to-understand areas of advanced sciences or technology or even in the heady offices in which sovereign power resides, can for long endure if it ignores such fundamentals. Hitler "planned" for the next thousand years, but was reviled within his own short generation.

In an article in April 1962 reviewing some ideas on higher education by an eminent professor and scientist, Raphael Demos wrote:

The scientist shares with everybody the fate of being human; what will be the place of his scientific work in the wider context of his life as a human being? Secondly, the scientist is also a citizen; what will be the bearing of his specialty to society? But these questions cannot be answered by his specialty. The scientist needs a general framework of values in order to answer them; now such a framework is one of the concerns of liberal education.

In my opinion, the achievement of knowledge and of specialized skills on the one hand, and the awareness of the vast area of uncertainty on the other, are two complementary facets of education. . . . Our nation should seek ways in which to kindle in young minds the sense of the vast complexity of things, the sense that inquiry is never finished, the sense of doubt and of ignorance, the sense of the limitations imposed upon our aspirations to know by our own finite nature, even the sense of the final mystery of things.

These would seem to be words of wisdom alike for the scientist and for the economist, the specialist planner, and the manager himself.

The greatly constructive function of the specialist in planning is his capacity, from his own research and discoveries, to *teach* his associates throughout the organization to pull their respective oars more effectively—in the planning aspects of their work and in teamwork, just as in all other aspects. His least useful long-pull effort will be to try to do their planning for them, and then have them reward him as it fails later by saying it was no good in the first place because it was his and not theirs.

Long-range planning is one of the basic hopes for progress in tomorrow's ever more sizable, diversified, and complicated organizations. There is almost an infinite field still to be investigated, formed, and learned in the area of how to do it well and in time—and over longer future stretches in which "normal" conditions will be changing fast.

The manager's opportunity is to use his developing knowledge and skills, against the background of his firmly entrenched values, to anticipate crises and make them manageable. Long-range planning as visualized here can be one of the most fascinating features of his current and future managerial work, ever more professionally performed.

8
Planning: Establishing and Working Toward Dynamic Objectives

TERMINOLOGY OF PROFESSIONAL MANAGING

In reviewing the contributions to professional managing that have been made over a period of many decades, it is significant to note that planning and organizing have always appeared in the literature.

Although the concepts of both planning and organizing have undergone changes—and, in fact, enlargement—over the years, the concepts of integrating and measuring are relatively new.

Older terms such as coordinating and controlling, as previously cited, have begun to pass out of the literature, because they have not been found to express adequately the plus values in the mutual efforts of people working together. Nor have they denoted the need both to get information and to make it available to the man whose performance it mirrors for his own measurement and his own creative action, rather than for the purpose of his manager telling him to alter his course.

Based on a speech at Presidents' Course, American Management Associations, Colgate University, July 31, 1957.

104

IDENTIFIABLE PARTS OF PLANNING

The six identifiable parts of the managerial work element of planning as a necessary antecedent step to organizing may be defined (over-briefly) as:

1. Determining objectives.
2. Establishing policies.
3. Formulating plans (including schedules) and standards of performance.
4. Making known the objectives, policies, plans, and standards.
5. Using the results of measuring to keep readjusting the work of planning.
6. Exercising judgment and making reasoned, objective, and timely decisions to effectuate the planning process.

All should be approached in the dynamic context of the future and not geared to a static study of present affairs and outlook. Figure 1 summarizes the concepts in the six elements of planning. A few words on each will help to make the ideas and their relationships plain.

I Determining Objectives
The determination of objectives involves taking into consideration all of the environmental factors likely to affect the future of the enterprise. In addition, it should consider the best balanced interests of all persons or groups who contribute to, or benefit from, the enterprise's output of goods or services. These interested "contributor-claimants" are:

◇ Customers, who exercise freedom of choice in purchasing the enterprise's products or services.
◇ Share owners, who have invested their capital.
◇ Employees, who contribute their work and teamwork.
◇ Suppliers and distributors, who furnish parts and services.
◇ The public, who benefit directly or indirectly from all advances, including government agencies as representatives of the public.

It is clearly academic to consider that an enterprise may be able to make contributions—or even consider making them—to the common good of all contributor-claimants, unless it is itself in a position to stay in business and grow from where it is to something better.

In short, *profit* is basic to an ability to fulfill the objectives of an

Figure 1. The planning elements of the work of the professional manager.

I Determining Objectives
◇ Making sharp, clear analyses of past and present trends.
◇ Thinking ahead—making sound, practical forecasts.
◇ Anticipating, rather than merely forecasting; so as to make and not simply meet the next situation with perception, imagination, courage, and faith; looking to the future hopefully, constructively, and creatively; combining originality and boldness with capacity for thinking clearly under pressure so as to take full advantage of all opportunities and avoid costly mistakes.
◇ Choosing the best from possible alternatives, considering both long- and short-range advantages and disadvantages.
◇ Selecting and stating optimistic, difficult goals, for the component, or the whole enterprise being managed, in terms both of service to be rendered and profits to be earned and of the inseparable relationships between them.
◇ Avoiding confusion, rigidity, stagnation; accepting change, flexibility, and progress; and looking to the future creatively and constructively.

II Establishing Policies
◇ Developing, formulating, and affirming sound policies; reflecting broad understanding of human values and keeping good perspective and balance between long- and short-range goals, as well as between each job and component and the whole enterprise being managed.
◇ Determining priorities and maintaining a realistic balance among specific objectives, recognizing that conflicts among overall interests are normal from time to time.
◇ Anticipating obstacles or difficulties to be encountered, and requiring persistence and confidence in selecting the best practical steps to overcome them.
◇ Expecting high standards of performance from self and all associates.
◇ Expressing policies—and their factual background—so as to secure acceptance loyally within, and understandingly without, the component, or enterprise, being managed.

III Formulating Plans (Including Schedules) and Standards of Performance
◇ Finding the right way by orderly research, a factual approach, and analyzing problems resourcefully, intelligently, and aggressively; assembling and presenting adequate facts so that they may be available to all concerned, in advance, as a basis for making reasoned decisions coolly, impersonally, objectively.
◇ Selecting and stating tasks to accomplish objectives.
◇ Determining programs, including time schedules; and developing patterns of objectives and work of the business that are clear enough to facilitate accurate visualization and understanding participation by all employees.
◇ Expressive programs in budgets for
   Manpower—managerial, other professional, and other.
   Facilities and equipment.
   Operations—sales and income, outgo and expenses, net profit, and return on investments.
   Cash and financing, including new money required.
◇ Making definite development plans for individual managerial, professional, and other associates.
◇ Developing and expressing factors, units, and standards for measuring performance of individuals and of components; establishing valid criteria to assess significance of accomplishment and growth.

IV Making Known the Objectives, Policies, Plans, and Standards
◇ To all those involved or concerned with their performance.

V Using Results of Measuring to Keep Readjusting the Work of Planning
◇ Of objectives, policies, plans, schedules, and standards.

VI Exercising Judgment and Making Reasoned, Objective, and Timely Decisions to Effectuate the Planning Work and Progress
◇ Taking reasonable risks confidently, competitively, courageously, and on own responsibility, on basis of facts available, choosing wisely from among possible alternatives as responsibility and need for decision arise.

enterprise as a basically economic, but at the same time a social, organization.

Determining objectives starts with making sharp, clear analyses of past and present trends and practical forecasts of the future. In some cases these forecasts may be based on studies of the economy as a whole, and on the various elements or subelements of the total economy that affect it. The relationship between the enterprise and the industry of which the enterprise is a part needs to be evaluated carefully and studied in depth in order to understand the true nature of its competition.

Businessmen often state, rather categorically, that they are engaged in a specific line of business. But it may be well at this point to pause and ask such questions as:

◇ Is this business a milk business? Or a dairy product business? Or a part of the food business?
◇ Is this business a railroad business? Or is it part of a larger transportation business?
◇ Is this a camera supply business? Or is it really part of the hobbies business?

Understanding the industry to which the enterprise really belongs and the real nature of its competition becomes increasingly important in an economy where perhaps 70 percent of the spending of the public is what the economists term "discretionary buying power." The customer can make a choice between buying a new car and taking a vacation; between purchasing shrubbery for the yard and redoing the kitchen; between going to more moving pictures and buying better books for the home library; between indulging in some luxuries and educating the children.

More important than mere forecasts, in view of the rapid changes taking place in the technological, economic, and social environment, is the process of anticipating so as to make and not simply meet the future situation. A combination of originality and boldness is required, with capacity for thinking perceptively so as to take full advantage of opportunities and avoid mistakes.

It is necessary to choose from alternatives and select and stand optimistically by difficult-to-attain goals, for the enterprise as a whole or for its various sections or departments, and in terms both of the service to be rendered and profit to be earned.

II Establishing Policies

It is necessary to develop, formulate, and affirm sound policies in order to realize successfully the objectives set for an enterprise and its various component parts.

One approach to policies is to regard them as means for identifying the common interests the enterprise will preserve and for defining the common purposes it will strive to attain. Thus policies may be used to indicate, and so to establish and maintain, priorities and realistic plans among specific objectives; recognizing that conflicts among overall interests are normal from time to time.

In addition, policies should reflect a broad understanding of human values and thus aid in maintaining a good perspective and balance between long- and short-range goals; as well as between each job and each component and the whole enterprise being managed.

So regarded, policies are not restrictions; they are written, advance indications of the basic interests of those responsible for the enterprise, which all decisionmakers throughout the organization will thus understand and be able to take into full consideration *before* making a specific personal decision.

In preparing and issuing policies, those obstacles or differences to be encountered should be anticipated that are likely to require persistence and confidence in selecting the best practical steps to overcome them. Policies can thus also be a means for setting high standards for performance on the part of managers as well as their associates.

When properly expressed and communicated so that they are accepted within and understood outside the enterprise, policies achieve the following results:

1. Provide effective advance information as to the broad course of conduct within which business activities are performed.
2. Achieve unity of purpose.
3. Make possible the principle of managing largely by patterns.
4. Increase the freedom of action of managers so that they can fulfill their responsibilities with a minimum of checking or reporting of details.

III Formulating Plans (Including Schedules) and Standards of Performance

As a prerequisite to organizing, it is essential to have objectives, policies, and then definite plans, because without them, the work and the corresponding teamwork needed in the business cannot be determined. Essentially, the plans, patterns, or structures required in order to realize an overall "business plan" are:

A product or salable service plan.
A marketing plan.
An organization and manpower plan.
A facilities plan.
A financial plan.
A corporate plan (where required by the size or nature of the business).

Each of these plans is likely to have a separately identifiable time element. Yet they must meet together in a complete and integrated pattern if optimum results are to be realized.

In the making of such plans, several steps may normally be discerned, including, for instance:

◆ Finding the right way, by orderly research, factual approach, and analysis of problems; and then assembling and presenting adequate facts so they may be available to all concerned.

◆ Selecting and setting tasks to accomplish objectives.

◆ Determining programs, including time schedules, and developing patterns of objectives and work of the business that facilitate understanding and participation by all employees.

◆ Expressing the programs for the business plan in operating, capital, and cash budgets. These should preferably be made on a long-range, such as a five- and ten-year, basis, as well as for the current year.

◆ Making development plans for individuals, including managers.

◆ Developing and expressing factors, units, and standards for measuring performance both of individuals and of component parts of the enterprise and establishing valid criteria to assess the significance of accomplishments and growth.

Measuring systems that merely make an annual audit of performance are not adequate in terms of today's challenges. What managers really need in order for decisions to be based on facts, and not merely on hunches, are systems of measuring that reflect the results currently achieved in the enterprise or the part of the enterprise for which they are responsible; and do so as a basis for anticipating the trends and future action to be taken. Many kinds of measures are needed, therefore, and it is unwise to rely exclusively on one kind of reporting. As Ralph Cordiner once said:

The manager who merely tries to keep his plans and policies up-to-date is already out-of-date. He must keep them up-to-the-future, where the objectives of the business will be achieved.

IV Making Known the Objectives, Policies, Plans, and Standards

Much has been written about it, and it is unnecessary to comment concerning the advantages of making known objectives, policies, plans, and standards to all those in an enterprise involved with their execution.

In order for the work of planning to be effective, details must be communicated so that those concerned know how their work fits into the total team operation. The dynamic advantages of wholehearted participation are thus realized, since the process of "making known" induces a two-way flow of communication. Again, as Ralph Cordiner put it:

The development of measurements is important, but is only one part of the immense problem of organizing and communicating the necessary information required to operate a large, decentralized organization to achieve defined objectives and known common purposes.

V Using the Results of Measuring to Keep Readjusting the Work of Planning

The work required in an enterprise—including the work of professional managers in realizing objectives, policies, plans, schedules and standards, and budgets—is dynamic and constantly changing. Flexibility needs to be maintained on an automatic basis through the "feedback" principle, whereby measurement of performance and the results of measuring are used to make continuous readjustments.

This is true no matter whether the business is growing rapidly or has reached a steady state with established markets, products, and methods of production.

VI Exercising Judgment and Making Reasoned Objectives and Timely Decisions to Effectuate the Planning Work and Progress

Throughout all the planning process, and in fact throughout all the processes involved in running a business, it is necessary to exercise judgment and to take reasonable risks confidently, competitively, and courageously; and on their own responsibility *for profit*, in the case of the managers of the enterprise—both functional managers and the general manager, alike.

It is often said that proper decisions can be made when all the facts are available. While this is true, all the facts are seldom available; and even then, choices must be made between alternative courses, the relative risks of which must be weighed carefully and constantly. As George Humphrey once said: "There are no bad decisions, only inadequate information."

Hence, the planning element of the work of managing is not a static phase. It goes on constantly and in close correlation with the organizing, integrating, and measuring elements of the work of a professional manager.

9
Organizing for Future Challenges and Opportunities

Organizing—that is, the creation of a dynamic, purposeful business organism that can "do things and go places" and of which customers, share owners, employees, suppliers, and the public and government will be proud—is not a mechanistic process. It is a dynamic, continuing process and therefore produces a dynamic result.

The purpose of organizing is related to something—something to be accomplished, and a field of activity—and, therefore, it goes on in close relationship with planning. The purpose of *having* the organization, when completed, is to *accomplish* the designated objectives—and to do so by carrying out the policies, completing the plans, and implementing the judgments that were formulated in the planning stage.

The heart of the organizing process is, therefore, accurate designing of work into positions and components so that the end effect of the organization produced will be dynamic, will produce the results desired, and will do so economically *and on time*.

Based on a speech at Presidents' Course, American Management Associations, Colgate University, July 31, 1957.

112

PRINCIPLES OF GOOD ORGANIZING

Any enterprise may be organized either on a centralized or a decentralized basis. A basic criterion in the organizing process is to decide the basis of decisionmaking. Are decisions to be made at the point where action is taking place? Or must all major decisions be made at headquarters by those immediately responsible for the overall managing of the company and who have overall responsibility for profit and results?

Those who have made a professional study of organization are widely agreed, although their language may vary somewhat, that the guiding principles of good organization in successful, profitable, continuing enterprises, which in effect are the objectives of the organizing process, are that they should produce:

1. Clear, fast, accurate communication in both upward and downward directions, by having a minimum number of levels—and so distortion points—in the organization structure.

2. Decisions made for best business results by having responsibility, authority and commensurate accountability assigned at the point where decision and action are taking place, at whatever level in the organization structure this occurs.

3. Responsibilities sharply delineated and accountabilities defined; so that the objective measurement of work results can pinpoint the individual position requiring attention when deviations are noted above or below agreed-upon standards—to the end that corrective action may be taken on his *own* initiative by the individual responsible.

4. Shared, or split, responsibilities eliminated; so that each position is an entity in itself, with both present and potential work and relationship responsibilities clearly stated—especially so as to avoid inability to perceive whether performance must be corrected when results are below desired standards.

By following such principles, the organization structure can be built on clean, easily understood lines of reporting relationships to facilitate integrating the work of all employees in the achievement of common objectives.

If an organization plan is then expressed in clear, simple organization charts—which show both the reporting relationships and also the overall description of the work to be done in each part of the organization—the resulting organization structure will be free from conflicting relationships such as:

1. Indistinct delineation of responsibilities so that two indi-

viduals assume responsibility for doing the same piece of work.

2. Involved reporting relationships for a given position so that an incumbent is not certain where to look for functional leadership.

3. Incomplete decentralization of decisionmaking so that decisions must be referred to higher levels for approval.

4. Ill-defined "staff" positions, with informal or implied but unofficial authority. For example, "assistant" or "assistant to" positions with informal or implied—but unofficial—authority that has not been made clear and, therefore, stands in the way of rapid two-way communication in both directions and in effect may add another layer to the organization structure.

There are also certain other basic principles, or commonsense rules, if you prefer, for organizing best results. These include, for example:

1. An individual should have only one boss.

2. A manager's duties and responsibilities should be written out, understood, and agreed upon.

3. A manager should have as many subordinates reporting to him as he can manage adequately; creating and preserving a sound and cordial man–manager relationship with each, but based on each doing his own work, and each building and increasing his own expertness to do so.

4. Executives of the enterprise should devote a majority of their time to forward planning, to policymaking, to setting objectives and measuring results in achieving them, and above all to creating and staffing a sound organization structure, rather than spending time on routine work and detail.

5. Organization should be made and kept as simple as possible. A good rule to aim for is not more than five levels between the president or head of the enterprise and the hourly-paid worker, even in the largest organizations.

The nature of the organization that will result from the organizing process will depend greatly on circumstances. It is obvious that there are bound to be great differences in the way different industries and different enterprises are organized because of the inherent nature of the disciplines that are fundamental to each business concerned.

For example, the fundamental disciplines in the process of making steel, where large quantities of raw materials must be put through a process requiring large capital investment, is very different from that of operating a large but local dairy. In one case, the process is difficult and dangerous, but substantially one basic kind of product is produced and sold to a relatively small number of customers. In the other case, the process is not so involved, but customers are numerous, and furthermore, there is a personal service aspect to the business that is fundamental to its success.

IDENTIFIABLE PARTS OF ORGANIZING

With the guiding principles of organization already stated, the process of organizing may then go forward in a logical sequence. The following eight parts—which together with the main subconcepts applicable for each are summarized in Figure 1—may be identified in this sequence.

I Determining and Classifying the Work Required and Dividing It into Manageable Components and Jobs
Organizing involves classifying and then grouping "work," and therefore:

A. The first step in determining and classifying work is to find ways of looking at the business—or a particular part of the business—as a whole, so as to evaluate the total amount required in order to accomplish plans or programs within the framework of designated objectives and policies.

Usually it is not necessary to go back to first principles in determining the total work required, because it most generally happens in an enterprise (unless it is new and starting from scratch) that it is possible to determine the total work required by the following process:

1. Carefully observing the work actually being done in all functions or parts of the business.

2. Cataloging or identifying additional work that ought to be done, but possibly is not being done, in order to accomplish the objectives of the enterprise.

3. Cataloging, or identifying, and eliminating unnecessary work.

4. Exercising judgment as to the number and kind of "full-time" jobs of work that need to be organized.

5. Generally structuring jobs into components so as to group logically like and supporting work together; and so as to have best continuity and stability in the resultant organization structure, per-

Figure 1. The organizing elements of the work of a professional manager.

I Determining and Classifying Work Required and Dividing It Into Manageable Components and Jobs

◇ Determining total work necessary to accomplish plans and programs within the framework of designated objectives and policies.

◇ Classifying total work into primary constituent kinds of work—research and engineering, manufacturing, marketing, financial, employee and public relations, legal and corporate (and operations research and synthesis, where applicable), and managerial; and into their respective subfunctions—as applicable.

◇ Dividing the work as so classified into manageable components, positions, and jobs.

◇ Combining the work to be done with facilities necessary for its performance to provide best channels for coordinated application of available effort.

II Grouping Components and Jobs Into an Orderly Organization Structure

◇ Grouping like work together into an orderly pattern or structure of distinct and dissimilar organization components and of individual positions or jobs within components in proper and natural relationships to other work.

◇ Making effective use of all resources of the business needed to accomplish objectives of each component and of the enterprise as a whole.

◇ Defining salary and wage structure for all positions and jobs.

◇ Defining responsibility and accountability for performance and relationships of each position or job, commensurate with authority assigned or delegated to such job.

◇ Specifically stating as to each job—in kind and in dollar or other number limits—reserved authorities, in accordance with written policies, for each position or job.

◇ Using such reservations and policies as a means for expressing owner interests in terms of guide rules within which each manager or other employee may exercise free initiative in performing his own work in the balanced best interests of the component and the enterprise as a whole.

III Selecting Individuals for Designated Positions and Jobs

◇ Specifying personal characteristics, skills and knowledge, and actions to be required of man to perform the work of each job.

◇ Selecting an individual—from the component, the enterprise as a whole, or elsewhere—to fill each job who is well qualified by the test of such candidate specifications; thus manning the organization structure to use the talents of individuals most logically and effectively.

◇ Finding what men do well rather than what they do badly, so as to fit round pegs in round holes with sympathy and understanding.

◇ Removing, after appraisal against performance standards and after proper discussion with the man, any individual who is inadequate either in performance or in compatibility.

IV Formulating and Defining Methods and Procedures for Performing Work to Be Done

◇ Seeking and describing the simplest and best way to do each task or kind of work, especially those kinds that are repetitive, so that all work may be done most quickly, easily, economically, systematically, and understandably.

◇ Conducting analyses and studies (including appropriate operational research) to find patterns of order in work and relationships that will facilitate understanding, communication, and economy of money and energy in performing all necessary work with greatest productivity rather than greatest intensity of effort.

V Organizing Manager's Own Work and Time

◇ Securing maximum balance and effectiveness in own efforts and in use of own available working hours.

VI Making Known the Organization Pattern, Staffing, and Methods and Procedures

◇ So manager and associates can perform as an effective, cooperative team.

◇ Specifying the need for common sense and good judgment so that contacts, and flow of information, between people and components are carried out in the simplest and most direct way practicable for prompt, effective handling of all company work.

◇ Noting that the organization structure indicates channels for flow of authority and of decisionmaking responsibility but not for such free flow of contacts and information; with each man expected to communicate to his manager and his associates as fairly and fully as they are expected to communicate to him.

VII Using Results of Measuring to Keep Readjusting the Work of Organizing

VIII Exercising Judgment and Making Reasoned, Objective, and Timely Decisions to Effectuate the Organizing Work and Progress

◇ Taking reasonable risks confidently, competitively, courageously, and on own responsibility, on basis of facts available, choosing wisely from among possible alternatives as responsibility and need for decision arise.

---

mitting flexibility in moving and promoting men into and out of jobs without need to reorganize and upset large numbers of people to be able to make such individual transfers freely and readily.

6. Determining ways of optimizing the effectiveness of both present and future work requirements and performance.

B. As a second step, the classification of work into constituent kinds of work, first the primary functions and then the applicable subfunctions, can be undertaken once a determination has been made of total work requirements; having in mind the principle outlined under A.5. just cited.

One such classification of primary functional kinds of work that has been found to apply pretty generally to businesses in the electrical industry is, for example, research and engineering, manufacturing, marketing, finance, public and employee relations, legal, operations research and synthesis, if and where applicable, and managerial. Other, and generally corresponding classifications, are usually found applicable in other industries.

The concept of *classification* in itself is a simple, logical procedure of sorting work into categories, on the basis of whatever criteria or standards of differences and similarities are needed for the purpose for which the specific classification is intended. Because work is not as easily classifiable as material objects, two well-known approaches to classification are:

1. In accordance with the inherent characteristics of the work.
2. In accordance with the purpose of the work.

The first of these approaches is on the basis of what the work is, its nature, the actual differences in the work process as it takes place. For practical purposes, however, not too much should be expected from such classifications. The basic reason is that it is difficult to distinguish purely physical human work from mental work. Certain kinds of mental work, such as creative work, are not simple concepts that can be sorted out on the basis of the work process.

There are extensive and useful classifications that *can* be made on the basis of what the work is. But this is more often accomplished through analogies such as training and knowledge requirements, social and personality aptitudes, and statutory professional requirements.

While this approach has its uses, it has the disadvantage that analogous relationships may not hold true over the full range of a position; nor may they fit future requirements arising from inherent changes with respect to the work itself or the work of the position.

The second approach to classification is based on the purpose of the work or why the work is being done. This is a broad point of view looking down through the whole enterprise toward a point of action. This is classified by business, product, or salable service with emphasis on the end result, rather than how it is accomplished. In this case classifications are made by direct observation of the differences and similarities in the purpose or objectives of the work. The problems encountered in classification are therefore related to accomplishing objectives and achieving results, rather than to the nature of the work itself.

For example, all concerns require a certain amount of statistical work to be done. Such work is to be found in several functions; in the financial function almost certainly, but to an increasing degree also in marketing, engineering, manufacturing, and others. Yet the purposes of the statistical work in these functions will be different.

The question arises therefore as to whether the personnel in a statistical "department" or "section" will in all cases approach the inherent problems and work objectives of all functions with the same interest and feeling of purposefulness that the personnel of these specific functional components would exhibit if they did the statistical work themselves. How far do you go on "specialization" as such? Should there be one central company section to sharpen lead pencils? Or not? Is the basic reason for doing so just to get pencils sharpened well and cheaply? Or is this incidental to using them to facilitate engineering, or marketing, studies and plans?

One solution in the structuring of work in such cases—and particularly where, for reasons of economy, necessary office equipment is to be concentrated in one place—is to have the statistical department or section, in effect, "under contract to" the other functions to perform the work according to specifications and time schedules that those responsible for such other functions, needing such services, prescribe.

One aspect of the classification of work, to which particular attention needs to be given, is to distinguish clearly between the work of managers and the work of those who are not managers.

A number of different titles have been used, but a convenient title to describe such nonmanagerial positions is "functional individual contributors." Some elaboration and analysis of the precise nature of managerial work is, therefore, itself important and necessary as a vital part of the organizing process.

The attainment of the most effective pattern of order in the relationships of work, resources, and changing environment is the distinct contribution or result of the manager's own work toward achieving the objectives of an enterprise.

That is what gives economic justification to a manager's position. Not only does he need to manage so as to achieve objectives through the work of others, but he needs to manage so as to achieve such objectives in a constantly changing environment.

A high content of a manager's own work is:

1. Looking perceptively at the environment ahead; appraising the opportunities and difficulties it presents to the business and developing an overall balanced, timed plan, to use those opportunities to contribute toward profitability—in other words, to do more than anticipate so as to adapt; instead, to anticipate so as to be able to shape the future in which that business will be functioning. We know from our experience that what we are today is itself a definite result of decisions taken yesterday, and *before!*

2. Formulating and deciding upon specific and short-term objectives, policies, plans, schedules, and budgets.

3. Formulating and deciding upon an overall resources plan as already described; and determining the financial, facilities, product, market, and organization structures for best marshaling, use, and profitability from and for such resources.

4. Formulating and deciding upon an organization and manpower plan.

5. Organizing according to the plan.

The work in functional individual contributor positions is concerned with aiding the decisionmaking of the manager by supplying information, analyses, points of view, and recommendations with respect to those areas of managerial work just enumerated; and from these data he selects the best alternative and makes decisions. Of course, as to functional decisions within the field of the individual contributor's own expertness, the specific responsibility for decisions—or at least for recommending a decision, if it will have serious impact beyond areas for which he can reasonably have adequate information—may properly be delegated to him.

The manager, of course, is responsible for the actual achievement of necessary results of the enterprise, or of that part of it for which he is responsible, and for actually doing his personal work as a manager. He can delegate parts of such responsibility, for direct performance, as the work of others; but, of course, this still leaves him with the responsibility for getting results through the work of such others.

Thus the manager primarily spends his time in blending thought and action in decisionmaking, and by otherwise leading the individuals in the enterprise, or his component part, toward objectives by being sensitive to each individual's needs, abilities, potential, and performance of both work and teamwork responsibilities.

In so doing, the manager devotes much of his time to leading by being out in front conceptually; looking ahead so as to create a climate in which leadership by persuasion can be accomplished without undue backward looks, except where this is necessary to improve objectives and performance.

The extent to which his leadership actually achieves this climate goes far, in turn, in determining the speed with which he himself and those responsible to him are able to move and to accomplish designated and desired performance and results.

The manager fulfills these responsibilities, therefore, by leading effectively a sufficient number of other individuals to require the full-time effort of one capable manager for this kind of work. He works more effectively this way than if his work of managing were diluted by setting up a mixed position in which he had a dual role of personally maintaining leadership in doing truly managerial work and simultaneously maintaining expertness in, and performing, certain kinds of specific functional work.

Naturally, in managing the functional work for which he is responsible, and in order to do his own work of managing professionally, the manager needs to have knowledge and understanding of the:

1. Objectives and scope of the totality of the functional work in the business.

2. Functional work to be performed and the work process necessary for the accomplishment of objectives, in general depth.

3. Purpose and objective of each position; and also of its teamwork or relationships responsibilities.

4. Kinds of skills and disciplines of personnel needed to be put in place.

5. Work and teamwork of each position, in order to arrange relationships responsibilities—and thus to provide for teaching and multiplying skills and for encouraging *self*-development by *all* employees.

C. Thus, as a third step in classification, the principle of "full-time positions" is recognized in the determination and classifying of work into either full-time managerial positions or full-time functional individual contributor positions.

No longer, then, can a manager soundly "be made" simply by giving the title to an individual with the sole qualification that he is the best individual expert in a functional field; in fact, this may be the very best reason for giving him opportunity and compensation to grow in that field rather than to change his vocation under such circumstances to take over the different work of managing, unless it is both his free choice and his likely full competence to do so.

There are many new developments constantly arising in the rapidly growing science of managing that create a great requirement for continuing study in order to maintain managerial knowledge, skill, and competence. Ability and willingness to specialize in managerial work, as such and as a primary professional field of work itself, and even at the expense of renouncing functional leadership in a previous functional specialty, are essential if such progress is to be assured.

At the same time functional individual contributors today, more than ever before, need to be much more than "specialists" in any narrow or limited restrictive sense.

Rather, such work calls increasingly for concentration of individual effort in the chosen field, fitted to the needs of the business, followed by continuing effort to learn as much as possible with respect to current developments in this chosen area.

Then to develop further, by personal growth, an increasing sensitivity to opportunities as the basis for forward-looking leaps in progress, and in new advances by building on what others have learned before, is continually essential.

D. As a fourth step, the classification of full-time positions and jobs is combined with the facilities necessary for the performance of the work so as to provide the best combination for integrated application of available effort for the company to avail itself to the utmost of *both* the human and the material resources of the business.

II Grouping Components and Jobs into an Orderly Organization Structure

Once the process of determining and classifying work required and dividing it into manageable components and jobs has been done, it is necessary, as indicated earlier, to group like work together into an orderly pattern of distinct and dissimilar organization components, and of individual positions or jobs within components, with proper and natural relationships to other work.

Before so doing, some questions may arise that point up the need for further organization work. Some of these have already been covered or inferred in the classification process. Typical ones are:

◇ Does the basic organizational setup of the business appear outmoded?

◇ Is there an apparent lack of integration among major activities? That is, do the principal departments function too independently?

◇ Do executives and managers have a hazy knowledge of their own and others' responsibilities? And if so, does this part of their work go undone?

◇ Are there delays in reaching decisions?

The answers to such questions as these may definitely point to the need for a more detailed and penetrating organization study, the objectives of which would be decided on the basis of the information that has been revealed, and that will ultimately suggest the principles underlying a plan of organization that needs to be developed.

Such a study should also contemplate making best use of all the available resources, including both human resources and natural resources. It is commonplace experience to find executives of businesses thinking in terms of factories, tools, transportation equipment, inventories, and bank balances. But in any plan of organization it is even more vitally necessary to think first in terms of the human beings who, in the last analysis, constitute the only resources that will keep the business going and growing.

In order to determine how to obtain best use of the human resources, particularly for individuals occupying key positions, it may be necessary to undertake a personal appraisal of such individuals, both from the point of view of how they have been fulfilling their present responsibilities and from the point of view of their capabilities, personal ambitions, and capacity for future growth.

The grouping of individual jobs into an orderly organization structure involves the preparation of "position guides" or "position duty lists" for the individual positions represented on a typical functional organization chart. A basic pattern in preparing such guides or lists would embrace:

1. *Scope of the Position*

A clear delineation is made of the broad function, or mission, of the position; and also a precise statement of its scope which sets it apart from all other positions.

2. *Objectives of the Position*

The objectives or purpose of the position—that is, why it exists at all—must be consistent with the objectives of the business, or the part of the business within which it is structured. These objectives will be derivable from the manager's own organization planning; with the position fulfilling a particular set of "work and teamwork" responsibilities that constitute a full-time job and are needed to contribute to the achievement of component objectives. Thus the contribution expected from the work of the incumbent represents both functional and relationships responsibilities from which may be derived valid measures of accountability.

3. *Functional (or Work) Responsibilities*

This describes the precise kind and degree of personal work responsibilities the incumbent is expected to fulfill.

4. *Relationships (or Teamwork) Responsibilities*

This section of the position guide describes precisely and delineates the teamwork situations of major consequence to the achievement of objectives. For each such situation described in the incumbent's position guide, there should correspondingly be described in the position guides covering each other position in which such teamwork is involved the precise reciprocal roles of the incumbents of these positions.

Preparation of position guides provides the greatest opportunity—and they are excellent tools—for the avoidance of either overlaps or gaps in the total work of positions required to accomplish objectives.

5. *Authority of the Position*

The general principle to be followed is that the authority for a position is complete as needed to fulfill a designated responsibility, except where some aspects of authority may be specifically reserved, in writing, to a higher manager or managers for specific cause—either because of the nature of the decision reserved, or because of lack of full feasibility and practicability as yet to make economically available to the position incumbent needed information on external impacts of a decision as well as immediate consequences in the area of his own work.

6. *Measures of Accountability*

This section of the position guide constitutes the basis for appraising the incumbent's performance with respect to the results he has achieved. In general, for each principle identified as a responsibility in the position guide, the nature of criteria and standards by which the incumbent's performance of each such responsibility is to be measured and accounted for should be stated.

Finally, in addition to the work of organizing already described, it is necessary to develop a salary and wage structure for all positions and an adequate and appropriate nomenclature—or position and component naming—system.

The salary and wage structure should be related to the "worth" of the work of each position, when competently performed, in contributing to the attainment of the objectives of the enterprise. An adequate salary and wage administration plan also needs to be developed.

The process of selecting a suitable nomenclature, or naming, system to apply to all positions—and components—throughout the organization, assumes significant importance once the preceding steps have been taken.

There are a number of theories concerning nomenclature systems that it is well to examine. Such a system for naming positions and components needs, especially, to be reasonably commonly based and used throughout the organization, both in order that there may be maximum opportunity for individual cross-promotions and personal growth, and that clear work naming may be of maximum aid to facilitate ready and cooperative teamwork.

In general, an even deeper purpose—and usefulness—of a sound naming system is to aid every individual to identify himself with his work and also to place him and his work in the fairest and most accurate light before his associates in the organization and before any interested people outside it. In general, inaccurate—or false "prestige"—titles should be avoided; since they result in a confusion of relationships and very often are found actually to mislead by meaning different things to different people, even within the organization itself.

The preparation of adequate, accurate, thoughtfully designed individual position guides will itself be found to contribute greatly to the development of a logical naming system. Such an approach—which plainly names the work for "what it is," and not for where it is or who does it—both describes the work of each position and at the same time defines it clearly so as to satisfy the natural desires of the incumbent concerned to be recognized for the work, for the contributions expected from it, and for its true dignity arising out of its actual nature, rather than out of any false attempts to give spurious "status" by a kind of "title inflation" whose patent insincerity is soon apparent to all, and damaging in proportion.

III Selecting Individuals for Designated Positions

An obviously fundamentally important element of organizing is the selection of an individual for each designated position, including that of the manager for each component.

But this should not be done until work has been classified, and components grouped into the simplest, most orderly organization structure.

Specifying personal characteristics, skills, and knowledge and actions to be required of a man to perform the work of each particular job is not always easy. Selecting an individual from the enterprise as a whole or elsewhere to thus man the organization structure, using the talents of individuals most logically and effectively, and finding out what men do well rather than what they do badly—so as to fit round pegs into round holes with sympathy and understanding—all demand careful and logical thought.

A helpful approach to the problem of selection is the preparation of a careful "candidate specification" for each position.

The elements of such a specification are quite similar for both managerial positions and functional individual contributor positions, since, as already described, either position must comprehend the basic approach to work of the other for effective teamwork. But the emphasis required in the different qualifications will vary with the type of position under consideration, and with the specific responsibilities and accountabilities described in the corresponding position guides.

A typical candidate specification includes such elements as the following—the exact list varying with due regard both to the qualifications required to perform the work and to the particular patterns or standards of attitudes, personality, and emotional and other factors desirable so the incumbent may fit successfully, and basically compatibly, with the other members of the particular organization.

1. *What the candidate should be*
   a. business–social personality
   b. basic personal characteristics
   c. leadership characteristics

2. *What the candidate should know*
   a. education
   b. human relations
   c. managerial experience
   d. functional know-how
3. *What the candidate, as an incumbent of a defined and designated position should do*
   As described in the position guide, for the position under consideration.

A final factor in the placement of an individual for a designated position involves providing means for replacement or removal if, after a fair trial, appraisal against performance standards, and proper discussion with the man, any individual is found either inadequate in performance or incompatible for desirable teamwork relationships. New balance and judgment is required here to avoid overemphasis on conformance rather than performance, on the one hand; and to obtain optimum diversification of ideas, skills, reactions, and emotions for best overall climate and progress, on the other hand.

A vital advantage of written position guides—and similarly of written candidate specifications—is that if these have been well prepared, the measures of accountability serve automatically to focus attention on the strengths and weaknesses of an individual incumbent.

All incumbents should be appraised from time to time, on a recognized and reasonably regular basis; and with ample opportunity to increase competence, to correct deficiencies, and to prepare for greater future responsibilities through appropriate measures—and agreed action plans—for continuing self-development.

IV Formulating and Defining Methods and Procedures for Performing the Work to Be Done
The work and process of organizing involve continually seeking and describing the best or simplest way to do each task so that all work may always be accomplished quickly, easily, economically, systematically, and understandingly—the aim, as the work simplification experts put it so graphically, being to "work smarter, not harder."

Position guides or position duty lists, which define the contribution and work of the position, functional organization charts, which describe the contribution and work of components, and organization charts, which show channels of responsibility and of reporting relationships, but not of flow of information, ideas, or contacts, are all helpful and meaningful aids in the organizing process already described.

Methods and procedures go well beyond this and into each subfunctional area. They get into such matters as accounting procedures, payroll procedures, and others so that repetitive work—especially in connection with cross-functional as well as intrafunctional flow of work or papers or materials—can be singled out, and can be placed on a uniform normal basis without having to determine how a job is to be done all over again each time it is done. For, as one great philosopher so crisply said:

Civilization advances by increasing the number of important operations we can perform without thinking about them.

Another aspect of formulating and defining methods and procedures is, therefore, conducting analyses and studies to find patterns and order in work and relationships that facilitate understanding, communication, and economy of money and energy—again so the necessary work is performed with greatest productivity rather than merely greatest intensity of effort.

V Making Known the Organization Pattern, Staffing, and Methods and Procedures

To draw up organization plans and charts, to prepare position guides, to develop organization procedures, and to perform all the other elements in the process of organizing are of manifestly little avail, unless these are also made known to the men and women of the organization.

Opinions differ as to how far and how widely such information should be made available to those within a particular organization. A general rule to follow would seem to be that the limit is reached *only* when distribution no longer aids the manager and his associates to perform as an effective team.

Certain types of information should, of course, clearly be restricted. It is generally accepted good practice that appraisals of personal performance and what a man earns are private affairs; although generally the fundamental ranges and structural relationships regarding relative remuneration between one job and another are reasonably well comprehended and, preferably, should be authentically available rather than "known" but in distorted form by being left only to grapevine and surreptitious circulation. The bad news gets around anyhow, so it is unwise not to give the sound facts equal circulation.

In general, it may be said that organization charts, functional organization charts describing the work of each component part of the enterprise, and position guides may safely be made known to all concerned. In fact they aid greatly in the integrating efforts for the accomplishment of objectives.

Broadly speaking, mystery and secrecy usually do far more harm than good. Men respect facts and frankness. They are going to *think* in any event. The wise manager early realizes that giving them the truth will lead to sounder work, sounder relationships, and sounder emotional attitudes than actions that let either ignorance or suspicions reign.

Above all, it is desirable that a manager specify the need for common sense and good judgment so that channels of contacts and flow of information between people and parts of the enterprise are carried out in the simplest and most practical way for the prompt, effective handling of business.

The organization structure and the organization chart indicate channels for flow of authority and decisionmaking responsibility. But they do not and should not inhibit free flow of contacts and information, as each man is expected to communicate to his manager and his associates as freely, fairly, and fully as they are expected to communicate to him.

There are, however, certain types of situations where resort to organization channels is both desirable and essential. Four of the most common of such situations where it is the duty of each employee to keep his manager informed promptly include any matters:

1. For which his manager may be held properly accountable by others.

2. As to which there are, or which are likely to cause, disagreement or controversy, especially between different components in the enterprise.

3. Which require the advice of his manager or integration by his manager with other components of the enterprise.

4. Which involve recommendations for change in, or variance from, established policies.

VI Organizing the Manager's Own Work and Time

Upgrading of competence and sharpening of the awareness of the responsibility of individuals through position guides and other means has real added value to the manager in enabling him more easily and fully to organize his own time and work.

Managers primarily spend their personal time in the following kinds of activities: thinking ahead, doing work that cannot be delegated, working with those on the same and higher organizational levels, and working with those on lower levels.

The portion of a particular manager's time devoted to each of these activities varies greatly between managerial positions—and also from time to time in the same position.

The majority of a first-line manager's time is usually spent in working with those at the lower functional individual contributor levels and proportionately less of it in thinking ahead. The president of a business, or the manager of a large company component, by contrast, spends a majority—possibly 75 percent or more—of his time in thinking ahead, doing work that cannot be delegated, and working with those on the same, or higher levels if the man's job is below the president's.

This work may well include the work he does with men in other businesses, such as his suppliers and vendors, with other community leaders, with his bank, and with the board of directors of the company in the normal-sized enterprise; or with division general managers, executive vice-presidents, the treasurer, and services or staff oganizations, where these exist, in the case of larger companies.

Unfortunately, far too many "managers" today are victims of the fact that they have not made clear to their subordinates that his, the manager's, most important function is thinking ahead, anticipating, and taking the "forward look" with respect to all aspects of his business to be able to steer rather than merely "run with the weather" in setting the course for the future.

An interesting analysis of "Work Simplification at the Level of the General Manager" was reported a while ago by Rolf Nordling, president of a substantial French chemical and detergent manufacturing firm. Mr. Nordling drew upon his own experience and upon an actual time analysis made for a group of Swedish industrialists by Professor Sune Carlson of that nation that showed the small amount of sustained time they were actually able to spend in forward planning as they performed the activities to carry out the normal work of their respective positions.

It was found that the most important functions of the manager—which were described in language not too different from leading by persuasion, by blending thought and action in decisionmaking, through planning, organizing, integrating, and measuring as the elements of the work of a professional manager—received usually only a fraction of the time of these executives, whereas the exact opposite should have been the case. Professor Carlson, in fact, drew this classic conclusion at the time when the Swedish studies were finished:

> Up to now I had imagined the head of a business as a conductor leading an orchestra, but today I see him clearly as a marionette whose strings are pulled by an unorganized mob.

And in concluding his report, Mr. Nordling makes this penetrating observation:

> As a matter of fact, only by considering the job that he holds as a leader of men, producer of goods, and guardian of the future of a business that has been entrusted to him by circumstances, will the head of a business be able to build up his own work so that it will correspond to the real role that life has assigned to him.

*VII Using the Results of Measuring to Keep Readjusting
the Work of Organizing*

Measuring, and readjusting, the seventh part of organizing, are not *exclusively* the work of a manager.

When all individuals in the organization have access to information on their work and teamwork, it permits them to correct themselves in advance of any external action that may force them to make corrections.

Such feedback gives the manager, as well as all functional individual contributors working for him, a constant feeling of the nature of the activity within the enterprise. Thus, both they and the manager can make necessary adjustments in his organization structure that if left unattended could threaten the profitability, even the existence, of the business.

The work of managing, in particular, requires such continued self-regeneration. It is truly a dynamic, "closed-loop" process, requiring—for continuing successful performance and results—constant sensing of events and trends, and equally constant and dynamic refinement and reinvigoration so that decay does not limit or prevent live and healthy growth.

VIII Exercising Judgment and Making Reasoned and Timely Decisions to Effectuate the Organizing Work and Progress

Confident then of his own competence, of the competence of his associates, and of the fact that he has the information needed for decisionmaking, the manager can choose wisely from among possible alternatives, and do so as the need for decision arises.

In this respect he and all the individuals reporting to him take such risks confidently as they act with initiative, self-discipline, and competence.

SUMMARY OF ORGANIZING

Thus, organization becomes the end product of the process of organizing, which results in the creation of a *dynamic* organization that has legitimate standing with *all* the contributor–claimants on the business.

In addition, however, good organizing brings advantages both to managers and to functional individual contributors throughout the enterprise. Good organizing provides time for good leadership and for the compounding effects of professional managing, which cannot be realized when much of the day is devoted to routine matters, the responsibilities for which should be assumed and performed by others.

The most challenging task of leadership is education. It is teaching, as the faculty of being able to educate and the ability to lead are closely related.

One of the larger functions of leadership, therefore, is to translate the goal of an organization into concrete and stimulating terms so that those who are "followers" will perceive the validity of the group objectives and see in its accomplishment an honorable self-fulfillment—thus creating that genuine legitimacy of leadership that arises out of the resultant commonness of purposes of leaders and followers together!

10
Organizing for Decentralization of Responsibilities

Bases of Decentralization

Many in our generation have thought deeply concerning the responsible decentralization of our social, economic, and political institutions. In this period it has been possible also to observe, or actually to experience, many "experimental" organizations.

Italian experience with the corporate state during the twenties and thirties, for instance, has been among these specific examples through which we have added to knowledge in this respect. We have also seen certain basic theories concerning the place of man in society and his ethical and moral relation to his government propounded and tried out in various portions of Europe and Asia and in other parts of the world.

Comments to the Council for International Progress in Management (USA) Inc., for VIII National Annual Conference of UCID, Unione Cristiana Imprenditori, Rome, Italy, January 27, 1957. Mr. Smiddy gratefully acknowledged the aid and collaboration, in preparation of these comments, of his business associate Robert W. Newman.

The sociologists, historians, economists, and we business owners or managers ourselves are, however, not the only observers of organizational structure. The physicists, chemists, astronomers, and others are also taking giant steps in understanding certain aspects of "organization" in this universe of ours.

At the turn of the century the great French entomologist Jean Henri Fabre published the findings of a lifetime of observation in his treatise "The Social Life in the Insect World," which displayed a "perfect" social organization among certain classes of insects. Here were vast societies in which each member played his role and made his contribution with very little, if any, apparent show of force. An ideal existence—but was it?

From such a wide and diverse scope of observations, an increasing number of thoughtful managers and other leaders have been coming to a common view with respect to at least one of the principal bases for soundly establishing and organizing our social and economic structure; namely, that one must begin from an ethical or moral base.

What is and what should be the relationship of man to his created organizations?

What is the place of freedom of individual action, freedom to think and experiment, to anticipate, to create, to change purposefully in our social structure?

What are the purposes of our social, economic, and political organizations in terms of man, and his purpose?

A second basic aspect of economic organization, which is similarly being appreciated by critical observers of our day, stems from the technological developments and the multiplying complexity of mid-twentieth-century living, with its increasing awareness of overall social responsibilities in our economic as well as in our political institutions.

Employers, managers, and employees less readily accept, for example, the arbitrary varying of the direct labor in a manufacturing facility as a responsible way of compensating for avoidable errors in manufacturing or distribution scheduling. Or, for another example, we now recognize that excessive taxes frequently limit the reward incentives obtained from successful ventures and reduce the possibility of recouping the losses incurred in the inevitable risks and ventures that are unsuccessful.

In the same vein, the competitive economic climate and the continual increases in technological development have broadly reduced the useful life cycle of most equipment and have considerably increased the risks involved in long-term investment; and as is now being even more widely sensed, progressive automation dramatically combines many of these elements.

With larger investment requirements and greater futurity of rewards from these investments, the multitudes of family and owner-managed firms that are forever being started by proprietor-minded men are tending in turn to change status in the more developed countries as they attain material size, frequently being absorbed into, or replaced by, popularly held stock companies managed by professional managers rather than owner–entrepreneurs.

Such managers have a different relationship and responsibility to their employees from the one held by the former owner–managers. Today's corporate managers, then, are typically also employees themselves in enterprises of substantial scope. And even owner–managers of incorporated ventures have to realize that they wear two separate hats, with distinct and diverse obligations, when acting in each of their dual capacities.

Day-to-day operations can no longer be directed by the owners of the business in minute detail. The managers of the business need to be primarily involved in the continuity of the business itself; in its basic strategy, in its long-range planning, and in the firm's policy relationship with the rest of the society and economy in which it functions—with its employees, with its share owners, with its vendors, and with the public and the public's representatives, the government.

The needs for decentralization under such circumstances became increasingly more evident. Accordingly, the specific purpose of these comments, after displaying such needs, is simply to explore how we can better understand how to design real *and responsible* decentralization into a practical business organization. Such a framework seems highly essential for helpful and useful understanding and discussion of the actual problems of attaining genuine, responsible, and accountable decentralization.

Faced with such growing and pressing needs one major American company, which has made a great deal of progress in this field, developed the following three basic premises concerning decentralization:

1. Decentralization must protect and enhance the dignity, the creative ability, and the human and moral qualities of all the men and women making up the organization; recognizing—as Ralph J. Cordiner, president of General Electric Company, puts it in his 1956 book on *New Frontiers for Professional Managers*—that:

Any sensitive observer must agree that the human potential in business has never been unleashed. The great dream of the professional manager is that some day he will find a way to share with his associates a mutually deep vision of what a truly inspired human organization can achieve.

2. Decentralization must be designed to give the managers and executives of the business greater time for longer-range planning, contemplation, and thinking about the business, since, again quoting the same book:

The hallmark of *leadership* is the ability to anticipate the reasonably foreseeable needs of tomorrow and beyond tomorrow with at least some clarity and confidence.

3. Decentralization, despite any possible inference from the title of these comments, should not consist of decentralizing responsibilities *alone,* but also requires decentralizing, along with responsibility, the sister aspects of both adequate *authority* and measured *accountability.*

REQUIREMENTS OF DECENTRALIZATION

From the three basic concepts ten principles of decentralization have evolved that seem of general enough usefulness to be presented here. According to this philosophy, decentralization:

1. Puts authority to make decisions at points as near as possible to where actions take place.

2. Is likely to achieve the best overall results by bringing the fullest and most directly applicable knowledge and most timely understanding actually into play on the greatest number of decisions.

3. Works only if real authority is delegated; and not if details then have to be reported, or, worse yet, if they, in fact, have to be "checked" first.

4. Requires faith and confidence that associates in decentralized jobs will have the capacity to make sound decisions in the majority of cases; and this confidence and faith is required jointly, as a matter of deep personal conviction, both by higher operating executives and by higher functional executives. The officers especially need to set an example in the art of full delegation.

5. Requires understanding that the main role for members of

services (or of staff) components * is the providing of help and advice through a few experienced people, so those operating managers responsible for making decisions can themselves make them correctly.

6. Requires realization that the natural aggregate of many individually sound decisions will be better for the business and for the public than centrally planned and controlled decisions.

7. Rests on the need to have general business objectives, policies, plans, organization structure, and relationships known, understood, followed, and measured; while recognizing that definition of policies does not necessarily mean uniformity of methods of carrying them out in decentralized operations.

8. Can be achieved only when higher executives realize that authority genuinely delegated to lower echelons cannot, in fact, also be retained by them; and that belief in "decentralization" down to themselves, but no further, while actually reviewing detailed work and decisions and continually "second-guessing" their associates is but a travesty on responsible decentralization in fact, and represents only lip service to the genuine concept—with the inevitable result of keeping the organization in confusion and preventing the growth of self-reliant men.

9. Will work only if responsibility commensurate with decision-making authority is not only delegated but is also truly accepted and exercised at all levels.

10. Requires personnel practices based on measured performance, enforced standards, rewards for good performance, and removal for incapacity or sustained poor performance.

In these relatively brief comments it is feasible to examine only two of these principles in greater detail.

Principle No. 7 states: "Decentralization rests on the need to have general business objectives, policies, plans, organization structure, and relationships known, understood, followed, and measured"; and principle No. 1 says: "Decentralization puts authority to make decisions at points as near as possible to where actions take place."

What do these two principles imply?

From principle No. 7 comes the concept of "managing by objectives." This implies that each manager, after taking due counsel

* Editor's Note: The reference to "members of services (or of staff) components" in this paper, addressed to an international audience, should not be interpreted as reflecting General Electric's concept of the services role.

with and thus making use of the knowledge and expertness of his associates reporting to him, should make statements of clear, precise, consistent, measurable objectives for the organization component—or the business—he is managing.

The premises on which such objectives are based need to be sound. The objectives themselves need to be compatible and attainable. Attainment of one should not seriously jeopardize any other.

Functional objectives—as, for example, for engineering or manufacturing or marketing work or components—need to stem from those of the overall business; and to formulate these more specific functional objectives, those of the business need to be defined with adequate clarity and detail. The purpose of functional objectives is to generate functional action plans that will result in their attainment.

Here, then, is a complex, interlocked set of business and functional objectives, premises, and action plans that the managers need both to generate and to analyze as a set; and to modify and revise over periods of time with due appreciation of their interlocking, or "systems," characteristics.

To achieve the goal of managing by objectives—rather than by command as daily situations pop up—each manager needs to have available, therefore, and on an organized basis, adequate information that describes the business as a whole, as well as the interrelationships of its parts.

With such information the manager can contribute, understandingly and rationally, to the whole complex overall set of objectives, premises, and plans, since it allows time truly to obtain a "common view" of the business "system" of which his own component's work needs to be an integral and an organic part.

With such a communicable "common view," the "common interests" involved become visible, and the objectives can take on the nature of common purposes arising specifically out of such common interests.

Out of principle No. 1 are derived the requirements of decision-making in a decentralized business.

Implementation of principle No. 1 requires that decisions be made at the lowest organizational level where the necessary skills and competence on the one hand, and the needed information on the other, can reasonably and economically be brought together. This information needs to be up-to-date and sufficiently complete, and needs to cover adequately the significant impacts of the decision both within the component, or business, being managed and in the larger environment of which it is itself a part.

There is more to this principle than the usual act of simple delegation. If decisions are to be made as near as possible to the direct point of impact, the managers need to *design* their organization structure—both as to individual jobs and organization components— to ensure that, along with the responsibility and authority for making a particular decision, all the really pertinent available information relative to the decisions is either generated by or made available to the decisionmaker.

This means, on the one hand, a clear, concise, *communicable* expression of any significant factor influencing the decision so that the individual to whom the responsibility for making the choice of risks involved has been delegated can do so on the basis of all necessary available facts. On the other hand, it also means keeping a neat economic balance between the cost and critical usefulness of the information provided and between the volume and quality of information that can reasonably be brought to the point to which decision-making responsibility is delegated.

A vital key to the achievement of sound and responsible decisionmaking under decentralization, then, is information. And this is particularly true of information that defines organizational interrelationships, and so permits the man making the decision to do so with an understanding of the full significant impact of his decisions throughout the business. The development of information of this kind is, therefore, a prerequisite to satisfactory definition and practical attainment of selected component, and business, objectives and goals.

THE ROLE OF THE PROFESSIONAL MANAGER

One cannot sensibly think in terms of decentralization entirely abstractly; or without considering *what* is being decentralized and fully comprehending the other and interrelated elements of the business "system" involved, including the whole of the applicable organizational theory, structure, and concept of managing. Indeed, it is the manager who by his action and philosophy permits and facilitates decentralization.

In line with this concept, we view the work of managing in today's corporate, and other, business enterprises as, itself:

◇ A distinct and professional kind of work; namely, leading by persuasion rather than by command; and by blending thought and action in decisionmaking through planning, organizing, integrating, and measuring,

◇ As the elements of the dynamic work of the professional manager himself,

◇ In the balanced and effective use of all of the human and material resources,

◇ Of the particular component, or of the whole enterprise, being managed,

◇ With due understanding and balanced application of the skills and knowledge required to manage its particular activities or operation,

◇ With best pace, synchronized flow, timing, and turnover; all

◇ To secure balanced results through the specific functional or managerial work of other people, who themselves are also

◇ Acting with initiative, self-development, self-discipline, and competence as to both their personal work and their voluntary teamwork, and two-way communication; each

◇ Seeing the individual job and its relationships to the whole component, and enterprise, imaginatively and in true perspective

◇ Consistent with the current and potential economic, social, and political climate (or environment, or "society") of the component or enterprise being managed,

◇ To achieve desired performance and results; namely,

◇ To accomplish successfully, economically, profitably, and on time, challenging and difficult-to-attain objectives of the component, and of the enterprise as a whole, in the balanced best interests of customers, share owners, employees, suppliers, and the public, including the public's representatives, the government.

As Ralph Cordiner emphasized in his book, cited earlier,

The separation of ownership and the managerial function—increasingly common in business today—has important consequences.

The work of managing is tending to become professional, as a distinct kind of work in itself. It is becoming a job that requires a great amount of specialized thought, effort, and training in the principles as well as the techniques of managing. For the manager has the challenging task of getting results through the work of other men and women, rather than directly by his own effort.

This professional approach requires, in fact, a dedication of the man's self and service not only to the owners of the business through his board of directors, but also as a steward to the company's customers, its industry, its employees, and to the community at large.

The professional manager must consciously place the balanced best interests of these ahead of his own personal interests. The corporate manager today thus has an opportunity and an obligation for service comparable to the highest traditions of any professions in the past.

Communicating Common Purposes

In order to lead by persuasion, rather than by command or dictation, and to provide the necessary working climate for effective, creative, and self-disciplined decentralization, the manager needs both to decide upon and also to make known his objectives, goals, theories, policies, plans, organization structure, and delegations.

By "making known," the manager communicates objectives as a basic step in establishing common understanding of those objectives, so that pursuit of them may truly be voluntary and cooperative by manager and functional individual contributor alike. Such clear understanding of the purposes of the overall work to be done coupled with specific organizational assignments of work and responsibility, are essential for each man in each component so that he may contribute to results with optimum initiative, creativeness, and economy in the use of both human and material resources.

In his book *Management and Morale,* Fritz Roethlisberger points out that:

Maintaining internal equilibrium within the social organization of the plant involves keeping the channels of communication free and clear . . . . This involves getting the bottom of the organization to understand the economic objectives of the top; it also means getting the top of the organization to understand the feelings and sentiments of the bottom. . . .

The development of concepts, or of theories, in readily communicable form is thus badly needed, though as yet purposefully done in all too few cases in modern business.

But, as one distinguished writer has concluded: "The man who says he has no time for theory is either using a theory someone else has developed, or even a theory someone else has discarded."

The manager's perpetual dilemma, of course—like that of his nonmanager associates—comes from his perpetual, practical necessity to exercise judgment, to choose among alternative risks, and then to make reasoned objectives and timely decisions on the basis of facts available as the responsibility and need for each decision arise.

By putting together such information as is available, analyzing it, and then developing or synthesizing it into an integrated and unified concept, a manager is in a far better position, first, to get a situation or objective understood, and second—if required—to utilize corrective measures in a purposeful fashion. For, as the frequently misunderstood Vilfredo Pareto, in commenting on Kepler, has observed: "Give me a fruitful error any time, full of seeds, bursting with its own corrections. You can keep your sterile truth for youself."

From a managing viewpoint this means that we need to find ways of permitting both managers and functional individual contributors, in all functional fields of work, to manage their jobs by the principle of selecting, and seeking to achieve, objectives in accord with principles commonly accepted. In this way the maximum of decisions and work may flow in a manner allowing routines to satisfy the requirements for the normal situation without thwarting the need always "to find a better way." There is also time to think through finding a better way in the exceptional cases or in truly new conditions, precisely because good methods and standard practices make it unnecessary to reinvent the wheel for repetitive situations.

As William James observed in his *Principles of Psychology,* routine and habit are essentials in our society. Yet man must be freed from these routines in order to be innovative and creative:

Habit is thus the enormous fly-wheel of society, its most precious conservative agent. It alone is what kept us all within the bounds of ordinance. . . . Genius, in truth, means little more than the faculty of perceiving in an unhabitual way.

Thus, in a society and in a decentralized company, common purposes are required as a foundation for orderly work and progress on a voluntary and practical basis. These common purposes can be defined expressly, after participation in their formulation by those whom they affect, as policies. They need to be precise so that genuine decentralization of authority to accomplish chosen goals within the spirit and framework of such canons may itself exist; yet without fragmenting and losing the overall advantages—to the customers and the public as well as the share owners and employees—that the competitive, modern, technological, corporate enterprise can and does provide.

Policies, therefore, are an aid to managers of decentralized components, or businesses, specifically because they represent definite statements, by the owners' own representatives, of what are conceived to be the owners' interests in designated business fields.

Such policies are issued so that the managers and the functional individual contributors, alike, of such decentralized business components may exercise the broad responsibility and authority delegated to them from the owners. And they may do so in ways that are compatible with the stated interests of these specific owners as made clear in policies in *advance* of the need to make decisions, rather than as reserved power to second guess a manager after he has met his practical day-to-day need to make decisions to operate.

As Frederic Hayek so succinctly put it: "Common acceptance of formal rules is indeed the only alternative to direction by a single will man has yet discovered."

The determinant level for responsibility and authority to make a particular decision should, as noted earlier, be the lowest organizational level at which both the needed skills and competence on the one hand, and the needed information—embracing understanding of both direct and environmental probable impacts of the decision—on the other hand, can reasonably be brought to exist and actually to be used in choosing wisely from possible alternatives, again "as responsibility and need for decision arise."

This is both the real meaning and one of the greatest problems of sincere decentralization.

The possibility of reaching such a goal thus becomes a test of our ability to see that the information or available facts that are needed to form a fair basis for personal decisions by responsible individuals— both managers and nonmanagers—is the best possible information for the maximum number of jobs and situations.

Principles of common understanding and of need for information about a business are obviously not new. As a matter of fact, one of our more important modern managerial tools, which early permitted some degree of decentralization and greater uniformity in an understanding of the business, has really been borrowed from thinking and practice of years long gone by, like so many other elements of our industrial society. In 1494, soon after the distinguished navigator from Genoa first put his foot on the continental soil of the Americas, Luca Paccioli published his "Systems of Double Entry Bookkeeping"

(*Summa de Arithmetica, Geometria, Proporcioni e Proporcionità*), which for nearly half a millennium has been, perhaps, the single most important tool of management.

Paccioli's concept provided common information, to managers and to others, permitting decentralized decisions to be made with a better understanding of the consequences to the whole business.

Unfortunately, many such accepted and important, but simple, concepts are becoming less useful today for decisionmaking purposes. The reason is essentially that business decisions, in this modern technological age, have increasingly come to require consideration of greater numbers of interlocked variables, and with greater futurity, than was formerly the case.

Happily, however, new methods, skills, and techniques are being developed and are being made available for providing the needed information, the "systems" view, the common understanding, that are required as much as ever but are thus far more difficult to achieve under today's more complex and faster paced conditions.

By research and analysis into the business operation, and by the systematic synthesis of the data, concepts, and facts from such studies, into organized information and theory, it is still possible and practicable today to obtain the material required for successful decentralized decisionmaking as part of the work of meeting this immense problem of organizing and communicating the information required to operate a large, decentralized organization to achieve defined objectives and known common purposes.

Again quoting Mr. Cordiner:

This deep problem of communication is not solved by providing more volume of data for all concerned, or even by faster accumulation and transmittal of conventional data, or by wider distribution of previously existing data, or through holding more conferences. Indeed, the belief that such measures will meet the *communications* challenge is probably one of the great fallacies in business and managerial thinking.

What is required, instead, is a far more penetrating and orderly study of the business in its entirety to discover what specific information is needed at each particular position in view of the decisions to be made there.

Operations Research and Synthesis

One promising approach to this problem is the discipline that has now become known as operations research and synthesis. Operations research first came into prominence during World War II, when it was applied with great success to such involved problems as analyzing and predicting enemy submarine attack patterns, and working out the most efficient and economical form of defense.

Since that time, a number of companies, including General Electric, have been studying ways to apply and extend operations research philosophy and techniques—including the techniques of mathematics, formal logic, and scientific method—to the analysis, measurement, and anticipation of business activities.

These techniques will be helpful in dealing with such matters in each of the business functions. Their original applications for fact-finding, or research as such, are being amplified to discover patterns and principles from the facts, which is synthesis. Such principles and patterns should have value in anticipating and guiding the future course of the enterprise.

Those who are studying operations research and synthesis are increasingly convinced that its greatest values may thus lie in helping both the general manager and functional managers to see the business as a whole, to plan its course more confidently, and to communicate such plans more clearly.

The approach requires that each decentralized business be viewed as a rational process or system, whose assumptions, objectives, and patterns of operation can be productively subjected to scientific analysis. From such analysis, with the aid of mathematical and scientific techniques, the manager is able to synthesize a progressively clearer "model" of the business that will enable him and his associates to measure and guide its progress with steadily greater accuracy and consistency.

A word of caution is also in order here, as was cited in noting that better measurements aid, but do not replace, judgment. To adopt a system or approach that relies primarily on statistics could easily foster a dangerous tendency to assume that anything which cannot be expressed numerically does not actually exist. Such a highly theoretical approach could lead to excessive rigidity, and to overlooking many of the most important factors, especially the human factors. Neither research nor the manager can ignore such human factors.

General Electric is steadily building experience in operations research and synthesis studies, and is constantly reevaluating its possible long-term usefulness. It is a field of great promise, and its use in the specific situations to which it has been applied has encouraged the company to continue exploring the possibilities of its future success as another significant aid in managerial decisionmaking.

Decentralization of responsibilities admittedly leads to problems, which can be handled more readily when such organized, purposeful research and synthesis into the operation is planned and achieved.

The results of using this kind of work to provide the needed information, understanding, and "systems" concepts, which permit true integrated decentralization, can allow us to cope successfully with increasing technological complexities; and thus to meet the challenge of our day. This idea was ably stated by Dr. Zay Jeffries:

Our progress depends to a considerable extent on seeing to it that the simplifying processes move forward in approximate balance with the complicating processes. If this can be accomplished, then individuals with given ability can expect to go forward indefinitely without becoming casualties of their own complexities.

CLIMATE FOR DECENTRALIZATION

It is part of the manager's role to provide the managerial climate in which other individuals will self-develop. It is *not* the manager's role personally to educate each one of his people as to all the new functional knowledge they should acquire or develop and possess.

The manager needs to have deep faith and confidence in the abilities of the people in the component, or business, he is charged with managing. I believe it is in this sense that we will come to understand the distinguished educator who said recently that "Democracy is faith in extraordinary abilities in ordinary people."

Without this kind of confidence, decentralization—and indeed democracy—could not exist; and we would be faced with recognizing the alternative, which leads, as Lord Acton has observed, to the situation where "All power corrupts and absolute power corrupts absolutely."

And yet, by decentralization we do not mean anarchy, but rather true liberty in the sense of Clemenceau's significant words: "Liberty is the right to discipline oneself in order not to be disciplined by others."

There is no doubt that, naturally—as has already been noted—decentralization itself has complicating features, as well as its thoughtfully developed advantages. It *does* limit authority to components of a scope that available managers can usually get their arms around. It *is* a limit to any genius who happens currently to be charged with an area of responsibility of specific, basic proportions.

It does tempt the fast operator to edge over the boundary, and take for his own, decisions that are really only properly made in cooperation with others whose interests are also affected. This is doubly annoying if—as can always be the case at a given time—the other manager involved is less speedy in his gait, less sure that the first manager sees the overall company interest whole, or, possibly, is himself incompetent but not yet replaced.

If managers approach this fundamental problem logically from the standpoint of the human being, rather than only the work and the knowledge about the work, you have to come even more firmly to the same conclusion. That is, you cannot treat people as though they were mere cams in some big machine rigidly structured into place by some master designer and therefore permitted only to oscillate in a pattern described from somewhere on high.

This is the basic reason the excesses of some "efficiency experts" brought failure to their efforts when they tried to atomize jobs to the point where, on the one hand, the resultant job duties didn't challenge individual human beings, or, on the other hand, their content became so repetitive as to be repulsive to a creative human being.

Hence, there is a deep requirement to seek solutions for living in our peculiarly complex industrial society today in directions that give recognition to the human factors involved and to the dignity of every *individual person,* whatever type of work he is doing. This means that the real demand, from this human viewpoint no less than from the work viewpoint, is for decentralization.

The essence of a sound managerial approach to practical decentralization, therefore, roots in the development of men.

This calls, first, for self-development; for each manager, as part of his job, to challenge and guide those reporting to him in their own self-development planning, but with the spark and the initiative being provided by the man himself. At the same time, the manager needs to establish a real and inspiring climate for growth, and to do so on a serious, organized, systematic basis. Intention is not enough here. It is part of the manager's own work to make the analysis and to take the steps so that such a favorable managerial climate actually does prevail.

Let us recognize, however, that decentralization, to be successful, does not lead to mere conformity or necessarily even to uniformity, even when policies and information are available; nor should we want it to.

In the mid-1950s, the U.S. Air Force Survival Training School released a report entitled: "Function of Expressed Disagreement in Small Group Processes" and concluded that its research suggested the following meanings in managerial activities:

First, management needs to accept the fact that task-oriented disagreement is almost always "good." You have been long conditioned to believe that it is "bad." Parents become quite disturbed if their children argue or fight. Teachers, managers, and supervisors behave similarly.

I think one extremely valuable application for management comes from the findings concerning individual performance and willingness to oppose others. Willingness to disagree is a major characteristic of the aces—the high achievers. It also characterizes those best able to meet frustration, those most willing to take calculated risks, and those who have the most "will to fight."

In spite of the fact that most really outstanding people appear to have this characteristic, many of them fare rather badly at the hands of management both in business and in military situations. They are seen as threats by superiors and are frequently not tolerated. Too often the greatest rewards are for conformity.

Perhaps we need a new definition of "group unity." I submit that what we are looking for is a group which can tolerate disagreement without becoming emotionally involved. A group in which disagreements are *not* expressed may be the most emotional group.

The Air Force studies, and conclusions, bring us fairly to grips with the manager's everlasting paradox—the parallel needs to organize for effective collective action and to preserve the dignity, the initiative, the creativeness, the voluntary participation of each individual in the organization. The manager has these conflicting needs no matter what the organization's size or task, and whether or not some individuals in the organization are currently acting either selfishly (some always are) or without any real concept of the need to play their own role as responsible team members, no less than as free individuals.

Here the manager, and especially the manager of the decentralized operation, comes squarely into the whole challenging area of human motivations—of why people work, either together or alone, and of what satisfactions or rewards they expect to find in their work.

People being individuals—and *only* individuals finally have the capacity to reason and to make rational decisions—the overpowering need in modern industrial society to decentralize in order to bring decisionmaking as close as possible to the work itself becomes even plainer, no matter what difficulties may be encountered in attempts to achieve decentralization.

Approach for Responsible Decentralization

In closing, seven points seem worthy of reemphasis. Decentralization of responsibilities results in many more problems than it needs to, unless:

1. Goals or objectives are set by the manager after mutual consideration and participation by himself and the men in the component, or enterprise, being managed.

2. Policies are clearly and explicitly stated and made known.

3. Jobs are carefully designed and defined, and evaluated for fair and adequate compensation and rewards.

4. Ideas and information are communicated both ways.

5. Research and synthesis into the operation being managed are purposefully organized to obtain and process the best available information needed for decisionmaking and common understanding of the whole.

6. Measurements are established, agreed upon, and understood.

7. And, most important, the manager recognizes that the human requirements and human purpose are a moral and ethical part of his managing work.

As Guglielmo Ferrero pointed out in his famous treatise on "The Principle of Power," in discussing the legitimacy of governmental power:

Above all, both government and subjects must realize that, principles of legitimacy being human, limited, and conventional, they must be applied in loyalty and good faith for what they are, and not with deception in the intent to use them as instruments of domination and obtain results contrary to their nature. Honesty should become the supreme virtue. . . .

11
Integrating and Motivating for Effective Performance

Although the usual procedure in a paper of this kind is to grasp frantically at the Webster definition of the subject word, I suggest we pass it by with a simple bow to its validity. The dictionary is necessarily too general to provide, in the increasingly complex and sometimes chaotic conditions of today's business world, more than a generic springboard for a whole series of techniques that, in the aggregate, give meaning and applicability to integrating as a business concept.

What do we mean by integrating? Is it a "thing" in the sense that you or I can sit down at our desks once a day or once a week and say, "Now I'm going to get the integrating cleaned up," and then put it aside as a job well done? I think it will become very clear to you that such an approach is completely valueless because, in fact, we cannot "do" integrating as a discrete and isolated function, but only as part and parcel of every activity that contributes to our business effectiveness, including especially our managerial effectiveness.

Based on remarks made at the Executive Leadership Conference, Cornell University, Ithaca, N.Y., February 18, 1955.

Integrating stems from the concept that true leadership is found in accomplishing the common purposes of the business and of all members of the business by example, by participation, and by persuasion rather than by command. It is, in essence, the interpretation and unification of the aims and activities of individuals and groups in order to ensure mutual and voluntary cooperation, teamwork, and self-disciplined unity of effort toward common goals.

Perhaps I can clarify our understanding of this elusive concept by bringing to your attention these classic words of Mary Parker Follett:

> As conflict—difference—is here in the world, as we cannot avoid it, we should, I think, *use it*. Instead of condemning it, we should set it to work for us. . . . There are three main ways of dealing with conflict: domination, compromise, and integration. Domination, obviously, is a victory of one side over the other. This is the easiest way of dealing with conflict, the easiest for the moment but not usually successful in the long run.

> The second way of dealing with conflict, that of compromise, we understand well, for it is the way we settle most of our controversies. . . . Yet no one really wants to compromise, because that means a giving up of something. Is there then any method of ending conflict? There is a way beginning now to be recognized at least and occasionally followed: when two desires are integrated, that means a solution has been found in which both desires have found a place.

What is important for us in Miss Follett's statement is the fact that integrating must spring from a clearly understood necessity to bring seemingly divergent strengths into an harmonious direction. Its value, as a managerial technique, is that it totals the strengths of an enterprise rather than eliminates those that seem, at the moment, to be pulling in the wrong direction.

Integrating is, then, the active creation by the managerial leader of an organization, or a component of an organization, of an atmosphere in which a coalescence of individual and personal intents, desires, skills, and energies and of corporate and component objectives is encouraged to take place voluntarily in the attainment of broad overall objectives. It cannot be achieved by executive order or command, since such compulsions destroy or dilute understanding by their very nature. And it is understanding, "one for the other," at all levels and throughout all levels of a business, that is the simple result of the integrating activity.

EVOLUTION OF THE INTEGRATING CONCEPT

I think we all draw a certain strength for our ideas and enhance our confidence in their probable rightness when we are able to trace their validation and revalidation through the course of history and business experience. Let me relate this Aesop fable to you both for its historical importance and for its contribution to our understanding of the integrating process.

In former days when all a man's limbs did not work together as amicably as they do now, the Members generally began to find fault with the Belly for spending an idle luxurious life, while they were wholly occupied in laboring for its support, and ministering to its wants and pleasures; so they entered into a conspiracy to cut off its supplies for the future.

The Hands were no longer to carry food to the Mouth, nor the Mouth to receive the food, nor the Teeth to chew it. They had not long persisted in this course of starving the Belly into subjection, ere they all began, one by one, to fail and flag, and the whole body to pine away.

Then the Members were convinced that the Belly also, cumbersome and useless as it seemed, had an important function of its own; that they could no more do without it than it could do without them; and that if they would have the constitution of the body in a healthy state, they must work together, each in his proper sphere, for the common good of all.

Aesop, and probably many before his time, recognized with varying degrees of perception the necessity for integrative action in the achievement of objectives. The concept has been variously expressed and applied to group activity as far back as our records and legends will allow us to venture. Indeed, its elements were applied to military conflict in a primitive and instinctive way from the beginning of recorded time until the scale and technical nature of modern warfare made it necessary for military leaders to take positive action to substitute trained and specific understanding of motives and objectives for the apathy and unconcern that was otherwise manifest in the body of their armies.

We, of course, are concerned with integrating as it applies to modern organizations, and so we may properly shorten the lines of history to our modern day and our modern industrial society. It has been only within the lifetime of many of us—the past 70 years—that clear recognition of the integrating concept as a distinct instrumental element, and as a basic motivating force, in the work of managing has come about.

It is always difficult to analyze so complex an amalgam of efforts as those that constitute the work of successful and professional managing. We need to try mentally to "stop" an apparently continuous process energized by many diverse forces in an effort to see and understand the parts that make it whole. We must, in these instants of observation, draw heavily upon our experiences in order to give meaningful classification to what we see, and in order to reference it into our system of thought with ample definition.

The concept of integrating as an element of the work of managing has evolved from the slow and painful synthesis and analysis of all the elements that are combined in the work of the manager. Originally, in the early part of the century, the elements were considered to be planning, organizing, and usually some other factor most frequently designated by the word "command."

It is this last element, command, that held the embryonic beginnings of the modern managerial principle with which we deal today.

The basic concept was, of course, there, but the name—command—was awkward in its implications and served to cloud the true nature of the function. Unlike planning and organizing, which deal more largely with facts and more readily measurable results, the integrating phase was difficult to pin down as to its philosophical principles or functional content, and hence, as to standards and measurements for its specific performance.

An examination of standard books on organization quickly confirms that whereas the duty of a manager to plan and to organize was recognized early and broadly accepted—and with reasonably common conceptual consent as to the work connoted by these two words—the remainder of the manager's task and function was much less clear or commonly conceived.

This is significant but understandable. There is a notable difference between the planning and organizing work of a manager and the balance of his function. These first two elements of his overall job tend to deal more essentially and primarily with either the internal or the structural phases of his work, whereas the rest of the job embraces those more dynamic factors that come from the fact that the end and distinguishing goal of managerial activities is to get planned and chosen results through the work of *other* people, rather than by purely personal effort.

Consequently, those parts of a manager's job concerned with the motivation that causes others to work with common purposes are under discussion here.

THE PHILOSOPHICAL JUSTIFICATION OF THE INTEGRATING CONCEPT

The endless search and repeated reference to the problems of integrating group activities that we find in the philosophical literature of our own and other societies should lead us to the conclusion that there is more to be found in its exploration than a simple methodology, or work technique, for getting a job done.

As you may readily guess, its praise is sung by parable and exhortation through our Bible and the theological documents of the other great religions of the world. It appears, if you will read them so, in the books and folklore of all people wherever there is concern with the motivations and actions of people who must work for a common good and live in common circumstances.

You will concede, I think, that it is a generally accepted fact that you can't have one set of ethics for one part of your activities and another equally justifiable set for another part. It is a parallel fact that the processes of business are specific and special examples of the workings of social processes in general. Paraphrasing Socrates, each of us needs to remind ourselves, "I am not a student of the business or the economy, but of the society." It is in this light that the problems of integrating have been the concern of the social scientist as fully as of the business scientist.

We need not look outside our own experiences—though yours and mine may have been somewhat different—beyond our own experiences of World War II, to understand the penetrating and all-pervading implications of the need for integrating.

Suddenly, there was a common cause, an inescapable necessity, pressed upon us all. War production, while it meant little change in the actual work of many people, provided a complete change in the meaning and importance of the purposes of the work. Production, with preservation rather than pay as the dominating stimulus, reached a magnitude that is hard to believe even in retrospect.

Industrial experience after the war was equally revealing. Because we, as managers and leaders, found it more difficult to make known with equal persuasiveness the meaning and importance of peacetime objectives in terms of the workers' needs and ambitions—in other words, because we were not able to integrate and show unity between the objectives of business and the objectives of people generally—we were unable to sustain the same spirit of voluntary contribution that showed the true proportions and potential of our industrial productive capacity.

One of the most revealing examples of the active power of integrating divergent wills and attitudes by setting acceptable and fully understood objectives came about in another way. It is an example I use to demonstrate further the effect of integrating, and I suggest that whatever other implications it may bring to your mind be set aside for the moment. They, in themselves, form a subject so difficult and so complex that we cannot touch upon it here, although eventually it, too, must be faced and reasoned to solution.

There is a book that I think might well become a part of your business library. It is called *The Nature of Prejudice* by Dr. Gordon Allport of Harvard. Because it serves to define the causes of prejudice that exists in us all to a greater or lesser extent, and because prejudice toward our associates, our customers, our competitors, and our government underlies—sometimes rightfully, I might add—so much of our business thinking, I think you will find it worth your time.

Dr. Allport describes a survey made by the army in its attempt to make the most effective use of our forces by integrating soldiers of various races. For those in segregated units there was a 60:20 vote against such a mixture, while those who had shared the perils of combat with men of other races voted overwhelmingly in favor of integration. What had happened? There had been no statistical disparity in educational status, in geographical background, or in general intelligence.

I think the answer is plain. An integration on the emotional and intellectual level had taken place because these men who were thrown together were given understanding—by the enemy as well as by their leaders—of the truly common quality of their goals.

How We Can Understand the Integrating Process

Just as we have broken the work of the professional manager into its four basic elements of planning, organizing, integrating, and measuring, it is also possible to examine each of these elements in turn and to state with reasonable precision the subelements that make up its organic character.

We must remember here, of course, that we are dividing the integrating process so that we may examine it better, but that these divisions are, in fact, parts of a single matrix that cannot, in practice, be so neatly divided or chosen, one without the other (Figure 1).

What we are going to do is to look at integrating in terms of its work content—in other words, in terms of what we do in our managerial way of life to accomplish it. As we progress, in what I hope will be an orderly and understandable fashion, I believe that the reasons behind each step, or subelement, will become obvious, and that we will see, at the end, a final fabric of the managing task made up with the parallel threads of planning, organizing, integrating, and measuring as its warp, and with the functional work of a business, such as research and engineering, manufacturing, marketing, finance, employee and public relations, and legal and corporate work, as the woof or weft of the same overall business fabric.

I. Interpreting and Making Understood

The first identifiable part of the integrating phase of the managerial leader's work is the interpretation and communication, to the point of mutual understanding, of the meanings and purposes of the planning, organizing, integrating, and measuring elements that constitute that work in its overall sense.

Interpretation and communication are a dual and indivisible responsibility of the professional manager, whether he is responsible for some functional or subfunctional component or for the overall organization. It is not enough that he, alone, understand and guide his activities in the direction set by the objectives of the organization, for then his relationship with those who report to him is necessarily one of command. Common objectives require an unequivocal statement and a voluntary acceptance of the common purposes that will bring them into being. In the words of Albert Lauterbach:

In order to be translated into action, a general incentive must crystallize in specific expectations. From the viewpoint of business practice the expectation concept of economic theory usually requires far-reaching adjustment and *amplification* in order to be meaningful. To begin with, any static assumption that expectations are always realized must be eliminated. . . . We approach business practice more nearly in J. R. Hicks's concept of "elasticity of expectations."

Figure 1. The integrating elements

I Interpreting and Making Understood the Planning, Organizing, Integrating, and Measuring Elements of the Dynamic Work of a Professional Manager
◇ Showing the common purpose that integrates all activities and all components of the enterprise and makes an organic whole of the enterprise, all of whose parts must function and grow in balanced accord.
◇ Interpreting company and component objectives, policies, and plans and explaining the work and responsibilities of others.
◇ Explaining to each individual his assigned portion of work and the relation of his work to the total work of the component and of the company.

II Listening: Facilitating Full Frank Communication to the Manager
◇ Keeping close contact with, and making optimum use of, ideas of employees, associates, customers, suppliers, and the public, including the public's representatives, government.
◇ Giving men the right to be heard, with open-minded patience and tolerance for objections and differing opinions.
◇ Consulting men before making plans or decisions that affect them.
◇ Having consideration for and regarding human values as precious assets worthy of preservation and development.

III Obtaining Sincere, Voluntary Acceptance of Work Assignments, Responsibility Relationships, and Accountability from Individuals
◇ Inspiring willingness, freely expressed, to perform work and teamwork within the determined organization pattern and relationships.
◇ Obtaining from each individual voluntary acceptance of the responsibilities and commensurate accountabilities that go with his work assignment.
◇ Or arranging for the transfer of the individual to another type of work for which he is better fitted and has more interest, in or out of the component or enterprise being managed.
◇ In accomplishing the above, listening for, being sensitive to, and understanding the individual's desires, objectives, feelings, ideas, and suggestions and seeing if, and how, these are consistent with the common purpose of the enterprise as a whole.

IV Creating and Maintaining a Friendly, Cooperative, Dynamic, and Productive Working Climate
◇ Engendering high morale and fostering continuing individual and team productivity.
◇ Encouraging, stimulating, and inspiring thoughtfulness, initiative, and individual productivity rather than demanding only intensity of work.
◇ Expecting men to recommend decisions rather than merely ask for decisions; and to bring wrong decisions back for review and correction instead of merely complying blindly.
◇ Teaching, coaching, advising, and counseling as to means for individual self-improvement and best known ways of doing the necessary work.
◇ Delegating responsibility and authority genuinely and continually.
◇ Making sure that work is rewarded by recognition, status, and compensation in accordance with accomplishments.
◇ Representing and supporting the men who report to him strongly and well.
◇ Basing decisions on established principles, facts, and the "authority of knowledge," rather than on position, rank, or expediency.
◇ Deserving and earning the respect of associates because of actions as well as words and because of his own integrity, ability, and consideration of others.
◇ Settling differences by finding a better way, not by *domination* (in which one gets victory over another—temporarily at least) or by *compromise* (in which neither gives nor gets all and neither is satisfied) but by integrating, *inventing another way of serving the best purposes and interests of all;* this being one of the most important elements of a manager's job—and one of the hardest.

of the work of a professional manager.

V Encouraging Individual Self-Development
◇ Carefully appraising each individual's strengths and weaknesses, suggesting on-the-job and off-the-job plans for self-development, and discussing appraisals and self-improvement plans in a frank and friendly manner.
◇ Holding each man to high standards of performance and encouraging self-appraisal, self-discipline, self-control, self-motivation, and self-improvement; thus helping each man to attain his own personal objectives and release his own best efforts.
◇ Teaching men that the work of managing can be learned and that leadership ability can be developed.
◇ Challenging others to do their best and thus leading them to greatest achievement.

VI Relating the Interests of the Individual, His Component, and the Organization to the Interests of the Industry, the Community, the Nation, and the World
◇ Knowing and explaining how our industrial society raises the standard of living of all citizens and provides social benefits to the community and the nation.
◇ Making and encouraging others to make reasonable contributions of time and effort to the work of outside groups whose purpose is general social and economic growth and improvement in the theory and practice of the work of the professional managers.
◇ Realizing the need to fit the behavior of the enterprise constructively and imaginatively to the general economic and social progress of community, nation, and world.
◇ Recognizing the "sovereignty of the people" as the great legitimatizing principle of modern politics and government.
◇ Being willing to grow and to deliver more and better service at constantly lower unit prices in terms of currency of stable value.

VII Achieving Successful, Economical, Profitable, Integrated Performance by All Individuals and Components
◇ Delving into snarls and untangling them successfully and profitably.
◇ Reuniting, harmonizing, synchronizing, and blending the portions of work that were divided and assigned in planning and organizing.
◇ Getting integrated and balanced results with good pace, flow, timing, and turnover.
◇ Utilizing all human and natural resources of the business well and in good balance.
◇ Carrying out objectives, policies, and plans of the component and of the company in long-and short-term best interests of customers, share owners, employees, suppliers, and the public, including the public's representatives, the government.

VIII Making Known the Integrating Concept and Work

IX Using the Results of Measuring to Keep Readjusting the Work of Integrating

X Exercising Judgment and Making Reasoned, Objective, and Timely Decisions to Effectuate the Integrating Work and Progress
◇ Taking reasonable risks confidently, competitively, courageously, and on own responsibility, on the basis of facts available, choosing wisely from among possible alternatives as responsibility and need for decision arise.

It is this "elasticity of expectations," the organic changes in growth and intent of the enterprise, that give the integrating process its dynamic nature.

It is necessary to define the common purposes that are the integrators of all activities and all components of the enterprise and that make a living whole of that enterprise, all of whose parts must function and grow in balanced but dynamic and organic accord, not in static discord.

The interpretation of the organization's objectives in order that those who work may understand their work and their responsibilities in terms of a total organization's accomplishment is a part of this first stage of the integrating process. It requires, for those who would do it well, a personal relationship between the manager and all those who report directly to him. Also, it implies an unbroken ladder of two-way communication between the top and the very first level of the organization, in order that the business goals be known as fully as is possible and necessary for effective action.

The work of any job in an organization structure is composed of two parts. The first of these is what we do ourselves, no matter what position or status we enjoy; the second is how we reference our personal activities into the work of others. It is this teamwork that is brought into being by integrating—by the proper and effective interpretation and communication of the business objectives, as well as by the other parts of this process—that we will discuss in turn.

II. Listening; Facilitating Full, Frank Communication to the Manager

The second part of the integrating process is by far the most difficult for most of us. It is plain and simple *listening;* that is, facilitating full and frank communication to the manager. Although few of us doubt the importance of this part of the two-way communication process, which is necessary to an effective measuring technique, we tend, by our natures, to honor it in the breach.

Listening has another effect, best expressed by the phrase "giving men the right to be heard." The desire to be part of a social or business unit is found in all of us, and we are only partly satisfied by the exercise of our assigned work functions.

We want to contribute—create might be a better word—a part of the destiny of those with whom we are identified. It is a clear responsibility of the manager–leader to provide the climate within his organization that allows such attitudes to flourish. Listening, consulting, accepting counsel, honoring differences as well as agreements—doing it with open-minded patience, tolerance, and even occasional forbearance—are the practices of the *professional* manager and *inspiring* leader.

It was Shakespeare's King Henry IV who said, and I think we have reason to note it: "It is the disease of not listening, the malady of not marking, that I am troubled withal."

III. Obtaining Sincere, Voluntary Acceptance

The third part of the integrating process is concerned with problems of obtaining a sincere and voluntary acceptance of the work assignments and the relationships responsibilities, as well as with clear recognition of what we can best call the accountability factors by which the accomplishment of assignments and the maintenance of relationships may be evaluated.

At this point, I think you can see why I warned you some time back about the perils of isolating the nondiscrete parts of a continuous whole. The gaining of acceptance is, of course, intimately connected with the interpreting and listening parts of the integrating process. Rather than removing it from the environment that gives it identity, we can only examine it fairly in the general context of the whole.

I suggest to you that what is necessary in order to gain the voluntary acceptance of work and responsibility is a contribution of inspiration on the part of the manager to those whose work he guides. We must inspire willingness, freely expressed, to perform work and teamwork within—and this is very important—within the determined organization pattern and essential relationships.

The gist of this is that the worker being managed needs to have a managerial attitude and vision himself to be able to do even his personal work well. Especially where his work is itself technical is this attitude deeply essential. Such men, like the manager himself, are stimulated by the professional character of their own work. Yet, only too often, there is failure—frequently on both sides—to sense the mutual as well as the distinct duties for which each is responsible.

The functional professional especially wants to feel that he is "part of management." Yet he far too frequently fails to take time to set his own important contribution precisely in the integral whole of which it is a part and to see himself as a partner in the overall team on which he is a player. It is, in such familiar circumstances, peculiarly the professional manager's province to help such an individual to perceive plainly his external as well as his more personal responsibilities; and to gain his voluntary and self-disciplined acceptance of the teamwork responsibilities of his job as no less a part of his personal accountabilities than his functional or technical contributions.

We need, in this part of our work, to be sensitive to the individual; that is, to recognize and adapt our communication to his capacity to understand the requirements of the task—that is, the degree of maturity of his response—and his willingness to accept the burden of it. And we must be ready, when there is no other course, to move the failing to more suitable work, even against a storm of abjuration or protest. Essentially it is a transitive kind of action that is required, difficult at best, but always necessary to the fulfillment of common objectives.

IV. Creating and Maintaining a Friendly, Dynamic, and Productive Working Climate

The fourth part of the integrating process is concerned with the manager's function of creation and maintenance of a friendly, cooperative, dynamic, and productive working climate. Again, it is interlaced with the three parts we have discussed and with the parts that are yet before us.

Because the concept of this climate-creating phase is long, and there are many things to do, perhaps we can fix them most easily in our minds by listing them in a kind of verbal shorthand:

First, there is engendering high morale and fostering continuing individual and team productivity.

Second, there is encouraging, stimulating, and inspiring thoughtfulness, initiative, and individual productivity rather than demanding only intensity of work.

Third, there is expecting men to recommend decisions rather than merely to ask for decisions, and expecting them voluntarily to bring dubious or wrong decisions back for review and correction instead of merely complying blindly.

Fourth, there is teaching, coaching, advising, and counseling as to the means for individual self-improvement and the best known ways of doing necessary work.

Fifth, there is delegating authority and holding individuals to both their work and their teamwork responsibilities genuinely and continually.

Sixth, there is making sure that work is rewarded by recognition, status, and compensation in accordance with accomplishment and performance.

Seventh, there is basing decision on established principles, facts, and the "authority of knowledge," rather than on position, rank, or expediency.

Eighth, there is deserving and earning the respect of associates because of actions as well as words and because of one's integrity, ability, and consideration of others.

Ninth, and last, there is settling of differences by finding a better way—not by domination or by compromise, but by integrating in the fullest meaning we can give that word.

It was O. Henry who suggested that "We may achieve climate, but the weather is thrust upon us." In our business activities our weather is the forces that impinge upon us, but our climate is that which we create in the process of giving and receiving the knowledge, the understanding, and the vitality that are everywhere about us in our enterprise.

V. Encouraging Individual Self-Development

The fifth part of integration, the encouragement of individual self-development by every member of an organization, may well be its most important part in terms of long-range survival of the enterprise.

A business continues to exist as a dynamic organic entity only so long as it is able to find within itself the resources of continuing imagination, increasing knowledge, and developing skills.

The structure of a corporation, of course, has no physical reality, but is actually only a clarifying classification and concept whose statement happens to be the physical properties of people, plants, and products.

It is clear, I think, that such a corporation may enjoy a place in our society only so long as those charged with its perpetuation look to its health and to its profitable growth. Charles E. Wilson—Electric Charlie—expressed it this way some years ago:

> The primary purpose of good corporation management is to keep a company in business indefinitely. They must look ahead and plan. . . . They must grow reserves . . . improve and lower the cost of their products, stabilize the security of their workers as much as possible, and make the public like and desire their company as a community and national asset.

The successful manager needs to know not only that there is a necessity to foster and encourage the self-development of individual men to meet these objectives, but also the ways in which it can be done. He must, in other words, develop in himself the skills of adult education along with the many other skills that bear on his work.

Educational and industrial institutions have devoted a surprising portion of their resources to this basic problem of "how to learn," for it must be known before "what to teach" can be given life.

We have been given new understanding of the learning process from such studies, and it is, without a doubt, a prime responsibility of a leader to learn, to understand, and to apply these principles. We know that men grow from within; that is, from a personal desire to win improved status and expanded trust in their activities. Ralph Cordiner expressed this conviction when he said:

The process by which men grow and develop into better leaders and managers is necessarily a self-development process. The company, and its managers, do not—in fact cannot—develop anyone. The initiative and the drive must spring from within the individual. Any system that urges development upon the individual against his inner desires and willingness would be gross paternalism, entirely contrary to the company's managerial philosophy and finest traditions.

The method of encouraging self-development will seem relatively simple as I describe it to you here. It has been our experience, however, that even in the hands of its most able and experienced practitioners, it is an intricate and time-devouring job, one that requires conscious allocation of adequate manager man-hours for successful performance, recognizing thus that it is a part of the distinct work of a manager as such.

Careful appraisal of each individual's strengths and weaknesses must be made periodically to explore both dormant and latent possibilities for growth. The individual needs to be encouraged to look within himself to find the physical and psychological factors that lie at the bottom of both his strengths and his weaknesses. He needs, with the help of the manager, to develop, to subscribe to, and to implement a personal plan of self-development that is, at once, directed toward his own objectives and toward those of the enterprise.

Standards of performance and of accomplishment must be established that are high but not discouragingly beyond the reach of each man as he is. It is challenging to those who do this work—and you are certainly among us—to realize that there is no single standard for human performance. Even more important is the realization that there is, in fact, no standard that can remain fixed and yet offer continuing challenge.

Each man needs to be made aware of his objectives and needs to be aided in learning the values of continuing self-appraisal, self-discipline, self-control, self-motivation, and self-improvement in actually attaining those objectives. It is recasting, revaluing, reexamining, and reorienting. It is endless but, above all, it is necessary.

The manager must personally discharge the ultimate responsibility of providing for the continuity of his work. Churchill was not entirely right when he said, "The world does not end with the life of any man." The world and the things of the mind and spirit that are in it will certainly end a recognizable existence unless those of us who are presently creating its pattern are willing to communicate our experiences and our perception of basic causes and principles to those who will follow us.

But if we will strive to do so, the work of managing can be defined, described, and learned; and leadership ability can be developed. We can, in sum, take personal, specific steps to aid the transfer of skills of creative and innovative thinking to others as our own time as individuals to create draws toward an end.

This obligation was pungently phrased by Virgil Jordan in his powerful 1940 Presidential Report to the National Industrial Conference Board, when he said:

The individual human, even in the most primitive community, is inevitably a part of the social organism in which he lives. His way of making a living, his way of life, his physical existence, its material substance, his knowledge, emotions, ideas, habits, customs, and institutions are created by contact, intercourse, and cooperation of individuals in the community. Those individuals are born and die, but the social organism in which they live is continuous.

Finally, in the matter of encouraging individual self-development, therefore, there is the matter of personal conduct. The manager cannot escape the fact that he is the embodiment of the challenge to others to do their best. It is hardly enough to suggest the ways of self-discipline and development while we, ourselves, lie secretive and secure in the things we have always known and always done.

VI. Relating the Interests of the Individual, His Component, and the Organization to the Interests of the Industry, the Community, and the Nation

The sixth part of the integrating process is concerned with the relation of the individual to his company, and of himself and the company to the larger and enclosing spheres of the community, the nation, and the world.

Business cannot be divorced at will from a social structure that has been fashioned to a great extent upon our unique and irreplaceable strengths. This point was ably presented by Kreps and Wright, who wrote:

Business . . . is a way of life, a system of providing goods and services. It is not a segment of the community, cooperating or warring with other segments, such as labor, consumers, or farmers. . . . It is the community engaged in getting its daily bread. Its goals, its ethics, its welfare are inseparable from the goals and aspirations and welfare of the community. . . . The fundamental and organic unity between business and the community is indissoluble.

And, in extension of this idea, Henry Ford II has said:

Business and industry have a political problem and responsibility. The problem is to gain and maintain the confidence of the American people so as to survive as free institutions.

This is the situation and the demand upon the sixth part of the integrating work of a professional manager. There must be first, within each of us, a belief—perhaps I should call it a faith—in the essential moral and ethical honesty of the competitive enterprise system.

We need to be able to distinguish, in absolute terms, those things that result from our awkwardness and errors—that only reflect our human failings—from those that are inherent in the system itself.

We need, in this thing we have created, to make it strong by conquering *ourselves*—our weaknesses as individuals, our prejudices, our jealousies, and our avarice.

We need to know where we are going; why we have chosen this particular path toward the common good. We need to define what we mean by the common good itself; including a definition of the need of business to operate profitably as a basic prerequisite to its being able to continue its creative role in the community and to continue to afford a focus for the efforts of all—customers, owners, employers, suppliers, and the public—whom it serves.

As managers and leaders, furthermore, it is our responsibility to communicate those things that we have accepted to others, everywhere. The horizon here is not the periphery of the enterprise; it is as far as we can reach and as far as we can be heard. As Norbert Wiener so sharply said, in today's complex technological age, "The statesmanship of management cannot . . . stop at the edge of each individual firm."

There are many ways in which this kind of integrating can be performed, but I think you will agree that only one can have a telling and lasting effect. It is fairly easy to stand off and criticize a situation or condition; easy and *meaningless.* We must, instead, encourage those about us and ourselves literally to plunge into the work of building a better world. We must provide time, and devote energy, to studying our society; to choose an area, or many areas, in which our aptitudes, talents, and skills can be employed effectively; to recognize the needs, purposes, and objectives of a job, and, finally, to do it with all our hearts.

VII. Achieving Successful, Economical, Profitable, Integrated Performance

Achieving an integrated performance in a business as an organic unit is the seventh part of the integrating process. It can be, properly performed, an example of the "problem-solving" science that is of the highest order.

We come to grips, in this part of our analysis, with the kind of integrating, as an element of the work of a professional manager, that is intimately tied to the actual operation and progress of the business itself. In a sense we are dealing, now, with those things that are the business of business itself rather than the impinging and modifying or altering forces that surround it.

There is a tendency to forget fundamental purposes in the freshening, speeding stream of our newly awakening industrial humanism. Let's look back for a moment to examine Mr. Wilson's statement, "The primary purpose of good corporation management is to keep a company in business indefinitely." As important as the self-development of men, there is this corresponding responsibility of the manager to achieve successful, economical, and profitable integration of all parts of a business in an overall display of the intrinsic unity of the organization.

The picture and the pattern are nearly obvious. There is a delicately linked chain of materials, resources, time, men and skills, machinery, plants, processes, markets, and customers that must somehow fall into an orderly relationship within the angle our intellect subtends. The view must be broad because it is only in this way that opportunity and objectives can be seen together. And yet the view must be rich in detail, for the total enterprise is the summation of many incremental activities.

This is the nasty, necessary work of keeping anticipated work on schedule and of digging into trouble, of untangling it, of setting things right—successfully, profitably, and on time. It is the work of reuniting, harmonizing, synchronizing, and blending the portions of work that have been divided and assigned in the manager's task of planning and organizing.

It is getting integrated and balanced results with good pace, flow, timing, and turnover, of utilizing all human and natural resources of the business most effectively. It is, finally, the implementation—in each individual organization component and personal job no less than in the enterprise as a whole—of business objectives that are the very justification of business existence.

VIII. Making Known the Integrating Concept and Work

The eighth part of the work of integrating may, at first glance, strike some of you as either rhetoric or mere redundancy. It is hard to express this concept otherwise, however, because we are applying a process to itself. Integrating is a work function as fully as the running of a lathe or the planning of a schedule. It must be, like every other facet of our activities, itself integrated into the total work of the manager. You'll remember my earlier references to the truly indivisible nature of the "work of a professional manager" as it is applied, and I think that we have it demonstrated here in full fashion.

Integrating is done to bring people, objects, and objectives together, but that alone can't satisfy its purpose. Having seen a unity and coherence in the enterprise, the manager must work, in fulfillment of this eighth part, to return this vision to the points of application.

In each of the other three primary elements of the work of a professional manager—that is, in planning, in organizing, and in measuring work—there is a need for making known the nature and content of the work to all those in the enterprise who will translate the results into courses of productive action through their own particular functional efforts.

It is clear, I think, that organizing is done in the light of the desired objectives determined by the planning work, and that measuring provides the review and test of the validity and effectiveness of such work. Integrating, however, is the substantive process that brings these separate elements into practical and useful alloy.

It is because integrating is the work that gives life and dynamics to the other parts of a manager's work that it becomes so necessary that its *own* concept be understood fully, and that the techniques of its application be clearly demonstrated to all within an organization.

IX. *Using the Results of Measuring to Keep Readjusting the Work of Integrating*

One important key, of course, to assuring progress toward a set of objectives is the measuring process. As the name implies, this is the work of looking at what has been done in the light of what needed to be done in a way that not only provides a baseline against which performance and accomplishment may be measured, but also provides a way in which the baseline itself may be readjusted and refined continuously to provide greater precision in the measuring work.

Thus, the results of measuring need to be applied as fully to integrating work as to all other elements of a manager's work, and I think the reasons are obvious. Although we are dealing with a function whose results are largely measured "once removed," that is, by the testing of our planning and organizing work, these latter elements are, as we have seen, completely dependent upon proper integrating for their effectiveness.

We can apply measuring to integrating by looking at the success with which we bring together into a common direction the needs and objectives of the business and the resources at its command; the desires and aspirations of its people and the attainment of these personal objectives within the basic intent and purpose of their contribution; and, finally, the objectives, both short- and long-range, of the business as a whole and the demands of the society in which it operates.

Integrating uses the results of the manager's measuring work to test its own vitality and accomplishment, feeding back, through itself, the appraisals of all the work of the enterprise in a process of cross-fertilization that is necessary to continuing dynamic growth.

X. *Exercising Judgment and Making Reasoned, Objective, and Timely Decisions to Effectuate the Integrating Work and Progress*

Integrating, like every other part of the manager's work, is an exercise in the "exercise of judgment." It requires the making of reasoned, objective, and timely decisions. There is an evident necessity to take reasonable risks with confidence, to take them competitively, courageously, responsibly, intelligently, and promptly on the basis of facts available at the time each individual decision is needed from, and should be made by, the manager.

Out of the inevitable host of possible solutions to any situation, there is often only one that is fully right in the integrating sense—one, that is, that serves every desired objective and answers every possible need.

Frequently, of course, there is none that provides a totally perfect answer. It is here that the ability to separate and select the usable and necessary purposes of the business and of its people that can be successfully integrated into a common direction becomes of paramount importance. It is a measure of managerial competence and performance in "blending thought and action" in taking risks and in making timely decisions.

You might, I think, consider that this tenth part is also part of the technique of integrating integrating, for it is judgment applied properly to the correlation of business circumstances that gives this element of the work a practical reality and meaning in the dynamic life of the enterprise.

The Personal Challenge

Let us now isolate and describe those subelements of integrating that are divisible in an abstract sense, because they relate to different aspects of the operation of business. These subelements are:

First, interpreting and making understood the planning, organizing, integrating, and measuring elements of the dynamic work of a professional manager.

Second, listening; facilitating full frank communication to the manager.

Third, obtaining sincere, voluntary acceptance of work assignments, responsibility relationships, and accountability from individuals.

Fourth, creating and maintaining a friendly, cooperative, dynamic, and productive working climate.

Fifth, encouraging individual self-development.

Sixth, relating the interests of the individual, his component, and the company to the interests of the industry, the community, the nation, and the world.

Seventh, achieving successful, economical, profitable, integrated performance by all individuals and components.

Eighth, making known the integrating concept and work.

Ninth, using the results of measuring to keep readjusting the work of integrating.

Tenth, exercising judgment and making reasoned, objective, and timely decisions to effectuate the integrating work and progress.

The managerial work of integrating is a challenge that I have only barely expressed. In every human being there is a desire to do well in all that he does, and in managerial work, as fully as in any place of which I conceive, there is also the *necessity* to do well. You may know this pertinent quote from "Our Town":

Every time a child is born into the world it's Nature's attempt to make a perfect human being. Well, we've seen Nature pushing and contriving for some time now. We all know she's interested in quantity; but I think she's interested in quality, too.

I suppose there is some meaning in everything we remember. Perhaps this quote is worth remembering because I think that we, as managers, can emulate this search for perfection and this concern with quality in the things *we* do in the separate, smaller worlds we each create in our daily jobs.

12

"Measuring" as an Element of a Manager's Work of Leading

RELATION OF MEASURING CONCEPT TO OVERALL BUSINESS PHILOSOPHY

There probably are few fields of human relations in which there are more clichés, and a greater tendency to camouflage with words the stubborn continuance of traditionally based managerial practices and habits, than in those activities of managers loosely described by the words "control" and "controls." The literature of the accountants, management societies, and university researchers and writers is full of such words.

Today, however, I will be discussing "measures" and "measuring"—both as better terms or handles and as approaches deliberately rooted in more soundly conceived managerial philosophy, principles, and practices. The results sought by the older concepts of "controls" and "controlling" can be attained more harmoniously and profitably by this consciously chosen alternative route.

Speech at Executive Controls Program, Syracuse University, College of Business Administration, August 9, 1957.

170

These managing terms are not offered as just a superficial face lift, or even as a kind of glamorized "selling" label for older managing practices and habits, which themselves, in all fairness, have often been fairly effective and reliable in the past.

Instead, "measuring" has a far more encompassing and unique meaning. It is geared to the more complex mission and work of the manager in today's increasingly technological, competitive environment and in the changing business world of tomorrow that is so plainly foreshadowed for us.

To be able to examine in depth the reasons this measuring approach should be preferable, despite its requirement to go beyond older working practices, we need first to take a look briefly at the whole evolving and complex business and social environment in which business enterprises will have to function and in which such measuring may be expected to be effective.

Second, we need a little deeper look at the fundamentals and principles of professional managing, based on a rational and an ethical managing philosophy, which are the needed basis for a professional manager's work.

Finally, we will go in reasonable depth into the measuring process itself, as conceived and practiced under such a philosophy and approach.

Many aspects of managing seem often to come back to two fundamental factors:

1. Of all the resources the manager has to blend by his leadership, through his own work and teamwork, to accomplish results that are both competitive and profitable in the marketplace, the people in the organization are the only resource the manager can actually influence and develop so as to be themselves initiators of progress beyond his own capacity.

The people in the enterprise, then, are the variable element, and by this I mean *all* the people—all functional individual contributors and all managers alike; and both professional workers and nonprofessionals alike.

The manager accordingly needs to manage so that he creates such a working climate that the people in the business will themselves voluntarily perform to their best abilities, both as to quality and volume of output and results. To give a new twist to a common expression, the manager needs to know how to inspire people so that they will get the most work out of themselves and by the best application of their initiative and talents, not merely by more intensity or duration of personal effort.

2. Throughout the ages, no scheme, formula, reports, or other mechanisms—in fact, even threats of penal confinement or worse— have been nearly as consistently effective in achieving both economic and social progress as the voluntary efforts of inspired people who are thinking and acting with high morale just because they know what they are doing; and who, accordingly, are—of their own free will— constantly integrating their individual work and mutual teamwork, and measuring their progress as they go, both to keep it in line with objectives and to keep refining and improving those objectives them- selves whenever new insights permit.

I believe that there is a planned professional approach to bring- ing about this well-adjusted situation, and I will explain it.

THE BUSINESS ENVIRONMENT

Growing Complexity and Interaction of Business Factors

As industry becomes more complex, each employee uses assets of greater value and each employee's work impinges more and more on the work of more and more other employees. The enterprise itself becomes larger and more complex.

All will be working in a business environment that has less inher- ent stability and is subject to quick and accelerating technological changes. In fact, the education and self-development of most employ- ees will be, and will need to be, almost continuous, and will need to have a built-in acceleration factor.

Need for Communication and Participation

The manager will need to summarize and sincerely and clearly communicate to all component employees information. This informa- tion will enable them to determine what the changing business envi- ronment is, what is happening when it changes, what the business— and the employee's particular component within the business—has as specific short- and long-term objectives, what the resources are to gain component goals, what obstacles have to be overcome, and what the chief strengths and weaknesses of the business, including those of the employee himself, are.

Managers need, regularly, to discuss the prevailing situation frankly—and on a participating and listening basis—in channels at all levels. In the process they need consciously to bring all employees in on the determination of goals for their component so that the other employees see the situation as the manager sees it and the manager sees it as the other employees see it. In this way managers can achieve that genuine legitimacy of leadership that exists when both leaders and followers are pursuing common goals and objectives.

The final objectives, plans, programs, and schedules will represent unified balanced goals enriched by the viewpoints, ideas, and suggestions of each employee. Each employee will be responsible for doing a specific satisfying part of the work, for contributing a known and specific result toward accomplishing the specific broader objectives he has helped to establish. And such personal responsibility will include working voluntarily with other employees toward the common objectives of the component and the enterprise.

With this philosophy and approach, each defined yet interlocking segment of the total work to be accomplished to attain the chosen and agreed-upon goals can be looked at in terms of specific measurement standards, identified with individual positions whose incumbents understand and voluntarily accept the responsibility, and the corresponding authority and consequent personal accountability for both work and teamwork results.

Use of Data Processing Equipment

Computers and similar automatic processing equipment, of course, are largely and increasingly taking over repetitive, tedious, mechanical-type tasks not requiring creative skill or original thinking, and will greatly facilitate the timely presentation and better analysis of more complete and useful managerial and other work measurements, data, and information of all kinds.

Hence, despite the increasing complexities of the work of running an enterprise competitively and properly, such new tools—and new and improved principles for using and applying them—will allow managers and other workers alike to cope with the greater number of variables arising and to do so more rapidly and usefully than their predecessors of earlier days could devise and use the more elementary information methods and equipment that sufficed at the time.

Changing Employee Capabilities and the Manager's Mission

To an amazingly broad degree, the employee himself is changing in the competence he brings to the job. Basically, in the near future, employees will be better educated, with perhaps 50 percent completing college and 50 percent having a high school education and often further technical training.

A high proportion of this literate group will have been exposed to psychological, sociological, or economic thinking in considerable depth. Such educated employees will expect a high mental content in their work; will bring a professional orientation to their positions; and will be better adjusted to make the best contributions, especially when the managing itself is of correspondingly better and more professional quality.

Increasingly, managing will be regarded not as a higher level kind of work, but rather as a different kind of work—a kind of work both unique and professional in itself—as illustrated, say, by the difference in a very large hospital between the manager with a professional doctor's training and a pathologist.

The future manager will also be working in a scarce labor market—scarce both as to virtually all skills and as to total available population of working age. Therefore, the manager will need to manage so as to attract, hold, and develop employees and their skills, as well as to earn their understanding and their continuing—and freely tendered—support.

Furthermore, with this approach each employee can and will be depended upon to self-integrate and self-measure his own actual progress toward assigned and accepted goals. More and more he will be acting with self-initiative, self-discipline, self-confidence, and self-development.

As a result the manager can assume a larger span of managerial responsibility and yet have closer, more satisfactory human relationships with each employee at the vital man-to-manager contact point. And—precisely because the functional employee thus takes on his own responsibility for forward-looking expertness and for making able and rational decisions in his functional work field—the manager spends more of his time on his true managerial function of thinking through the most challenging objectives, plans, and programs and organized efforts for improving products, lowering costs, increasing customer values, and making the best integrated and measured use of all the available human and material resources.

This will be professional and scientific managing—accomplished by persuasion and not by command—with maximum decentralization to functional individual contributor positions of responsibility for conceiving and performing varied, interesting, challenging, de-

cisionmaking, and risk-taking work, and with maximum participation by all concerned.

The manager, in this philosophy, is *not* the "thinker," with the others "doers." Both managers and functional individual contributors "create and produce" in their assigned areas of accountability to accomplish results: the managers by planning and organizing to get optimum results through the work of others; the functional individual contributors by thinking and acting to achieve able and high personal performance—with both alike integrating, and always measuring, to keep the whole process going steadily forward at a satisfactory pace.

These broader ideas—that all functional individual contributors both think and act, that they participate in planning, and that they are experts themselves in their functional work field, who take risks and make decisions—have a great effect on best organizing, particularly in the managerial steps of designing individual positions and grouping them into components of the organization structure, in staffing such positions, and in then aiding and motivating all employees to self-develop on a continuing basis, and to have the highest quality knowledge, skill, and understanding in actually doing the work, and teamwork, of each position.

As part of the planning element of his own work, the manager, as one initial part of his own approach, specifically develops and expresses factors, units, and standards for measuring performance of both individuals and components, and he establishes valid criteria to assess the significance of the accomplishments and growth of the individual in his work and in his potential, as subsequent measuring data and analyses permit comparison of actual results in terms of such standards and criteria.

Thus the basis for mutual use of the highest quality of measuring work is, so to speak, built into each job—for manager and functional individual contributor alike—as a foundational element of the design of the basic organization pattern for the whole enterprise.

Other Significant Changes

I will also note here, but not further belabor, those trends familiar to all of you that are bringing about, on all sides, multiplying technological, economic, political, and social changes. These will also require changes in the future manner in which a manager manages and, therefore, in the manner in which he measures.

Modern Terms

It was with a clear understanding of such evolving conditions that Dr. Harry Hopf named planning, organizing, coordinating, and controlling as the four primary elements comprising professional managerial work.

And it is through building on this foundational advance that our research and practice in General Electric brought us to evolving integrating from coordinating, and measuring from controlling, to indicate best the *attitudes* as well as the *attributes* of the professional manager's leadership work, in rounding out the dynamic phases of his job, to complement his planning and organizing efforts.

These work element names are, in a real sense, therefore, evolutions rather than mere changes of words.

Integrating reaches beyond compromise or mere coordination for that "plus value" in the mutual efforts of men for which Mary Parker Follett was striving, as disclosed in her writings. For example, she said:

There are three main ways of dealing with conflict: domination, compromise, and integration. Domination, obviously, is a victory of one side over the other. This is the easiest way of dealing with conflict, the easiest for the moment but not usually successful in the long run.

The second way of dealing with conflict, that of compromise, we understand well, for it is the way we settle most of our controversies; each side gives up a little in order to have peace, or, to speak more accurately, in order that the activity which has been interrupted by the conflict may go on.

Compromise is the accepted, the approved, way of ending controversy. Yet no one really wants to compromise, because that means a giving up of something. When we compromise, something is always lost.

There is a way beginning now to be recognized at least, and even occasionally followed: when two desires are integrated, that means that a solution has been found in which both desires have found a place, that neither side has had to sacrifice anything. . . .

The integrating work done by a manager as a leader, as thus derived, in turn has several significant cross-links to the fourth, or measuring, element of his unique work; especially:

1. Interpreting organization and component objectives and policies, and explaining the work and responsibilities of others.

2. Explaining to each individual his assigned portion of the work

and the relation of his work to the total work of the component and of the organization.

3. Inspiring willingness, freely expressed, to perform work and teamwork within the organization patterns and relationships.

4. Obtaining from each individual voluntary acceptance of the responsibilities and commensurate accountabilities that go with his work assignment.

5. Holding each man to high standards of performance and encouraging self-appraisal, self-discipline, self-control, self-motivation, and self-improvement, thus helping each man to accomplish his own personal objectives and release his own best efforts.

Measuring and Leadership

Measuring, the fourth primary element of the professional manager's work, is literally the feedback and sensing element in that work; the red-and-green lights, as it were, that indicate simultaneously to the manager and to all associated functional individual contributors the effectiveness of the manager's thinking and decisions under the planning, organizing, integrating, and measuring elements.

Measuring also forms the basis for new manager decisions under all those elements of his own work of leadership that may be necessary to accomplish the component objectives. Measuring is thus the manager's own work element that ties together all his other work.

Measuring also communicates, for each functional individual contributor and manager, the tie-in of the results of his own work and teamwork to that of other functional individual contributors and managers; and it shows the specific contributions through the work and teamwork of each toward accomplishing component objectives.

Measuring, therefore, denotes the need both to get data and information and also to make it available first to the man whose performance it mirrors—for his own self-appraisal and his own creative action—rather than to the manager who will *tell* him to alter his course.

Understanding the Measuring Process

This is, you will surely agree, a long foundation-laying job on which to erect an understanding of measuring, and of its key place as one of the four primary elements of the work of a professional manager. But perhaps, by thus defining its conceptual place in the manager's work

Figure 1. The measuring elements of the work of a professional manager.

I Devising and Establishing Measuring Systems and Media
◇ Creating and effectuating measuring systen.s and media for orderly recording and reporting of measurement facts, information, statistics, and accounts.
◇ Giving specific attention to need and ways to measure operating (including income, cost, and profit), functional, and managerial performance—both long- and short-range—for all key areas to which managerial attention needs to be guided to develop strengths and eliminate weaknesses; and to improve current and future planning, organizing, integrating, and measuring, continually using a research approach to find a new and better way.

II Recording and Reporting Performance of People and of Components
◇ Recording actual performance of people and of components in a form comparable with the factors and units determined as standards for measuring such work and results.
◇ Reporting recorded results promptly and understandably.
◇ Transforming detailed information as rapidly as possible into condensed measuring facts, comparisons, and variances as it moves upward in the organizational structure, thus making it possible for managers to function, and to deserve respect, through authority of knowledge rather than authority of position.

III Analyzing, Appraising, and Interpreting Measured Results
◇ Analyzing data and comparing plans and performance with opportunities.
◇ Comparing performance and results with plans, including schedules, and with standards.
◇ Determining both basic performance and deviations (or variances) from standards.
◇ Analyzing data and comparing performances with standards.
◇ Formulating and interpreting results of such analyses to indicate actual or probable causes for results and variances wherever possible.
◇ Making facts, comparisons, analyses, and interpretations available quickly and clearly to those responsible for performance and for taking any actions required in the light of such measuring work; and especially so that adequate facts may be available to all concerned, in advance, as a basis for making reasoned decisions on such facts rather than on opinions, so far as feasible and practicable.

IV Making Known the Measuring Systems, Media, and Results
◇ To all whose performance is measured or who can use results of the measuring process for better understanding, planning, and performance of their own work.

V Using the Results of Measuring to Keep Readjusting the Work of Measuring
◇ Improving measuring systems and media and their use continually to keep managerial planning, organizing, and integrating current with the dynamic progress, needs, and potentials of each component and of the enterprise as a whole.
◇ Using the measuring work and process as a feedback for continual reappraisal and readjustment of the entire work and performance.

VI Exercising Judgment and Making Reasoned, Objective, and Timely Decisions to Effectuate the Measuring Work and Progress
◇ Taking reasonable risks confidently, competitively, courageously, and on own responsibility, on basis of facts available, choosing wisely from among possible alternatives as responsibility and need for decision arise.

---

so fully, time can be saved in defining the actual content of the measuring element itself. We believe there are six essential parts to such content. These six subelements of measuring, and the respective principal conceptual ideas within each, are outlined in condensed form in Figure 1. A few words here on each of the six principal headings is, however, useful at this point.

I. Devising and Establishing Measuring Systems and Media
What needs to be measured, how and when to measure it—all need careful systematic planning and creative thinking. The ap-

proach, of course, is to devise an orderly, structured measuring system that aids the attainment of objectives through what information it furnishes, when it furnishes it, and to whom it furnishes it. This is a never-ending research area, but certain criteria seem to stand the test of time.

The organization needs to determine first the significant or key result areas of performance in which success or failure is critical to the enterprise. Such key areas of competitive performance, in which the business enterprise as a whole strives for leadership, and to which all managerial and functional work contributes, are eight in number:

1. Profitability
2. Market position
3. Productivity
4. Product leadership
5. Personnel development
6. Employee attitudes
7. Public responsibility
8. Balance between short-range and long-range goals

Measurements, therefore, need to be developed, and agreed upon, to show the degree of progress toward accomplishment of specific objectives currently established (in the planning work element) both for the enterprise as a whole and for each component position thereof in each of such key result areas. These specific measurements need, in turn, to show both short- and long-term progress, and at the same time proportionate use of resources, including time.

In a sense, planned objectives will break down into two broad classifications as to work results to be measured. One is the acceleration in the rate of improving strengths and overcoming weaknesses in doing the work under generally established patterns, procedures, methods, and insights.

The kinds of measurement factors used here—such as ratio of rejects, extra work labor, expense ratios, and so on—can usually be determined by applying normally available operating experience. In addition, it is usually a similarly practicable task to agree upon fair standards of performance and on challenging goals for progressive improvement. It would, naturally, be possible to offer long lists of such widely tested "nuts-and-bolts" kinds of work measures. But the best for you will be those you develop—as near the work point as possible—in your own sphere.

The other classification—which often represents the real

opportunity—is a breakthrough to an entirely new way of doing things so as permanently to change and improve methods, processes, insights, patterns, and procedures of work. Planned results from such innovating projects are thus likely to be a major factor on the position attained in the eight key result areas.

Such projects are the focus of creative innovating effort. The degrees of success are not uniform and cannot be guaranteed. The measuring systems need to give early and true indications, accurately and promptly during the course of the work, of the degree of planned accomplishment, in proportion to time schedules and use of other resources and in time and in a way for such measurements data to have decisionmaking value to the functional individual contributors and managers responsible for the particular piece of leapfrogging progress or innovation.

The essence of the "measuring system and media" approach here is to think through in balance to determine the most economical, quickly available and understandable measuring information, generated closest to the point of action. This will both indicate the degree of real progress in accurate comparison with the planned stage of advancement and highlight critical areas for further attention.

II. Recording and Reporting Performance of People and of Components

Measuring too much and too often wastes money, interferes with more creative work, and tends to put the manager in the position of virtually peering over each man's shoulder as the man makes every decision. This kind of measuring would effectively nullify the original delegation to the man of the responsibility for accomplishing the result or making the specific contribution to progress toward objectives.

In any event, there are distinct limits to the usefulness of measuring what has already happened for the manager whose task is increasingly to look and plan for the future.

As Ralph Cordiner put it once:

The manager who merely tries to keep his plans and policies up-to-date is already out-of-date. He must keep them up-to-the-future, where the objectives of the business will be achieved.

On the other hand, the measurements system should cover enough significant spots in each significant project or performance area and be done often enough to prevent any probably irrecoverable operating situation of critical significance to the enterprise—or to the component—from arising without the man doing the work himself being able to see it.

That calls for measurement information that enables him to see that it *is* in fact a critical situation that he should face up to, solve—or review with his manager if he sees no solution of reasonable probability of success with planned resources, or no probability of getting back on the original time plan for the finished project.

Scientists say you can observe but not creatively understand natural phenomena that you cannot measure. Likewise, the quality of results of human work cannot be measured solely on opinions, especially if the qualifications for a *particular* opinion are not fully clear. It is important also to record actual performance of people and of components factually in a form comparable with the factors and units determined in advance—and agreed upon, on a participating basis— as standards for measuring such work and results.

Such agreed-upon measurements become like the thermometer element in an air conditioning system, impartially stating the temperature for feedback to other parts of the system for their appropriately designed system interaction.

The functional individual contributor actually doing a particular piece of work needs more frequent measurements in more detail for his own information and his own decisions with respect to thinking, acting, and measuring to guide his own efforts than his manager—or his manager's manager—needs.

Therefore, detailed measuring information needs to be transformed as rapidly as possible into more condensed measuring facts, comparisons, and variances as it moves upward in the organization structure. This flow of condensed measurement information makes it possible for managers to function, and to deserve respect, through authority of possessing knowledge they understandably need to do the manager's work of leadership, rather than through authority of position.

III. Analyzing, Appraising, and Interpreting Measured Results

Measuring data, and comparisons of plans and performance, should be analyzed from a constructive perspective; namely, to determine the degree to which the full opportunities for contribution toward objectives inherently present in the work were sensed and utilized.

Here a sharp distinction needs to be made between agencies—whether mechanical processes or human work—for effectively recording and developing data and information and making meaningful comparisons, however effective they may be; and the entirely different responsibility to study, and to think through, all measurements information as the *whole* measuring element in the manager's work of leadership. The latter forms a rational basis for manager planning, organizing, and integrating decisions in order still to accomplish the results originally planned on time, with planned use of resources, and in balance with other planned objectives.

The first, while of importance as to accuracy and completeness and as to being done economically and well, is nevertheless a fact-gathering, analytical, supporting function that should be synthesized, patterned, and mechanized as much as possible. It might be described as the procedural side of measurements system design and operation.

It is only one factor, however, in the overall measurements systems design, since the primary determinant is the great variety and blending of measurement information that managers and functional individual contributors need to have to do their work, to make their decisions, and to take risks intelligently and on the basis of thoughtful judgment exercised to choose wisely among alternative available courses.

We should never expect the inertia of fact-gathering and analysis, or of a so-called "control" system, somehow to take managers or functional individual contributors magically in the right direction or to turn them around fast enough to the right direction.

Any such system is too insensitive to human reactions; so centralized action and communication will always lag behind that of a decision system based on those closest to the work, but holding themselves directly and voluntarily accountable for measuring their own contribution, for thinking through the changed situation, and for making decisions to achieve chosen objectives.

Here, indeed, is the fundamental weakness—namely, the less powerful drive—of the checkup or audit approach in the "control" concept.

In contrast, the "measuring" approach is based on sincere and expressed belief in the fundamental willingness and capability of people to do a job for which they are responsible—and accept themselves to be accountable—with self-motivation, self-integration, and self-development.

IV. Making Known the Measuring Systems, Media, and Results

Everyone in an organization whose work is being measured, or who has any working use for particular results of the measurement process, should be informed of the measuring systems and media, and of specific measurement results. The same need for frankness and good communication exists here as in making original plans.

The results of measuring interact with the planning, organizing, and integrating elements. The significance of measurement results needs to be fully understood and discussed. Only in this way will there be the most effective and timely understanding, planning, and performance of each man's own work by everyone in the organization.

V. Using the Results of Measuring to Keep Readjusting the Work of Measuring

Perhaps here we can relax a little and consider Ring Lardner, Jr.'s famous remark about the ballplayer who "made the wrong mistake." The measuring systems and media—as well as their use—need to be reviewed critically and improved on a planned basis for two purposes:

1. To bring to light any gaps in measurements that did, or might, lead to mistakes in decisions; that were not bad judgment, but bad information as to what was being accomplished. This is, of course, using the results of the measuring feedback to redesign the measuring feedback element itself.

2. Looking toward the measurement requirements of the future—to keep managerial planning, organizing, and integrating always *current* with the dynamic progress, needs, and potentials of the enterprise as a whole, and of each component, in the changing environment.

VI. Exercising Judgment and Making Reasoned, Objective, and Timely Decisions to Effectuate the Measuring Work and Progress

The output of the measurement system is an orderly pattern of facts and data as to progress, and of specific indications of strengths and weaknesses in progress toward accomplishing objectives.

Functional individual contributors and managers then have—each and severally—the responsibility to use that information pattern to take reasonable risks confidently, competitively, courageously, and on their own responsibility, on the basis of facts available, and personally to choose wisely from among possible alternatives as responsibility and need for decision arise.

Hence, fundamentally this concept of measuring, as a primary element of both managerial and other work, also contemplates, as in decentralization of decisionmaking, that the best measurements be made directly available at the point of the action or work.

Thus, each employee acting with self-discipline, self-confidence, self-motivation, and self-development measures the results of his own work and teamwork, and takes corrective action as required, before such action is, or needs to be, imposed from above.

Correspondingly, the measuring system, with all its complex interlocks, is rooted in the idea mentioned earlier, and these measurements, as thus initially available at each individual position, will be increasingly summarized as they flow upward to executive managers in the organization structure.

Such summaries then will include not only the measurement but also the corrective action already taken or contemplated by those directly responsible for the specific contributions toward component objectives.

Hence their managers are alerted to new trends—which also, of course, need to be reflected in the next higher summaries of measurements—and can then devote to their work those efforts that deal with the activities required or desirable beyond the corrective action already contemplated.

CONCLUSION

I was once asked for remarks on the subject of the evaluation and measurement of business performance. In reply, I noted:

As a word of warning, I am probably the world's worst to talk on "control"—it is just a bad word for me, usually used inherently to imply the kind of top-down masterminding that I think businessmen most need to discipline themselves to use most sparingly.

Our approach is to urge "measuring" as a far more fundamental way to tackle the manager's growing needs to get, analyze, and understand more and deeper information—but made available to, and used by, the man whose work is being measured and not by some higher authority either to second-guess him or to take the real responsibility of his own work "upstairs" and away from him.

In closing, therefore, may I leave that simple thought with you—that the real managerial task is not "control" by him of others, but rather making sure that the best information, as a solid basis for decisionmaking, should be spelled out through a measuring system. In this way, decisions may be decentralized, and still competently made, at the closest possible point to the area of work to which a particular decision applies, yet made also with sound factual understanding of the external or environmental—as well as the local and immediate—probable consequences and benefits, or harm, of that decision.

And, I suggest—finally—that if the separate, individual decisions are made by that approach, the larger results that will add up from such decentralized decisions will allow you greatly to simplify your own higher-ranking managerial tasks.

13

General Electric's Philosophy on Manager Development

Publicity for AMA's 1955 General Management Conference "to prepare for sound, strong company growth" noted that "General Electric has worked out a plan for developing executive talent that contains many pointers for small companies." Orienting this paper to the viewpoint of the managers of a typical American Management Associations member company—not a General Electric, but a so-called "small company," which, incidentally, would probably itself be called "big business" anywhere in the world outside these United States—is not as difficult as one might think, for two simple reasons.

The first is that General Electric is not a single operation, as many might casually assume, but is rather a kind of cooperative federation, within a common corporate charter, of a number of highly decentralized, individually managed, manufacturing and selling enterprises; each very much like, in size and characteristics, the kinds of businesses that most AMA members actually do help to build and to manage.

Reprinted from General Management Series No. 174. Copyright 1955 by American Management Associations.

The second reason is that these decentralized General Electric businesses can only grow, profit, and progress by competing successfully in the marketplace not only with companies like those of typical AMA members but, in a substantial number of cases, actually *with* those very same organizations.

For the peace of mind of those observers of American industry who sometimes worry that "bigness" as such (necessary as they now recognize it to be in today's technological age) may tend either to eliminate small business by sheer weight of resources or else to adopt methods of mechanization and automation that will make small business uneconomic, it may be interjected here in all sincerity that if it is possible to discover ways for the managers of General Electric's decentralized businesses to thrive in the face of the competition that such small companies do provide, and even to keep up with the mechanization, automation, and other innovations such small-business folks always seem to be risking so aggressively, we will be glad indeed. And in turn we will also be quite willing to continue to take our competitive chances with those larger companies we have been meeting and matching, in seeking customer understanding and approval, for many decades.

General Electric's "Approach for," Rather than "Program of," Manager Development

Before going into detail on how it is hoped to develop managers under the actual conditions prevailing in General Electric, it is an author's privilege to amend the originally announced title of his paper a little; and so to call this "General Electric's Philosophy and Approach for Manager Development"; substituting the words "approach for manager development" for the phrase "program of manager development" that appeared in the printed conference program.

Only two words are changed, but both are significant. After literally decades of search and practice in this field we neither have nor want "a program of General Electric manager development"; but only an "approach for" that purpose through which the individual manager—in whatever decentralized business or functional component he is charged with responsibility for what we now consider to be the distinct, and the professional, work of a "manager"—can plan, guide, and persistently improve his own self-development in that unique, challenging, but not too well-understood kind of work.

The Word "Development"

This is a good time to pause for one step that is an indispensable key to finding areas of mutual comprehension, communication, and accord; namely, defining our terms so that we are both sensing closely the same thing as the words and the concepts in this analysis flow and take form.

The two key words here are, first, the word "manager," and second, the word "development."

Taking them in reverse order, the dictionary says that "development" is "the act of unfolding; growth; expansion; evolution"; and that is the rigorous sense in which the word is used in this discussion of "General Electric's Philosophy and Approach for Manager Development."

For further clarity please make a little mental note, as you turn that phrase "the act of unfolding" over in your mind, that it is the manager himself who performs that act, and who does the unfolding.

So "manager development" in this connotation differs from and goes beyond that important effort we all embrace in the word "training," which means "thorough instruction and practice along some special line."

The noteworthy difference hinges on that word "instruction," which—in turn—automatically puts the emphasis on the instructor who is teaching, informing, or even directing the person being "trained"; whereas "development" puts the stress and the responsibility on the manager himself.

Let's go on, therefore, in spelling out our terms to the other key word; namely, the word "manager" itself.

The Word "Manager"

In General Electric the work of a "manager"—as such, and irrespective of the product or the function at which such managerial work is specifically pointed—has a precise meaning; and since this is quite detailed, let's take it slowly and distinctly.

"Managing," as a distinct and a professional kind of work, is leading

◆ By persuasion rather than by command, and by blending thought and action in decisionmaking

◆ Through planning, organizing, integrating, and measuring—as the elements in this work of a professional manager—

◆ In the balanced and effective use of all the human and material resources

◆ Of the particular component, or of the whole enterprise, being managed

◆ With due understanding and balanced application of the skills and knowledge required to manage its particular activities or operations;

◆ With best pace, synchronized flow, timing, and turnover; all

◆ To secure balanced results through the specific work—be it research and engineering, manufacturing, marketing, financial, employee and public relations, legal and corporate (or operations research and synthesis, where applicable), or managerial—of other people, who themselves are also

◆ Acting with initiative, self-development, self-discipline, and competence, as to both their personal work and their voluntary teamwork and two-way communication; each

◆ Seeing the individual job and its relationships to the whole component, and enterprise, imaginatively and in true perspective

◆ Consistent with the current and potential economic, social, and political "climate" (or environment, or "society") of the component or enterprise being managed;

◆ And doing such managerial work to accomplish desired performance and results; namely,

◆ To achieve successfully, economically, profitably, and on time, challenging and difficult-to-attain objectives of the component, and of the enterprise as a whole,

◆ In the balanced best interests of customers, share owners, employees, suppliers, and the public, including the public's representatives, the government.

You may think, after that definition, that there must be easier ways to make a living, and you could be right. But such a definition brings out another point that is vitally important to get clear.

PRECISE DEFINITION AS A TOOL OF SIMPLIFICATION

By now, you well may feel that this kind of precise and detailed definition of what is meant by the work of a manager complicates what you already know to be a hard and many-sided job.

On the contrary, such a definition simplifies. And it is important to come right out and say so, and for all of us to know so, if we want to make genuine progress in this trying field of thought and effort.

The complication and the confusion that stimulate able managers to take the time from their busy days to come by the hundreds to management conferences arise precisely from the absence of such exact definitions of the distinguishing nature of this vital managerial work in which we are all engaged.

The powerful need for such far-ranging and deeply probing care in defining the work of a professional manager, in companies like yours and mine, arises because the principles involved for sensing and understanding it clearly are difficult to discern and to delineate in specific detail so that they can both be taught and be learned by individual managers to help themselves improve and grow in ability to apply such principles to their practical day-to-day business problems.

Elements of the General Electric Approach

The General Electric approach for manager development is, therefore, rooted in the need to aid every General Electric manager—be he foreman, president, or in-between—to give a better managerial performance on the job he now holds.

This approach, accordingly, is not limited to the kind of managerial manpower planning that tries to estimate how many future managers will be needed, but doesn't come fully to grips with how to get the right number for the right jobs at the right time.

Nor does it try—by some occult process, never clearly exposed—to pick "crown princes," give them a quick whirl through functional areas in which they are weak, and then anoint them some morning as presumably well-rounded managers.

So much for what manager development in General Electric is not. Now let's see what it is; at least so far as some 75 years of practice, topped since 1951 by three years of intensive reexploration of available knowledge, permits.

Need for a Philosophy of Manager Development

A review of the organization history of American businesses that have advanced consistently through the churning economic seas of the past 40 years shows that, fundamentally, their physical growth has come parallel to, but following, a growth toward what you might safely call "managerial maturity."

Without risking the classic "the chicken or the egg" debate about this, there is persuasive evidence that skillful, creative management has been the necessary forerunner of enduring corporate growth, not only in this dynamic country of ours but on an increasingly worldwide scale.

An old cliché of politics says that men and ideas are adequate only to the needs of the time. It implies that we are barely able to keep up with our environment and are hard put to bring forth enough of knowledge and of understanding to sustain an essentially static political or social situation.

Hence, it intimates that it is best to be practical, to hang on to the "tried and true" with which we are so comfortably familiar; ignoring alike Disraeli's reputed maxim that "a practical man is one who continues to practice the mistakes of his predecessors" and the pithy comment of a recent writer that the man who says he doesn't believe in theory is inevitably using someone else's theory, or more likely a theory that someone else has already discarded.

This old cliché, in fact, because it denies the clearly creative and the deliberately positive aspects of the progress so visible all about us, is a patent fallacy. It falls in the face of the historical advances that have been made in our political and social, no less than in our economic, institutions.

There has been a parallel condition in our developing industrial community. No few industrialists still believe that there is no "science of managing" that will ever be more than an academic toy; that, in the glaring light of "reality," leadership falls to the gifted few who have the faculty, or luck, of being on hand when and as the need for their services occurs.

Because this viewpoint presupposes no meaningful change in the conduct of business, because it assumes that the accidental sources of business leadership will continue to meet the demands of tomorrow, this too is but a cliché and fallacious. Even if it had some applicability when business was done largely in personal proprietorships, it is erroneous and dangerous in this day of diversified corporate enterprises and institutions.

Rejecting such clichés, General Electric is striving to evolve instead a positive and creative philosophy and approach for manager development.

After a searching study, we are casting aside our doubts of the essential need to detach a specific and a significant part of our think-ing and time from the important day-to-day challenges of designing, producing, and selling electrical equipment and to direct it toward the more abstract, more obscure, yet even more pressing problems of designing, producing, and selling the concrete organizational philosophy that we know we must have as the vehicle for:

◇ Bringing work simplification to the task of the manager himself;
◇ Making the manager's job more manageable; and thus
◇ Finding how to meet the imperative requirement to reverse the tendency toward increasing the hours and adding to the frustra-tions of these precious managers of our industrial operations and enterprises.

Over and above such qualitative requirements for evolving a posi-tive philosophy of manager development, General Electric's problem also has its quantitative aspects. Under the company's concept of con-tinuing decentralization to get decisionmaking itself decentralized to the points at which work is done and action takes place—which pat-tern of organization Ralph J. Cordiner, our company president, de-tailed in his fundamental talks to AMA's General Management Con-ferences in 1945 and again in 1952 *—the number of General Electric operating department businesses has steadily been increased from eight at the end of World War II to more than ten times that number today.

Thus General Electric needs a philosophy of manager develop-ment that recognizes operating decentralization in the fullest possible sense. And because these decentralized business organizations—with responsibility and authority placed at the lowest possible level not only of the overall company organization but also within every component—are truly much like the businesses most AMA members manage themselves, it seems a tenable premise, as AMA's conference program indicated, that this General Electric philosophy may indeed contain many pointers for smaller companies.

If so, however, this can only be because *you* see such parallels in your problems and ours. All we can do, or want to do, is to share with you the experiences we have gone through, which we do know have applicability to our own situations; but which can only be helpful or

* See "The Implications of Industrial Decentralization," AMA General Man-agement Series No. 134; and "Problems of Management in a Large Decen-tralized Organization," AMA General Management Series No. 159.

applicable in your businesses if you sense parallel problems to which parallel solutions may apply.

The point, and the specific manager development need, therefore is for a philosophy that will light a path so that men who have merely "supervised" before—that is, executed decisions communicated to them from one or more levels above—may be helped (now that they are called on to do the full work of a manager, as defined so specifically above) to learn and to find how to:

◇ Gather and weigh information
◇ Plan, organize, and delegate
◇ Integrate resources and objectives
◇ Exercise judgment in making decisions
◇ Measure their own performance fairly, and
◇ Be willingly accountable for their success in attaining chosen and desired results, primarily through the work of others rather than by purely personal performance.

But from where are these men to come? We need them in the thousands, and we have historically been developing them in the hundreds. Neither idly nor without cause did Mr. Cordiner warn us,

Not customers, not products, not plants, not money, but *managers* may be the limit on General Electric's growth.

So, for three years now, we have carried on an intensive study to evolve our present philosophy and approach for manager development.

THE THREE PHASES OF THE MANAGER DEVELOPMENT STUDY

This study can be divided into three phases; distinct and separable from each other more in manner or form than in their relation to the passage of time.

Research
The first phase was one of research. It began with a full-scale investigation and test of our needs, of our resources of knowledge within the company to meet those needs, and of the resources of ideas, information, and practices outside the company that seemed to offer promise to the same end.

This research activity seemed to divide itself into a study of three basic sets of questions:

1. What is a manager? Can managing be distinguished, as such, from all the other, functional kinds of work required in the operations of the company's businesses? Can basic principles of universal applicability for guidance in such work be discovered, delineated, and codified for decentralized and repetitive use?

2. Why do managers need to be "developed"? Doesn't the very nature of managing require that kind of initiative and desire to improve, which of itself creates both the will and the capacity to assume and meet such responsibilities? Isn't the process of learning, therefore, only that of "doing and deduction," case by case, until confidence and growing proficiency are attained?

3. If principles of managing can be established in such a way that they can be stated unequivocally, and if it can be discovered that such principles are within the capacity to learn, understand, and apply to the great majority of interested employees, is it then possible to accelerate the transfer of this knowledge over the threshold of utility by fashioning adult educational activities of sufficient potency to gain the voluntary interest and cooperation of the needed numbers of managers, and potential managers, of all functions and levels of managerial work?

To find usable answers to these questions, the need to wipe the slate clean of both prejudgments and opinions early became clear; as did the lack of likelihood of quick or simple analyses, or of commitments in any direction without the most penetrating search of the whole available literature and practices of business.

The study team was formed initially from men within General Electric who were well-versed with factors of organization and employee relations, and therefore suitable to institute such a search. They were joined quickly, on a "for the duration" basis, by a small corps of leading consultants and experts in the fields of management, psychology, and education in business administration. As the work progressed, this joint team called freely upon other sources of counsel and experience—both in and outside General Electric—as particular needs and questions arose.

After the study scope was carefully formulated, the slow process of fact gathering began. More than 50 major companies—and a sizable number of universities, business schools, and management associations—were interviewed at length.

These depth interviews were designed both to identify the substance of what those companies and institutions were doing to develop managers and to determine the permissible variations in conceptual philosophy within which favorable results apparently could still be secured in reasonable measure.

It is a real pleasure to offer public thanks and tribute to all of those business firms, educational institutions, and management society staffs without whose willing cooperation and probing questions our progress must have been limited to areas far narrower than those they so wisely and so generously opened before us.

In three years of this intensive research over 300 General Electric managers also contributed liberally—sometimes even argumentatively, it may be added—of their time and thoughts in similar depth interviews, aimed at seeking the patterns of managerial success in the personal context of how it had been factually experienced. Detailed experience records of over 2,000 of their fellow General Electric managers were also compiled and combed in the hunt for similar pattern identification clues and factors.

Finally, in this first or research phase of the study, the voluminous literature of writings that bore directly on the concepts of managing and of manager development, and the even more copious material that only touched on these topics, were patiently explored.

Analysis
The second phase, starting almost concurrently with the research work, was one of analysis. Despite care in phrasing the study questions, and discrimination in selection of seemingly pertinent items, the information gathered was overpowering both in its bulk and in the disparity of ideas that somehow had to be distilled to an acceptable and practical essence. Suffice it to say that the wheat was finally winnowed from the chaff, though the yield seemed at times relatively low for the tonnage handled.

Conceptualization and Implementation
The third phase, in which we are engaged presently, can perhaps best be called the conceptualization and implementation stage. This is in addition to,. rather than in replacement of, the research and analysis phases, however, because knowledge and understanding of modern manager development are clearly still low on their growth curves when measured against the ever-expanding needs of your companies and ours. The study process is consequently not so much

finished as institutionalized, as *one* of the clearly required findings of our deliberations to date.

THE PROFESSIONAL AND ETHICAL VALUES DEMANDED IN MANAGERIAL WORK

In the meantime, parallel research and study projects have progressively indicated and blocked out the evolving nature of the work of a professional manager, along the lines summarized in the definition cited earlier in this paper.

As that summary makes plain, this work of a manager in today's competitive and technical business enterprises—as both AMA's able President Lawrence A. Appley and our General Electric President Ralph J. Cordiner have so often told us—is truly both a distinct and a professional kind of work, in and of itself and irrespective of the product business, the functional component, or the level in the organization structure where such managerial work is actually being performed.

Being a professional kind of work, and being aimed at guiding and integrating the work of other people by persuasion rather than command, it requires above all that conscious perception and employment of ethical values that alone can constitute lasting foundations for its continuing validity, acceptance, and self-disciplined practice.

THE NEED FOR ORDERLY MANAGER DEVELOPMENT

So much for the study. Before setting forth the highlights of its direct findings, there is one more question to be directly answered here: namely, *did* it indicate that an organized process of manager development is indeed essential, in your business as well as in General Electric?

Or is all this current talk, which bears down on us from all sides, mere chatter on a currently "fashionable" subject that will shortly—as some say, and probably no few hope—be superseded by some new "cure-all" for managerial problems and progress?

The question then is: *do* managers need to be "developed"? Is a formal and vitalizing approach necessary, or at least desirable and economical, to accomplish this end?

Or is it reasonable rather to assume that all those needed for leadership positions will be driven by ambition, and enabled by sheer practice, to search out and apply for themselves the principles and working techniques for discovering and learning to use required managerial insights and skills?

What is wrong, if anything, with the traditional methods that have always, somehow, brought men to managing tasks? Why has this natural process become inadequate, or less useful for the future than it has been for producing the past industrial growth and material progress so familiar to us all?

If time permitted, some instructive, provocative, and at times even amusing quotations could be invoked to show the enduring character of these particular kinds of questions. In the fundamental "Ten-Year Progress in Management" reports of the American Society of Mechanical Engineers you find them in 1911 or 1921 no less than in 1941 or 1951. Only the names of the proponents change. The refrain is the same from decade to decade. Or at least so it seems at first look.

Yet closer examination quickly shows two other, and highly pertinent, factors. First, many of the particular "new" ideas challenged in one decade have shown a hardy tendency to become almost basic tenets of managing but a few years later.

Second, the four forces of multiplying technology, of ramifying competition (often in end service to the customer rather than in kind), of big government, and of individual and public opinion, buttressed by constantly new wonders of transportation and communication, bring new aspects and complexities to the task of the manager at an ever-accelerating rate.

And no longer can he limit his chore by resolutely confining himself to his own company's affairs. For as Norbert Wiener so succinctly said, after pointing out the interlocked social and economic impacts of modern technological discoveries, "The statesmanship of management cannot, in the face of radical changes like that, stop at the edge of each individual firm."

So our study clearly brought out that the assumptions of adequacy of "natural progress" implicit in such questions never were valid for an expanding economy.

The archives of business failures are strewn with the records of those who learned this the hard way. The records of successful businesses that have continued to grow through successive generations of managers have, as noted earlier, shown that such growth followed a parallel growth toward "managerial maturity"—toward a steady evolution of a definite company philosophy of objectives, policies, organization structure, and well-formulated managerial concepts and leadership.

While we laugh with some justification at the owner's son who "progresses" from floor sweeper to president in a few short months, candor compels the question of whether many corporate methods of managerial anointment, rotation, and "arrival" have not at times represented distinctions without differences.

Only too often, in promoting men, hindsight reveals how easy it is to place too optimistic a value upon the simple willingness to take decisive action. While this is a commendable and necessary side of the desirable managerial aspirant, common observation, no less than our patient study, shows that there is an even more important quality of willingness, and competence, to come to the level of decision through the painstaking process of:

♦ *Thinking ahead* before accepting the completeness and validity of the problem as presented.

♦ *Thinking whole* on the nature and the relationships of the problem, as realistically defined.

♦ *Thinking through* to the far-reaching implications of the alternative courses of action or decision available, in exercising balanced judgment to make the best decision in the light of the best information available at the time.

The General Electric study confirmed, therefore, that in spite of the pressing twin needs for more managers and for more competence in each manager, the so-called "natural selection" process supplies neither need in even minimum adequate quantity. In its pointless parsimony, it limits opportunity to too few; and it fails to search for or stimulate that latent talent for leadership and—as Erwin Schell said—that normal human "wish to participate in the . . . management of affairs [that] is one of the deepest desires of men."

In its essential formlessness and in its typical limitations of offering training in only a limited set of cases and techniques, it fails likewise to meet the realistic pressures in our expanding world, where everything under the sun seems at least partially "new"; and very specifically it fails to help the managers it typically produces to be adequately capable of taking the "big look" today's environment so frequently demands, even for our seemingly smaller business problems.

Except for the rare and talented few, with the intuitive understanding to develop for themselves the necessary scientific attitudes, the "natural selection" process for managers, therefore, characteristically produces too few, too late.

In frank exchanges with the 300 General Electric managers who participated directly in the study, some of the most revealing information came in answers to the simple question: "How did *you* come to *your* present level of responsibility and authority?"

In almost every case the successful manager remarked that, one way or another, he had been "helped"; not by being pushed or commanded, but by being given better and sharper opportunities to sense and understand precepts that would allow him to meet the managerial problems of his component more squarely or correctly. And, curiously enough, it was the demanding type of manager—rather than simply the cheerful but then unrequiring delegator—who was very frequently credited by these men with having stimulated their efforts and their search most effectively and rewardingly.

Yet the most typical among even these successful managers commonly remarked that his development had been based upon principles that were instinctively felt rather than wholly understood; and that the organization of his work lacked the simplification and clarity that would permit him to realize the results of his energies in the fullest measure. Because the climate of his managerial education had been so highly personalized, it often tended to make him think in terms of "who was right" rather than of "what was right."

Repeated review and replay of these frank comments made it cumulatively clear, as the study went along, that a newer, more comprehensive approach to the development of men—particularly for managerial work—is deeply needed and heartily desired; and by present managers no less than by those still looking forward to their initial managerial jobs.

This persistent probing for ways to develop new managers in the quantity, and of the quality, demanded by the future, and for concepts under which present managers may learn to replace habits of years with new ways of personal action rooted in firm principles for managing as a distinct and as a professional kind of work, was a significant and pervasive factor running all through the General Electric study. It pointed up forcefully that there *is* a plain and present need for more effective, more orderly, and more widespread manager development. So General Electric's philosophy and approach are formulated to cope more adequately and systematically with that plain and present need.

Objectives of Manager Development in General Electric

The main objectives at which this philosophy and approach are aimed are only four in number. They are by no means either easy or beyond our faith in our capacity to attain them. They are:

1. To provide all managers and potential managers in General Electric with challenges and opportunities for maximum self-development on their present jobs and for advancement in the future as earned.

2. To work toward improving skill and competence throughout the entire manager group so as to help General Electric managers become equal to the demands of tomorrow's management job.

3. To operate to furnish the company with both the number and kind of managers that will be needed in the years ahead.

4. To encourage systematic habits and procedures to make it simpler for each manager to discharge his manager development responsibility.

This approach consists, therefore, not of *one* General Electric plan, but actually of as many plans as there are individual managers. Each individual manager has the dual responsibility to develop himself and to create the best managerial climate in his own organizational component for those other men whose stimulation for their own self-development he must foster.

This approach, therefore, integrates three essential elements:

◆ The individual manager's desire for his own improvement.

◆ His responsibility for the development of the men in his own component.

◆ The company's needs for adequate and competent managerial leadership.

Principles Behind the General Electric Approach

The principles on which this approach is founded, as evolved through the manager development study, are seven in number. They are short enough to quote here in full:

1. The General Electric manager development approach is founded on continuing systematic research.

2. The focus of the approach is on the individual.

3. Responsibility for the development of men is part of every manager's job, and is specifically written into all manager position guides.

4. All managers and potential managers come within the scope of this approach.

5. Manager development in practice operates for and through the decentralized components, both general product–business components and single-functional or subfunctional components.

6. Manager development requires comprehensive and selective application.

7. The General Electric approach recognizes managing itself as a profession that is learnable and teachable.

Perhaps the most provocative of these seven principles is this last one. But the study said plainly to us, despite fears to the contrary, that as the job of the manager has become more complex, it has also become more indentifiable and more learnable.

No longer is it true, in our reasoned judgment, that experience alone can teach the work of managing adequately and in time. Managing is no longer merely an art. It is unlikely ever to be an exact science either. Yet it is fast acquiring the character of a profession. And this means that its principles can be increasingly discovered, stated, verified, and taught systematically. They can be learned, and they can be applied.

The experience an individual acquires in his work as a manager can be organized in an orderly way so that he may derive general principles from it. He can apply such principles to improvement in his present job, to different jobs, and to different work.

The company's organization, its objectives, goals, and management philosophy—all these things and others—can definitely be taught systematically and learned systematically.

Some people will always be better at developing men than others. They are the "naturals." But today enough is known about what encourages people to develop into effective managers so that *each* manager can systematically be aided to discharge his manager development responsibilities adequately.

We can, in other words, diagnose fairly accurately both the individual's development needs and the impact on him of the climate of the organization—its spirit, its policies, its management methods. Hence, it is feasible to plan for maximum development opportunities and to measure actual development progress.

PURPOSES OF SYSTEMATIC MANAGER DEVELOPMENT

The study further proved that the need for more systematic manager development exists, particularly for these five purposes:

1. Decentralization requires managers capable of carrying greater responsibilities.

2. The company's growth plans call for greater numbers of competent managers.

3. Increasingly complex business problems have intensified the need for "professional" managers.

4. Developing managerial leadership is a social, as well as an economic, responsibility.

5. The job of developing managers itself needs to be simplified and made more systematic.

Looking at these needs and purposes, their implications can be boiled down to the simple requirement that General Electric managers today do not have any real choice between doing manager development or not doing it. Their only realistic choice is between being overwhelmed by this part of their job or being master of it.

To master it calls for the individual manager to organize his manager development skills in four specific respects; and since these are truly the essence of General Electric's "Philosophy and Approach for Manager Development," the remainder of this paper is devoted to pointing out the scope and nature of these four key areas for practical day-to-day implementation of the company's philosophy and objectives.

They deal, respectively, with the managerial climate of the organizational component, with self-development planning, with manager manpower planning, and with manager education.

KEY AREAS FOR IMPLEMENTATION

The Managerial Climate of the Organizational Component
The study demonstrated beyond fair doubt that what we have come to call the "managerial climate" of an organizational component—or in turn of a business as a whole—is created essentially:

◇ By managers by their attitudes and behavior.
◇ By policies and practices from above.

◇ By two-way communication between the manager and the men he manages.
◇ By the standards for such climate the managers themselves set.

Analysis and improvement of climate is both feasible by orderly managerial action and a required, regular duty of every manager.

The climate in which a man works may thus encourage self-development, speed its growth, and guide it in the right direction—or it may stifle development potential and wastefully misdirect human efforts. And, since men tend to manage as they have been managed, they tend to perpetuate the climate under which they themselves came up.

The General Electric approach, founded on these factors, is that the managerial climate of any manager's component can be appraised and can be improved; and that it is the job of the manager of that component to see that this is done.

This necessitates systematic, and periodic, examination to discover the attitudes and behavior of the manager himself, as well as to review calmly and critically the policies and practices in and impinging upon the component that are responsible for the climate that actually exists—be it good or bad; be it getting better or worse from year to year.

Climate is thus created by managers, individually and collectively. It directly reflects their attitudes and their skill as managers. It is a measure alike of each manager's capacity to express himself to the individuals reporting to him so that both their work and their teamwork responsibilities may be crystal clear to them; and of each manager's ability to make two-way communication real by listening well, by giving men the right to be heard in a sincere and genuine sense, and by trying to understand what they are thinking as well as what they are saying when either observing them or listening to them.

Finally, the managerial climate of the component will be a function of the standards the managers themselves set and follow in this respect. One of the most curious, yet possibly most obvious, findings of the study was indeed that continual but fair and realistic raising of the standard of what is considered adequate performance is of itself a potent spur to climate improvement.

There are few, if any, managers who do not sincerely intend to create the right spirit and policies in their components—or who do not sincerely believe that they are doing just that. But to have a good climate, and to improve it steadily and persistently, more than good intentions are required.

To improve the spirit of the organization, or his managerial policies, a manager has to find out what is amiss and how to go about correcting it.

The first key element in the General Electric approach to manager development, therefore, is that each manager has the personal responsibility to do this, to do it in an orderly and systematic way, and to review and appraise both his climate and his progress at regular intervals, in all cases taking a complete inventory in this respect at least annually.

Self-Development Planning

The second fundamental of the General Electric approach to manager development is equally personal, and equally direct. It is that each manager is responsible, first, for his own self-development, and second, for providing both opportunities and challenges to all the men whose work he manages.

This responsibility also calls for periodic and comprehensive appraisal by the manager to discover each individual's strengths, potential, and weaknesses; and then to use planned challenges and opportunities to help a man to fill needs, to acquire additional strengths and qualifications, and to correct weaknesses or move to other work in which they are not a detriment to his performance and his progress.

The foundation of this part of the General Electric approach is that the manager actually does sit down and make the required appraisal of each man reporting to him; and then builds with that man a personal plan of development—based on his demonstrated needs, qualifications, and appraisal potentials. The secret of this is not in devising some magical or uniform appraisal sheets, but in doing it the hard way, year by year, man by man, manager by manager, component by component.

The participation and confidence of the man appraised is as vital as the appraisal itself, in order both to find the facts about the man's qualifications, potentials, and problems and to build a personalized yearly plan for him that really will motivate him to effective self-development efforts and guide those efforts in sound and right directions.

Without a systematic appraisal, high visibility rather than outstanding performance can too easily result in injustices for men and company alike. Sometimes a good man, absent such regular appraisal, can even be overlooked simply because he does not create problems that engage his manager's attention. Or a man's good performance may deprive him of an earned promotion by seeming to make him indispensable.

Systematic appraisal, therefore, is needed to save the manager's time and energy, no less than to ensure fairness to the individual and best use of the manager manpower available to the company.

Finally, lest anyone erroneously think that this is some kind of purely Pollyanna process for promoting pale people to potent places, the appraisal calls also for getting firmly into such critical factors as these, for every individual managed:

◇ Is this man willing to pay the price of success?
◇ Does he stick to the job, keep it moving, see it through?
◇ Does he do more than is required?
◇ Is he willing to take calculated risks?
◇ Does he usually avoid serious mistakes of judgment and of timing?
◇ Does he learn from the mistakes he does make?
◇ Does he organize and make effective use of his time?
◇ Is he effective and cooperative in working with others?
◇ Do people like to work with him?
◇ Does he gain the confidence of people?
◇ Is he persuasive?
◇ Is he a good listener?
◇ Is he effective in communicating and persuading at all levels, inside and outside the company?
◇ Is he successful in working as a professional manager himself; in planning, in organizing, in integrating, and in measuring to attain balanced and defined objectives profitably and on time through the work of others?
◇ Does he know the functions and the products with which his managerial work is concerned well enough so that he can manage competently in his particular component or business?
◇ Is he in the right place, the right kind of work, and the right present job for him?
◇ Does he have growth potential beyond his present job?
◇ What specific action—and what specific self-development plan— is right for this man at this time?
◇ If he is not on the right job, after a fair opportunity to perform

and to improve, should he be transferred to some more suitable job in the company?

◊ Or should he be released to find work more suitable to his particular interests and capacities outside the company?

This is by no means an all-inclusive list, but it does give a serious idea of why the General Electric philosophy and approach for manager development puts such powerful emphasis on self-development planning as a key element in the whole process of the development of men, whether managers or nonmanagers.

Manager Manpower Planning

The third element in the General Electric approach consists of orderly manager manpower planning. In this respect the approach is generally consistent with those used in the majority of American companies that do such planning regularly today.

Since so much has been written in this particular field, it need only be noted here that General Electric planning in this respect has three distinct, though interlocked, phases:

1. Long-range manager manpower planning, with a time span of anticipation and planning of at least five years, based on the required organization structure for the component, or business, not as it is today but as it will need to be to cope with then-anticipated conditions.

2. Short-range manager manpower planning, focusing on specific needs of the particular component for the 18 months next ahead; to provide for orderly filling of vacancies and for proper promotion and placement of men, companywide as well as in each decentralized component.

3. Planning for continuity of managerial leadership, in a sound organization structure—the integrating and measuring phase of the whole manager manpower planning process.

This kind of analysis not only ensures having a manager manpower plan for each component and for the company as a whole, it also shows whether the managerial team has adequate "depth"; whether there are "thin spots" and where they are; and whether General Electric's policy of companywide equality of opportunity for promotion to higher-level positions is actually implemented in planning for and in filling managerial, and equivalent functional or specialist, positions.

The unifying characteristic of the three basic elements of the overall General Electric approach to manager development so far outlined is their complete decentralization of responsibility to the individual component of the organization structure, to the individual manager, and to the individual men or managers reporting to each manager.

The fourth element, namely, manager education, is similarly decentralized in its basic concepts.

Manager Education

The study team, of course, encountered a few hopeful souls who still nourished the illusion that they could somehow "read a book" and soon thereafter be fitted to take over Mr. Cordiner's job and pay. But the record always said bluntly that the way to learn to manage is by doing, just as the way to learn to think is by thinking; and especially to learn to manage professionally by applying the principles of professional managerial work in the earliest and the lowest managerial jobs, specifically those like that of the foreman–manager on the first rung of the managerial ladder.

There are two simple reasons for this. The first is that you can only learn to manage, as you can only learn to do any other work, by trying; and since human judgment in decisionmaking is fallible, by making mistakes as one way of making progress. So the mistakes you can make in the lower-ranking manager jobs are both easier to correct and less costly in consequences than those in the more responsible managerial positions.

The second reason is that the man who waits too late, and then tries to start too high on the managerial ladder, tends far too frequently to have his mind so rigidly geared to some single functional kind of work and discipline that in practice he finds himself unable effectively either to see the picture whole and with all functions and subfunctions managed in good order and balance or to sense clearly the fact that "managing" is itself a distinct and full-time job, to get results through the work of others, and hence requires delegation to those others of the fascinating functional work that has been his life and his joy so long.

This is a good place to interject the caution that our intensive study of, and emphasis on, managerial work and manager development at General Electric emphatically does not indicate that we think managerial work is more important than other kinds of work, such as engineering, manufacturing, marketing, financial, employee and public relations, or legal work.

Quite the contrary. If you think any of these are not important, try stopping them for a while and you'll see only too soon why managerial work is but one of the many kinds of necessary work, all important, for continued competitive growth and profitable operation. The answer is that if any work is not important you shouldn't be doing it at all. If you need it, then it *is* important whatever its functional nature, managerial or otherwise.

And, in passing, this is a good spot to make the record clear that managing in General Electric means doing your assigned managerial work yourself, without any so-called "assistants" trying to do, without responsibility, some work you can't do yourself in your available hours—and so carve out of your job and delegate directly and with authority to others. Managing also means doing your work without any so-called "coordinators," whom we define as "third parties with a vested interest in keeping two people apart whom you are paying to work together."

If managing, then, is so very personal and if proficiency only comes by doing such work yourself, what is the place for manager education in a well-rounded philosophy and approach for manager development?

The answer to this dilemma is not as complicated as you might think. It is well expressed in these words of the late Dr. Harry Arthur Hopf, who made so many illuminating contributions to earlier AMA General Management conferences:

The successful exercise [of the functions of management today] presupposes the availability of new types of executive personnel whose assumption of the responsibilities of management is fortified not by comprehensive knowledge of one or more technical disciplines, however valuable these may be, nor even by long years of service accompanying a slow but steady rise to the top level of authority, but rather by *thorough grounding in the principles of management,* proficiency in their application to new and varying conditions, and possession of the ability to apply the tools of management in charting the course of the business and keeping it headed with the proper degree of momentum toward the appointed goals. . . .

The manager must succeed not through the "authority of position" but through the *"authority of knowledge."*

It is to aid General Electric managers to best—and earliest—awareness and acquisition of the essential knowledge already available as to such principles of managing professionally that the manager education parts of our philosophy and approach for manager development have been given a primary place in such an approach.

There are four chief features of manager education in General Electric; namely:

1. *Individual Reading and Study Plans.* Each is founded on the elementary concept that development is first and foremost the responsibility of the individual himself. Such plans are highly flexible and are worked out specifically for each manager or potential manager by his own manager in the course of the annual appraisal process.

These plans are highly flexible and really have in common only the need to help each man more easily, and earlier in his career, to learn how to mine systematically and discriminatingly the copious store of material at hand today in the fields of organization and management, both generally and in each particular company.

2. *Local Professional Business Management Courses.* Each carried out at the location and level of particular decentralized company businesses and organizational components; and each going into such topics as

◇ The company's history, organization, and managerial philosophy.
◇ New methods available to managers.
◇ The work of a professional manager as such.
◇ The component's place in the business, social, and economic world.
◇ What the department and the company expect of the component.
◇ What customers, owners, and suppliers expect of the company.
◇ The responsibility of the business enterprise in American society.
◇ Economic education and other steps to better employee relations.

3. *Outside Management Courses and Activities.* These embrace a wide range of other educational opportunities for manager development, including especially:

◇ Courses offered through other functional divisions of the company.
◇ Courses of study offered by leading universities and business schools, full or part time, in which General Electric's historic participation is actively continued.
◇ Useful educational programs and other constructive activities of-

fered by management societies, both nationally and through local chapter programs and forums.

◇ Sensible participation in the affairs of such outside organizations as professional societies, community and civic groups, and similar organizations that can contribute significantly to the self-development of an individual.

4. *General Electric Advanced Management Course.* This is a new approach projected to be given at the General Electric Management Research and Development Institute currently under construction at Crotonville on the Hudson, some 35 miles north of New York City. When it gets under way, about a year from now, this course will run uninterrupted for successive 13-week periods, with participants from the ranks of General Electric managers in residence and freed of all other responsibilities for that period. Plans call for five teams organized principally in work sessions of 15 men each, making 75 at a time or 300 per year.

This advanced course at the Institute is thus to be in session on a year-round basis, under the guidance of a full-time faculty of professional educators with demonstrated leadership capacity in the field of adult education; brought together at the Institute for this purpose and aided freely by visiting professors and consultants, as well as by experienced managers from all parts of the General Electric organization and from other companies and institutions.

This advanced management course will focus on the specific tasks of General Electric managers, and will cover such subjects as:

The challenge to General Electric managers.
Basic concepts and managerial philosophy.
Broad responsibilities of General Electric managers.
Elements of the work of managing.
Improving teamwork among company components.
Development methods and procedures for managers.

In summary, the four main manager education elements of General Electric's philosophy for manager development are designed as instruments for the individual manager that will help him to attain the habits of an orderly approach to his responsibilities in this respect, and to guide his authority into channels that allow and require proper regard for its relationship to the accountabilities and authority of others throughout the General Electric organization, and indeed outside that organization also.

Goals of the General Electric Approach for Manager Development

So that is the best summarization feasible in this condensed paper of General Electric's philosophy and approach for manager development.

If it seems to you to be somewhat long on theory, we can only confirm that this is deliberate and is intended to walk into the teeth of the classic condition in business that Walter Bagehot, the famous nineteenth-century English economist, described so well in these pungent words:

The abstract thinking of the world is never to be expected from men in high places. The administration of current transactions is a most engrossing business, and those charged with them are but little inclined to think on points of theory, *even when such thinking most nearly concerns those transactions.*

The cumulative complexities that have come to business in the ensuing hundred years have steadily decreased the possibility and increased the risk of managing by ear in this way, until it represents today a luxury of irresponsibility that is neither economically sensible nor socially permissible.

The simple fact of life is that the decisionmaking work of a manager now affects so many other people that it can no longer justly and fairly be left wholly to cut-and-try methods.

And the teamwork that is absolutely required for sound relationships both within our individual components and businesses, and equally among even the diversely owned firms and enterprises in today's interlocked and specialized economy, can no more rightly be left to chance than the intricate plays of a winning football team can be left solely to the intuitive and instinctive resourcefulness of the individual players.

An organized and orderly approach to manager development is, then, not an option of those of us who are following the calling of "manager" today. It is not even some onerous or disagreeable chore that is added to our already baffling and diverse responsibilities. Instead, it is a necessary route to work simplification for ourselves so that we may be able to realize our goals.

14
A Perspective on Operations Research and Synthesis

Operations research and synthesis is steadily commanding an increasing amount of attention in both technical and managerial circles. But we should not let this sudden awareness obscure the established history of the science involved or its fundamental association with business and industrial life since at least the time of Frederick W. Taylor. Truly, the philosophy and techniques now crystallizing under this name have been an important concern of social and business philosophers for many decades. And their pioneering work has contributed more than the "basis" or "roots" of the science so many of us are now so lately sensing and defining.

I think that what has really happened is rather that the name "operations research" itself—or, more definitively, "operations research and synthesis"—has been claiming an increasing amount of current attention. We have gathered the facts; we have added to the facts; we have given a body of knowledge this newly descriptive and

Presented at the Operations Research Conference, September 29, 1955, New York City.

impressive name; and more of us have become aware of its usefulness and applicability in our practical business world. But let us not forget that we are truly dealing with a science that is older than any of us.

The Meaning of Operations Research and Synthesis

I'm sure you have heard many definitions that call to mind the attitude of Thomas Carlyle who, in that nineteenth century of intellectual soul-searching, heard one of his contemporaries cry in an orgy of self-acclamation, "I acknowledge the UNIVERSE." Carlyle turned to a friend and said, "By God, he'd better." We will be far better off here if we merely acknowledge the very widespread applicability of operations research and synthesis; and turn to what it is in relation to the kind of specific demands our modern, complex, and exacting society places upon us as active and progressive businessmen.

Operations research and synthesis (OR&S) is a part of the social sciences and, in particular, is a branch of what has been firmly established in its own right as the science of management. In itself it is two things, or has two parts, if you will. There is *attitude* and there is *method*.

The Attitude Concept of Operations Research and Synthesis

Let us look first at OR&S as an attitude. Melvin Hurni, writing a few years ago about this "next step in management," tied OR&S processes back to a logical and acceptable philosophy when he said:

What is unique about this approach is not the techniques employed but the attitude of mind that brings these techniques into play. The concept is based upon the belief that,

1—If an operation is thoroughly explored and the facts documented in an understandable manner, its broad guiding principles and factors or parameters will be disclosed.

2—If such principles are disclosed, in many instances these may be defined quantitatively and, hence, manipulated with some foreknowledge of the consequences.

3—If such principles are disclosed, there will result optimum procedures and processes, substantial work simplification, more precise direction, and better management.

The first part, "exploring an operation thoroughly," is a most important and characteristic part of the OR&S attitude. A tendency, which is all too frequent, is to consider OR&S as a way to unscramble a bottleneck in the West Overshoe, Indiana, plant, or a way of doing bookkeeping with push buttons.

OR&S says rather that the Indiana bottleneck is symptomatic, or at least indicative, of a general managerial problem, and that its rectification might best be achieved by looking first at the business itself, as a whole and total process.

The OR&S attitude says in the same vein that bookkeeping is itself essentially a symbolic common language by which we record and measure performance, but that it is only by understanding, once more, the business as a whole that we can safely and successfully redesign its "language."

Simply enough, then, the fundamental OR&S attitude is one that encourages understanding of the interaction and interdependence of our many kinds of work processes as well as the discrete techniques of each.

One of the principal limitations nature imposes on us in our rational thought processes is the inevitable burden of things we do not know or fully understand. No situations we are liable to encounter in everyday life, including those on which you and I still must make business and technical decisions daily as we go along, are complete as to either necessary information or reliability of information.

Recognizing this, the OR&S attitude takes sensible cognizance of the limitations of determined courses of action as fully as it does of their probable effectiveness. By separating fact from judicious "guess," it permits taking the measure of each and using them both, yet distinctly, at their full and very different values.

Finally, in this matter of OR&S attitude, there is a need to consider how it takes into account the apparent success of what we think of as decisionmaking by intuition.

There is every probability that a careful analysis of most such "decisions by intuition" would reveal a far more complex kind of process. Most successful intuitive decisions are made rather, I suspect, as a choice between alternative courses of action that have been built out of the stuff of known facts, consciously and doggedly stored away in the successful businessman's memory over his years of earlier experience. This, of course, is a matter of "feel," but we need to realize that bringing ourselves to a point where we can "feel" our decision with reasonable certainty is clearly necessary if we are successfully to fill posts where our decisions affect large numbers of other people either directly or as owners of the capital resources involved.

The human brain programs and computes so intricately and so fast, in fact, that we too often tend to see its "answer" without sensing or remembering its full operating process. So we tend to assume that this "answer" is achieved by sheer intuition, and, as a result, we overlook its high logical and rational content.

Perhaps I can illustrate what I am getting at by a simple kind of example. Suppose I were to ask you, "Should the John Smith Company move its operations from Vermont to Texas?" A pure intuitive decision—the kind that is found only in the intimate view of big business created by some of our TV and play writers—would require a yes or no answer, now.

Yet no reasonable man would care to give such an answer, which, in its execution, might affect the lives of many people and eventually touch upon the economy as a whole. Think for a moment of the questions you would ask—of what the John Smith Company manufactures, how big it is, where its markets are, where its material sources are, what skills it needs, why it was located in Vermont in the first place, why a move to Texas is even being contemplated. I could go on endlessly, and I'm sure you could add to the list.

Here, then, is the point. Pure, unsupported intuition is a highly questionable, maybe even a nearly useless, gift in the normal workaday business world. OR&S, by defining a problem in terms of what is known and unknown, by establishing both possible action and probable consequence, by bringing a problem to the point of final decision along identified and pretested paths, helps to minimize the hazards in exercising the managerial, or technical, judgment that attends the final "intuitive" decision.

The OR&S attitude, therefore, is not a denial or rejection of the powers of intuition, but it does far more than simply take such intuitive judgment into account. By recognizing intuition for what it is—by noting its faults and limitations—we are able to blend in its virtues as an essential ingredient of the sound OR&S attitude.

OPERATIONS RESEARCH AND SYNTHESIS AND
THE WORK OF THE MANAGER

We are coming slowly to know, with increasing precision, the distinct and essential role of the manager in a business society. Beginning with the work of Taylor, Fayol, Gantt, the Gilbreths, and others, the evaluation of history has postulated increasingly that managing is both a distinct and a professional kind of work; and that there is a science of managing that deals with the special discipline of accomplishing a manager's work—whether he is manager of a whole business, of a functional section of a business, of a geographic plant or office, or of any other organized component in which his basic responsibility is to get results that are in line with chosen objectives, through the work of other people.

We can assume the process of managing is complex from our own experiences, and therefore our concern with it is justified. Happily, we realize, as we think more penetratingly about it, that it is also rational; and that it therefore lends itself to scientific study and analysis.

Clear, too, is the fact that all our businesses are "managed" in the sense that decisions are reached and action is taken. The science of managing deals with how we do our work and the criteria by which we may assure its optimum effectiveness and contribution with regard to the enterprise, and its maximum satisfactions with regard to ourselves as individuals.

Let me suggest, as a beginning, this concept of this particular science: The science of managing is the application of ethical principles by qualified professional managers to the problems of creating and maintaining a complex pattern of order that serves, in optimum fashion, the common interests of people closely concerned with the enterprise, whether as customers, owners, employees, suppliers or the public through its representatives in government. It is a key and characteristic element of today's industrial society.

With respect to this "application," we can establish the following rational managerial functions, specifically assuming that we are dealing with managing as leadership of men by persuasion to inspire and receive their voluntary participation and performance, and not by command or dictatorship:

1. *Planning*—the determination of objectives, the establishment of policies, and the formulation of programs, plans, and standards of performance.

2. *Organizing*—the determination and classification of the aggregate work required, the division of such work into manageable components and jobs, the grouping of such components and jobs into an orderly organization structure, the selection of individuals for the jobs, the definition of methods and procedures for performing work

to be done, and the organization of the manager's own time and work.

3. *Integrating*—the interpretation and communication of planning and organizing, and the motivation of people so as to achieve common objectives through their work; in other words, the development of voluntary, two-way teamwork as an element of the duties of every job, fully parallel with the internal work contents of that job.

4. *Measuring*—the devising and establishing of measuring systems and media and the examination of the performance of people and components to develop refinements of principles and practices for modification and improvement of the subsequent work phases of planning, organizing, and integrating.

Coupled with our identification of managing as a process of leadership rooted in these four rational elements, we still need, of course, assurance that they can be exercised in situations that in themselves, are essentially rational. Some years ago, Harry Arthur Hopf, who contributed greatly to our present understanding of the nature of business and who was a distinguished past recipient of SAM's Taylor Key, wrote as follows after a long and meticulous quantitative study of the optimum relationships of size and success in modern business enterprises:

When an individual institution has reached a certain state of maturity, it will be found to conform to a definite pattern which for a given economic epoch appears to undergo little if any change. Recognition of the particular pattern exhibited in a specific instance is a prime requisite in the establishment and operation of a program dedicated to the attainment of enhanced operating results.

To net it down, we have covered thus far that managing is a rational kind of work; and that business itself is essentially a rational kind of activity. We have not, however, shown how managing is to be applied to business yet.

Our premise, then, is that operations research and synthesis as an attitude, rather than as a kind of work, is the bridging element that allows the successful application of managerial work to business operations. OR&S is not planning, organizing, integrating, or measuring, nor, in fact, even the particular way in which these elements of the work of a professional manager are performed.

OR&S is an approach to such work that constantly keeps awake every individual manager's realization that reasonable and progressive decisions on significant matters can best be reached through the aid of soundly identified premises and carefully constructed logic.

This realization is, of course, tempered by the facts of business life. The manager's burden is that he has to make each particular decision with the best information already available to him at a time when "getting on with the job" requires a choice of action; to do so after an exercise of judgment, rather than further procrastination in the hope of being bailed out by some miracle of new information or change of circumstances. This burden need not be overwhelming, however, because few decisions are totally irreversible and new decisions are still to come.

THE METHODOLOGY OF OPERATIONS RESEARCH AND SYNTHESIS

Let's turn now to operations research and synthesis as a methodology that can be applied to the operation of a business. The attitude, which we have seen as a characteristic of the work of the professional manager, needs also to be a part of the intellectual makeup of those who will apply its methods. This is because time to use its results is as important as recognition of the need for OR&S in the first place, in the successful conduct of the business.

Oversimplified, the process of OR&S rests usually in the establishment of an analogy between a given situation and some known logical structure, and the subsequent transfer of the standards and criteria provided by the logical structure to the situation.

Does this sound somewhat frightening? Really, we are only talking of the familiar work of building a "model" of the business, or of a particular part of it, out of material that can be studied and manipulated. Indeed, one authority on managerial accounting practices suggests that the day-to-day operation of a business can be viewed as a "continuing experiment." This is an odd and interesting proposition. It suggests to us that an understanding of the methods of OR&S can best be realized by recalling how the scientific method of experimentation operates; and by thinking how the "feedback" principle can be applied more systematically to our own work as managers.

As a first proposal, I suggest that you visualize a circle whose quadrants are identified by hypothesis, prediction, experiment, and analysis; and that these quadrants be connected by arrows indicating flow in the order I have named. More precisely, as you will see, we are going to generate a spiral, for the intention of the scientific method is to start with an hypothesis, and, by the process, land someplace else than where we started. In other words, proof of the original theory necessarily will provide new knowledge and this cannot help but modify that initial theory to some extent.

It is easy, now, to see how the operation of a business can be likened to an experiment. The business as a whole and each of its operations are based on a set of initial objectives and an interrelated framework of initial assumptions. They include, for instance, the existence of a demand for a product or service, the facilities for its production and distribution, the people to carry on its work, and similar basic and necessary characteristics.

The managerial team thus anticipates that the enterprise can produce and sell in terms that will produce a profit. Then they describe this objective or anticipated result by constructing a plan of action and by implementing this plan in the experimental phase of the method. Finally, the team measures the results, compares them against the prediction, and analyzes any variances to determine their causes.

Applying Operations Research and Synthesis to the Business Experiment

The cycle I've described is, of course, an oversimplification of the process of scientific experiment as it applies to business, both as a whole and in its primary work functions and components. Not only does the simplest enterprise involve a spiral that describes the experiment on the business as a whole interacting with the many spirals of its several and discrete processes, but all of them are developing at different and sometimes random rates and phases.

The managerial problem is to apply suitable methods to every part of the total business experiment. You will concur, I am sure, that none of us who manages a business with merely mortal intelligence or energy can hope individually to have all of the endlessly ramifying knowledge it seems necessary to have in the complex environment of modern business. Nor will you dispute me, I am confident, that as our enterprises, our functional work, our technologies, our relationships, and our scopes of competition become ever more complex and ever more interramified, none of these developments makes the variables less numerous or makes the manager's fields requiring decision less confusing and complex.

It is to cope with this factual situation that we turn now—with a well-justified hope in my personal judgment—to the attitudes and the methodologies of OR&S for help.

The application of OR&S methods requires a combination of skills that need to be learned, and I would like to speak a bit later about the kind of men I think will be needed to do this unique work. At this moment, though, let's limit our look to some of the ways in which OR&S methodology is useful in the business experiment. Let me suggest four such ways to help give us the picture in this respect.

First, business assumptions and hypotheses can be enumerated systematically and tested for reliability and consistency.

For example, through use of OR&S methods, the nature and behavior of a market can be more adequately described, the confusing relationships of price and volume with time and demand more successfully estimated, and the dynamic response and volume-mix characteristics of the manufacturing and distribution systems more clearly established. Out of these advances, definitions of basic business objectives and mutually consistent functional goals and projects may, in turn, be derived.

Processes such as these involve careful description and extensive survey-oriented research. As such, they call for integration of the skills of business and of the scientific method; in short, for the methods of OR&S.

Second, managerial planning crystallizes objectives into anticipations such as policies, programs, and procedures. They are aptly classed, for each then really predicts that the objective will be achieved if the behavior it specifies is followed.

OR&S, as a distinct methodology—and indeed as a new primary functional kind of work in itself—can help in the planning function by testing and evaluating, for a manager, the various alternative programs that might be developed out of a body of basic assumptions. Here again, I think you will see the need for men trained specifically for the rigors of the work, since highly technical methods—linear programming or game theory, for example—are often employed in the simplest kind of situation; without, as a word of warning, forgetting that common sense is still to be applied first, and may often cast light, in even complicated technical problems.

It's pretty well recognized that the real world offers few opportunities to choose the single "right" decision and leave behind a forgotten residue of totally "wrong" decisions. Managing is, therefore, increasingly recognized as being a problem in optimization—of choosing the best of the many good or even of the "least worst." So here again, a significant function of the OR&S method is to facilitate examining policies, programs, and procedures in the course of exercising managerial judgment to determine their probable impact upon the optimality of any actual or postulated course of action.

Third, a pertinent application of OR&S methodology to business is in the area of bringing together, into harmonious and productive organization, the personnel and other resources available to the business. The processes are very similar to those used in the evaluation of policies and methods, and require similar kinds of special knowledge and skills.

Consequently, the design of a communication system, the determination of advantageous organizational relationships, and the specification of sources and kinds of appropriate data to weld the enterprise into cohesive unity and into voluntarily integrated teamwork can clearly be advanced by the use of operations research and synthesis methods. I rather suspect, in fact, that fewer of the situations of present-day business than we ordinarily realize can be analyzed with other than a fortuitous kind of success by much less scientific techniques.

Fourth, in the application of OR&S to the business experiment lies the method of analysis the science can bring to performance statistics. Our accountants assure us that, in many of our businesses, accounting and recordkeeping techniques are themselves at the threshold of significant changes and advances.

In our efforts to make them work, however, we commonly see attempts to make them more complex and bigger, and even, with the aid of modern data-processing and computing equipment, to recentralize them to "justify" the considerable costs of such machines. I wonder, here, if we may not be creating a danger of the tail outgrowing and outwagging the dog or even of creating such an unnatural combination as the tiger tail on old King Guz.

Might I suggest here that you look over carefully a thoughtful paper by Cuthbert C. Hurd on "Computing in Management Science" in the January 1955 issue of *Management Science.* In it, Dr. Hurd called attention to the differences in machine design requirements for repetitive volume engineering computation and for processing data for ordinary diverse business transactions.

Noting the resultant emergence of "two essentially different classes of automatic machines," Dr. Hurd went on to make the significant statement that:

There are now indications that the differences in design objectives are only temporary. That is, on the one hand, many of the techniques now being applied in the development of management science require that more arithmetic, including multiplication, be performed on a given piece of input data; thus the data-processing machine moves toward a computer.

On the other hand, much of the work carried out heretofore in scientific computing and in the fields of chemistry and physics has now proved so successful that the results are now being applied to engineering design. In the scientific work, one idealizes both with respect to coordinate systems and boundaries. As these idealizations are made to conform more and more closely to real live physical designs, the amount of input–output data increases as do the number of logical choices.

    With basic machine design conditions thus still so fluid, is it not a time to look forward thoughtfully in our increasingly decentralized businesses and to avoid premature overcentralized machine installations that—divorced from the actual managers and personnel of the particular business—may trade a theoretical computing efficiency for the greater efficiency of direct participation by men on the same managerial team with those encountering, and responsible for solving, the problems of the particular business or function of that business?

    Is not the real need to keep the machines—whether simulators or computers—themselves decentralized so that, properly coupled and integrated, the models they work on shall themselves be those of the actual operations involved, as visualized directly by those men responsible for such operations? From the start, should we not all insist that it is the productivity and profitability of the business itself that is our end, not merely the efficiency or unit output cost of our new machines as such? I happen to think myself that some of the most significant "mechanical brain" installations today—the ones to watch for their impact on the future—may well be those in some of our independent smaller companies or in decentralized departments of some of our larger enterprises, where the machine is kept close to, and at the direct service of, the men and managers of the particular business.

    Here again, then, a scientific OR&S approach should, and can, be of assistance, since, rather than follow the classic pattern of cut, patch, and try, it concerns itself with the purposes of accounting, with the minimum tools and the most simplified language that is needed to satisfy that purpose, and, finally, with the integration of those tools and language into the business and into all phases of its measurement activities directly at the point at which the business itself is being operated and managed.

The Concept of Operations Research and Synthesis as a Distinct Kind of Work

It thus seems increasingly apparent under today's conditions that OR&S has a place in the organization of a business. Having thus discussed (and I hope indicated) the requirement for such work, we need, now, therefore, to determine where in the organization it can best be done.

The first question to ask is why, if OR&S is so closely related to every aspect of the business, its work may not be conducted solely in the already established functions of that business, that is, in its engineering, manufacturing, marketing, accounting, or other usual functional sections. The realities of the situation, however, can also suggest sharply a distinctly different conclusion. The normal capacity to learn and to apply learning itself imposes practical, as well as time, limits on each of us.

Certainly, problems, on the solution of which OR&S can be helpful, arise in individual functional fields as well as in interfunctional or overall enterprise areas. Actually, today, most OR&S pioneers are working on relatively limited problems in particular functional components and there seems no likelihood of lack of future need for similar efforts and personnel.

Two other factors stare us in the eye, however, as we now think into the future to visualize the best lasting placement of OR&S work and workers. First, OR&S itself calls for knowledge, skills, attitudes of mind, and access to information that have a heavy bearing on its optimum placement. Second, the distinctive and characteristic work of each of the older and established primary functions is itself becoming—in all cases—progressively more complex, more technical, and more in need of primary attention, study, and specialization, by those charged with its planning and performance as their own fundamental activity.

Hence, while applications of OR&S will continue to fall in all functional areas and while men who understand its narrower uses in single functional situations will indeed be needed, and in growing numbers, in such areas, the general manager now needs in more and more businesses to face the equally plain fact that both from an overall business and from a "unique technology" standpoint, there is already a place for men and components, at the primary functional level, making operations research and synthesis work their full-time objective and calling in a professional sense.

In other words, the growing technical and political complexities of our real business world are plainly emphasizing our need to split the total work of the business into portions that can each be done in a practical way with normally available talents; and because of this we are steadily required to look at OR&S as itself a kind of professional work that is really separate and distinct from the older activities of our typical businesses. We are now recognizing in more and more product and business fields, for example, that:

♦ There needs to be a component of the organization of a particular decentralized business assigned to the business research activities contemplated by the OR&S concept.

♦ Such a component needs to be equipped with personnel and resources to use predominantly, though by no means exclusively, the formal scientific methods of research and study; and especially with men able to synthesize as well as to analyze, in the face of given facts, alternatives and situations.

♦ This component needs specifically *not* to have responsibility for managerial operating plans or decisions that are assigned to, or fall within the functional competence and interest of, existing functional components; but only for devising and providing for availability of the integrated information useful in making, or underlying the preparation required in making, such plans and decisions.

♦ Finally, the research to be done needs to be of a continuing character that repeats with the repetitive cycle of managing itself, so that it becomes a supporting partner in the rational processes of each manager's work—including that of the manager of such an OR&S component itself.

In such a perspective, the concept of OR&S assumes enhanced meaning with regard to the definite limits of its own contribution. It becomes, however, more than a simple office for isolated "problem solving," and instead becomes a part of the full and continuing process of managing the business, as a whole, in terms recognizing it as an ultimately indivisible entity and as an enterprise with chosen long-range objectives, not merely expedient short-range goals.

Our sights can be raised, therefore, from the restrictions of isolated problems to the overall business situations that lie at the root of such problems. This is another powerful reason those with the greatest OR&S skills and experiences will be needed more and more and will be able to make their most profitable contributions in a new primary functional OR&S component, rather than within the framework of our older functional sections.

The Work of Operations Research and Synthesis

An evaluation of OR&S, such as we have been developing here, would be incomplete without our touching at least briefly on the kind of men who are needed to do this progressively difficult work of operations research and synthesis.

Where are these men? Fundamental to a successful performance of the work, there necessarily should be a display of the schooled techniques of the scientist as well as of the enormous resourcefulness and inventiveness that are part of the successful scientific personality. Mathematicians, physicists, and many engineers are gifted in such matters. Yet this is not enough.

OR&S work needs, in addition, an intimate acquaintance with the business itself at its most pedestrian level. This comes primarily from operating experience and from operating know-how in all functional fields of the business.

While we can speak of the basically experimental nature of our business enterprises, it is essential to realize that their ordinary factory or office activities are carried out in an environment usually quite different from that of the typical scientific or research laboratory.

In his book *Management and Morale*, Fritz Roethlisberger points out that:

An industrial organization is composed of a number of people with characteristics and relationships which vary from person to person. Many different persons—bosses, technical specialists, supervisors, factory workers, elevator operators, and scrubwomen—are interacting daily with one another, and from their associations certain relationships are formed among them.

OR&S work, in the face of such actual circumstances, thus requires emotional maturity, for it deals in the formulation of policies and plans that affect the well-being of all these people and takes into account their apparent need for establishing relationships peculiar to their respective work and personalities. By the same token, it requires increasingly an understanding of the purposes and objectives of society as a whole and of the function of our industrial enterprises in contributing to the changing expectations of this society.

Men who can do OR&S work in such a practical environment are not rare phenomena, however. We know of many who have already done this work either under its own banner or in one of its constituent disciplines. Many, perhaps even most, of you here combine these talents in quantity and in balance. What is still lacking, although its light now shines strongly on our horizon, is widespread awareness among our business leaders of their own need for OR&S work as a progressive requirement of survival and growth, both for their businesses and for themselves.

I believe that this light is definitely dawning, and that with it, more opportunities for formal self-development in OR&S work are steadily being provided, so that your ranks will be steadily augmented, not only by the force of numbers but also by the strengths of disciplined new knowledge.

HISTORICAL PATHS

OR&S is a new kind of name, characterizing a particular state of intellectual organization of one part of the work in the developing science of managing. Let's look briefly at the mainstreams that have contributed to the present status of this work.

Pioneers in Scientific Management, going back as far as 1825 with the mathematician Charles Babbage, and followed by Taylor, the Gilbreths, Gantt, Dodge, Alford, Persons, Follett, Dennison, and valiant other practitioners and theorists too numerous to list here, gave us our early insights into the essentially rational nature of business processes and relationships.

Such theorists of management and organization contributed to our knowledge a realization that the functional elements of the work of managing can be identified, and that the work of carrying out these elements can be structured by logical methods. The history of management and organization theory existed at least as early as biblical times, with Jethro, and traces its developments through the ages to the work in the last half century of such pioneers as Fayol, Fremenville, Limperg, Wallace Clark, Griffenhagen, Harry Arthur Hopf, McKinsey, Maynard, Appley, and, again, their pioneer colleagues too numerous to list.

The economists, beginning with Adam Smith and tracing the

stream through the work of Walras, Cassel, Pareto, Snyder, Garrett, Woodlock, Morley, Hayek, Von Mises, and countless contemporaries, taught us the elements of a language in which we could deal and communicate in the concepts of the business entity—its resources, its purposes, and its objectives.

The mathematicians and statisticians refined the language of the economists and contributed new symbols and tools that aid us now in the reasoning process. Einstein, Von Neumann, Danzig, Tucker, Boole, Cantor, Wiener, and Shannon are the bare beginnings of a contemporary list of people to whom we owe a debt. Through their analytical work, the general principles of computers and data processing have been revealed.

Finally, there are the behavioral scientists—such leaders as Mayo, Tead, Whitehead, Mooney and Reiley, Mary Niles, Bush, Mosteller, Schell, McGregor, Argyris, and Simon—who have contributed insights beyond value into the nature of the individual and his relationship to his society and environment.

Looking at so wide a range of scientific disciplines and the degree to which they penetrate all business activity, perhaps we can state, in conclusion, the following five principles with an "operations research and synthesis" kind of assurance:

1. It is possible to conduct a systematic inquiry into the large and complex organizations that are typical of businesses today.

2. There is, underlying the business patterns, a structure useful in better visualizing and understanding the nature of these patterns and processes.

3. The sheer number and diversity of the elements of today's and tomorrow's business structure indicate the need for a component of specialists to obtain competence in the requisite basic disciplines, organized as an OR&S entity in the organizational structure of the overall business team.

4. There is a need for a scientific generalist to manage such a component in order for the multiple skills of individual members to be integrated in a balanced and effective force.

5. The OR&S component, through its manager, should work intimately, and on a par, with other primary functional components of the organization of the business in order for the views, interpretations, and contributions possible with the scientific method to be constructively applied, and not lost or distorted in the functional fields and components.

Operations research and synthesis work, so set up, is definitely able to make a significant contribution to a business. Even in circumstances where its best relationship to other functions of the business is not yet realized in an ideal structural sense, its mere presence in an organization as an attitude of individuals, if nothing more, is sure to have a meaningful impact.

What we may learn most, then, by exploring here together, is that operations research and synthesis work becomes significantly important and its contribution truly unique when it is frankly recognized as a primary business function in a sound working partnership with the older primary functions, such as engineering, manufacturing, marketing, financial, legal, or employee and public relations work. So understood, it can, in turn, be directed to improving each manager's visualization of the business, of its functions, its subtleties, its resources, its people, and, especially, of its risks and opportunities.

15
The Effect of Continuing Technological Change on Corporate Organization and Management

The difficulty with continuing technological change is that—so far, anyhow—it doesn't stop, but accelerates. For present purposes, the assumption is made that this trend will go on. But before exploring probable consequences, a caution is in order that it might not. There are sober observers of history who feel that dramatic twentieth-century changes—as in travel, communication, and weapons—cannot continue at present rates, even for the 15 or 20 years ahead. Their reasoning is that the curve of growth obviously cannot continue indefinitely in any field; that the exponential curve bends over and flattens out into the more general "S-curve" or "logistic curve" of

Presented to the Second Systems Engineering Conference, Chicago, Ill., September 20, 1965.

growth; that plateaus are likely in sciences, technology, communication, and travel as outstanding fields of accelerating change; and that while life will go on being different it will be in the direction of improving quality of life rather than wrenching apart its very nature and interactions. A challenging offering of this view is summarized most readably in an article by John R. Platt in *Science* for August 6, 1965. He ends on this note:

It is a tremendous prospect. Hardly anyone has seen the sweep and structuring and unity and future of it except perhaps dreamers like H. G. Wells or Teilhard de Chardin. It is a new state of matter. The act of saving ourselves, if it succeeds, will make us participants in the most incredible event in evolution. It is the step to Man.

The potential is thus pointed out that "continuing technological change" itself may change. The effects on organization and management consequently may have asymptotic limits that are nearer than we think. An eye to these fences of the future is in order, but on the still visible record it is pertinent to explore here the effects if current winds of change continue to blow.

More optimistically, the systems approach may be alternatively considered as an extension of the spirit of technology from purely physical properties to the volitional economic, social, and political communities of human life—and thus a hopeful portent of a new order of opportunities for engineers and of new potential benefits for their associates.

The need for such a new scope of technological thinking is great. So is the need for technology to be seen as a source of hope to mankind, rather than only of calamitous weapons or of emotionally upsetting vehicles of human disorder.

More than three decades ago, in a treatise on "The Salvaging of Civilization: The Probable Future of Mankind," H. G. Wells, whom Mr. Platt quoted so approvingly—after commenting on the relatively limited scope, and even some benefits, of wars in past history—said this:

. . . before this age of discovery, communities had fought and struggled with each other much as naughty children might do in a crowded nursery, within the measure of their strength.

But into this nursery has come Science, and has put into the fists of these children razor blades with poison on them, bombs of frightful explosive, corrosive fluids and the like. . . .

A real nursery invaded by a reckless person distributing such gifts would be promptly saved by the intervention of the nurse; but humanity has no nurse but its own poor wisdom. And whether that poor wisdom can rise to the pitch of effectual intervention is the most fundamental problem in mundane affairs at the present time.

A little later in Wells' stimulating analysis, he noted—prophetically, in the light of now-known developments in the intervening three decades—"The world of thought still hesitates to use the means of power that now exist for it."

Such is the challenge and opportunity of the corporate manager in dealing now with the effects of continuing technological change, so as

◇ To focus his wisdom, and that of his associates, as sharply as their expanding knowledge, and skills.
◇ To lead all in the enterprise to use responsibly, in their thinking, the means of power at their disposal.

A better title for these remarks might have been "The Effect of Corporate Organization and Management on Continuing Technological Change." That would, at least, emphasize the urgent need for fullest use of the leadership function of corporate managers in this sea of change. And it would require management to have the wisdom to anticipate and shape change and its impacts, not merely to cringe and adapt as it impinges.

The task is plainly one for corporate managers to tackle positively. The word bureaucracy actually means government by rigid and arbitrary routine. The effect of continuing technological change is to necessitate leaders who can use routine for repetitive actions so as to free precious time to cope with nonroutine matters and with change. These leaders must be equally alert to the need to change routines themselves before they become stultifying instead of supporting for progress and growth.

To try to bring so formidable a topic as "The Effect of Continuing Technological Change on Corporate Organization and Management" within the bounds of a short paper, one assertion is pertinent as a basic premise, and five areas of impact of change are noteworthy as representative of the topic's dimensions of impingement for men in all the functional work fields of corporate organization.

The assertion is simply that the mission of the corporate manager in these dynamic days has to be that of leadership of the organization, and leadership by the use of wisdom beyond mere knowledge, of belief beyond mere facts; and of motivation of increasingly educated followers through inspiration and persuasion beyond mere command authority. This will motivate those who follow to carry individual organizational responsibilities—for personal work and teamwork alike—by acting with initiative, self-development, self-discipline, and competence, voluntarily making such corporate responsibilities common with their personal aims and ends in their respective job contributions. To accomplish this calls for professional—that is, for ethical as well as skillful and knowledgeable—dedication by leaders and followers both.

The most basic nature of organization is that it necessarily differentiates men working together to accomplish common objectives from individuals working each for himself.

The dilemma of organizational restrictions is, of course, inevitably personal to every individual in the organization. So the more people in a particular enterprise, the greater the need to face it in terms of mutually acceptable philosophy and principles, expressed and made known to all, rather than by incident-to-incident approaches. Perhaps the greatest of all opportunities for management is to define and clarify applicable systems—or patterns for smooth flow of joint work—so as to ease the pains of organizational restraints and maximize the contributions and satisfactions of all participants.

So much for the assertion of a basic premise. Now what are the five aspects of corporate organization in which corporate managers typically need to anticipate and cope with the impacts of continuing technological change?

1. Scale and complexity of operations
2. Application of new knowledge
3. Degree of risk of resources
4. Time cycle of decision responsibility
5. Kind and timeliness of information

The effects of change on such business factors will fall on men in all the work functions into which corporate work is basically classifiable. Classification is vital for organizational understanding, but as a means to workable and reasonably stable organization structuring, not as just a fascinating mental exercise or, least of all, as an end in itself.

Such classification of work functions in modern organizations involves numerous variables and viewpoints. Looking through mere variations of nomenclature—too often even of jargon, scientific or otherwise—the operation of businesses of great actual and apparent diversity can be seen to embrace perhaps half a dozen substantially primary "work functions" and about ten times that number of reasonably widespread subfunctions. It is this kind of basic "classification" that is pertinent for organizing purposes and continuity.

The reason is that a fundamental purpose of formal, and known, organization is to fit the needed work relationships, in the basic organization structure, to patterns and trends that, normally, are longest lasting, change most slowly, facilitate continuing personal career development, permit confinement of special, temporary project organization structures to truly transient incremental activities, and, overall, consequently offer a framework for teamwork least likely to require frequent upsets in working contacts, and personal give-and-take, that at best take time to get flowing in a smooth groove with the least wasteful frictions.

For practical reasons, and with a sincerely respectful bow to countless alternative classifications, the following seven "functions" will be taken as continuing to be primary for industrial manufacturing organizations:

1. *Research and Engineering*—to conceive, innovate, and design salable products and services.

2. *Manufacturing*—to procure, fabricate, and process the materials and other items necessary to make available in salable form the products and services of the business.

3. *Marketing*—to determine the markets that are available or developable and to promote, sell, and deliver the company's offerings to customers in such markets.

4. *Financial*—to raise and account for the capital required to carry on the operations of the business.

5. *Employee and Public Relations*—to recognize that the work of planning and living with the human resources of the business, and its markets, ranks on a par with other primary functional classes of work.

6. *Legal*—to ensure that the enterprise, and all of its work, is conducted in an environment, and in accordance with principles and actions, consistent with the basic laws, regulations, and ground rules defined by society or the public as a whole.

7. *Business Systems Research*—to discover the patterns and relationships in the total situation of the enterprise, and of its workers whether as leaders or followers in particular respects, in order to

facilitate the wisest choices and risks in setting corporate scope, goals, timetables, and operating efforts to reach optimum objectives successfully, profitably, and on time.

The use of quite a few such primary work functions as foundations for the continuity of the organization for joint human work has its own "systems" implications, especially since, on discerning review, many currently popular kinds of so-called "new systems" seem to be only a regrouping of such primary functions, less rather than more useful for organizational continuity and for both result and cost effectiveness.

In order for difficult teamwork relationships to be stabilized as much as practicable, for continuing productivity even when changes called for by product or process innovations and programs require shifts in emphasis on particular functions and subfunctions, it is important to keep in mind that *any* "system" is just a specific combination of elements or component parts.

With some 60 or so recognizably continuing subprimary work functions identifiable widely, the possible number of combinations is very high. Variable "systems," inherently subject to instability in components and of varying desirability over often short time periods, are likely to be poor bases for practicable and effective organization structures.

Rather, the greatest usefulness of systems work is to provide identification and clarity of understanding of the patterns and flow of work responsibilities and relationships among men pursuing chosen careers in basic work fields, not to serve as determinants of the work careers available. The chaotic human upsets, frequently to men of long professional education and competence, that have come about from passing "systems" off as organizational ends in themselves are an effect of technological change inviting most thoughtful managerial consideration.

Before discussing separately the five aspects of corporate organization selected as representative areas of impact of continuing technological change, a few further comments on "systems" as a concept are appropriate first.

The typical and continuing vision of "the engineer" is likely to be that of an analyst, a logical and rational-minded man who brings clarity to a puzzling technical situation by breaking it into its elements—identifying, classifying, and describing them so they may be more readily understood, more easily manipulated, and more beneficially used. When the subject of the analysis is purely physical material, certain rational methods of thinking and analyzing are applicable and workable, usually on the assumption that, for purposes of analysis, a "truth" once sensed can be verified in a reproducible experiment.

When the concept and practice of engineering are extended to apply to situations in which the free human will of fellow men is *inside* the area of analysis and experiment, different dimensions of analysis are required. In the field of modern organization, the structuring of work is only one element for its accomplishment. The selection of individuals for each designed area of responsibility introduces human dynamics into the working organization.

Consequently the design has to cover both the direct work responsibilities and the relationships or teamwork responsibilities, and increasingly has to do so for jobs with occupants who bring ever greater knowledge, skills, and professional values to their personal work in the organization.

As the engineer, through continuing technological change, creates more complex physical products and processes, the manager has to prepare an appropriate and corresponding economic, social, and political organization. It is leadership in this sense that is uniquely characteristic of managerial work, in whatever product, market, or functional work fields it is performed.

So, as engineering systems of profound technological content replace the simpler products and services of yesterday's economy, the manager's organization systems have to anticipate such progress or tragically waste the engineering advances. It is against this concept of corporate organization and management that the selected five representative aspects of impact of continuing technological change are now examined.

SCOPE AND COMPLEXITY OF OPERATIONS

Decisions on the charter or scope of the business—on what products and markets to get in, keep in, or abandon—rank in their call for managerial wisdom beyond sheer rationality with those on the selection, development, commitment, and motivation of personnel.

By designating this factor as "scope and complexity" of operations we deliberately skipped the word "size" as such. Brashly, perhaps, but practically today, principles of organization already known seem usable for continuing manageability of operations of any foreseeable size with normally available people, if only wise choices are made on the scope and composition of activities and on the placement and inspiration of personnel.

Size—especially with inadequate governing of attendant complexity—is an unwise objective in itself. As Ralph J. Cordiner, when he was head of General Electric, said,

> Important as economic growth may be, it is not an end in itself; rather it is a means by which all the people of the earth can lift themselves to a new life of dignity, freedom, and accomplishment.

Complexity of organization, and difficulty of teamwork, is a function more of homogeneity or diversity than of mere size of chosen scope. Workable complexity, more or less irrespective of aggregate size, depends rather on judgment in anticipating changes in such areas as:

1. Long-range emphasis on purposes and objectives rather than on detailed means of subsequent performance.

2. Genuine decentralization, and sincere acceptance, of decision responsibilities.

3. Deployment of skills and information at original work faces, so both work and teamwork decisions can be made right in the first place, with consequent lowest costs and timeliest competitive impact; with concurrent minimization of so-called "staff" personnel external to the basic work functions and flow—and with particular avoidance of duplication of staffs at each echelon of the organizational hierarchy so they become blockages rather than channels for decision flows and work progress.

4. Blending of wisdom and lore with factual knowledge in consciously developing focus and affinity of operations versus proliferation, amorphous diversity, or scatteration.

5. Organization, around continuing career work classifications, for synthesis and continuity of work and results as current analyses, experiments, and projects flourish and fade.

6. Making present structure and personnel develop and perform rather than trying needless changes that sacrifice competitive time when a little more persistence and skill in getting men to do their best in relationships they already know can often get quicker results in work output and in satisfaction for all concerned.

7. Making long-range plans in terms of what is the essential, and probably the most stable, structures of the organization, the ones most

subject to optimum anticipatory guidance. Such structures include those of product and market scopes, corporate and financial structure, information and report structure, structure of facilities and material resources, general organization structure of the human resources and of the managerial and other leadership they need, and the overall enterprise in the structure of the larger environment and communities of which it is itself a component part.

8. Recognizing that in modern organized efforts, with ever more educated participants, personal authority is legitimatized by authority of knowledge rather than that of rank; and that with skilled specialists in all work functions, decisions flow in "circuits of authority," in the words of Richard Armand of France, rather than in the "lines of authority" characteristic of simpler organizational times. "Circuits" indicates flow and the dynamics involved as the authority of knowledge for a particular decision shifts in real-life situations, whereas "lines" emphasizes the more static or bureaucratic aspects of organization structure.

9. Finally, minimization of the number of echelons in the organizational structure, so that two-way interlevel communication is simplified; and so that individual manager jobs have sufficient spans of responsibility to require full time on truly managerial work and to inhibit either kibitzing or, worse, second-guessing by the manager's own follower or leader associates.

Such are the vital issues as continuing technological change calls for wise choices of scope and complexity of operations. The principle of decentralization of decision responsibility to individuals of currently pertinent decision competence has the significant incidental benefit of automatically limiting unbridled personal power at *any* echelon. This is the same benefit achieved so notably through the checks and balances of the legislative, executive, and judicial branches in the national governmental structure.

APPLICATION OF NEW KNOWLEDGE

New technology may either improve or replace earlier applications. For a fast introduction, it may be assigned to present personnel at first. However, it is preferable to give it to new people, fired up and anxious to use it, if it makes present knowledge obsolete and threatens the work security of present incumbents. In any event, like the generations in life, the new has to be blended in rapidly with the old; the show must go on.

It is vital to nibble always at the far fences of today's knowledge; they'll be in the well-trodden middle of the pasture only too soon. If time is given as a hostage while technological progress proceeds, normally it must be dearly bought back later from competitors who moved faster. Today's manager has only one choice here. In President Truman's famous phrase, "If you can't stand the heat, stay out of the kitchen."

Research is now as essential in all other functional fields as it is in science and engineering. It is a bad maldistribution of brains organizationally if creative mental resources are heaped up in one function and absent in others.

Such old professional fields as accounting and the law are no longer exempt. They, too, are critically in need of upsetting, innovative research today, so that the advances of technology do not get smothered in any smugness that needed concepts and practices have immutably been developed. Interproduct and international competition prescribes fresh approaches, elimination of obsolete and retarding practices, and multifunctional teamwork in applying the fruits of technological change. Significantly in point is Chief Justice Earl Warren's remark,

I for one believe we can create just as mightily in the law field as our scientific brethren did in the field of science.

This era of change calls for youth in the application of technology, but youth of spirit, not calendar age. The inertia of a man who stalls off a new application until his own retirement, dumping his delays on his successor, is organizational fat where lean, hard muscle should be.

As mechanical, chemical, and electrical energy minimizes physical labor, and as automation progressively displaces repetitive mental skills, increasingly innovative mental work comes more and more to predominate in the organization. Managerial innovation is demanded in proportion to devise ways of measuring such mental contributions and to use measurements to pressure continuing operational and cost flexibility. There are few "piece rates" in this league and the managerial task is correspondingly compounded.

Systems engineering, now burgeoning in all directions, is likely to be an instinctive response. But it is an application of technology that itself needs as much managerial measurement and guidance as any other organizational work.

Synthesis of knowledge here has to keep pace with its analytical derivation. As such engineering probes beyond physical into volitional systems, synthesis in these relatively imprecise fields is doubly useful. The "inventory of scientific findings" in the area of human behavior, as listed in the book called *Human Behavior* published in 1964 by Bernard Berelson and Gary Steiner, is a splendid illustration of potentials for accelerating application of such new technology, deserving wide emulation by more systems engineers.

Human delays can flow either from entrenched beliefs, cultures, and interests or from lack of information to sense and understand new potentials from technological change. Codification of systems engineering contributions helps close the informational gap. The content of such contributions—hopefully stripped of jargon from pride of authorship—can clarify how established cultures, beliefs, and interests can be enhanced and enriched rather than only threatened. The manager and the systems engineer share potentials for progress through both approaches.

DEGREE OF RISK OF RESOURCES

Realistically, today's world of continuing technological change seems long on population and short on capital. It offers new organizational opportunities for a more creative use of human resources and for a more flexible, and productive, deployment of capital resources. Here, too, wisdom beyond data and logic is essential, especially as risks are multiplied by incursions into new product, process, or market areas where the safeguarding inheritance of touch or feel from past experience is missing.

Innovative financial and accounting thinking is imperative as conventional concepts of costs, recordkeeping, reserve accrual practices, and noncontinuous periodicity of information become progressively obsolete. Variable direct production costs of hourly labor diminish, and vanish, as an escape valve for managerial mistakes of anticipation or choice. With human foresight and wisdom still limited, the necessity for cost minimization and flexibility remains. It might even be said to mount, as technology brings a wider scope and complexity and longer decision time cycles to the operational scene.

In a savings- and capital-short world, with new scales of consumer versus producer claims for capital resources, the financial function faces fresh forces to focus firmly on its primary responsibility of economically raising, supplying, and safeguarding appropriate money resources.

The design of systems, parallel in the equipment and organizational spheres, for flexibility of application and for building-block variability with standardized, adaptable component elements is essential, and is a proper and mighty menace to selfishness or thoughtlessness in systems engineering.

Wholly new fields of "make or buy" decisions arise, and challenge managers, engineers, operators, personnel experts, and accountants simultaneously. The small, creative, and ingenious vendor, subcontractor, or distributor—of either products or services—has a new place in the large corporate picture as an antidote to both bureaucracy and muscle-bound organizational cramps. A flexible balance of relatively rigid payroll and capital costs and variable purchased service expenses shrieks for truly innovative thinking as technological changes bear down.

Just as one sharp example, the technology that makes basic computer machinery so large, fast, and capable as to necessitate centralized installations at the same time removes the need to finance it on company premises, whereas peripheral or terminal components were necessarily located at scattered operational work sites. Thus a steel or a chemical company today has no more genuine need to divert scarce capital from its own unique new production machinery or distribution facilities to major information processing or communication equipment than to a company-owned electric generation or transmission plant.

The place government has in technological risk taking also needs a sharp new look. A philosophy rooted in limiting the area of the economy with which the bureaucratic risks and the sovereign power exposures of government are concerned remains vital for freedom and progress.

Ways to provide new forms or amounts of excess-liability or backup insurance, or even of high-volume seed money, until currently unappraisable risks can be quantified in the fires of experience, are one thing. But an automatic way to transfer such insurance and equity-supply risks progressively to nongovernmental shoulders as early as feasible is a potently required alternative to an unchecked expansion of the governmental sector of the overall economy. And, in passing, I may say that excessive diversion of academic and university personnel on the ferry of loosely provided governmental "research" money, away from their basic educational mission, should get an equally fishy eye.

In this general field of government participation in the introduction of technological change, the striking invention aspects of the COMSAT development seem tremendously significant. The use of private capital and management, with restrained government intervention, contrasts hopefully with the fuller government operation and control in earlier ventures like TVA.

Through such an approach, brand-new spheres for organized enterprise open in such vast vistas as better land and water usage; environmental conservation for health, safety, and beauty; international integrated energy, communication, and transport systems; peaceful uses of nuclear energy; decentralization and reconstitution of spreading urban/suburban communities; and countless related, multiplying new support activities.

Research and understanding in political science are as essential for such potentials as they are in technology and in the social and economic sciences. Public and personal interests cry jointly here for a continuing safe balance between technological progress that eats up huge capital resources and prudent limitation of sovereign power against possible misuse.

Visualizing people—both as individuals and in responsibly organized enterprises—as the greatest resource for continuing progress, production, productivity, and earned capital-creating profit for values delivered is management's clear responsibility. People are the only resource available to take or contain the risks already apparent; the only resource to permit, as H. G. Wells said, the world of thought to use the means of power that exist for it, yet safely to surmount the hesitation to do so that he decried.

TIME CYCLES OF DECISION RESPONSIBILITY

Large organizations, in particular, have to be managed on the basis of long-cycle objectives, policies, and plans. Manager tenure in a specific job commonly becomes shorter than such cycles, especially in supersized government operations, where noncareer heads come and go at quite brief intervals. Executive turnover separates a judgment by the currently responsible manager from the day when its effectiveness can be measured. The temptation is serious to play it safe for the tenure period rather than risk courageously for a time when credit can only fall to a successor. This temptation has to be staunchly resisted.

The opposite is the tendency in a practical situation today—while trying to make a decision but feeling frustrated by the aftermaths of someone else's previous decision—to think, "Well, it's too bad; if he'd been just a little less stupid, my life could be easier here today." Too seldom does the countervailing thought flow: "Well, if I'm not a little brighter, that's also too bad, because somebody in this chair ten years from now is going to be looking back and wondering how I really was doing here this morning."

In essence, personal teamwork responsibilities flow from predecessors and to successors in this time of accelerating change, and resultant—often currently unquantifiable—decisions have to be taken in consciousness of the continuity of relationship responsibilities.

At the other extreme are the decision responsibilities on the operation of an orbiting vehicle, with fellow workers aboard and millions of coquarterbacks listening in. The vehicle moves hundreds of miles in a single minute and a decision may be substantially irreversible.

At both extremes, the organizational necessity is to be sure the right individual does make, and bear responsibility for, the particular decision. Old rules of operating practice become obsolete fast. Nor are real-time, instantly available figure data necessarily determining. Managerial obligations compel the application of wisdom beyond logic and of an ethical dedication and leadership that go beyond mere knowledgeability.

When on-line, real-scale, real-time information has to be applied with judgment to operations that will be over in seconds, on the one hand, or in decades, on the other, past organizational and management decision practices have to be amended or replaced, even where the underlying philosophy for decision foundations is still timeless.

Impacts on the accounting function are also critical. How to relate cycles of measuring to those of decision responsibility, and still provide an incentive for that continuing current profitability whose absence can make future results of academic concern only, challenges penetrating research attention. When current financial statements are a mix, in unstable proportions, of ascertained current facts and of estimates for uncertain future impacts, conventional record and report approaches need a rapid review and, probably, radical revision. The amounts justifiable for the permanent preservation of transiently significant but also transiently used factual data call for a nice sense of balance on what to record at all; how, where, when, and through whom to use the records; and whether or not to retain them. Similarly, bases and costs to consider in pricing judgments call for a most thoughtful reexamination.

Time cushions permissible for updating personal cultural lags, teamwork thinking, and the balance of beliefs and logic in approaching work get smaller and smaller as the effects of continuing technological change on personal performance multiply. Organization and management practices have to be kept in gear with such changes in reality. Lip service will not be enough.

KIND AND TIMELINESS OF INFORMATION

The first industrial revolution multiplied the energy at each worker's disposal. The hopeful product of today's successor revolution is its capacity to multiply the information usable in organized work.

The hardware for such information is still sprouting, and it is so fascinating that it can easily divert managerial perceptivity from the deeper nature and implications of the information output. Two aspects of this situation have different claims on managerial attention.

The hardware to sense, communicate, process, store, and retrieve information is of positive but secondary managerial concern, to be viewed like a manager's automobile, watch, or any other tool that he can use without having to be an expert in its design, production, or mechanical functioning—unless by happenstance that is his field of expertise.

On the other hand, creative understanding, interpretation, and application of the information produced are of primary managerial significance. For the first time in history, the timely availability of information that can impact on both work and teamwork decisions and provide real alternatives becomes feasible for all in the organization, and on a real-time, real-scale basis.

There is no valid reason to expect managers or their associates to know how to behave yet in so startling a confrontation. They literally have nothing to go on but wisdom—no examples to copy, no road map of the route ahead. This is the opportunity of our time, the golden fruit of technological growth, the potentially positive organizational payoff from change.

But, like trying to swallow an apple in one bite, one can gag on the information rather than be nourished if the information is not perceptively, intelligently, and wisely apprehended and processed.

The crashing advent of today's computer-communication systems brings its own excited welter of reexamination of the feasibility and desirability of recentralization within widening potentials for getting, comprehending, using, and dispersing business information.

As a long-time enthusiast for the development and introduction of computers, I feel that they do bring a wonderful new dimension to managerial potentials. They can make available information of a scope and timeliness never before feasible about work and teamwork plans, possibilities, and performance in a complex organization.

Easy mental extrapolation might postulate centralized managers making operational decisions they could not risk making before and downgrading materially the decision responsibilities, or even the number, of middle- and lower-echelon managers. New theories that advance this organizational concept have evolved in profusion.

But do we have among us any really universal geniuses? Do we have people who can marshal in one body and mind the energy, knowledge, skills, and values to make decisions (irrespective of the breadth and timeliness of factual data at hand) across all areas of products and markets; of business, technological, functional, and managerial lore and resources; and of the diverse human emotions and values responsible managers and employees in a sizable show can cumulatively bring to bear on the ever-shifting, highly interlocked, innumerable daily operational situations that are the very body and blood of any dynamic and successful business?

So, I gladly recognize that the computer is here to stay and opens up imaginative new potentials for effective human organization. At the same time, I feel that these potentials can best be attained by sensing one truth; namely, that the computer-communication system that brings current information to central computer equipment at the speed of light can and should also be used to get the computer's pertinent output back to the people at the actual work points with equal speed.

By thus enabling each of them to have fuller, more timely information on the progress, trends, and implications of both their work and their teamwork responsibilities, we are also enabling them to make better, faster decisions, of a scope and import previously impossible, at their individual work stations.

This, in turn, can relieve upper- and corporate-echelon executives so that they may devote more of their limited time and wisdom to those fewer corporately significant decisions on goals, policies, personnel, and plans that are unlikely to be made well, on time, or at all unless they become the executives' primary responsibilities.

SUMMARY

To summarize, the basic viewpoint here is that it is a uniquely managerial leadership function to be sure that the progress of science and technology is perceived and used as a source of continuing benefits for all people, and that to this end both wisdom and knowledge are interspersed in the managerial process of the modern corporate organization.

Engineering emphasis on systems—on the synthesis of knowledge as well as on its analysis—is a hopeful trend for corporate progress if it senses that empiricism and experimentation are means rather than ends in themselves. Significant was Dr. Gordon Allport's warning to the American Psychological Association to:

. . . beware of galloping empiricism, which is our occupational disease. . . .

It has no rational objective, no rational method other than the mathematical, reaches no rational conclusion. It lets the discordant data sing for themselves. . . . we are faced with the task of rational explanation. . . . the tide is turning away from itsy-bitsy empiricism.

Leaders of American sociology observed, at about the same time, that behavioral scientists are too devoted to the bits and pieces of life and too little concerned with integrating their ideas.

This systems engineering conference shows, just by its very existence, that engineers know that they must integrate their ideas—and so bring synthesis and analysis into balance in their work, their aims, their contributions, their progress, and their relationships.

The responsibility to integrate as a personal commitment of work in organized enterprises is common and reciprocal to both the functional contributor—thinking and acting to contribute through his own work and teamwork—and to the manager—planning and organizing to provide inspiring leadership for the functional contributors.

The obligation and the willingness to bring the combined power of wisdom and empirical knowledge to organized work are at once the governor and the flywheel for converting continuing technological change into beneficial human progress. This is a duty falling—like the rain from above—on manager and engineer alike in partnership in the organized work community.

Proper use requires an understanding of systems beyond their mechanics or methodology and a realization that systems of growing complexity and interlock are the normal stuff of modern enterprise—to be taken in stride as they form, flourish, function, and fall by the wayside in these exhilarating days of accelerating technological change.

16
What's Ahead in Managing?

In theory, at least, "principles of management" are settled rules of action or conduct. However, "settled"—with today's world electronic communication—no longer holds its old meaning of free from doubt or uncertainty. Instead, change is the order of the day. So it is timely to take a look around, beyond any national boundaries, to try to see what different ideas and trends are evolving that may well offer an opportunity for matching the evolution of "principles of management," to keep them progressively in phase with the situations to which they have to be applied.

In some ways old national barriers, even "cold wars," recede or become penetrable. In other ways, the old trends may simply progress under new names or forms. Hence, an indication of such affairs (for example, "new" Marxist movements), notably in Europe, prompts reflection and suggests trying to think through a bit on what *is* happening and on implications for managing.

1. Contemporaneous events in Europe—and in NATO—do deserve perceptive attention. As William Safire wrote on "NATO After Yom Kippur" in *The New York Times* on November 29, 1973:

Now that the Soviets are beginning . . . to exert pressure on West European governments, American influence would be more effective if our presence were not taken for granted. . . .

Emery Air Freight Educational Foundation Visiting Professor lecture delivered at Manhattan College, Riverdale, N.Y., January 31, 1974.

A committee of democratic governments, each made up of coalitions of bare majorities, is a frustrating, unnerving, self-centered group to deal with; and the great bold strokes must be replaced by small stroking, tickling and prodding.

. . . Pandering to greed, suffering foolishness, and swallowing ingratitude is part of the price Americans must pay in order to lead—and occasionally to manipulate—the motley aggregations of mainly free people who make up the Atlantic alliance.

2. Today's big organizations, of all kinds, often appear to be mere "motley aggregations" rather than self-disciplined institutions. They are not easy either to manipulate or to manage. It's like trying to get an elephant to smile by passing a law—the beast just may not want to.

The managerial lesson—for leaders in unions, colleges, and governments no less than in business—is that laws (like managerial commands) are useful to codify custom rather than to create it, to use new science (organized knowledge) rather than to bring it into being. The temptation to try for giant government "problem solving," especially with gobs of paper money, is great.

Over three decades back, in the depression of the 1930s, when U.S. electric utilities were in national trouble, S. R. Inch said, "national issues start as local issues and to be resolved they must again be localized."

This is why current efforts, for instance, like some by Rome's International University of Social Studies—Pro Deo—are fundamental in "organizing a large-scale long-range offensive against economic illiteracy to offset the new Marxist movements in Europe and Latin America, which, strangely, are now headed by educators, organizers, and journalists who naively declare that Marx . . . is the only one who gives the clue to the realization of Christian social justice."

Such movements work through highly decentralized local efforts, and have to be countered accordingly. As 50 years of Soviet difficulties show, giant central "master plans" often build more bureaucracy than progress. The latter finally has to be cumulated from the combined results of local personalized approaches. Like the elephant, the "motley aggregations" just do not smile at top "command."

3. A parallel continuing lesson is that both democracy and freedom are fragile. To keep them, it is vital, in a democracy, for the opposition or the minority to "carry its own burden of responsibility for preserving popular freedoms and popular choice" (*Wall Street Journal* editorial on Greece, Nov. 27, 1973).

The visible limitations of excessive long-range forecasting and planning do not mean that imaginative attempts to anticipate and avoid problems, to sense and seize opportunities, and to try to use available resources wisely are unnecessary in either government or business organizations.

A constructively intended effort is thus a new U.S. Commission on Critical Choices for America, to anticipate coming developments as the nation enters its third century. The commission's aim is to address itself systematically to the nature and direction of events, seek a new perspective on the emerging problems and forces at work in the world, develop new concepts within which we can cope with them, and thus help chart the future for America.

Similar forethought is timely for all sizable organizations. But the actual work, habits, ideas, and aims of people in broad groups still do not change explosively, only evolutionarily.

4. References to journalists as heading new movements in Europe are equally applicable in America. They dramatize the place of today's communication media as instigators, not just reporters of change.

Writing in *The New York Times* on November 18, 1973, John B. Connally noted:

. . . change has already occurred in the political life of the United States. The news media have emerged as an even more profound influence on the political system . . . ; the structure of two-party government has been weakened by public disapproval of party politics and partisan politicians.

To be frank, the institutions of America are under siege with greater intensity than before. . . . Yet . . . the shock waves of change are not a sudden occurrence and not limited to the United States.

The impact on managers and on manager education is proportionate—and in all kinds of institutions. In taking up advocacy journalism so widely, with recent college graduates as reporters, the media too often pontificate more loudly, in compound cumulative fashion, and more superficially (with slogans and overbroad clichés like "the energy crisis"), than their real data, information, knowledge, or wisdom warrant. But the power they exert on public opinion is no less potent, and all managerial leaders would now ignore such influences only at a very high risk. As emphasized later, managing today has to factor in affairs external to the organization no less than those within it.

Curiously enough, this is as true for managers of today's media as for those of other institutions. Vice-president James Reston of *The New York Times* organization, in the *Times* of September 9, 1973, perceptively wrote that if the press does not put limits on its own right to print, on the basis of "sources" only, public privacy will force government restrictions to obtain media responsibility.

5. The weaknesses of relying too much on big government are well dramatized in the condition of the Soviet Union after 50 years of centralized rule. Two major conditions become clear worldwide. First, Soviet progress in nonweapon technology lags badly behind that of Free World nations. Second, Soviet progress in broadly effective management lags, too.

History will surely show that the great success of the Soviets has been in *educating* a previously illiterate peasant population. But the price of that success has been the dissipation of discipline under authoritarian direction. They have let the human minds out of the cage by education—even if the education has been narrowly specialized. Now that these minds have learned to think on their own, the people cannot be waved or pushed back into the cage. Sooner or later, the resultant Soviet problems will force them to focus their attention on what is happening at home instead of in other nations. So it would be doubly tragic to let scheming abroad go unopposed in the interim.

6. Since modern managing consists of leading rather than problem solving in a world of increasingly educated and specialized co-workers, the manager has more and more to become a negotiator and an integrator rather than either a commander or a mere coordinator or amalgamator-mixer. As Max Lerner put it in the *New York Post* recently (referring to the achievements of Henry Kissinger), our "leadership fund" has to rely more on "representative men" and less on "hero cults":

A representative man is one who, in his person and career, gathers up the energies, trials and aspirations of his society and age. . . .

What makes him representative is his essential character as *negotiator*. We have had explorers, pioneers, politicians, tycoons, astronauts, sports idols, men of war. But in a time of nuclear weapons when cold wars need ending and hot wars need preventing and when the world has grown totally interdependent and, therefore, totally fragile, the negotiator must come to the center of the stage.

As Kissinger himself told the European allies:

The specialized concerns of experts and technicians have a life of their own and a narrow national or sectarian bias.

The preservation of organizational harmony (without a fair measure of which progress is impaired) consequently calls more and more for the manager, as leader, to cumulate and integrate the contributions of all in the enterprise. However special individually, the contributions necessarily add up to more than the capacity to contribute of any single boss, no matter how able or brilliant he may be. The leader has to be pertinacious, but in negotiating the greatest common effort, not in dictating his own ideas alone.

7. The dangers in failing to grow such leadership adequately are cited in a lecture by Maurice Stans in *Saturday Review-World* for December 18, 1973, under the head "The Heedless Passage Toward Social Disintegration":

The larger self-interest of all nations today is inevitably merged in the inescapable web of interdependence that characterizes the technological civilizations. This requires a cooperative approach to *managing* the interacting relationships between resources, . . . technology, . . . and the minimal needs for sustaining decent standards of human life; and protecting the environment on which that life depends. These interlocking subjects must move to the top of the world's agenda for thought and action. And they are ultimately inseparable from the issues of war and peace and national security that preoccupied us up to now.

The managerial lesson in this analysis is that institutional structures in which normal human beings function together in orderly and effective ways and take time to build to functioning patterns are dangerously disrupted by sudden changes not yet desired or understood by participating personnel. Furthermore, they usually cannot be replaced quickly by hastily thrown together new organizations even when backed by immense sums of government money. Therefore, they are best based on trends that are longest lasting and shift most slowly, foster career- rather than project-long personal development, hold temporary projects to incremental dimensions, and thereby provide the best framework for continuing amicable teamwork.

8. Another serious handicap to the continuing manageability of democratic government organizations comes from the frequency of public elections—usually at one- to five-year intervals—with consequent twin difficulties for the acceptable continuity of work. First, "next-election" pressures realistically force current political leaders to overemphasize short- versus long-term aims. Second, swings in voter performance may cause the introduction of green and maybe inexperienced top leaders at critical times when competence and stability of managerial leadership are most essential. To put it bluntly, limits to

government are no less fundamental than limits to growth.

9. In the face of such limits to government, modern worldwide urbanization is a burgeoning by-product of technology, causing two organizational problems. First, removal from the self-supporting possibilities of living on the land not only makes people more interdependent, but also more dependent on government welfare approaches, especially as basic agricultural skills do not transform automatically to those needed for urban commercial or industrial work. Second, the political popularity of wide "welfare" handouts puts powerful pressure on politicians to push such spending to seriously inflationary levels, to the detriment, as money depreciates and prices jump, of the poor even more than of the rich.

10. Resultant worldwide, politically generated *inflation* has outrun the capacity of gold (in both quantity and national ore locations) to continue as an accepted solid medium for use in exchange for national currencies. Hence, international money chaos tends to spread. The absence of any world sovereign power—though itself probably a blessing in the face of the apparent unmanageability of even national governments—inhibits the creation of any continuing world pooling of reserves of money across national boundaries. Therefore, it stops the use of any universally acceptable paper currency like Federal Reserve bank notes within the United States, for instance. The world need for managerial-type leadership to create a compatible world currency exchange system looms proportionately.

11. Both the specific socialization of some governments, with private property ownership diminished, and the undertaking even in democracies of more economic (but not fundamentally "sovereign") functions by government introduce the need for new orders of scope for government "managers." These managers must learn to operate without the automatic backing of the usual "sovereign authority" needed for military, police, fire, and similar activities.

The line, if any, between "sovereign" and "economic" operations is usually not neat or clear. Government managers have less and less "command" authority, but they usually don't have the training or capacity to function without it.

Such phenomena as labor strikes against the government (even at times in police, fire, transport, utilities, and other operations involving the highest public interest and need for service) become a naturally evolving by-product of the politicizing of unions and of collective bargaining for either money or productivity.

When deficiencies in business leadership brought public depression in the 1930s, government began to put limits on its leaders.

Similar checks and balances on excessive union leader power, especially if misused to wide public disadvantage, seem sure to evolve.

If freedom, rather than totalitarian dictatorship, is to prevail, unions, as organized institutions themselves, had better undergo better operational management. The need to evolve recognized managerial principles to new situations thus becomes another factor forcing the constant evolution of such principles.

This is of double significance for educators. They should be leading the struggle to improve those principles; and, for reasons distinct from those for unions, universities need better management than they are getting.

12. The usual tendency of governments when laws do not work is to try to correct the problems by passing more laws. For two clear reasons, managerial leadership should urge alternate approaches.

First, as overcentralized government gets too big and too complex, operating decisions (and plans) get too far away from the people and the communities they affect. The better cure would be to decentralize more government operations, including financial responsibility, to local areas, where both needs and cures are more readily visible and amenable to interested voters' scrutiny and direction and there is a greater understanding of community reality.

Second, with "full employment" more and more a goal of both social justice and political expediency (odd bedfellows, to be sure), leaders need to watch the easy tendency to try to counter dips in volume of business and other activities with inflationary "emergency" government spending.

Using such spending rather than a variable return on equity investment as the flywheel for stabilizing the economy tends to reduce the risk investment, with its inherent profit-and-loss incentives, to a mere loan or debt equivalency with the return regulated in good times and bad. The combined effect is higher private and public debt. But the history of government debt is that the next generation does not want to pay for its parents' flings. People know this instinctively. So currency depreciation is expedited, and such "redistribution of wealth" usually misses "social justice" by a wide mark.

13. Going back to look at manager education in the light of world trends like those cited, the need for more teaching and more learning on two topics seems to stand out ever more clearly. The first is political science. As government and politics intrude more confusingly on economics, technology, and sociology, all managers, both in and out of government, need to be more knowledgeable about political principles. The second is theology, a theology beyond ethics or

morals. As the need grows to recognize man's spiritual and emotional capacities over and above his mere rationality, we need a new understanding to go with the recognition.

14. Publicity reflects a growing concern, everywhere, for developments dubbed by such labels as participatory democracy, sharing in the decisionmaking process, and worker self-management. These really seem to be different degrees of a common trend, and to have three significant common characteristics, characteristics which managers urgently need to take into account.

(a) They are natural developments as all workers attain higher levels of education and knowledge.

(b) They are necessary, to a steadily greater degree, as the proliferation of knowledge specialties passes the comprehension of any one person, even a top manager.

(c) They are progressively dangerous to organizational continuity if all involved, managers and nonmanagers alike, do not voluntarily, and in advance, consider the implications of all decisions for teamwork, for overall organization effects, and for community impacts, rather than narrowly, for only their own specialty job interest.

Hence, worker councils, codetermination groups, dual supervisory boards, and so on, especially in Europe today, respond to real organizational problems. But, however well meant, they need to be used with care and thought, lest they disperse operating authority beyond responsibility and compound rather than cure the problems. These approaches, if not applied with balance, can produce the kind of results seen only too often in the U.S. Congress or in NATO. They can put so much diverse talent into so many ongoing operational acts (as distinct from into policy formulation) that they paralyze any effective operations consensus and continuity.

15. Particularly when "ownership" is socialized and divorced from individuals or private corporation groups of share owners, the need (cited above) to distinguish the truly sovereign from the economic activities of government is great. One development, in the face of such trends, is very thought provoking. It is well pictured in a 1972 English book entitled *The State as Entrepreneur: New Dimensions for Public Enterprise—the IRI State Shareholding Formula,* edited by Stuart Holland. As developed in Italy, the concept means that the state tries to combine the advantages of private corporate management and operation of entrepreneurial activities with government financing by ownership of corporate shares rather than of corporate property and assets as such.

This is clearly a "most important new dimension in public enterprise" that calls for constructive managerial attention, scrutiny, and understanding. However such initial ventures develop, they at least represent willingness to take a risk to try to integrate the capacities of the public and private sectors of national (and maybe international) economies rather than to rush them to reckless confrontations.

The basic philosophical approach at issue was well put by the late H. I. Romnes, former Bell Telephone System chief executive:

If we in business can say to a bureaucrat that he never met a payroll, it can also be said with equal justice that we never carried a precinct. We have a lot to learn from each other.

Such thinking was consistent with Mr. Romnes' overall managerial approaches, as summed up in *The New York Times* of November 21, 1973.

Among his favorite themes were the ideas that even sudden change can be rationally managed; that taking time to know the other person better and to listen to him tends to diminish difficulties; that institutions have no rights except through performance; that long-term consequences are of more importance than quick results; and that even in a complex society one man can make a difference.

16. In today's world, it is pertinent to note that, generally, nationalism separates nations, whereas trade crosses national boundaries, seeking areas of common (rather than diverse) interest. This is why the modern multinational corporations currently get growing attention from both business and government leaders, and why, despite avid presentations of both their benefits and "dangers" (even in some minds to threats to the sovereignty of nations), the multinational corporations continue to grow in size, diversity, and geographic scope.

Although such popular critiques as Anthony Sampson's book, *The Sovereign State of ITT,* do get notice for such claims as "some multinational corporations get too big and cunning for even a large country to control," better research and reporting are found in such volumes as Raymond Vernon's *Sovereignty at Bay; The Multi-National Spread of U.S. Enterprises,* which presents, as per its jacket text, "the first really adequate picture of these revolutionary institutions, their myriad organizational forms, their varied adaptations to developments in technology, transport, and communication and, above all, their phenomenal economic efficiency—a book (for) business man, social scientist, or student of foreign affairs, etc."

Another interesting book is one from England, *The Multinationals* (1972) by Christopher Tugendhat, who fears that nations may lose control of their economic destinies to multinational corporations unless they act positively to harmonize the interests of the resident multinational and the host nation.

Possibly most perceptive in identifying points at issue among national political, social, and business structures is Richard Eells' *Global Corporations: The Emerging System of World Economic Power* (1976). For a short, yet comprehensive, picture of the emerging multinational corporations, few presentations are more penetrating and clear than Eells' summary, in seven "propositions." Especially significant is the sixth on "the search for congruence" between future international political boundaries and the corporate domains of indispensable multinational firms in an ecologically sound world.

17. Such ongoing corporate and political trends, as all kinds of organizations get larger, only further emphasize the growing opportunity for *managerial* advances to foster changes to use better modern education and technology, to lead the larger-sized private and public institutions cropping up all over well, to define the nature and contributions of teamwork as plainly as those of functional work, and, in the process, to improve and extend the capacity of the manager's own work at all organizational levels.

18. As Max Lerner said in the *New York Post*, we do live in a "time of nuclear weapons." The most fundamental change of today's era focuses on the technology that has created a nuclear age.

For the first time, man has the knowledge to destroy (whether purposely or accidentally) the whole planet Earth, all its nations, all its people.

The implications, still only intuitively sensed by most people, do generate wide fears, both consciously and otherwise. A not-to-be-skipped by-product may be much of the current violence and irresponsibility, if only on the basis of "we might as well romp before we go." Out of the possibility of such a short-range reaction grows the deeper universal responsibility to cope with and contain the underlying realities.

For government leaders particularly—most of all in the more powerful nations—such potentials call for *early* cooperation to form sensible new world alliances as the old World War II alliances and leaders vanish. Specifically:

(a) They should cut and limit military weapons, huge armed organizations, and their costs.

(b) By doing so, they would both restrict the danger of holocaust and gain chances to redistribute savings to better purposes.

(c) They should do so expeditiously, if only because today's communication media make politics more volatile—even at national levels—at the same time that old religions, ethics, and morals seem to be fading as inhibiting limitations on perverse human conduct.

(d) At the same time, they should avoid substituting economic resources—whether metals, food, or oil—as world weapons instead of the more obviously dangerous military arms, because the human disruption from such alternative "weapons" can be just as disastrous for all.

19. There are good reasons for leadership to expect constructive results if such steps are taken. Widely sensed by many, such reasons are well summed up in a quarter-century-old book by Arthur Koestler, *Insight and Outlook*. In it, reporting years of reflection and research, he views man's long evolutionary progress from individual to family group, to tribe, to nation, to modern multinational institutions with art, invention, and ethics all components of that evolutionary human process.

The gist of Koestler's conclusions is that all men have opposing urges within them: one, self-assertive to be independent and competitive; the other, self-transcending to take a place as part of a greater whole. He also concludes that, in the light of history, the self-transcending drive wins out for long-run progress, though at an evolutionary, rather than revolutionary, pace.

History, of course, can be read many ways, but it is hard to fault Koestler's reflections. Current evidence shows a growing emphasis on such themes as social responsibility, even for essentially economic institutions, and for social justice as a goal of religious congregations.

The constructive tendencies in such trends, in efforts to have managers integrate social and economic ends rather than set them in conflict, are ably boiled down in Neil H. Jacoby's *Corporate Power and Social Responsibility* (1973). While granting the growth of competition in the international field, Jacoby sees both expanded governmental regulation and the rise of new, competing interest blocs as combining with corporate responses to changing social values and priorities to increase the stability of world order and promote the growth of regional and worldwide political organization.

20. Obviously the flow of adequate, as well as accurate, informa-

tion has to be a necessary lubricant for such progress. Both the technical advances involved and the functioning of modern media, already noted, play a role.

The computerization of information makes it possible to put needed facts at the beck of all organizational decisionmakers, however decentralized, as well as supply appropriate data on the potential impacts of their decisions on others. However, an excessive haste to expedite technology can cause errors and delays as well as advances.

To a large degree computer programming is still an infant science. The substitution of oversimplified "models," indices, and statistics for the human complexities of real-life organizations and components can work two ways. Used with judgment it can allow people to deal with scopes of variables not earlier practicable. Used too hurriedly or unwisely it can lead to bigger mistakes.

Oversimplified assumptions—whether by individual operators, management scientists, even "think tanks" of brilliant intellectuals or aggressive advocacy journalists—can help to widen our horizons but can also be seriously misleading if taken too literally as truth.

21. It seems doubly vital not to misuse modern statistics and information in government circles, where quick enactment of sovereign legislation to "cure" social situations by fiat—backed by big appropriations and spent by green organizations and agencies—so often results in substituting worse messes for familiar ones and squandering savings and human resources, expediting inflation in the process.

Not idly does the *U.S. News and World Report* for January 7, 1974, in its column "A Look Ahead From the Nation's Capitol," report that:

Rising too is a feeling that bigger and bigger government doesn't hold answers to all the country's troubles. There's impatience at official failure to get a grip on the economy. Price–wage controls are widely judged a flop . . . that's to be reflected in stubborn opposition to new taxes, new government programs. Criticism of waste in welfare costs won't end. Other spending targets will include education, defense, foreign aid, and space programs.

The common sense and intuitive human wisdom of ordinary voters are, incidentally, further exemplified in that same column, thus:

Tougher public attitude extends to labor. In Detroit—a strong union town—people are sore about truckers blocking highways, pulling wildcat strikes on grocery stores. Such actions are resented, seen hurting ordinary people.

22. Despite such public reactions, the trend to governmental socialization has by no means run its course; and managers need to pay attention proportionately.

The public desire to develop, apply, and exploit new technology more rapidly than private enterprises can, and therefore to provide needed risk capital and risk insurance, is not, surely, bad in itself. The ultimate great danger is that repeated lunges of that kind build such cumulative dimensions for government operations—with their normal bureaucratic and inflationary aspects—that real and permanent progress is distorted, delayed, or missed.

Excessive "national planning," as Will Rogers said in the thirties, can also mean that "Hereafter we're going to make our mistakes on a national scale where up to now we've made them for ourselves."

Possibly managers should be directing their thoughts to ways of getting activities out of government operations—especially those for which technology, financing, and risk dimensions have been established—with the same aggressive drives that have, often beneficially, put new programs into government in recent decades.

Maybe, to keep overall government size manageable, some kind of a "one out for one in" criterion or policy is needed whereby any new proposal has to pass a test to prove that it is so persuasively in the public interest as to warrant transferring some present government operations, of equivalent resource requirements, to the private sector. Examples of such trends already exist, such as the COMSAT venture for global communication satellites and more recent changes in U.S. postal services. Managers of the future, though, should surely seek to foster such moves in a positive, not merely a passive or incidental, manner.

23. Again, though, any overly casual chatter about a business and government "partnership" in such ventures needs examination. The final characteristic of government is sovereignty. If it is to be kept legitimate, to have public acceptance and backing, it is critical both to limit the scope of government to activities that would genuinely fare better under the sovereign approach and to keep the sovereign status of such affairs clear of the legal concept of partners, in which each would have total responsibility organizationally and total authority in proportion. Nongovernmental organizations should neither seek nor get such sovereign authority. They can act as contractors for, but not legal partners with, their government.

24. For over six decades the American Society of Mechanical Engineers has promoted summaries of managerial progress for each

ten-year period. Paper No. 10 (WA/Mgt-10) wraps up the review for the sixties. In thinking of "What's Ahead in Managing," we should find the summary of that paper to be pertinent:

The Sixties saw notable progress. NASA's decentralized approach landed man on the moon. The United States economy functioned at substantially a trillion dollar annual level. Yet, regional, racial and religious conflicts persisted, even to spreading violence currently on campus and streets. Political leadership was overtaxed; inflation varied only in degree in old and "new" countries. Noneconomic institutions—universities, unions, hospitals, even churches—grew to use large human and material resources, but too often with ineffective managerial guidance. Notable progress, or lag, is indicated in five fields:—general gains, and drops, in the sixties; managerial advances in business and government; manager education; information for managing; managerial concepts for the future. In conclusion, the lag of classic authority to produce needed new orders of organized teamwork becomes startlingly visible, but does so just as the supply of trained brains and the availability of needed new kinds of information take on dimensions already component to keep order ahead of chaos while still keeping man free.

25. More recently studies like that on *Limits to Growth* made at M.I.T. under Club of Rome sponsorship, emphasized by developments like changing Arab oil policies, have stimulated fresh thinking on managerial and institutional aims, policies, techniques, measures, and trends.

In particular the managerial need both to respect human values and to improve productivity in order to limit the waste of any resources comes on strongly today. Earlier comments above about "productivity" are especially to the point under such conditions. The type of "efficiency" advocated by managerial pioneers of the days of leaders like Taylor, Fayol, Gantt, or the Gilbreths has undergone some popular criticism, even derision, in recent times.

Actually Taylor sought "harmony, not discord" and "cooperation, not individualism" as intensively as "efficiency"; and was pioneering properly on both fronts. But whether it is called "efficiency" or "productivity," the leadership ability to use resources well and not wastefully becomes ever more timely.

Surely a key area for managerial advances is to clarify productivity concepts for applicability and acceptance in organizations where "output" is more mental than manual and "input" is often not measurable merely in man-hours. That the measure needs to be of value added from effort applied, and that "value" is often harder to measure or judge (or even guess) than costs are only more powerful reasons to concentrate good leadership talent to make progress in this respect. This managerial requirement is bound to grow, not diminish, in decades ahead.

26. Under such conditions, educators, like managers, cannot hibernate in historic habits. Here, too, imagination and innovation are imperative. This is particularly true at the college level in the education of "professionals."

As professions themselves proliferate, yet interlock, as practice calls for institutional beyond individual resources, classic professional loyalties become impossibly narrow. For professionals no less than for managers, it has to be both, not either/or. Without giving up loyalty to the professional discipline, a parallel loyalty to the organization and the community is required for manager and nonmanager alike. The essentiality of disciplined dedication and teamwork as well as of a professional specialty is no longer avoidable or permissible to try to avoid.

27. Another factor that deserves future managerial attention involves changes in property ownership not only by transfer to socialized status but also, within the private sector of the economy, by interposition of various "fund" institutions between individual investors and corporate share ownership.

Hence, the character of "ownership" shifts in parallel ways to both public and private institutions. But securities markets transactions by institutional investors tend to be of higher orders of magnitude than those of personal owners of securities. A curious parallel trend is for so-called "institutional investors"—all necessarily working from more or less common information for their respective value analyses—to move in the market on more of a herd than a single basis. Predictably, they made security markets more rather than less erratic.

Such factors, combined with the continuing effects of inflation, give new dimensions to managerial decisions on institutional financing—especially on the need to reconcile the classic debt-to-equity ratio in financing growth. The degree of uncertainty imposed on decisions that necessarily have to be made with plans—or at least rather definite anticipations—for substantial future periods makes precedents of ever more questionable help. Managing has always involved risks for the future, but the rather interesting thing is that with more data and information than ever before, risks seem to become less clear rather than clearer; executive responsibilities become greater in proportion.

As the record in such economies as that in the USSR reveals, "national planning" runs into about the same uncertainties, and confronts them with even fewer entrepreneurial skills.

Thus, as "ownership" gets divorced from property both owned and dispersed on a cumulative basis, the responsibility of the institutional managers gets more and more pluralistic.

The need to see and to balance the continuing interests of diverse groups, even though the individuals in such groups overlap in multiple degrees, takes on new managerial meaning. Owners, workers, customers, voters, politicians, educators, and others all impact on the organization managed. The "rights" of all—majorities and minorities alike—have to be considered at all times.

The net consequence is that the executive and managerial goals have to be directed toward optimizing, synthesizing, and truly integrating such multiple interests—not just, as of yore, toward seeking profit maximization as a single overriding aim and measure of performance. Thus, both education for and practice of operational managing for the future have to be based on balancing diverse short- and long-range pressures and opportunities.

28. Interestingly enough, similar diversities have an impact on religious, as well as on economic and political, leaders. And multiple choices and complex optimization priorities demand similar leadership, imagination, and judgments. The dilemmas are well noted in these pastoral comments by Monsignor George A. Kelly of the Church of St. John the Evangelist on November 25, 1973:

One of the big things in our day is "Sociology in Religion." Sociology is a social science that studies the situation as it is, not as it ought to be, not as people would like it to be. So it is not interested in Christ as the Son of God nor in the truth or demands in his teaching, but rather the social processes that brought him to social power and the social forces he became (mostly through his followers) in the ensuing generations.

For the sociologist, therefore, Christ is explained in much the same way as Moses, Luther, Napoleon and Mao Tse-tung. The presence of movement of the Holy Spirit in Christian history is not important because the Spirit is really a religious myth which defies scientific study.

No one can quarrel with this approach by a scientist, but it is a fact that most sociologists are unbelievers and thus inclined (like the doubting Thomas) to debunk everything they see, including the sacred.

The trouble begins, however, when the faithful and their leaders act like sociologists expect them to act.

The consequent scrambling of earlier "value" rules has an impact on lay organizational leaders no less than on religious leaders. The place of normative influences on decisions and operations gets more uncertain along with other conditions of the operational world.

As a result, managerial planning and forecasting increasingly have to see, sense, and settle for such scrambled uncertainties. The capacity to anticipate alternative potentials and to be as aware and able to ride tail winds as to force your way through against headwinds calls for corresponding managerial flexibility, reinforced by a dose of stubbornness.

29. Particularly in older cultures in Europe, as distinct from the 200-year-old, but still younger, United States, the need to localize decisionmaking to match the visibility of applicable risks more closely has grown accordingly.

Although at times it has seemed popular to ascribe European problems to foreign forces—as in J. J. Servan-Schreiber's *The American Challenge* (1965)—modern approaches like operations research and so-called "management science" in decisionmaking can help modern managers to assess such situations more realistically. As is well put in the book *The Management Revolution; Management Consulting and Computer Aided Decision-Making* (1972) by three French consultants (R. Armand, R. Lettis, and J. Lesourne), the "development of decision assistance has been extraordinary both in its speed and in its diversity." Both the book's text and its conclusion are as useful for American as for European managers, not least the concluding phrases:

We must structure, adapt, and simulate in a determinedly international frame of mind. . . . The task is not as great financially as it appears, but it is immense as regards structure and manpower. To succeed in it we must break free of several centuries of administrative centralization. We must forget many of the reflexes we have acquired . . . the proof being that it is the countries which make most fuss about humanism which turn out to be least capable of managing properly the products of the mind.

Like all the great undertakings, this one must begin with an effort at self-improvement.

30. But if individual self-improvement is to have a chance, the managerial authority of older days has to undergo fundamental improvements.

The opportunity to learn by doing, as well as by studying—even the right to make rational mistakes in so doing—has to be available to, and respected by, everyone in the managed organization.

Also, personal rights to privacy—for individuals in and out of particular organizations—need sharp new recognition, especially as computerized data banks, simultaneous tape recordings (openly or clandestine), and modern media and government forces bring order-of-magnitude shifts from old cultural conditions. Once again, mutual—teamwork—interests and rights assume new managerial dimensions.

31. In perceptive analyses of the leadership of Red China, in *The New York Times* on November 18 and 22, 1973, C. L. Sulzberger dubbed Mao "chairman of the board" and Chou En-lai "managing director." He characterized Mao as "semiretired in terms of administrative routine but still the ultimate boss for major policy decisions, and said that Chou applies on a practical basis the revolutionary theorems worked out by the top leadership in accordance with Maoist doctrine. But he suggested the limits of such an approach—as a possible example for managers in other institutions—by noting that Mao "has often produced an amalgam (that is, a mere mixture) of others' ideas rather than a synthesis. . . ."

For lasting progress—in other words, to try to avoid the extreme upsets so typical in China in late years—tomorrow's managerial leaders in sizable organizations will more and more need to seek and secure a solid synthesis, or integration, of the diverse talents and interests of all co-workers at all organizational levels.

To try to attain such results, the late Richard Armand of France once aptly noted that customary concepts of "lines of authority" increasingly need to be thought of rather as "circuits of authority." This aptly recognized that the diversity of disciplines now spreads the scope of knowledge beyond the personal comprehensions of even "top" executives, however smart or educated. The required decentralization of both information and decisions—but with known policy binders to aid all in achieving known common organizational interests—is the heart of the synthesizing concept.

32. Equally as essential as the synthesizing process is the growing executive mandate to keep the entrepreneurial spirit—so common in small personalized forms—alive, dispersed, and functioning as an enterprise grows in size and dynamics and tends rather naturally to degenerate to bureaucratic "play it safe" or "let George do it" habits and practices.

Few future managerial imperatives are as vital as to preserve—to paraphrase recent words by James L. Hayes, president of the American Management Associations—the needed sharing of enthusiasm for achievement and commitment to the goals of the organization and to prevent that sense of commitment and of individual participant creativity from withering after a while.

33. As resources become more limited, the need for imaginative managerial leadership, as also noted earlier, becomes as powerful in noneconomic as in business institutions.

With technology—or the ability to apply more widely and scientifically organized information—growing, but with physical resources, on the one hand, and savings for capital purposes, on the other, not growing at equivalent rates, the competence to deploy human, material, and financial resources most productively has to become a prime aspect of managerial leadership. The need to update manager education leadership is also great.

With knowledge proliferating and making itself obsolete at the same time, "lifetime learning"—beyond classic school, college, or university classrooms—becomes the norm. This trend may well limit on-campus education and transfer much future education to work-site learning. Both college and business leaders already have a duty to rethink their respective operating and educational objectives, functions, and methods accordingly. Here, most likely, it is already later than we think.

As Dennis Gabor noted in his thoughtful book *The Mature Society* (1972), "Till now, man has been up against nature; from now on he will be up against his own nature."

As Dr. Gabor goes on to show, science and old economic virtues have brought man face to face with an age of leisure for which he is psychologically unprepared. Man's inherent ability to respond to challenges and his irrational capacity to behave best in adversity justify faith in what can still be done, but they in no way eliminate parallel leadership calls for far-reaching changes in education, employment patterns, fiscal policies, and attitudes that he believes will result in a "mature society, stable in numbers and in material production, in ecological equilibrium with the resources of the Earth . . . a world which maintains the maximum amount of individual freedom compatible with social stability." The aim—as Dr. Gabor puts it for managers and educators alike—is for each one to "develop a visceral feeling for evolutionary ethics . . . and feel in his bones that this hard-earned civilization is worth preserving."

34. The wide present-day breakup of classic family, moral ethics, and religious customs will not go away by itself. Instead, the very personal drive of all molders of opinion and leaders of men—whether media, church, parents, managers, computer or calculator makers and programmers, even those who hijack for a cause—will be needed.

The ability to get public attention by noise and clamor does not absolve anyone from direct human responsibility for the results of the clamor. Even if notions—for example, a mandate to use auto seat belts—get put into statutory form, they will not succeed if the vast, diverse public citizenry is not in accord. And it should not be necessary to repeat America's constitutional prohibition of the use of alcoholic beverages to see this point. Although history does not repeat itself exactly, its lessons are still significant. As an old colleague, Lem Boulware of General Electric, once said, "It is not necessary for us all to start in the Garden of Eden."

35. To conclude, therefore, the *continuity* of human organizations—to meet deep human callings—has to be sensed, provided for, and achieved in modern managerial leadership. This remains as true in a "knowledge economy" as it was earlier in agricultural and industrial economies.

The need to marshal resources to get a current cash flow for continuing operation across economy dips is as essential—or, in human terms, even more so—when organizational "fixed costs" are for payroll as they were earlier, when they were for land or capital equipment.

Changes in entrenched "make or buy" decision processes—earlier habitualized and shaped for different economy characteristics and relationships—have to be developed and applied in and across all modern organized institutions, however "owned."

As "socialization" makes employment and personnel costs more and more inflexible, new managerial criteria to decide whether to put people on the particular organization's payroll or to contract for their services from parallel institutions have to be developed.

In many respects, direct employment may best be used only when there is a high annual load-factor use for each specialist's services. But this can itself help to curb unwieldy organizational size and to decentralize more and more specialist personnel—only intermittently needed in most specific operations—to corresponding specialist organizations.

The result, intelligently steered, can be mutually beneficial to the individuals concerned and to the overall economy by limiting the excess concentration of people in oversized organizations. Decision-making can be both decentralized and improved, especially by being more frankly individualized. This is the inner nature of "participatory democracy."

Part II
THE EVOLVING SCIENCE OF MANAGEMENT

Melvin Zimet

17
Introduction

Management has been variously described as an art, as a practice, and as a science. Clearly, it is all of these things, involving a joint effort on the part of practitioners, academicians, and researchers. The amorphousness of management as a discipline stems, to a large extent, from its eclectic nature. It derives its substance from such fields as economics, mathematics, psychology, sociology, anthropology, and many more. Academicians and researchers develop and provide the material that is absorbed into the study of management.

The role of the practicing manager, as distinguished from the field of management, however, is far from amorphous, and lends itself more readily to definition. Although this definition is stated in different ways by different people, there is fairly general agreement that the manager is responsible for planning, organizing, staffing, directing, and controlling.

Defining the management process in these terms is the keystone of the operational school, which has its roots in the work of Henri Fayol. One of its staunchest advocates is Harold Koontz, who contends that operational management and science theory provide the core for a structure which can include group behavior, interpersonal behavior, mathematics, the various components of the systems approach, and the clinical experience of practitioners. It is therefore superior to the numerous approaches that have sprung up which limit themselves to one particular facet of the managerial role.

To carry out his functions, the manager relies to an ever increasing degree on the disciplines mentioned above. This does not mean that the manager is a passive user of developments that have been provided through the spontaneous efforts of academic researchers.

269

On the contrary, the manager has been the dynamic element that has motivated research in directions that the practitioner could apply. It is in this sense that the manager provides the impetus toward a science of management.

As Smiddy and Naum point out, the relationship between the practitioner and the academic disciplines was established at an early stage of modern management. Frederick Taylor, for example, was not at all reluctant to take his steel plant data and his speed feed formulas to mathematicians for solutions. Elton Mayo, a psychologist, conducted the studies that provided the foundation for the human relations approach to managing at the Hawthorne plant of Western Electric. And it was no mere coincidence that Max Weber, a sociologist, was defining the characteristics of the "ideal bureaucracy" at a point in history when the trend toward large-scale business enterprise had clearly begun to change the course of economic events. More recently, the seminal work of Claude Shannon on the communication of information was conducted at and under the auspices of Bell Telephone Laboratories.

In his chapter, "The Behavioral Dimensions of 'Span of Management' Theory," James Worthy, whose pioneering studies on the impact of differences in span of control were conducted at Sears Roebuck, discusses a structural concept that has commanded the attention of management theorists for the past 50 years. The notion of an appropriate span of control goes back to classical theory. However, the question of what constitutes an appropriate span of control continues to stimulate research by behavioral scientists.

Meeting the physical requirements of production was among the earliest responsibilities of professional managers, a responsibility which certainly still exists today. In meeting this responsibility, managers relied, at first, on the physical scientists—in chemistry, in metallurgy, and the like. Later, managers came to recognize the importance of the behavioral scientists in motivating workers to higher levels of productivity. With the growing maturity and power of the business organizations they serve, managers have learned that society now imposes responsibilities that go far beyond the classical ones.

Each in his own way, Professor Mee, Professor Steiner, and Father Morlion trace the transition from economic man to social man. Professor Mee describes economic man as engaging in a struggle to survive and acquire property, wealth, and income. Social man, on the other hand, seeks satisfaction not from heroic individual effort, but rather from participation in a social process. Our nation, says Professor Mee, has become a nation of employees. What motivation, he asks, can management provide for social man to replace the financial incentive that motivated economic man? It is not unreasonable to expect that managers will turn to the behavioral scientists for the answer.

In a similar vein, Professor Steiner compares the classical business ideology, which has its taproots in the concepts of Adam Smith, to the socioeconomic managerial ideology. A statement by the Committee for Economic Development conveys the essence of this latter concept: "Business functions by public consent, and its basic purpose is to serve constructively the needs of society—to the satisfaction of society." Professor Steiner contends that the modern corporation still has to establish its legitimacy with the American people, and it is not likely to do so by giving its allegiance to a classical ideology that fails to respond to their aspirations. The reconciliation of the needs of the business corporation with the aspirations of the American people presents economists and social scientists with a challenge worthy of their skills.

Father Morlion traces management through three phases of industrial revolution. The early phase established the primacy of the machine over manual labor and, as a result, the supremacy of the entrepreneur over the worker. The second phase established the right of people in the enterprise to participate in the decision-making process through their unions and through government intervention. The third phase is characterized by government by the people through civic and public relations which express the public philosophy of the enterprise. Father Morlion argues that managers must be trained not only to be good socioeconomic managers of the enterprise, but also to be leaders in the community.

This is a concept that adds the skills of the political scientist to those of the behavioral scientist on the list of disciplines upon which the manager of the modern corporation will have to draw. As a matter of fact, the concept of codetermination, as Herbert Hicks points out, is already a reality in several European countries.

Codetermination is the sharing of management by persons representing the workforce with persons representing ownership in an industry. In West Germany, this concept has been credited with having been a major force in West Germany's postwar recovery. After World War II, Germany was faced with the task of rebuilding its industrial complex. Several German state governments requested and received permission from the zonal military governments to make comanagement compulsory in industry. Subsequently, a series of codetermination laws, the most recent of which was the New Codetermination Act of 1976, expanded and defined the process of codetermination. Volkswagen is just one of the companies that have operated with considerable success under this system.

West Germany is not alone, however, in the adoption of codetermination. The Dutch have also adopted their own form of codetermination. In France, a committee appointed by President Giscard D'Estaing has proposed using a form of cosupervision rather than the German model of codetermination. Hicks concludes that codetermination is a profound experience that appears to deserve the close attention of government leaders and managers throughout the world.

The chapters that follow suggest the increasing variety of problems that practicing managers face today. In finding solutions, they rely more and more on scientists in fields that at one time were, at best, only tangential to the experience of businessmen. The essays also suggest that although there are problems that are general to all organizations, the solutions are not the same for all of them. To bring the variety of knowledge and expertise that has been developed over the years to the solution of these problems in all their complexity is the special skill of the management consultant.

Peter Drucker compares this skill to that of the doctor or the lawyer who is able to bring the knowledge that he has acquired through his training and his experience with many different patients and clients to each new case. At the same time, he is able to maintain his objectivity because of his professional detachment from the patient or client.

The profession of management consultant is a relatively new one. Two of its foremost pioneers are Lyndall Urwick and Harold Smiddy. Fortunately for the future of the profession, these men have provided a role model which is thoroughly compatible with that of the researcher, academician, and scientist with whom they work. It is through the combined efforts of men such as these and those of enlightened managers that we move toward a science of management.

Harold Smiddy and Lionel Naum

18
The Evolution of a "Science of Managing" in America

Wherever people have gathered to pursue a common and desired end, there has been an inevitable necessity to organize minds, hands, materials, and the use of time for efficient and contributive work. Man has learned that individual and personal rewards derive largely from an harmonious combination of individual work and teamwork in a soundly organized frame of reference, and thus the core of the history of "scientific management" is formed from his search for the techniques of joint but voluntary participation while still preserving individual initiative, creative imagination, and increasingly productive output.

Any historical survey, to be of more than passing interest, and to be more than a simple chronology of dates and names, needs to seek out the philosophical drives which both stimulated and limited the progress of such a scientific approach to more rational conception and performance of managerial work, that is, of securing results through the organized efforts of others.

While it is important to know when things happened, this knowl-

Reprinted from *Management Science*, October 1954, pp. 1–31.

edge only becomes significant and usable when it is understood *why* things happened. This chapter, therefore, is intended to outline the gradual historical development of the search for the basic principles of a science of managing, and thus of scientific management, rather than to be a simple recounting of experiment, methodology, or significant writings in that field.

THE SEARCH FOR PRINCIPLES OF MANAGEMENT

The philosophical sciences, and that dealing with the work of managing is one of them, deal with concepts and abstractions not *easily* tested or proved quantitatively, especially on a current basis, and not *readily* subject to exact delineation, definition, standardization, or measurement. The abilities to observe, to classify, to synthesize, and to act are at least partially inhibited by the relationship and reciprocal impact of the observer and his environment.

The observer deals with the classic study of man, and he deals with one of its most complex branches, the seeking of orderly process out of divergent wills, unclear or even contradictory objectives, and transient and often unmeasurable forces. Because each observer is an integral factor in his own study, complete objectivity is impossible, and he is often faced with the conflict of that which reason tells him must be so and that which emotion tells him should be so.

But, by acceptance of the limitations in method, rather than rejection because of the difficulties, cumulative progress has been consistently sought and progressively achieved. As a result, a "management movement," which lived only in the hopes of a relatively few dedicated volunteers as recently as only five decades ago, has, as of today, grown irresistibly to an organized and intensifying worldwide drive and to an increasingly international educational force.

Despite such visible and accelerating progress in so short an historical era, the science of managing, when compared to the physical sciences, may still seem slow in evolution and uncertain in direction. Yet, fairly judged, it is neither.

The apparent slowness has only reflected the normal systemic inertia encountered wherever tradition and prejudice guide men's actions and wherever there is deliberate observation of cause and effect. Uncertainty and delay in such progress has really been the result neither of any lack of a true goal nor of unwillingness to follow a just direction, but is, rather, the result of a need to consider every avenue of possible study and, by the very nature of things, to reject far more than can be accepted.

What is being sought? Certainly not the solution of isolated problems or the rectification of each pressing business or social exigency. That would be in the nature of art. Certainly not merely the kind of "progress" determined by ability to answer the simple questions: "Will it work?" "Can you get by with it?"

What has been, and still is, sought in all these recurring efforts to define and develop a true science of managing are, rather, those kinds of fundamental principles which are the essential scientific foundation of all generalization based on classified observations and which give meaning, accuracy, and dependability to formulation of rules of action or policies that, given a particular set of conditions, can be used or applied as guides with confidence in their effectiveness.

In other words, the search of the organized management movement and of the growing thousands of individual participants, both scholars and practitioners, is for principles, distilled out of what is now increasingly widely recorded experience in the social sciences, which can be applied to any and all situations involving the demand of leadership by reason and persuasion rather than merely by rank or dictation.

To consider the shop, the office, or even the total business as something apart and unique from the more general problem of *organizing for accomplishment,* is, therefore, to take the short and unproductive view. The stubborn refusal of disciples of scientific management to fall into that kind of mental trap is itself one of the firm reasons for the growing understanding and acceptance—locally, nationally, and internationally—that management principles can be applied to guidance of all kinds of organized efforts and can be a base for management education which leads to professional rather than whimsical managerial responsibility.

How is this "search" being conducted? Essentially, it has gone forward on two levels. First, there has been the elemental, "action" group whose members will always be necessary to avoid crises, but who rarely have time for rigorous thought. They have been putting out fires rather than developing methods of fire prevention. At best, they keep the work of the day from lagging, and they provide data for the file of experience.

Second, and more important, are those who, by time and circumstance, are determined to find and follow carefully measured paths, distinct though not remote from immediate demands.

Fortunately, this latter group is increasing both in size and influence, and in recent years their work has been credited with growth from deep roots and not merely from a knowing wave of the hand. It is because such men, and women, have boldly and persuasively demonstrated that there are basic truths which underlie the study of the relationships of men in common effort, and have shown that these truths can be demonstrated, applied, and measured, that acceptance of the needed fundamental study to develop an accepted science of managing is being won.

There are still many who regard the idea and concept of a "science of managing" as a scholarly diversion, a type of *post hoc* rationalization that is created and dies in the confines of the lecture hall. But, especially in the United States, while there have been, to be sure, the theorists and while their contributions have been indispensable, there have also been the practical men, and more often than not, both theoretical concepts and practical applications have found common spokesmen. In the complex organization of modern technological society, there has been a necessary division of thought and labor, and yet the carefully balanced alloy of the philosopher and the practitioner has been the metal for forging the characteristic industrial society of today.

Although, as Dr. Albert Einstein has pointed out, "We now realize, with special clarity, how much in error are those theorists who believe that theory comes inductively from experience," [1] the immutable demands of science are such that new concepts inevitably bear at least the subjective imprint of past experience, and that, inevitably, there must be a commingling of theory and practice.

In sum, the object and method of the search are clear. They are to establish a true science of managing based upon a valid, moral, and ethically acceptable philosophy of management by the impartial observation of social components as discrete entities within and related to a total common purpose. The search, especially in business and little less in government, has been, and will continue to be, conducted in a climate of reality for:

Life cannot wait until the sciences may have explained the universe scientifically. We cannot put off living until we are ready. The most salient characteristic of life is its coerciveness: it is always urgent "here and now," without any possible postponement. . . . [2]

History as a Guide

There have been many definitions of "scientific management," or as we prefer to phrase it, of a specific "science of managing." Mostly, they have been reflections of their time and frequently have served the needs of brevity more than of understanding. Yet awareness of the need for managing skills dates back, of course, beyond the beginning of recorded history. There are three phases, however, which, at the risk of rather obvious oversimplification, can be divided in time.

Before the nineteenth century, industry and business as we know it today were basically craft, individual, or, at best, guild matters. Dominating other aspects and counting above other endeavor usually was the organization and pursuit of territorial conquest. The energy of creative leadership was devoted in large part to the expansion of geographic horizons and the consequent need to discover, to take over, and to govern new territories.

Thus, there is evidence of "management" in military structures as in the conduct of civilian public affairs, but it was a type of management in which thought over and above the satisfaction of immediate requirements was usually of minimum proportions or impact. This era was perhaps the clearest example of management as an art; that is, the application of knowledge without systemization, and ordinarily on a definitely personalized basis.

The second period, on this scale of classification, began in the early part of the nineteenth century, following closely upon the heels of the introduction of the power loom and the steam engine. Here the first clearly definitive movement toward understanding the managerial, and even the broader social, implications of rapid technological progress was made, although nearly always in the light of just adequate and immediate solutions.

The information necessary to establish a true science of managing was still not at hand. The implications of constructive and successful steps taken in the direction of sound and rational organization were largely overlooked. Controlled experiment, accurate observation, and statistical correlation of human processes sometimes fell far short of more than lip service. Those who had created the industrial revolution, however, were concerned with the changing world they had brought into being, and the writings indicate at least a growing realization of a serious, impending human problem.

In the last half of the nineteenth century, therefore, they talked hopefully of a "science of management." But, because they dealt only with specific fragments of a complex problem, the principles they accepted are seen by the broader view of hindsight to have been overly narrow and superficial; and the science they established was, by today's dimensions at least, only a quasi-science.

A more serious danger inherent in the limited understanding of the nineteenth-century mechanists has been pointed out by Professor A. N. Whitehead:

A factory with its machinery, its community of operatives, its social service to the general population, its dependence upon organizing and designing genius, its potentialities as a source of wealth to the holders of its stock is an organism exhibiting a variety of vivid values. What we want to train is the habit of apprehending such an organism in its completeness. It is very arguable that the science of political economy, as studied in its first period after the death of Adam Smith (1790), did more harm than good. It destroyed many economic fallacies, and taught how to think about the economic revolution then in progress. But, it riveted on men a certain set of abstractions which were disastrous in their influence on modern mentality. It dehumanized industry.[3]

Many historians mark the first decade of the present, or twentieth, century as the beginning of the work of investigating the principles of management along lines which provide statistical validity; although even casual analysis, especially of papers on cost accounting and on work analyses before such bodies as the American Society of Mechanical Engineers, shows clearly that the foundation studies for such investigation had been developing for at least 20 years previously.

The examination of work skills in terms of output, which has thus received growing attention in the last quarter of the preceding century, was progressively restudied and carried forward with remarkable diligence and with increasingly startling results.

Resources in men and materials were expended in a great surge of discovery, but, unfortunately, the comparative abundance of the things man needed to make, to build, and to expand was in effect an embarrassment of riches. In the haste to make mightily, men fell too often into ways of leadership by command and by compulsion. The latent power of the people, which Gustave LeBon termed the "psychological law of the mental unity of crowds," [4] was accordingly marshaled in a pattern of social revolt, directed at such industrial methods because, while they did produce mightily, they tended to distribute inequitably and to make advances with inadequate regard for human developments.

Students of social status, customs, and trends became concerned with the creation, maintenance, and growth of the business, and specifically of the industrial enterprise as perhaps the most significant of current social phenomena. They realized, at last, that the total equation of civilization was heavily, perhaps even dominantly, affected by its business and industrial factors.

It is within the last 40 years, in consequence, that we have at last turned our primary, rather than our incidental, attention from *the* man, *the* machine, *the* product, to total enterprise, and even to industrial society, as an entity.

Those concerned with the science of managing are going back, now, over the accumulated knowledge and experience of centuries with new attitudes to discover the basic principles and patterns "which, like the great religions of the world, have the power to arouse the faith and hold the support of the great body of individual men and women throughout the ages."

Early Pioneers and Associations

The birth of the organized movement in search of a rational and cohesive science of management is generally credited to Frederick Winslow Taylor.[5] His book, *The Principles of Scientific Management,* published in 1911, and synthesizing and advancing the theses developed in his earlier experiments and writings from around 1880 to that time, seriously upset many traditional concepts of management.

It is interesting to study Taylor's development as, in the course of a long and productive life, both as a practitioner and engineer in and as a writer on the work of managing, his attention and emphasis shifted from the exploration of discrete facets of industrial processes to a search for underlying principles which governed the operation of those processes. It is, in a sense, the condensed pattern of the development of a real management science.

Taylor was born in 1856 and, after a rather cursory education, became apprenticed to the Enterprise Hydraulic Works in Philadelphia in 1874. He became concerned with the serious gap between the potential output and the actual output of shop workers and when he became a foreman, he determined to study the means of increasing productivity.

His early attempts were penetrating studies of the machine as a unit of productivity. Carefully controlled experiments were made on metal cutting techniques at Bethlehem Steel, at first alone and later with the aid of such associates as Carl Barth, Henry Gantt, and William Sellers. Every conceivable variation in speed, feed, depth of cut, and kind of tool was made and an empirical understanding of optimum combinations was established. And, in parallel with these empirical advances, it is significant that Taylor also sought the aid of able mathematicians of the day to find theoretical explanations and formulas from the abundant data with its complex and baffling variables, which their work amassed.

Encouraged by the success of the metal cutting work, Taylor made many other studies which dealt with the techniques of production. His work, during this period, was characterized primarily by his concern with end results, yet also by significant parallel attempts to deduce basic meanings. However, just as the metal cutting experiments dealt with what was happening more than why it happened, he failed, for the moment, to perceive the full general implications of his studies as an example of one of the elemental processes of scientific management.

Paralleling Taylor's and other early explorations, Frank and Lillian Gilbreth undertook a remarkable series of studies, which were distinguished by the fact that they definitely recognized and recorded with persuasive clarity that the basic unit of productivy had to include the worker as well as the machine and on a quantitative and specific basis. In 1909, for example, they published a work entitled *A Bricklaying System* and, in 1911, followed it with the more comprehensive *Motion Study*.

Their work, while of tremendous importance in creating an understanding of motion economy, of the techniques of increasing output by reducing incremental effort, and of the tools of measurement, is of deeper and more lasting importance in that it showed the significance of integrated thinking. They found and preached for all to know that it was the optimum combination of worker skills and machine operation, rather than the best of either alone, that could narrow the gap between potential and realized production.

The full import of the contribution of the industrial psychologist was not at first recognized. In reviewing the history of the American management movement, Colonel Lyndall F. Urwick gave this warm evaluation of the Gilbreth team:

If they (the ASME) had not been (aware of human problems involved)—and Taylor either failed to encounter, or to recognize the significance of, the early work in industrial psychology contributed by Walter Dill Scott, Hugo Munsterberg, and others—there was the amazing fact that one of them, Frank Bunker Gilbreth, happened to fall in love with a girl who was a psychologist by education, a teacher by profession, and a mother by vocation. I know of no occurrence in the whole history of human thought more worthy of the epithet "providential" than that fact. Here were three engineers—Taylor, Gantt, and Gilbreth—struggling to realize the wider implications of their technique, in travail with a "mental revolution," their great danger that they might not appreciate the difference between applying scientific thinking to material things and to human beings, and one of them married Lillian Moller, a woman who by training, by instinct, and by experience was deeply aware of human beings, the perfect mental complement in the work to which they had set their hands.[6]

As such work and that of many other pioneers progressed steadily, it is significant that Taylor, too, increasingly appreciated the fuller meanings of his work, and out of such developing awareness he offered this concept of "the manager" in *The Principles of Scientific Management:*

These *new* duties of the manager are grouped under four heads:

1. They develop a science for each element of man's work, which replaces the old rule-of-thumb method.
2. They scientifically select and then train, teach, and develop the workman, whereas in the past he chose his own work and trained himself the best he could.
3. They heartily cooperate with the men so as to insure all the work being done in accordance with the principles of the science which have been developed.
4. There is an almost equal division of the work between the management and the workmen. The management takes over all work for which it is better fitted than the workmen, while in the past almost all of the work and the greater part of the responsibility were thrown upon the men.

And, in that same treatise, he ably summarized the powerful concepts which he had evolved and clarified in his more than 35 years of resourceful, persistent, and classified studies in these memorable words:

The writer is one of those who believes that more and more will the third party (the whole people), as it becomes acquainted with the true facts, insist that justice shall be done to all three parties (employer, employee, public). It will demand the largest efficiency from both employers and employees. It will no longer tolerate the type of employer who has his eye on dividends alone, who refuses to do his full share of the work and who merely cracks the whip over the heads of his workmen and attempts to drive them into harder work for low pay. No more will it tolerate tyranny on the part of labor which demands one increase after another in pay and shorter hours, while at the same time it becomes less, instead of more, efficient.

And the means which the writer firmly believes will be adopted to bring about, first, efficiency both in employer and employee, and then an equitable division of the profits of their joint efforts, will be scientific management, which has for its sole aim the attainment of justice for all three parties through impartial scientific investigation of all the elements of the problem.

For a time both sides will rebel against this advance. The workers will resent any interference with their old rule-of-thumb methods, and the management will resent being asked to take on new duties and burdens; but in the end the people, through enlightened public opinion, will force the new order of things upon both employer and employee. . . .

Scientific management does not necessarily involve any great invention, nor the discovery of new or startling facts. It does, however, involve a certain *combination* of elements which have not existed in the past, namely, old knowledge so collected, analyzed, grouped, and classified into laws and rules that it constitutes a science; accompanied by complete change in the mental attitude of the working men as well as of those on the side of management, toward each other, and toward their respective duties and responsibilities. Also a new division of the duties between the two sides and intimate, friendly cooperation to an extent that is impossible under the philosophy of the old management. . . .

It is no single element, but rather this whole combination, that constitutes scientific management, which may be summarized as:

Science, not rule-of-thumb
Harmony, not discord
Cooperation, not individualism
Maximum output, in place of restricted output
The development of each man to his greatest efficiency and prosperity

The time is fast going by for the great personal or individual achievement of any one man standing alone and without the help of those around him. And the time is coming when all great things will be done by that type of cooperation in which each man performs the function for which he is best suited, each man preserves his own individuality and is supreme in his particular function, and each man at the same time loses none of his originality and proper personal initiative, and yet is controlled by and must work harmoniously with many other men.

Both Taylor and the Gilbreths had thus restated, and indeed proved, two basic concepts which set the pattern of the industrial revolution over a hundred years before. Adam Smith, in *Wealth of Nations,* 1776, suggested the principle of the division of labor:

This great increase of the quantity of work which, in consequence of the division of labor, the same number of people are capable of performing, is owing to three different circumstances; first, to the increase of dexterity in every particular workman; second, to the saving of the time which is commonly lost in passing from one species of work to another; and lastly, to the invention of a great number of machines which facilitate and abridge labor, and enable one man to do the work of many.

This, of course, was the historical precedent of the work in the early 1900s which was concerned with the organization of production skills and which has since been extended and enlarged by the contributions of Engstrom, Maynard, Segur, and many others in this country and by fellow scholars and practitioners in these fields abroad.

Charles Babbage, British mathematician and scholar, provided the second governing concept of *transference of skill* in his *Economy of Machinery and Manufacture,* published in 1832:

That the master manufacturer, by dividing the work to be executed into different processes, each requiring different degrees of skills and force, can purchase exactly that precise quantity of both which is necessary for each process; whereas, if the whole work were executed by one workman, that person must possess sufficient skill to perform the most difficult, and sufficient strength to execute the most laborious, of the operations into which the art is divided.

It is interesting to compare the statements of Babbage and Taylor. Superficially, they seem to say much of the same; actually, Taylor's four principles of managing introduced the means by which Babbage's "transference of skill" *might be accomplished.* While many still think of Taylor as a seeker of cold efficiency, the true scope of his work is more accurately envisioned in this prefatory summation from his 1911 book:

The principal object of management should be to secure the maximum prosperity for the employer, coupled with the maximum prosperity for each employee.

The words "maximum prosperity" are used, in their broad sense, to mean not only large dividends for the company or owner, but the development of every branch of the business to its highest state of excellence, so that the prosperity may be permanent.

In the same way maximum prosperity for each employee means not only higher wages than are usually received by men of his class, but, of more importance still, it also means the development of each man to his state of maximum efficiency, so that he may be able to do, generally speaking, the highest grade of work for which his natural abilities fit him, and it further means giving him, when possible, this class of work to do. . . .

The majority of these men (employers and employees) believe that the fundamental interests of employees and employers are necessarily antagonistic. Scientific management, on the contrary, has for its very foundation the firm conviction that the true interests of the two are one and the same; that prosperity for the employer cannot exist through a long term of years unless it is accompanied by prosperity for the employee, and vice versa; and that it is possible to give the workman what he wants—a low labor cost—for his manufactures.[7]

Another milestone of considerable stimulative value was passed in connection with the testimony of Harrington Emerson, and other engineers before the Interstate Commerce Commission. In October of 1910, Louis D. Brandeis and Henry L. Gantt brought together a group of engineers to choose the most suitable designation for the new philosophy of management.

Mr. Brandeis was the principal attorney of freight shippers who were fighting the imposition of railroad rate increases. The essence of his strategy was to prove by competent testimony that a method existed whereby the railroads could not only reduce rates but could, at the same time, reduce costs and increase wages. He realized that the case would be strengthened if all his witnesses called the same things by the same names and would agree on a single name to designate the system of management they represented.

Mr. Emerson pointed out, under careful questioning by Mr. Brandeis, that the railroads of America could save at least a million dollars a day by the application of scientific principles to the operation of their business. Sudden realization among business leaders everywhere that the then proudest industrial achievement, the system of railroads, was actually something less than the flawless gem of American enterprise, brought at last the needed widespread attention and support the management movement had lacked and gave the newly chosen name, scientific management, an official introduction.

A conference of some 300 businessmen, consultants, and educators was called in 1912 at Tuck School at Dartmouth to discuss the possible courses of action uncovered by such new avenues of management thinking. The deliberations of these historic sessions, powerfully preserved by Harlow Persons, are considered by many scholars to mark the "charter" of an *organized* management movement in this country within which to progress and cumulate individual contributions in a meaningful way.

Almost overnight, scientific management became a matter of public concern and open debate. As so often happens, however, enthusiasm outran understanding. Although resistance to excesses was prompt, the "efficiency expert" became the apostle of exploitation in the eyes of the great body of labor, rather than a leader for mutual progress and agreement.

Among management people themselves there was still a further dissimilarity of enthusiasm, reflecting that human nature is the common characteristic of both the managerial and the individual worker. Traditionalists regarded the work of the management investigators as so much pap and set out on an active debunking movement, rooted in an attempt to maintain the only ways of work they could or wanted to understand. Progressives refused the challenge of a pointless battle and began to reevaluate their responsibilities as managers.

Contrast these two answers to a survey conducted by the American Society of Mechanical Engineers and quoted in the first of that association's *Ten Year Progress in Management Reports,* published in 1912, which from 1912 to 1932 were under the distinguished guidance of L. P. Alford. In response to a request for a definition of the new element in the art of management, the traditionalist viewpoint held:

I am not aware that a *new* element in the art of management has been discovered. . . . There have been no new discoveries in scientific management of industrial institutions. Common-sense men have used common-sense methods always. The term "scientific management" is a catch-word which assumes that industrial institutions have not been scientifically managed—which is not the case. My experience and the experience of my friends has been that there has been no new element injected into the art of management.

In the writer's opinion there is very little that is new about it (the art of management). There is hardly any part of it that has not been practiced by managers for the past 100 years. The trouble is there are not enough managers with sufficient initiative to set the system moving properly. . . .

The problem presented is not the adoption of something entirely new; but rather the extension to every detail of our work of something which we have already tried.

This was the classic pattern of the resistance. The writer made categorical admission of two basic hazards in the path of industrial development—the lack of adequately trained and inspired managers and the need for the extension of scientific method to the overall enterprise. He offered neither solution nor alternative and apparently was willing to believe that the changing nature of management was a fictitious academic dream.

The ASME Committee, with J. M. Dodge as chairman and Alford, himself, as secretary, rejected this concept of "impossibility" and selected from among the many favorable responses one which seemed best to convey the nature of the then so-new "science":

The best designation of the new element I believe to be "scientific manage-ment." This term already has been adopted quite generally and although frequently misused, carries with it the fundamental idea that the management of labor is a process requiring thorough analytical treatment and involving scientific as opposed to "rule-of-thumb" methods.

The writer ventures to define the new element briefly, but broadly, as: The critical observation, accurate description, analysis, and classification of all in-dustrial and business phenomena of a recurring nature, including all forms of cooperative human effort and the systematic application of the resulting records to secure the most economical and efficient production and regula-tion of future phenomena.

Stripped of technicalities the method of the modern efficiency engineer is simply this: First, to analyze and study each piece of work before it is per-formed; second, to decide how it can be done with a minimum of wasted motion and energy; third, to instruct the workman so that he may do the work in the manner selected as most efficient.

The Taylor System is not a method of pay, specific ruling of account books, not the use of high-speed steel. It is simply an honest, intelligent effort to arrive at the absolute control in every department; to let tabulated and unim-peachable fact take the place of individual opinion; to develop "team play" to its highest possibility.

As we conceive it, scientific management consists in the conscious application of the laws inherent in the practice of successful managers and in the laws of science in general. It has been called management engineering, which seems more fully to cover its general scope than a science.

The 1912 (ASME) Progress Report continues in reference to this second letter:

These quotations convey the ideas of a conscious effort to ascertain and study facts and systematically to apply them in instructing the workmen and in controlling every department of industry. Setting these against the underly-ing principle of the transference of skill, we conceive the prominent element in present-day industrial management to be: *The mental attitude that consciously applies the transference of skill to all the activities of industry.*

The work of the committee, advanced and comprehensive though it then was, of course still fell short of a full appreciation of the basic nature of scientific management. They rejected as inaccurate and muddled a suggested approach to a specific means of putting into practice the "attitude that consciously applies the transference of skill." In the light of present theory and practice, however, this statement by an unnamed correspondent of the committee is neither fatally inaccurate nor particularly muddled in conceptual understanding, even though the "functional foreman" concept which was advocated to permit specialization in skills has since been found to be less desirable than the single foreman backed and aided by functional staff specialists:

The regulative principles of management along scientific lines include four important elements:

a. Planning of the processes and operations in detail by a special department organized for this purpose.
b. Functional organization by which each man superintending the workman is responsible for a single line of effort. This is distinctly opposed to the older type of military organization, where every man in the management is given a combination of executive, legislative, and judicial functions.
c. Training the worker so as to require him to do each job in what has been found to be the best method of operation.
d. Equable payment of the workers based on quantity and quality of output of each individual. This involves scientific analysis of each operation to determine the proper time that should be required for its accomplishment and also high payment for the worker who obtains the object sought.

As a result of the interest in the railroad rate cases, of the Dartmouth meeting, and of the generally increased attention of engineers and the public, 1912 and 1913 saw the formation of many new associations. Most of them, at the time, were essentially either splinter groups broken off from the basic ASME body or else newly organized as a result of somewhat different objectives or the desire of specialists to emphasize special facets of the movement.

One of the most important of these new societies was also one of the most short lived. It was important because it numbered among its members of record that kind of mixture of outstanding industrial executives and business managers, as well as management scholars, theorists, educators, economists, and publicists, which has allowed theory and practice to crossfertilize each other as the American industrial society has evolved. Its name, the Efficiency Society, was unfortunate since the word "efficiency" had begun to have a rather caustic effect on the public. Its reasons for failure were, however, somewhat more fundamental. Charles Buxton Going, managing editor of *Engineer Magazine,* in outlining the purposes and objectives of the society wrote:

The essence of the efficiency movement is insistence upon a determination of standards of achievement—equitable and reasonable standards by which the ratio of useful result secured to the effort expended, or the expense incurred in any given case, may be compared with the ratio that should exist in a normal utilization of the agencies at hand. Efficiency does not demand or even encourage strenuousness. It does not impose or even countenance parsimony. It merely demands equivalence, equivalence between power supplied and work performed; equivalence between natural resources utilized and products obtained; equivalence between vital opportunity and individual or national health; equivalence between attainable degrees of security and the actual proportion of casualties; equivalence between production capacity and finished product.[8]

One can hardly take issue with the "insistence" or the "demands." Certainly they are only objectives which are approachable and beneficial to society.

Yet, there is an air of coldness and of compulsion about this statement which could hardly be expected to win understanding or reduce antagonism. What seemed to be essentially lacking was an adequate awareness that the man at the machine might value and protect his own conception of his own dignity—that in the last analysis any hope for a more efficient world would necessarily have to depend on making the worker aware and voluntarily appreciative of the fact that although his objectives and those of the enterprise might normally be different, both sets of objectives could only be achieved together; that is, that their desires were not mutually exclusive, merely different.

Requoting Taylor on this point: "Scientific management, on the contrary, has for its very foundation the firm conviction that the true interests of the two are one and the same. . . ."[9] Although, of course, Taylor generalized—the "true interest" often being overshadowed by the *apparent* interest—he clearly appreciated the nature and magnitude of the human problem.

So, also, did others. A. Hamilton Church and L. P. Alford, for example, wrote:

Some of the conditions of personal effectiveness are these: The individual must feel leadership; have adequate encouragement and reward; be physically fit and under good physical conditions; and receive a definite allotment of responsibility.

These conditions apply not only to the operative force but to all grades of employees. In fact, some of them apply with greater urgency to the man "higher-up" than to the actual worker.

The truth is, of course, that no single element of a system, or even a combination of half a dozen of such elements . . . more than touch the fringe of the questions. Highly organized systems may coexist with fine esprit de corps but the latter is not dependent on any form of system or organization.

Of all the conditions controlling a fine working atmosphere, leadership probably plays the most important part. . . . The weakness of one prominent school of management doctrine is that it pretends that it has superseded leadership by substituting therefor elaborate mechanism. Such a contention betrays a complete misapprehension of how men are constituted and of what the true functions of elaborate mechanisms really are. All such mechanism is but a collection of mechanical tentacles or feelers to enable the controlling mind and spirit of the management to be in several places at once. If personality behind these tentacles is a feeble one, the mechanism will not supplement its deficiencies in the slightest degree.[10]

This was the visionary concept which, in the hands of those who were to carry on the work, has been embellished and amplified as one of the basic tenets of the science of managing.

It found expression in the formation of such associations as the Society to Promote the Science of Management and the National Association of Corporation Schools, the latter group devoted primarily to the problems of training in industry. Somewhat later, in 1917, the growing interest in connection with war work led to the formation of the Society of Industrial Engineers.

Soundly conceived, these organizations grew in prestige over the years. The first and third eventually became the present Society for the Advancement of Management, and the second, also after mergers with others, became the present American Management Associations.

In reviewing the rise and fall of various management organizations, a possible key to their success or failure may be found in the answers to Professor Dwight Waldo's questions:

Are students of administration trying to solve the problem of human cooperation on too low a plane? Have they, by the double process of regarding more and more formal data over a wider and wider field of human organization, lost insight, penetration? Is formal analysis of organizations without regard to the purposes that inspire them but a tedious elaboration of the insignificant?[11]

Where the sights have been properly set, and the objectives honestly derived from the inherent obligations imposed on the work by the needs of society in general, and of individual human beings in particular, management associations have flourished. They are accepted now as a necessary and desirable professional component of our technological industrial society and are progressively expanding their contributions based on their sound foundation.

THINKING AHEAD, THINKING THROUGH, AND THINKING WHOLE

The years between 1912 and 1922, the date of Alford's second ASME progress report, were years of international unrest and of worldwide war. Demands on current material and human resources had required almost the total attention of management thinking, and the theoretical aspects of the report were, therefore, very nearly restatements of the 1912 report. *Practically*, however, it was an era of great advances, since the unprecedented demands of the war effort required the *application* of every organizational and functional skill at hand.

One of the characteristics of a science, the alternate play and shifting dominance of theory and practice as demanded by necessity, then became evident in the science of managing.

If it is possible to assess against one man the stimulation for making the theoretics of management into working realities during World War I, such appraisal would undoubtedly point to Bernard Baruch. Both in the specific structure of his War Industries Board, as it was finally constituted in 1918, and in substituting centralized and authoritative governmental planning for the free market and the law of supply and demand which in effect enforced efficient managerial attitudes by such devices as rigid priorities, fixed prices, and absolute schedules, he gave industry little choice but to streamline and clean house or to fail. Heavy production schedules and severely limited profits thus practically forced these industry leaders, who had not done so through foresight and conviction, to turn to scientific management as a means of survival.

Baruch seemed peculiarly gifted in his ability to look at the mobilization effort as essentially an economic proposition. He demanded, and finally received, authority to make decisions and enforce them over the total field of supply and demand of not only the materials of war itself, but over the total economy. Most important, however, he substantially avoided the inherent dictatorial dangers of such a concentration of power by delegating his authority to subordinates in order to put decision making in the hands of experienced economic and industrial experts who were close to the scene of action.

Out of the chaos of the 1914–1917 period, a time when the

president's Advisory Commission was in the untenable position of being asked to make decisions but prevented by charter from enforcing the decisions, the United States thus finally achieved the integration of its aims and its capabilities, aided, of course, by that terrible but effective commonness of purpose and spirit which the fires of war so rapidly forged. How it was done is summed up by James Tyson in these words:

The great principle followed throughout the board's dealing with industry was that of voluntary cooperation with the big stick in the closet. The biggest problem was to increase production so as to raise the output of industry up somewhere nearer the tremendous demands of the government. For this reason it was necessary to give business every encouragement, by allowing a margin of profit and also by attempting to arrive at an agreement with each trade before imposing conservation or other regulations. . . . From the time of his early attempts to bring producers together . . . he [Baruch] followed this policy of close alliance rather than one of arbitrary control.

Perhaps no better appraisal of the final forms of this cooperating could be found than the observation of Paul Von Hindenburg in his memoirs, when he said of American industry: "Her brilliant, if pitiless, war industry had entered the service of patriotism and had not failed it. Under the compulsion of military necessity a ruthless autocracy was at work and rightly, even in this land at the portals of which the Statue of Liberty flashes its blinding light across the sea. They understood war!" [12]

The principles of leadership include of necessity an understanding of the limitations of those who are led.

Whether these limitations are the result of tradition, of prejudice, or of apathy, they exist and have to be dealt with in an atmosphere of reality. That not every man wants to be or is capable of being captain of his own ship was demonstrated in the attempts of Edward and Lincoln Filene, who were both early theorists and early practitioners of scientific management, to put their famous Boston department store on a cooperative basis.

Edward Filene, described by one of his associates as an "ingenuous and ingenious idealist," embarked on a program in 1912 which, in the cold light of hindsight, was as noted for its impracticality as it was for its humanity. He and his brother tried desperately to encourage the interest and active participation of the workers in the enterprise by establishing a Cooperative Association together with plans for the eventual transfer of all stock to employees. Indifference toward the exercise of power and resistance toward assuming responsibility for their own corporate destiny on the part of the workers was so startlingly apparent that Lincoln Steffens facetiously suggested that Filene might have to hire some agitators to put his program across.

The effort to put the enterprise in the hands of the workers continued unsuccessfully for more than ten years. It failed, not because of basic violations of ethical standards or of public and employee interests, but because of the failure of the Filenes to establish a system of communication with their employees which would allow them to determine the employees' concept of the manager's and worker's common interests.

The failure, a personal disaster for Edward Filene, made nevertheless two significant contributions to the business community. It showed that managing is a mantle of responsibility not willingly accepted by all people. Moreover, it demonstrated the fundamental need for thorough and undistorted study of all the facets of a problem. Thus, it highlighted, for management theorists and practitioners, the importance of these three elements of business managerial thinking: Thinking ahead, thinking through, and thinking whole.

The Awakening of the Leadership Process

The awakening of the true nature of the modern American leadership process came about in the period following World War I. Now, at last, acute realization of the closely geared relationship of the business enterprise as an integral part of, and at the same time as a significant contributor to a general pattern of social development, was broadly achieved.

The story of this awakening in industry is, in large part, vividly reported in the gifted observations and writings of Mary Parker Follett. Her papers and lectures covering some 30 years of uniquely contributive observation are remarkable both for their breadth of application and for the penetrating understanding of motive and need.

She realized that the true quality of modern business leadership stems from the appreciation of the basic needs and aspirations and of the mutual dependence of men in a complex social organism. Throughout her long career Miss Follett was fortunate in having the friendship and advice of the many industry and business leaders, including especially many in the management of the New England Telephone and Telegraph Company, who shared with her the benefit of their experience, and for whom she was able to express the meaning and import of their work. Her relationships with the telephone system were especially fortunate because the gifted early managerial work of Theodore Vail, president of the parent company in the Bell System, had provided an environment of management by well-defined and far-seeing policies within a clearly designed functional organization structure that has in essence survived to this day and that was peculiarly appropriate for her perceptive observation and advice. Mary Follett received her formal education at Radcliffe College. Her work there and her subsequent contributions earned her a place among the college's 50 most distinguished graduates. Metcalf and Urwick, in their collection of her papers, *Dynamic Administration*, attempted to define the special quality of her attitudes which gave her work such significance. It is repeated here because it is, in a way, the definition of a rare managerial trait:

Mary Follett's outstanding characteristic was a facility for winning the confidence and esteem of those with whom she came in contact; she established a deeply rooted understanding and friendship with a wide circle of eminent men and women on both sides of the Atlantic. The root of this social gift was her vivid interest in life. Every individual's experience, his relations with others and with the social groups—large or small—of which he was a part, were the food for her thought. She listened with alert and kindly attention; she discussed problems in a temper which drew the best out of the individual with whom she was talking. The strength of the personal associations she thus built up were remarkable.

Miss Follett progressed from community activities to social work, and from there to vocational guidance and finally to business and industrial organization. In the latter work she drew heavily upon her experience in practical psychology, and her lectures and papers were strongly woven with the threads of understanding and sympathy. Her philosophy was, of course, the synthesis of the studies of many people concerned with the theory of organization.

In the meantime, Mrs. Gilbreth, like many others prominent in the history of the management movement, continued her analysis of industrial problems, delineating specific worker and manager attributes which contributed to the balance of the business economy. At the same time comprehensive full-length books began to supplement the shorter conference-type papers as the building blocks of the literature of management. Thus, such volumes as Mooney and Reiley's *Onward Industry,* and later their *Principles of Organization,* Fayol's *Industrial and General Administration,* Barnard's *The Functions of the Executive,* and Brown's *Industrial Organization* typify the magnitude and scope of the source material to which Miss Follett added her own observation and imagination. It is noteworthy also that these writers were practicing industrialists, two from General Motors, one from the mining industry, one from the Bell Telephone System, and the last from the Johns-Manville Corporation.

Such writings and those of many other leading industrialists, consultants, and educators afforded a firm base for the present comprehensive literature in this field. Thus, the following brief quotations from the Follett papers are, in fact, representative of the creative outpouring of an era rather than of a single person:

On conflict:

As conflict—difference—is here in the world, as we cannot avoid it, we should, I think, use it. Instead of condemning it, we should set it to work for us. . . . There are three main ways of dealing with conflict: domination, compromise, and integration. Domination, obviously, is a victory of one side over the other. This is the easiest way of dealing with conflict, the easiest for the moment but not usually successful in the long run.

The second way of dealing with conflict, that of compromise, we understand well, for it is the way we settle most of our controversies. . . . Yet no one really wants to compromise, because that means a giving up of something. Is there then any other method of ending conflict? There is a way beginning now to be recognized at least and occasionally followed: when two desires are *integrated,* that means that a solution has been found in which both desires have found a place, that neither side has to sacrifice anything.

On business as an integrative unity:

It seems to me that the first test of business administration, of industrial organization, should be whether you have a business with all its parts so coordinated, so moving together in their closely knit and adjusted activities, so linking, interlocking, interrelating, that they make a work unit—that is, not a congeries of separate pieces, but what I have called a functionwhole or integrative unity.

On the nature of power:

So far as my observation has gone, it seems to me that whereas power usually means power-over, the power of some person or group over some other person or group, it is possible to develop the conception of power-with, a jointly developed power, a co-active, not a coercive power.

On the psychology of consent and participation:

Many people are now getting beyond the consent-of-the-governed stage in their thinking, yet there are political scientists who are still advocating it. And, indeed, it is much better to have the consent of the governed than not to have it . . . but we are also recognizing today that it is only a first step; that not consent but participation is the right basis for all social relations.

The literature of management during the period between the two World Wars shows how completely Miss Follett's views gave expression to the framework which had become a fundamental part of the thinking of industry.

Although it would be impossible in this limited treatise to give even an indication of the wealth of writing done during this period, no paper on the history of management concepts would be possible without at least a partial mention of the many contributions made here and abroad. It is interesting to note the significant degree to which many of these fundamental books were the work of men whose professional careers had been directly concerned with business operations. Few of them were "writers," and it is almost by incidental and fortunate circumstances that their work is so readable, not discounting, of course, that clarity of conviction and of purpose are themselves no mean aids to such clarity of presentation.

Dr. Harry Arthur Hopf, whose own work will be discussed at a later point, listed 12 indispensable books, chiefly of this general period, and his reviews of five are so indicative of the form which the evolving "science of managing" was assuming that they deserve to be quoted here in part: [13]

The Philosophy of Management, by Oliver Sheldon (of Great Britain), was "written from a broad perspective; it stresses the importance of scientific and ethical principles, gives an excellent exposition of the social and industrial background, and deals in an authoritative manner with fundamentals of management."

Industrial and General Administration by Henri Fayol (a leading French manager of mining and industrial firms): "His masterly analysis of the essential functions of a business enterprise, his selection among them of administration for special treatment leading to a statement of five underlying principles, and his advocacy of the latter in the form of the administrative doctrine, combined to lay the foundation for a new school of thought known as 'Fayolism.' "

Top-Management Organization and Control, by Holden, Fish, and Smith (with combined experience in educational and industrial circles in California), "deals with a field which has hitherto been little explored. . . . On the strength of their research study of the management policies and practices of 31 leading American industrial corporations, the authors have performed the signally valuable service of bringing together, in admirably organized form, a great amount of factual and interpretive material bearing upon some of the most important and complex management problems with which large-scale industrial organization is confronted."

The Principles of Organization by Mooney and Reiley (of the General Motors organization) is a scholarly work dominated to a large extent by the historians' approach. It covers the history of the management effort as it has applied to the organization of the state, the church, the army, and industry. "This is not a work which may be readily mastered. Its careful study will, however, supply the reader with a sound framework of principles which will serve excellently the purpose of orientation."

Lectures on Organization by Russell Robb is a collection of the lectures delivered in the course on industrial organization at Harvard University. "The author, a distinguished engineer (connected with the Stone & Webster engineering, financing, and management organization) who died in 1927, brought admirably to expression in these lectures a varied experience distilled into a philosophy which, taken as a whole, constitutes perhaps the single most authoritative and appealing exposition stemming from an American to be found in the literature of organization."

Other indispensable books listed by Dr. Hopf were *The Design of Manufacturing Enterprises* by Walter Rautenstrauch, *Industrial Organization and Management* by Ralph Davis, *Industrial Management* by Lansburgh and Spriegel, *Budgetary Control* by James McKinsey, *Personnel Management* by Scott, Clothier, Mathewson, and Spriegel, *Functions of the Executive* by Chester Barnard, and *The Art of Leadership* by Ordway Tead. The role of these authors is also interesting, showing how such universities as Columbia, Ohio State, and Northwestern, as well as industrial firms, were centers of thought of the steadily evolving "science of managing."

In reading these books, the difference in emphasis in fundamental thinking during the twenties and thirties compared to that of the first two decades of the century is apparent. The essence of a deeper *philosophy* of scientific management was gradually being distilled and assembled out of the diverse objectives which had been the goals of early investigators. Overall planning and measurement were replacing the patchwork approach, and though detailed studies of particular situations were necessarily continued, they were increasingly referenced to the framework of the total social scene.

The basic developments of the period were those of bringing into closer blend a proper mixture of the workers' and managers' individual emotional needs and the requirements of an industrial enterprise constituted for the rigors of competitive life in an increasingly complex technological environment. The science of managing thus began to appreciate and encompass the techniques of multiplying human skills as well as mechanical power.

THE WORK OF HARRY ARTHUR HOPF

When the final review of the history of management during this half-century is written, perhaps it may seek a representative of the movement who, in his work and in his writing, symbolizes the search for the basic and irrefutable principles of the science. They will need to look no further than Dr. Harry Arthur Hopf. Except by an extensive firsthand study of his writings, which unfortunately consist of many separate talks and articles rather than bound volumes, it is impossible to gauge even closely the remarkable gifts he left as a legacy to the student and practitioner of today.[14]

Dr. Hopf, of English birth, came to America in 1898. His first job as a foreign language stenographer for an insurance company was an education in the unending frustration that was the normally accepted part of the nonmanagement employee in business and industry of the time. He observed the disorganization of enterprises devoted solely to the demands of day-to-day problems, the dissatisfactions that came from indecisive or arbitrarily decisive management, the absence of rewards and compensation related even vaguely to effort and contribution at every level.

Writing in *Net Results,* a regular publication of the Institute of Management he later established, Dr. Hopf said:

With courage (or was it foolhardiness?) and vigor I attacked several situations literally crying for improvement. It was then that I learned for the first time that the way of the reformer is hard, for it required years of the most arduous effort to win a sympathetic hearing for any suggestions. And with the advent of the new life insurance laws in New York State in 1907, my company, in common with other similar institutions, apparently surrendered itself to a case of paralysis of management which was destined to persist for some years. . . .

Arduous effort was the normal way of life for Dr. Hopf. His activity as an industrial and business advisor, his participation as founder and pilot of expanded management society activities, his work as a government consultant during both major wars, his seemingly endless capacity to study, to understand, and to offer solutions for the basic problems of the management science paint a picture of nearly legendary proportions.

Out of his many and varied contributions, two, perhaps more than any others, have earned him an enduring place in the annals of the management movement. Dr. Hopf in his studies of the life insurance business was concerned, of course, with the problem of net efficiency. He noted that the criteria of success were universally related to size, and that these criteria were both wrong and potentially disastrous. Investigations into other industries revealed that this universality was not confined to the insurance business, but that nearly everyone engaged in industry just assumed that the bigger they were, the better, the more efficient, and the more secure they were.

At the Sixth International Congress for Scientific Management, held in London in 1935, he suggested that the time was ripe for the strengthening of the science of management and its transformation to the more inclusive one: optimology—the science of the optimum. In this talk Dr. Hopf said:

Among the most profound problems with which society must concern itself under present-day conditions is that relating to the determination, achievement, and maintenance of optimal conditions in all types of organized human enterprise. The overwhelming economic disaster, from the effects of which the world is still suffering, halted with ruthless force an era of unparalleled expansion which, in the United States of America at least, assumed proportions indicative of a belief in the feasibility of unlimited growth and unchecked size.

As we falteringly proceed upon the road to recovery, we are faced with new political, social, and economic trends and doctrines which are evidently destined to bring into being forms of organization and control without precedent in our experience, and to call for qualities of cooperation and joint action on the part of businessmen, engineers, social scientists, government officials, labor representatives, and others, far beyond any need of the past. Having then narrowly escaped complete destruction upon the rock of Scylla, are we now being drawn with increasing force into the whirlpool of Charybdis?

Dr. Hopf defined the optimum—for government as well as business—as that state of development of an enterprise which, when reached and maintained, tends to perpetuate an equilibrium among the factors of size, cost, and human capacity which would provide ideal realization of the organizational objectives, and he pointed out that the optimum size was at this state of equilibrium rather than connected, in any way, with bigness alone.

Although Hopf placed no arbitrary limitations on size, he demonstrated that perpetuation of a growing enterprise depended upon the concomitant upward shifting of the equilibrium point. He emphasized that the natural economic barriers to growth are rarely reached, but that the limiting barriers were, most generally, organizational in nature.

In concluding his paper, Dr. Hopf restated a conception of a method of formulating a technique to determine optimal size and relationships which he had originally presented at a meeting of the Taylor Society in 1930. They have become almost a working code of the mid-century science of management:

1. Establish the objectives of the business in comprehensive terms.
2. Define those general policies which should be followed regardless of operating conditions or results.
3. Define the task of management in human terms.
4. Staff the executive group with members who are competent to perform successfully the tasks assigned to them.
5. Furnish the executive group with standards of accomplishment by which performance can be accurately measured.
6. Study operating results and establish trends of accomplishment.
7. Adjust the rate of replacement of members of the executive group in line with requirements for maintaining the standards set.
8. Consider particularly the factor of age in its relation to productive capacity of executives.
9. Analyze all dynamic elements so as to discern the possible operation of the law of diminishing returns with respect to any element, substituting measurement for judgment, wherever possible.
10. Establish the optimal size of organization at the level at which the most favorable operating results can be secured, within the limits of the predetermined objectives and policies and without causing an executive overload at any point in the organization.

Dr. Hopf argued vigorously throughout his life for new perspectives in management. He believed that managing, as such, had to become a special and professional activity. In speaking before the Society of Industrial Engineers in 1933, he quoted Dennison and Willitts' [15] classic definition of a profession:

1. A profession is an occupation which requires intellectual training as contrasted with mechanical skill.
2. A profession employs the fruits of science, uses the scientifc method, and maintains an experimental attitude toward information.
3. The professed knowledge is used by its applicant to the service of others, usually in a manner governed by a code of ethics.
4. The amount of financial return is not the chief measure of success.
5. The professions are given public and often legal recognition.

Dr. Hopf examined the work of managing in the light of these criteria, seeking to establish a system of methods which would allow the professional manager to apply the first three as operational techniques. He suggested four basic divisions of the work as forming the dynamics of management: planning, organizing, coordinating, and controlling, a significant and penetrating pioneer attempt to divide the overall work of the professional manager into primary constituent elements.

In describing the meaning of these four key words, Dr. Hopf continued:

The first of these (planning) involves subdivision of activities to a point where they are within the compass of performance by persons of moderate ability. Failure to observe the requirement is bound to result in the creation of undue supervisory burdens and in obstructions to the smooth flow of operating routines.

The second requirement (organizing) calls for proper relative evaluation of operating units and their grouping along related lines. When the maintenance of arbitrary lines of demarcation among departments, bureaus, divisions, sections, branches, units, etc., comes to be regarded as of greater importance than preservation of the integrity of operating procedures, only disorganization and consequent lack of coordination ensues. . . .

The third requirement (coordinating) is the establishment of clear lines of authority, responsibility, and reporting relationships. . . . Maintenance of clear lines of authority, responsibility, and reporting relationships under this type of control hinges to a large extent upon integration of the often divergent concepts held by the administrators of the manner in which their relationships to one another shall be composed and of the character of personal supervision over the organization which each shall exercise.

The fourth requirement (controlling) goes right to the root of the problem of administrative coordination. It involves the separation of planning from performance, a sine qua non of effective organization. Progress in undertaking such separation is often attended by conflicts between the points of view of the staff, which is responsible for planning, and the line, which is charged with the accomplishment of satisfactory operating results. Unless conflicts can be resolved in favor of cooperative action, sound conditions of administrative coordination are impossible.

Like other great concepts in the philosophies, this one is deceptive in its simplicity. Its value as a working thesis, however, is unquestioned, for, with relatively evolutionary changes, it points yet to most of the basic keys to successful and professional managing.

The range of Dr. Hopf's work encompassed practically all areas of business thinking in both its current and its historical and in both its national and its international aspects. He was at once the theoretician and the practical man, the dreamer and the doer, the pragmatic statistician and the adventurous explorer. These words of Woodrow Wilson on the nature of leadership, written many years before Dr. Hopf's death, well describe this "first universal man of management": [16]

That the leader of men must have such sympathetic insight as shall enable him to know quite unerringly the motives which move other men in the mass is of course self-evident; but this insight which he must have is not the Shakespearean insight. It need not pierce the particular secrets of individual men: it need only know what it is that lies waiting to be stirred in the minds and purposes of groups and masses of men.[17]

THE CONCEPT OF THE PROFESSIONAL MANAGER

The modern science of managing in its evolving full dimensions has come from this historical background, but is nonetheless a true product of our own current day.

It is the application of ethical principles by qualified professional managers to the problems of creating and maintaining a complex pattern of order which serves, in optimum fashion, the common interests of the people—that is, of the customers and the public as well as the owners, the executives, and the employees—and of the enterprise itself as a key and characteristic element of today's industrial society.

Inherent in the acceptance of such a statement is the responsibility to determine the ethical principles which govern a situation, the qualifications of a professional manager, the pattern of order, and the common interests.

The ethical principles can be briefed simply. To have meaning and to generate faith, a genuine science of managing can only exist in a climate of liberty, of reason, of morality, and of religion. Outside it—in an air of compulsion, force, materialism, and atheism—it is reduced to impotence and cannot exist any more than the civilization of which it is a part can continue under such circumstances.

Deeply grounded in the understanding of our position is the acceptance of the natural rights of the individual as a natural person and that these, coming to him as a person in his own right, transcend in importance these other rights of society as an organized grouping of such individuals where functions come from them to be exercised for them. The individual creates his society not by self-abrogation of these rights, but by his voluntary modification of his liberties derived from them. This is the common interest. This makes possible those kinds of common purpose which justify joint teamwork in organized activities.

Dr. Einstein describes the temperament of the individual as an essentially independent being who willingly becomes a part of and accepts the obligations of a social environment:

Man is, at one and the same time, a solitary being and a social being. As a solitary being, he attempts to protect his own existence and that of those who are closest to him, to satisfy his personal desires, and to develop his innate abilities. As a social being, he seeks to gain the recognition and affection of his fellow human beings, to share in their pleasures, to comfort them in their sorrows, and to improve their conditions of life. . . . The abstract concept "society" means to the individual human being the sum total of his direct and indirect relations to his contemporaries and to all people of earlier generations. The individual is able to think, feel, strive, and work by himself; but he depends so much upon society—in his physical, intellectual, and emotional existence—that it is impossible to think of him, or to understand him, outside the framework of society.[18]

In order to join his personal aspirations understandingly and satisfyingly with those of the society of which he is a part, it has become more and more necessary for man to seek for a rational pattern within which to guide and govern his actions. The patterns of order which constitute the goals of this elemental search of all people are achieved by the integration of the results of observation into generalized laws which can be applied with measurably successful results.

Writing of *Management and the American Future*,[19] L. H. Appley, then President of the American Management Associations, characterized the professional manager as "an individual who, because of his training, experience, and competence, is employed to develop and expand the assets and realizations of owners." His horizons might well have been widened to include every conceivable area of human effort where leadership is a necessity.

The concept of professional managing as leadership by persuasion rather than by command, and the codification of the professional manager's distinct and unique work into the four subfunctional elements of planning, organizing, integrating, and measuring, is another of the hard-won milestones in the development of a true science of managing.[20]

Speaking of the emphasis placed on developing professional managers by General Electric Company, Ralph G. Cordiner said:

In such an approach is plainly found one deep source of our basic business climate which has made possible the productivity and the better living standards for more and more people which have literally thrust our country into its present position of worldwide leadership and responsibility. But this in turn brings new need to seek how to do a better and more professional job of management.

J. Wilson Newman, President of Dun and Bradstreet, added further understanding of the significance of the professional manager concept when he said:

Free enterprise brings up the subject of free will and decisions. In our country a man can risk his money, time, and skill in business without restraint. That is the way it should be, but as suppliers we are morally obligated to help him with all the friendly guidance we can offer. There is increasing evidence, too, that the new generation of entrepreneurs are better equipped in experience and understanding than were their fathers or grandfathers, although the hazards they face today are certainly greater and more complex . . .

Yet the basic problem is human and emotional rather than statistical. All the fixed operating data can be offset by the intangibles of human nature. The impulse to business risk isn't generated in statistics. It finds life in the eye of the individual who sees an opportunity and measures the risk to achieve it. The quality of his judgment is tested by his ability to overcome obstacles.[21]

THE ADVENT OF AUTOMATION

During the years of World War II, a new understanding of the problems born of organizations came into being. As in the time of the first World War, the demands of survival speeded the acceptance of the theories of the science of managing. Again, practice caught up with theory, but this time a new technology brought time for new horizons.

Again, spurred by the fires of war, the managers of American business, together with the scientists as their partners, and with the spirit of both workers and soldiers to turn ideas and plans to reality, rose to new heights. Global logistics set the demands; the competitive enterprise system, modified once more by governmental production direction, met the challenge.

But this time the scientific sweat of the ensuing decades provided a lubricant that allowed a multiplication of output almost fantastic in retrospect. The *principles* of managing enterprises of wide span and great diversity proved flexible enough to meet the test; and to allow the approach of leadership by persuasion once again to vanquish the totalitarian, or command, bid for supremacy.

A most significant factor in this period was that the principle of "division of labor" was successfully applied to the work of managing, itself, to entirely new degrees. The whole philosophy of decentralization developed to new dimensions, not merely decentralization to new geographic areas and to new plants, or even decentralization to separate "product businesses" within a common corporate framework, but actually as Mr. Cordiner said in a memorable address to the American Management Associations in 1945, "the decentralization of decision-making itself," so that the authority actually to *decide* was as close as possible to the work or action specifically calling for decisions.

Once more Dr. Hopf was chosen to summarize these trends. In an article called *Evolution in Organization During the Past Decade,* presented at the first postwar International Management Congress of CIOS at Stockholm in 1947, he listed the following outstanding managerial trends and advances since the seventh CIOS Congress in Washington in 1939:

1. Development of the personnel function.
2. Decentralization of management and operation.
3. Increased recognition and application of general principles of organization.
4. Creation of new units of organization to meet increasing economic and social responsibilities.
5. Improvement of techniques for policy formulation and execution.

It is also important to note at this point that the United States management societies were active contributors to the war effort, satisfying the insistent pleas of industry for technical aid, and, at the same time, following a process of continual measuring, tempering, and reapplication of organizational and operating principles.

Such ability to handle problems—of overwhelming magnitude compared to those of the first war—and to simultaneously continue to advance the science of managing was due, in no small part, to the newly developing techniques of organizational communications. The engineer proved once again that the essential nature of managing was a derivative of the scientific method and that his place in guiding the affairs of men was essential to the vitality of the movement, not mere accident or prior right.

Scientists and engineers who had worked to establish a factual basis on which communications systems could be predicated came to realize the general resemblance of large social patterns to those of specific electrical or mechanical networks. Dr. Norbert Wiener, who is widely credited with leading the study and with coining the name "cybernetics" from the Greek word meaning the art of the pilot or steersman, said:

One of the most interesting aspects of the world is that it may be considered to be made up of patterns. A pattern is essentially an arrangement. It is characterized by the order of the elements of which it is made, rather than by the intrinsic nature of these elements.[22]

He went on further to point out that a pattern can be used to convey information and will usually convey more information than the statement of isolated facts since it also conveys interrelations.

Dr. Wiener made the penetrating observation that there is implied in the adoption of automation as an outgrowth of cybernetics a transcending problem, for economic and for political and social statesmen alike, in "handling the social-political responsibility to see that some way of handling their [the permanently displaced workers'] leisure is provided, to make them fit into a society that is a going concern—since, in the face of radical changes, the statesmanship of management cannot stop at the edge of the individual firm."[23]

Dr. Claude Shannon of the Bell Telephone Laboratories and others carried Wiener's structural concept into fields which provided the management scientist with working theories which would allow him to apply and measure the principles of professional management in rigorous fashion.

In the first place, they established the importance of effective communications as the key to proper operation of any system involving more than a single element. What was true of the electrical network was true in even larger measure of the corporate enterprise.

Thus, Wiener, Shannon, and their associates and contemporaries believed that "one of the lessons of cybernetics is that any organism is held together by the possession of means for the acquisition, use, retention, and transmission of information" and that "communication of information is a problem in stat..tics . . . and that the theory, of course, does more than express a philosophy of communication, it provides universal measures." [24]

The ability to transmit directive information to implement change and the ability to feed back the results of the change was shown to be a function of the use of optimum channels through the minimum number of transfer or recording points. In terms of the enterprise, as an organic whole, they showed that effective operation can only be achieved when directive information, the result of decision making, is created and applied as close as possible to the point of action, and when the channels of information, transmission, and performance feedback are soundly conceived. Thus, they further affirmed the soundness of the widespread decentralization of managerial authority and responsibility, so characteristic of this period, which has to an astounding extent allowed customer and public benefits from the combined social acceptability of the relatively small decentralized business and the technological and other resources of the larger modern corporation.

In the second place, the cyberneticists showed the possibilities of mathematical analysis in problems of business organization. Dr. Zay Jeffries, scientist and retired vice-president of the General Electric Company, said in 1951:

Our progress depends to a considerable extent on seeing to it that simplification processes move forward in approximate balance with the complicating processes. If this can be accomplished, then individuals with given ability can expect to go forward indefinitely without becoming casualties of their own complexity.

The simplification processes for scientific management are many, but are greatly multiplied today by the rapid emergence of essentially statistical, mathematical, and logical method. These latter kinds of developments are divorced from traditional actuarial methods by the special attitudes of mind that bring them into play. Three essential steps form the basic technique which distinguishes the work:

1. Thorough exploration and precise, understandable documentation of facts concerned in an operation will reveal broad principles and parameters, or governing factors and variables.

2. The discovered principles and parameters may, in most instances, be defined quantitatively and manipulated with predictable results, so long as the system of which they are a part is essentially stable, as the fairly mature business characteristically tends to be.

3. The disclosure of principles and the studied manipulation of parameters will provide optimum procedures and processes, measurable work simplification, great precision of guidance, and better management.

This is the technique of what is now coming to be called "operations research and synthesis." Thus, the mathematician provided the professional manager not only with applicable theories, but he has also provided him with an important working tool.

The general use of computers in speeding the analysis and interpretation of the operations research process is growing rapidly and is facilitating the managerial approach based on "thinking through" to an ever more useful degree; which incidentally but reaffirms the perceptive foresight of Taylor in taking his steel plant data, and his speeds and feeds formulas, to the mathematicians for solution even before the turn of the twentieth century.

Such use of today's modern electronics computers, moreover, progressively allows the pretesting of an almost unlimited number of variables to determine their interrelation and their individual effect on alternative end objectives. Scientific management has thus, in effect, been handed the priceless technique of telescoping the time required in analyzing its course to an entirely new degree.

OTHER CONTRIBUTORS TO THE MANAGEMENT MOVEMENT

This "history" of the evolution of the management movement in America has, by definition, concerned itself only casually and but little with the great and important contributions of the many theorists and experimenters in the field in Europe and other parts of the world. The development of basic principles has in no sense, of course, been a purely American effort, so, in fairness, it must be pointed out that the "history" written here is thus only one American expression of what has, in fact, been a worldwide search.

CIOS, the International Committee for Scientific Management, has acted in behalf of some 20 or more member-organizations of the free world. Since its foundation in 1926, it has been a potent force in sustaining international amity through trying economic and political times. The Gold Medal of CIOS is thus widely recognized as a symbol of the highest achievement in the management field.

Another omission, necessary since this paper has dealt with the concepts of the science of managing, has been the catalytic activities of our own government, except when government direction has superseded normal economic interplay under the stress of global-scale war. However, the national government, representing the interests of all the people, has had the responsibility of maintaining balance among all these interests and consequently has influenced sharply, by both positive and negative stimulation, the creation of a distinctly American form of capitalism which is now enjoined by its very nature from being monopolistic.

The resultant competitive atmosphere, inherent in this philosophy of capitalism, has been one of the significant spurring forces which has helped to move scientific management out of the library or classroom and into the shop.

Despite all the natural forces of both politics and bureaucracy, starting with the introduction of cost cards in the Frankford Arsenal in the 1880s by Henry Metcalf and continuing through to the present day, various departments of the government have made active use of the techniques of scientific management in their own operations.

Particularly notable are, of course, the long and constructive contributions of Mr. Herbert Hoover, who, as Secretary of Commerce in the mid-twenties, made significant steps in the elimination of waste in industry and in the standardization of products; and who, with the great first President Masaryk of the then new republic of Czechoslovakia, was co-sponsor of the first International Management Congress at Prague in 1924. As President, Mr. Hoover later began a program for the improvement of governmental bureaus, and, as Chairman of the Committee on Organization of the Executive Branch of the Government, he continued this work years later during 1948 and 1949, and again in 1953 and 1954.

THE PRESENT STATUS OF THE SCIENCE OF MANAGING

What, then, is the present status of the science of managing? Is it, in the words of Mr. A. M. Lederer, the "fifth force," equal to and as necessary as the forces for labor, owners, government, and consumers? [25]

It would seem, in practice today, impossible to deny the importance of management without denying simultaneously the factual nature and complexity of our current technological culture. In accepting the inevitable pattern which lies ahead, the place of such a fifth force is thus evident, and the character and quality of the professional manager who will both guide and discipline this "force" is of lasting moment.

In a paper written in 1951, *Notes on a Theory of Advice,* Lyman Bryson of Columbia University emphasized the important obligation of the professional manager with respect to the integration of knowledge and authority which are essential counterparts of the managing function:

The function of advice is one of the oldest in human affairs and certain abstract generalizations about it that could have been made in paleolithic times are still true.

Most of these generalizations, however, have not been made and, as far as can be discovered, no standard treatise in this field has ever been written.

There are mountain piles of books on salesmanship, which is not disinterested advice, and a molehill of books on leadership, but nothing on the technique and difficulties of trying to put knowledge at the service of power.

The right relation of knowledge and power is, however, one of the big problems of our age.

We need to give the closest scrutiny to the processes whereby decisions are made, and the effect on those decisions of rational information, if we are to master the difficulties of freedom in a time when power is so developed and knowledge is so dispersed.

The function of advice is one of the crucial points in that relation and on that account may well be studied first.

Peter Drucker, in the face of such conditions, well describes the threefold job of the manager in connection with today's business enterprise. By substituting country, institution, family, or any of the collective nouns which represent group entities for the word "company" and "enterprise," the universal nature of the "manager's" job, in this sense, is readily made apparent. As Professor Drucker puts it:

It is management's first responsibility to decide what economic factors and trends are likely to affect the company's future welfare.

The second function of management is the organization and efficient utilization of the enterprise's human resources. In the industrial enterprise it is not individuals who produce, but a human organization.

The third major function of management is to provide a functioning management. This means that management has to provide for its own succession. . . . It is tomorrow's management that will determine whether the enterprise will prosper ten years hence and indeed whether it will survive. . . . Today's management can at least make sure that there will be available to make tomorrow's decisions men who are fully qualified, fully trained, and fully tested in actual performance.[26]

Similar growing awareness of the necessity and almost universal applicability of the managerial functions in all areas of society has become truly international in scope. For instance, Mr. Lederer in mid-1953 described to members of the Council for International Progress in Management (U.S.A.) a renaissance of European industry which "finds its expression in a European management movement eager to catch up with a comparable management movement in the United States, which has its roots in the same philosophical belief and which has translated that belief into practical applications to an industrial society." [27]

The enduring place of the scientific management movement, therefore, seems assured. To those who have made a professional life of its study or practice, these further words of Lawrence Appley may serve as both encouragement and credo:

The future of America is dependent upon the caliber of management to be found in the ranks of business and industry. It is management that sets the pace and motivates labor to do its job. It is the combination of a courageous, competent management and a high-moraled, highly productive labor force that makes more things available for more people, and therefore, increases the standard of living.

This management competency which is able to motivate labor to greater productivity requires sensitivity to certain moral obligations to the community. It must be understood by such management that our present form of society can be preserved only when those on the receiving end of leadership experience that for which democracy stands. If people are to know what a democracy really is, then they must enjoy its benefits in their work, as well as in their play. They must really feel and believe that their bosses are interested in them as individuals and in their development to the fullest potential of character, personality, and individual productivity.

The greatest doctors, teachers, lawyers, and engineers are those who have some sense of the human values involved in their work. So it is and will continue to be with managers. The price of leadership is criticism, but its more-than-compensating reward is sense of attainment.[28]

In 150 years we have come from narrow and dimly perceived horizons into a world of limitless possibilities and new scientific, as well as human, frontiers. The science of managing is, like all true sciences, creating an expanding universe of concepts and principles. Because it has come to recognize its problems as a part of, and a party to, the nature of our culture, it will continue as an unabating challenge to thought and ingenuity so long as free men continue to join in common effort to achieve desired ends.

NOTES AND REFERENCES

1. Albert Einstein, *Out of My Later Years* (New York: Philosophical Library, 1950), p. 72.
2. Ortega y Gasset, *Mission of the University* (London: Kegan Paul, 1946), p. 146.
3. A. N. Whitehead, *Science and the Modern World* (London: Macmillan, 1925).
4. Gustave LeBon, *The Crowd* (London: Ernest Benn Ltd., 1952), p. 24.
5. References in this chapter to individual practitioners and writers on scientific management are made solely to indicate by example the progression of ideas that developed with changing times. This paper is not an attempt to mention systematically even the outstanding pioneers of the management movement. For a systematic listing of such pioneers, and for a comprehensive presentation of their contributions, see the *Golden Book of Management*, prepared by CIOS, the Comité International de L'Organization Scientifique, with headquarters at Geneva, Switzerland, which now represents the organized management societies of free nations at the international level. Any attempt to list even the leading current authorities in the field would require another large book in itself.
6. Lyndall F. Urwick, "Management's Debt to the Engineers," the ASME Calvin W. Rice Lecture.
7. Frederick W. Taylor, *The Principles of Scientific Management* (New York: Harper & Bros., 1911), pp. 9–10.
8. Charles Buxton Going, *The Efficiency Movement. An Outline*, Efficiency Society, Inc., Transactions, 1912, Vol. I, p. 13.
9. Taylor, *The Principles of Scientific Management*, p. 9.
10. A. Hamilton Church and L. P. Alford, "The Principles of Management," *American Machinist*, May 30, 1912.
11. Dwight Waldo, *The Administrative State* (New York: The Ronald Press, 1948), p. 211.
12. James L. Tyson, "The War Industries Board, 1917–18," *Fortune* supplement, September 1940, p. 16.
13. Harry A. Hopf, *Soundings in the Literature of Management*, Hopf Institute of Management, Publication No. 6.
14. A two-volume set of Hopf's writing is now available from the Hive Press, Eaton, Pa.

15. Henry S. Dennison, of the Dennison Manufacturing Company, and Joseph H. Willitts, of the University of Pennsylvania.
16. As he was called, in memoriam, in *Net Results* for October 1949. Alvin E. Dodd, Executive Vice-Chairman, U.S. Council of the International Chamber of Commerce and President Emeritus, American Management Associations, and many other business and industrial leaders paid a final tribute to Dr. Hopf through the medium of this little magazine which he and Mrs. Hopf had written for so many years.
17. Woodrow Wilson, *Leaders of Men* (Princeton, N.J.: Princeton University Press, 1952).
18. Einstein, *Out of My Later Years,* p. 126. It is significant that in still later writings, Dr. Einstein—now clearly established as one of the foremost scientists of the ages—goes on to reject the concept of a purely random and patternless universe, in the striking phrase, "I cannot believe that God plays dice with the cosmos."
19. *Management at Mid-Century,* General Management Series No. 169 (New York: American Management Associations, 1954), p. 5.
20. The modification of Dr. Hopf's earlier concept of "planning, organizing, coordinating, and controlling," and the rejection of such incomplete classifications as "planning, organizing, and commanding," is apparent. Coordinating is the bringing together of actions; integrating implies unifying to form a complete whole. Control, Dr. Hopf's word, involves the exercise of guiding or restraining power, but such action inherently denies the substance of other subfunctions. Measuring is the process of reviewing performance against predetermined standards for the predicted results of planning, of making such measurements known, and thus of providing a corrective feedback to the process, so that replanning, reorganizing, and reintegrating may proceed; thus recognizing the need in organized efforts for objectives, policies, and clear structure on the one hand and for dynamic and vital progress on the other hand.
21. *Management at Mid-Century,* p. 21.
22. Norbert Wiener, *The Human Use of Human Beings* (Boston: Houghton Mifflin, 1954).
23. Meeting of New York Chapter of the Society for the Advancement of Management, 1950.
24. Francis Bello, "The Information Theory," *Fortune,* December 1953.
25. Mr. Lederer, partner in the consulting firm of Morris and VanWormer, is President of the Council for International Progress in Management (U.S.A.) and Deputy President of CIOS.
26. Peter F. Drucker, *The New Society* (New York: Harper, 1949), p. 204. See also Drucker's earlier books on *The End of Economic Man, The Future of Industrial Man, Concept of the Corporation,* and his later work, *The Practice of Management.*
27. President's Report for First Six Months, CIPM, 1953.
28. Lawrence A. Appley, *Management and the American Future,* General Management Series No. 169 (New York: American Management Associations, 1954), p. 13.

Reginald H. Jones

19
The Evolution of Management Strategy at General Electric

As most people who knew Harold Smiddy are very much aware, he was heavily involved in the decentralization of the General Electric Company back in the early 1950s. As vice-president—management consultation services under Chief Executive Ralph Cordiner, Harold acted as the architect for a whole new management system for the company.

Much has been said and written about that reorganization [1] and it furnished an archetype which many other diversified companies later followed. Much less, however, has been documented regarding the quarter century of organizational evolution which followed that massive change. The General Electric Company of 1978, as we celebrate our one hundredth anniversary, is perhaps as different from the General Electric of 1955 as the newly decentralized company of 1955 was different from the highly centralized institution which preceded it. Yet much of the heritage that Harold, Ralph, and their associates passed on to the present stewards of the business is inextricably woven into our management fabric—as applicable today as it was 25 years ago.

In this chapter, I shall trace some of the major changes in General Electric over the past quarter century, relating these changes to

313

the philosophical backdrop provided by those in Harold's era. This can best be done by examining the evolution of what are today five of General Electric's most pervasive management strategy themes:

Diversification via organic growth
Manageability via controlled decentralization
Earnings growth via selectivity in resource allocation
Risk containment via diversification and selectivity
Renewal via anticipatory/evolutionary change

These management strategy themes were not the outcome of holistic philosophizing or even the result of integrated and objective weighing of alternatives. Instead, they emerged one by one in cumulative fashion over the years as our unique corporate personality and management ethic have developed.

1878–1955: A POTENTIAL GIANT DEVELOPS

General Electric dates back to 1878 when a group of investors joined to finance Thomas Edison's experiments with the incandescent lamp. Early in its history, the company grew largely by acquisition and merger. Later, as it evolved from a company concerned with lighting to a company dedicated to the benign circle of electrical power—the generation, transmission, distribution, control, measurement, and use of electricity—it trended gradually away from acquisitions and relied heavily upon growth from within.

While this organic growth understandably took the company into all facets of electrical manufacturing, it also led down several paths leading to diversification. For example, financing of appliances led General Electric into consumer and later into commercial credit businesses. Defense work carried out during World War II led the company from production of superchargers for propeller-driven aircraft into jet engines. Similarly, radar and sonar led to missile guidance and space exploration. A fertile research and development lab led to man-made diamonds, silicones, and engineered materials. A government contract to run the Hanford Atomic Power Operation led General Electric into commercial nuclear energy products.

By 1950, General Electric's sales were over $2 billion. Its policy of growth from within had already turned it into one of the more diversified companies in the nation. It was engaged in 13 of the 21 basic manufacturing industries then defined by the U.S. Department of Commerce and sold its products into all 21.

But President Charles Wilson saw that the company would never reach its true potential with a top-heavy, highly centralized, functional organization structure. The company's great diversity and growing complexity required a different decision-making pattern than centralization provided and a much more flexible organization structure. Wilson brought in Ralph Cordiner (who in turn brought in Harold Smiddy) to attack this problem. Their response: Decentralize the company into profit and loss accountable business units "small enough for one man to get his arms around." These business units, called product departments, would be like small companies each with specific competitors in the marketplace. Delegation of authority for business decision making to the general managers of these small product departments was high. Counterbalancing this delegation, however, were a set of corporate policies and a carefully developed system of measurements and financial controls. Thus the resources leverage of a large company would be blended with the agility and intense product/market knowledge of small companies. Decisions would be made at the point closest to the action, not up in the "ivory tower."

Nearly 100 of these product departments were defined and there was thus a need to provide span-breaking echelons between the president and the departments. Accordingly, the departments were aggregated into 23 divisions and the divisions into 5 groups—the groups and divisions being charged with longer-range planning and business development responsibilities as well as hierarchical management review and approval.

Thus, in five change-laden years (1951–1955), the company was decentralized to meet the anticipated needs and opportunities of the 1960s and 1970s. Interestingly, all of this was accomplished during a very healthy period for the company. Sales had grown by more than 50 percent and earnings had increased commensurately over the 1950–1955 period. By 1955, three of our present prime management strategy themes were already quite evident.

Diversification via organic growth
Manageability via controlled decentralization
Renewal via anticipatory/evolutionary change

1956–1967: THE POSTDECENTRALIZATION PERIOD

During the next 12 years (1956–1967), General Electric grew to nearly four times its 1950 size—to an $8 billion company in 1967. A generation of management had become familiar with the tenets of decentralization. Yet Fred Borch, who had become president and chief executive officer in 1963, grew increasingly uneasy as to whether the desired and targeted growth pattern could be sustained. Some product departments had grown to be very large and complex components, perhaps too large and complex for "one man to get his arms around." Thus, in late 1967, he took the major step of again reorganizing the company.

This reorganization, unlike decentralization in the 1950s, was more an arithmetical than a conceptual change. Group-level components were increased to 10 from 5, divisions increased to 45, and departments to well over 150. As a further example of diversification via organic growth, one of the 1967 group-level components—information systems—had not even attained department size in 1955. By 1967, GE had increased its participation in the 21 basic manufacturing industries from 13 to 15.

Also at this time, President Borch instituted an innovation at top management level: the president's office. Three seasoned former group executives were named executive vice-presidents and joined both the president and chief executive officer and the chairman of the board in the newly constituted five-man office. All the groups and each of the ten corporate staff components reported to the president's office as a body, but one of the members of the president's office was assigned "primary cognizance" for that group or staff. This was done in recognition of the fact that it was nearly impossible for one man, however hard-working and competent, to be appropriately aware of and involved in the multiplicity of activities required at the top of a very large, highly diversified company. It was anticipated that this office (later retitled corporate executive office in 1968 when Mr. Borch became chairman and chief executive officer upon the death of Chairman Phillippe) would also provide an improved forum for longer-range corporate planning and corporate policy formulation.

The 1967 reorganization, an anticipative move aimed squarely at improving manageability, both reaffirmed and gave new meaning to a couple of our management strategy themes:

Manageability via controlled decentralization
Renewal via anticipatory/evolutionary change

1968–1972: The Emergence of Strategic Planning

By 1968, General Electric's sales had risen to $8.4 billion—quadruple the sales of General Electric in 1950. Thus, in terms of size as measured by sales, the company continued to meet the growth target earlier set by Mr. Cordiner of doubling in size every decade. Earnings, however, had only doubled over the 20-year period.

The comfortable advantage of "20/20 hindsight" reveals some of the major reasons why sales growth over this period was not accompanied by commensurate earnings growth.

◆ During the 1960s, the company had taken on simultaneously three massive investments with very long payout periods: (1) computers, (2) nuclear power, and (3) commercial jet engines. The enormous investment needs of these large ventures caused a critical earnings drain. Each of these "bet your company" ventures *alone* would have been enough to tax the resources and resourcefulness of most large companies. The three acting in concert jeopardized the longer-term viability of even as resource-rich an enterprise as General Electric.

◆ Why did General Electric decide to take on three such massive commitments simultaneously? While it is true that the original plans did not contemplate that all three ventures would be in large loss positions at the same time, the answer gets much closer to the root cause of "profitless prosperity" (as it was known) than does the massive earnings drain which was in reality only the symptom. The answer relates to selectivity in resource allocation and the role of top-down planning in risk containment.

◆ Under decentralization, heavy emphasis was placed upon growth as a prime goal. Each department was expected to plan and implement its own growth. The implicit assumption was that earnings growth would follow sales growth, as it almost invariably had in the past in situations where volume leverage and high market share had been attained. Fixation upon growth coupled with ready availability of investment capital led the company to invest in too many low-yield areas. There was not enough selectivity in allocation of our financial resources. Nor was it often enough considered that a growth strategy might *not* be in the best long-term interests of either a particular department or the company.

◆ Furthermore, effective planning was much more bottom up than top down during this period. As a result, it was easier to gain entry into a massive open-end investment commitment than it was to truncate the drain once initiated. Without the strategic analyses that are now so common under our strategic planning mode, the magnitude of a commitment and the lengthy period that it would take until red ink turned to black were not highly visible.

The computer business in particular was a voracious cash-consumer. When a study team estimated that General Electric would have to spend at least $500 million more to stay in computers—and even then might not chip away enough of IBM's market share to get its money back—the decision was made to exit from the business. In May 1970, it was announced that the GE computer business was being sold to Honeywell. The combined component thus created was judged to have a far better chance to compete successfully than either of its constituent parts. The era of strategic planning at General Electric was thus initiated.

Nearly concurrent with the computer study was a review of the company's planning processes and organization structure, which Fred Borch had commissioned a management consulting firm and later a high-level internal task force to do. Heavy emphasis was placed upon the problems and opportunities projected for the 1970s. Based on this study, the first major conceptual changes in the management system since the early 1950s were implemented:

♦ The strategic business unit (SBU) replaced the product department as the basic *planning* unit in the company. In 1970, the company had grown to nearly 200 departments. For the corporate executive office (CEO) to allocate resources equitably to such a huge number of components was nearly impossible. Furthermore, many departments had become really only *pieces* of businesses. For instance, the major appliance group in 1970 was comprised of 7 divisions and 14 product departments (as well as many additional functional and support operations). Yet none of the divisions or departments could act independently, since all products were sold and serviced as a single line utilizing a common distribution system, pricing the line was done on a centralized integrated basis, facilities planning was done centrally, and so on. In essence, the *business* was the major appliance group rather than any of its constituent components or product lines. A detailed analysis of all 190-odd General Electric profit and loss accountable components utilizing a structured set of criteria revealed 43 SBU's—43 "true businesses"—rather than 190. The resource allocation job for the corporate executive office thus improved from "impossible" to "extremely difficult."

♦ A company-wide strategic planning process was developed and implemented. This process was much more balanced in terms of top-down/bottom-up iteration. Each SBU was challenged to examine its own business environment realistically—its competitive position, the longer-term attractiveness of its markets, present and potential alternative strategies, the resource implications of alternative strategies, the financial expression of the long-range strategic plan, etc. "What-if" contingency planning was made a mandatory element of each plan. In an annual process, each SBU strategic plan was reviewed by the corporate executive office. Then the potential aggregate company result was compared with corporate financial objectives. Frequently, gaps or shortfalls became apparent and had to be dealt with by selectively cutting back investment in those SBU's with lower long-term attractiveness or by harvesting or divesting the least desirable businesses. On the other side of the ledger, decisions also were made to sharply increase investment in the businesses where we had or could attain high market position in the product/market segments of greatest long-term attractiveness.

♦ Since an SBU did not have to meet arbitrary size criteria and could be at any echelon—department, division or group—a major issue emerged as to how the overall operating organization of the company should be structured. In a move consistent with General Electric's preference for evolutionary change, Mr. Borch chose to superimpose the SBU designations and the planning structure upon the existing hierarchal structure of groups, divisions, and departments. The latter would remain the basic building blocks for organization structuring purposes, while SBU's would constitute the basic building blocks for strategic planning and resource allocation purposes. Thus, while the company would be stretched over the next period to implement a new planning system, carve out new roles for staff personnel, deal with such new institutions as internal group executive boards, and the like, it would be operating with an organization structure which was time-honored and well understood. Looking back, this proved to be a very sound strategic move.

Thus, in 1970, General Electric embarked upon perhaps as deep and meaningful a change as decentralization had been in 1951. But it was a change more in the management system than in organization structure—a change more attuned to getting earnings growth aligned with sales growth and ensuring that high risk/high investment ventures were given proper visibility. Squarely aimed at dramatically improving our planning system at the true business entity level, it resulted in giving new meaning to the philosophy of decentralization. Returning a moment to the thesis of this chapter, we see four of today's five management themes:

Earnings growth via selectivity in resource allocation
Risk containment via diversification and selectivity

Manageability via controlled decentralization
Renewal via anticipatory/evolutionary change

1973–1976: MOVING AHEAD ON ALL FRONTS

In December 1972, I was selected to replace Fred Borch as chairman and chief executive officer. The implementation of the SBU concept/ strategic planning process was virtually complete. And a good thing it was, for very shortly thereafter General Electric, along with the rest of the nation, was significantly affected by the 1974–1975 recession.

A recession is never a pleasant experience. But even a recession can result in positive change—for instance, tightening up financial controls and inventory management practices, or improving cash flow to ensure desired liquidity. Like many companies, we had also let ourselves get a bit overweight in personnel and other costs during the boom of the early 1970s. The measures taken to bring our costs and cash flow under control during the recession were extended into the recovery period. As a result, sales during the 1969–1977 period increased 207 percent and, most important, earnings increased 357 percent.

While attention to management basics like measurements and controls played a large part in generating these good results, it would not have been possible without our strategic planning process. Our strategic planning tools and techniques had evolved rapidly through the early 1970s and our strategic plans became much more realistic and sophisticated. There was far greater differentiation and selectivity in our resource allocation—selective exit of least desirable businesses, managing mature businesses for maximum earnings generation and positive cash flow, and intensified investment in our most promising growth opportunities.

Increased emphasis was also placed upon evolving a corporate-level strategic plan in the mid-1970s. Given the diversity of General Electric, this was no small task. Today, we have such a plan. Although it's a quantum jump forward from our first attempts in the early 1970s, it still has a way to go before we'll be satisfied. A major problem has been relating the necessarily broad and global corporate plan to the much more specific and narrow areas of interest characteristic of an SBU strategic plan. Let me return to this issue a little later.

Our approach to diversification has also changed somewhat. First, the merger of General Electric and Utah International in 1976 represented a dramatic deviation from our historical management strategy of "diversification via organic growth." I believe that history will probably show this to be a very visible, very important, but non-recurrent happening. The kind of merger opportunity which Utah afforded occurs only once in a great while. While I wouldn't rule out selective future acquisitions, our primary growth pattern in the future will continue to be organic growth from within.

The Utah merger represented a major strategic move in these respects:

♦ It decisively advanced our planned program of diversification into fast-growing materials and services businesses. In 1977, 40 per-cent of our earnings came from materials and services rather than from equipment businesses. Interestingly, of the 20 basic manufactur-ing industries,[2] General Electric now participates in only 11 compared to 15 in 1968. This drop was largely because we selectively exited businesses. But manufacturing is only one of 11 categories under which *all* industry and commerce is classified. During the period our growth was heavy in such nonmanufacturing areas as mining, con-struction, and services. We now participate in 8 out of the 11 categories of industry and commerce. Thus, our total diversification has grown significantly, while our manufacturing participation has concurrently grown more selective. We now are less vulnerable to inflation and economic cycles.

♦ The merger strengthened and broadened our strategic and in-ternational thrust. Utah is most heavily concentrated outside of the United States. In 1955, offshore sales (mostly exports) were less than 10 percent of total company sales. By contrast, in 1977 about one-third of our total revenues were from international sources. Our in-ternational sales have been growing twice as fast as our domestic sales, yet international saturation is still low and we have ample room to grow. While we plan to continue our rapid international growth, we plan to do so in the same selective fashion that has typified our domes-tic growth.

♦ Additionally, the merger brought us into a major new area of opportunity—natural resources. It provides, via mineral reserves, a long-term hedge against inflation, and improved our earnings per share from the first day of the merger.

Another change in our outlook toward diversification related to internal ventures. We made a conscious choice away from the massive "bet your company" ventures of the 1960s toward a greater number of smaller ventures most of which are funded by the components of which they are a part. In addition to representing good growth, these opportunities are chosen with an eye toward effectiveness in counter-cyclical situations. Many of these small ventures significantly outperformed the company during the 1974–1975 downturn.

The management strategy themes which most typified the 1973–1976 period were:

Risk containment by diversification and selectivity
Earnings growth via selectivity in resource allocation

1977 TO PRESENT: STRATEGIC MANAGEMENT FOR THE 1980s

Back in 1974, I had asked our corporate staff people to review our organization and our executive manpower development practices looking toward the longer-term growth opportunities and manageability challenges projected for the 1980s. Our objectives were four:

◇ To assure continued manageability of the company.
◇ To retain our "one company" image wherein corporate staffs and top management clearly "add value."
◇ To afford necessary and appropriate development opportunities for those key people who represent our potential top management team in the 1980s.
◇ To fine-tune and optimize our management system based upon several years' experience since its 1970 implementation.

The study (which was carried on over a four-year period) revealed certain things it was imperative to retain, such as our multiple-role top management structure and our well-understood organizational nomenclature. Several areas emerged, however, which needed to be changed or improved, and these furnished additional design objectives.

◆ We needed to improve overall company manageability in the face of rapid growth by reducing the number of operating components reporting directly to the corporate executive office. A projected increase in size from 9 groups in 1976 to about 13 groups by the early 1980s would clearly result in an unwieldy span of control. While several alternatives were reviewed, the clear preference involved creating a new organizational component larger than a group—a component which could contain groups, divisions, and departments—and have a smaller number of these report directly to the corporate executive office. The term "sector" was utilized in describing these new components, since it had no previous use in the company. We could define it to mean whatever we desired without having to unlearn previous meanings.

♦ We needed to improve overall manageability and enhance top operating executive development by increased delegation from vice-chairmen to the new sector executives. We also wanted to improve the linkage between the strategic planning process and SBU concepts and the organization structure of the operating components. Fortunately, we were able to address these two issues simultaneously. As you may recall, in 1970 we superimposed the strategic business unit structure upon the hierarchical structure of groups, divisions, and departments. Thus, components designated as SBU's were located at all echelons from group down through department. During 1970–1977, the strategic plans of all 43 SBU's were reviewed at corporate level. This took up a great deal of top management time. The new sectors structure allows us to delegate much of the strategy review and detailed resource allocation to the new sector executives. This enhances sector executive development while concurrently unburdening the corporate executive office. Also, it was judged timely to organize the sectors' internal structure to align more closely with SBU concept implications. Wherever reporting spans allow it under the new structure, SBU's report *directly* to the sector executive regardless of size or designated echelon. The nature of the business relationship with the sector executive, rather than the size of the component, now governs sector organization structure. Obviously, this represents a considerable change from the homogeneity and symmetry of 25 years ago.

♦ We needed to develop a better bridge between the broad-scoped corporate strategic plan and the more specific SBU strategic plans—an unresolved issue I mentioned earlier. Since sectors were defined as macro-business/industry groupings with commonality regarding customers, products, markets, and strategic challenges—thus having good capacity for synergy—we made the sector a planning level in our system. Thus, the sector strategic plan could supply an excellent and needed bridge between the SBU plan and the corporate plan.

♦ We needed to provide motivation for SBU upward mobility without precipitating frequent realignment of the corporate superstructure. Since many SBU's report directly to the sector executive irrespective of size, it was now possible to develop sales/earnings/ complexity yardsticks which, if achieved on a sustained basis, could result in a department evolving into a division and a division into a group. Thus, we could now give SBU's a motivational challenge without precipitating frequent changes in reporting, either among sectors or within sectors.

♦ We needed to refine, tune, and optimize the management system developed in the early 1970s to enhance both the needs and opportunities presented by the new structure and the world business environmental trends forecast for the 1980s. This was accomplished with particular emphasis on business development and international integration mechanisms, resource planning, and multilevel planning *above* the SBU. Essentially, the revised management system moves General Electric from strategic *planning* as a process designed for one level—the SBU—to strategic *management* as a system for all levels, with each level adding value.

On December 1, 1977, we reorganized the company into six sectors and a realigned corporate staff and began the implementation of our revised management system. The six sectors are sufficiently broad in scope so that it is anticipated that the growth of the company can take place within them for many years without need for basic restructuring. In all cases, the sectors and senior corporate staff positions represent significant personal development challenges for the assigned executives. All have highly dynamic business situations to deal with. In some cases, the assignments represent "new turf" and hence a learning situation. Thus, we were able to provide very important broadening opportunities for these executives. We were fortunate in having generally high stability at the SBU level and also at the corporate executive office level, which made these staff and sector executive placements an affordable risk. All these changes are being implemented at a time when our corporate health has seldom been better, not hastily in response to crisis. We feel these changes will enable us to evolve a measured path into the challenging 1980s.

We anticipate the following benefits from the implementation of the sectors approach. The changes should:

◇ Strengthen our opportunities for sustained high quality earnings growth while managing and containing downside risk.
◇ Improve our capability to cope successfully with the manageability challenges of increasing diversity, complexity, uncertainty, and accelerating change.
◇ Assure development of realistic strategic plans and more comprehensive and meaningful strategy review, resource allocation, and operations control.
◇ Provide even greater assurance that new ventures get the attention, resources, and continuity they need in order to succeed.
◇ Improve linkage between the corporate strategic plan and the SBU strategic plans.
◇ Provide a more effective approach to the integration of our international activities.

◇ Improve management of our basic resources—human, financial, and technological.
◇ Provide improved development for our top staff and operating executives in preparation for institutional leadership.
◇ Blend desired changes with planned areas of continuity, thus enhancing the chances of successful implementation.

CONCLUSION

I have tried to demonstrate how five of our most pervasive management strategies at General Electric developed over the years, influenced by both events and forces in the business environment as well as by our own corporate personality and management style:

Diversification via organic growth
Manageability via controlled decentralization
Earnings growth via selectivity in resource allocation
Risk containment via diversification and selectivity
Renewal via anticipatory/evolutionary change

In closing, let me further reflect for a moment upon two of these themes.
♦ Decentralization is a basic concept in our way of life at General Electric. But decentralization does *not* mean either absolute autonomy or abdication of corporate leadership. Effective controls are absolutely essential. Our management system encompasses alternate cycles of decentralized and centralized actions: decentralized development of strategies and plans, centralized review and approval of strategies and plans, decentralized implementation of plans, and centralized monitoring and control of performance of approved plans. Decentralization procedures should not be uniform in regard to all people—for example the time-tested veteran versus the brand-new manager—nor should it be the same across all time phases of the business cycle. We like to call this "differentiated decentralization." Decentralization as a rigid doctrine blindly followed can be as dangerous as extreme centralization.
♦ Anticipatory change of an evolutionary nature, made in response to changing business environment trends and defined in a studied manner, has served well the profitable growth of General Electric. Future-oriented change undertaken in good times, which takes into consideration the vital interplay between strategy, structure, and

staffing—*not* sweeping revolution undertaken in response to present crisis—is the key ingredient here.

We are told that General Electric is regarded in business and government circles as a well-managed company. Perhaps our demonstrated willingness to "anticipate change with change"—to invest the time, money, effort, and the certain degree of disruption that implementation of concept-based change invariably involves—is the basis for this valued reputation. Companies are not alive and well and profitably producing at the age of 100 without continually anticipating and adapting to the changing world of which they are a part.

NOTES AND REFERENCES

1. See especially Ralph J. Cordiner, *New Frontiers for Professional Managers* (New York: McGraw-Hill, 1956).
2. In 1972 the government revised the classification of manufacturing into 20 instead of 21 industries.

Harold Koontz

20
Toward a Useful
Operational Theory
of Management

The French industrialist Henri Fayol, usually acknowledged to be the first pioneer to develop a useful theory of management, undertook in 1916 to codify what he had learned about management by organizing that knowledge around five managerial functions. Approximately three decades later, Harold Smiddy helped to develop another pioneering study of management which was published in four volumes under the general title of *Professional Management in General Electric*.[1] He had the strong support of Ralph Cordiner, who was then vice-president of the General Electric Company and who was charged with the task of reorganizing that company.

Although based partly on Ralph Currier Davis's earlier work, the attempt of the General Electric team to develop a general theory was apparent, especially in Book Three. And the attempt to make the theory operational is attested to by the organization of knowledge around the practical managerial functions of planning, organizing, integrating, and measuring.

Smiddy's profound contributions to management knowledge and practice were distilled from his years as a management consultant and practicing manager, as assistant to Mr. Cordiner, and later as vice-president—consultation services of General Electric. His early insights into management have led the way for many people.[2] In all his thinking, speaking, and writing about management, Smiddy expressed and supported an operational theory, that is, one which underpins and explains the total job of managing in a practical way, rather than dealing only with pieces of the task, like human behavior or relationships.

This operational approach has been somewhat unusual, as I found when I described the nature and characteristics of the "Management Theory Jungle." [3] What I noted then was that all the approaches to the study of management, except the operational or "process" school of management, were partial and specialized—they were not developing a theory explaining the *total* task of managers, as managers. Although the "jungle" still exists and today one can even find double the "schools" or approaches that existed in 1961, there are signs that some specialists are beginning to merge their partial theories into a general, operational theory of management. This, in turn, tends to reflect the early perceptions of such pioneers as Fayol, Davis, Smiddy, and Urwick.

The purpose of this chapter is to outline briefly the principal characteristics of an operational theory and science of management, to revisit the "jungle" by stating the current prominent approaches to management, and to disclose areas in special approaches where research and thinking are beginning to come around to the operational point of view. This does not mean that we can yet see a positive movement toward a unified theory of management, but rather that there are some findings and thinking moving in this direction. In other words, we now seem to be making some progress, even though slight, in clearing a useful path in this jungle.

The Nature, Goal, and Responsibilities of Managing

The starting point in identifying and developing an operationally useful theory and science of management must be to get a clear understanding of the task of managing. As common as managing and managers are in all kinds of societies and cultures, it is difficult to define the task. We can probably begin to obtain a clear understanding of what managing is by looking at such matters as the basic task of managers, the fundamental aim of all managing, the responsibilities of managers. We can then begin organizing this knowledge with a view to developing a useful theory and science of managing.

The Task of Managers. It is the basic task of all managers at all levels and in all kinds of enterprises to design and maintain an environment in which individuals, working together in groups, can effectively and efficiently accomplish preselected missions and objectives. To give an idea of what is meant by an environment conducive to performance, we can mention such important environmental elements as:

◇ Clear, actionable, and verifiable goals and objectives.
◇ Clear, supportive, and intentional structure of roles, since it is always best that people know the part they play in any group operation.
◇ An environment where each manager does everything in his or her power to remove obstacles to the performance of people.
◇ An environment in which people are led to perform, preferably because they enjoy doing things required, often because they perceive it to be in their own interest to perform, and sometimes because something *must* be done or not done.
◇ An environment in which managers recognize that people have feelings, desires, wishes, and habits of thinking or doing, but do not make the foolish mistake of trying to be amateur psychiatrists.
◇ An environment of clarity, since managers cannot succeed unless they and their subordinates understand such essentials as objectives or goals, policies, programs, delegations, inter-position responsibilities, and how well they are performing.

In other words, managers are charged with the responsibility of doing those things which will make it possible for individuals to make their most effective contributions to achieving group objectives. It is well known that most people are willing, even anxious, to perform well in a group setting if the climate is such as to encourage and assist performance.

The Goal of All Managers—"Surplus." In establishing this environment for group effort, the goal of all managers must logically and morally be "surplus." In other words, whether managers are in business or nonbusiness enterprise, whether they are presidents or foremen, their principal task is to manage in such a way as either to accomplish objectives with a minimum input of money, materials, effort, time, or human dissatisfactions, or to accomplish as much of a mission or objective as possible with resources available.

In business, "profit" is really a measure of "surplus" of sales dollars over expense dollars in carrying out a certain economic mission. In nonbusiness enterprises, such as a police department, as well as in departments of a business that cannot be regarded as responsible for total profits, such as an accounting department, managers still have missions or objectives and should strive to accomplish these with the minimum of resource inputs, or accomplish as much as possible with available resources.

Social Responsibility and Environmental Responsiveness. Managers are, of course, not responsible for all kinds of social problems. They are, rather, responsible for the effective and efficient accomplishment of missions or objectives that have been entrusted to them and the groups for which they are responsible. It is properly assumed, of course, that missions of every kind of socially approved enterprise are aimed at contributing to the social welfare. Businesses produce and distribute needed goods and services. Schools and colleges contribute to the education of people and the discovery of new knowledge. Police departments contribute to the safety, security, and welfare of a society. And so on.

Obviously, the managers of all these organizations, in setting and striving for achievement of missions and objectives, must interact with and be responsive to their entire external environment—market and economic, technological, social, political, and ethical. There are no closed systems in managing, and all managers and their groups must interact, respond to, and be affected by environments external to their operations. In a very real sense, social responsibility is social responsiveness.

Management as Science and Art: The Role of Theory

In managing, as in any other area—whether engineering, medicine, accountancy, architecture, or even basketball—unless practitioners are to learn through their own trial and error, there is no other place they can turn for meaningful guidance than the accumulated and distilled knowledge in their special field. This relationship of knowledge to practice seems to be accepted in almost all fields of practice. We even speak of a good basketball coach as emphasizing fundamentals.

Yet, in managing, there is still much confusion about the nature of management knowledge and how it should be utilized. Questions are still raised as to whether management is a science or an art, what theory is and how it can be useful to managers, how technology fits into theory and science, and why there are so many "schools" or approaches to management theory and knowledge. Managers are often uncertain and even confused as to the existence of a management science and wonder what they can believe and what can be useful to them.

Is Managing a Science or an Art? While this question is often raised, a moment's reflection will disclose that it is a rather meaningless query. Managing, like all other practices, is an art. It is "knowhow." It is doing things in the light of the realities of a situation. The most effective practice of managing must make use of underlying organized knowledge; and it is this knowledge, whether crude or advanced, whether exact or inexact, which, to the extent that it is well organized, clear, and pertinent, comprises a science. Thus, managing as practice is art; the organized and pertinent knowledge underlying it may be referred to as a science. Consequently, science and art are not mutually exclusive, but are complementary. As science improves, so should art, as has happened so dramatically in the physical and biological sciences.

To be sure, the science underlying managing is fairly inexact and crude. This is partly because the multitude of variables with which managers deal are extremely complex, and partly because there has been relatively little research and development effort in the field of management. But such knowledge as is available can certainly be used to improve managerial practice since there is ample evidence that many managers are not effectively applying what we do know.

Science and Theory. It has been emphasized that science is organized knowledge. The essential feature of any science is that knowledge has been systematized and distilled, usually through the application of scientific method. Thus, we speak of the science of chemistry, physics, or astronomy as involving accumulated knowledge and techniques developed from hypotheses, experimentation, and analysis.

Any meaningful and mature science first requires clarity and general acceptance of concepts—definitions of words and terms which are clear, relevant to the phenomena being analyzed, and meaningful to the scientist and practitioner alike. In physics, for example, volts, ohms, and watts mean the same thing to everyone. As yet, unfortunately, we do not have this same exactness in management, where such common terms as "staff," "line," "authority," "responsibility," and "policy" may mean different things to different people.

Given clarity of concepts, scientific method involves determining facts through observation of events and verifying these facts through continued observations. After classifying and analyzing these facts, scientists look for causal relationships which they believe to be true. When these generalizations are tested for accuracy and appear to be true, to reflect or explain reality, and therefore to have value in predicting what will happen in similar circumstances, they are called "principles." This does not imply that they are unquestionably or invariably true, but that they are believed to be valid enough to be used for prediction.

Theory is a systematic grouping of interdependent concepts and principles which give a framework, or tie together, a significant area of knowledge. Scattered data, such as those one may find on a blackboard after a group of engineers have been discussing a problem, are not information unless the observer has a knowledge of the theory that will explain relationships. As Harvard Professor George C. Homans has said, theory is "in its lowest form a classification, a set of pigeonholes, a filing cabinet in which facts can accumulate. Nothing is more lost than a loose fact." [4]

The Role of Management Theory in Organizing Knowledge. In the field of management, then, the role of theory is to give a means of classifying knowledge. For example, there are a number of principles that are interrelated and have a predictive value for managers who wish to design an effective organization structure. Some principles give guidelines for delegating authority, such as delegating by results expected, the coincidence of authority and responsibility, and the unity of command. Likewise, in understanding how to do effective planning, managers are aided by theory which discloses that decision making, while at the heart of planning, will be more effective if related to objectives sought, if made in the light of the expected environment in which the decision will operate, and if based on an analysis of the most promising alternatives.

Principles of management, like those in physics or chemistry, are descriptive or predictive, not prescriptive. For example, the principle of unity of command only states that the more an individual is responsible to a single superior, the more likely he or she is to feel a sense of loyalty and obligation and the less likely is there to be confusion in instructions. It merely predicts. It in no sense implies that an individual should *never* report to more than one person. But rather, as in the case of functional authority relationships, a manager must expect some possible negative effects and should take these disadvantages into account in considering the advantages of giving a manager, such as the controller, functional authority over other managers and departments that do not directly report to him.

Management Techniques and Theory. Techniques are essentially ways of doing things, methods of accomplishing a given result. In all fields of practice they are important. They certainly are in managing, even though there are few really important techniques that have been invented. Among these are budgeting (including program, variable, and zero-based budgeting), network planning and control (such as PERT and CPM), rate-of-return-on-investment control, managing by objectives, and linear organization charts. As ways of doing things, techniques reflect theory and also assist in creating an environment for performance.

Science and Theory Must Reflect Realities. As organized knowledge underpinning the task of managing, management science and theory must reflect realities. This is not to say that they need to be prescriptive in telling managers what to do under all circumstances. But it does mean that as science and theory become more accurate, more useful as a means of helping in designing solutions to managerial problems, and more understood by practicing managers, they become more operational. This must be the ultimate goal of those who would purport to develop and verbally set forth management science and theory.

Approaches to Management Science and Theory: The Continuing Jungle

That management science and theory are far from being mature is nowhere more apparent than in the continuation of what I called some years ago "the management theory jungle." What has happened to this "jungle" in the intervening years since 1961? At that time, I found six "schools": the management process or operational, the empirical, the human behavior, the social system, the decision theory, and the mathematical. At the present time, I find a total of ten clearly identified approaches to the study and expression of management science and theory. These are the empirical approach, the interpersonal behavior approach, the group behavior approach, the cooperative social system approach, the sociotechnical systems approach, the decision theory approach, the mathematical or "management science" approach, the systems approach, the contingency approach, and the operational theory approach. Each of these may be summarized in a paragraph or two.

The Empirical, or Case, Approach. This school studies management by studying experience, usually through cases. It is based on the premise that students and practitioners will understand the field of management and somehow come to know how to manage effectively by studying managerial successes and failures in various individual cases.

However, unless a study of experience is aimed at determining *fundamentally* why something happened or did not happen, it is likely to be a useless and even dangerous approach to understanding management, since what happened or did not happen in the past is not likely to help in solving problems in a most certainly different future. If experience is studied with a view to finding *basic* generalizations, this can be a useful approach to develop or support some principles of management.

The Interpersonal Behavior Approach. This approach is based on the thesis that managing involves getting things done through people, and therefore, the study of management should be centered on interpersonal relations. The writers and scholars in this school are heavily oriented to individual psychology and, indeed, most are trained as psychologists. Their focus is on the individual and his or her motivations as a sociopsychological being. In this school are those who appear to emphasize human relations as an art which managers, even when foolishly trying to be amateur psychiatrists, can understand and practice. There are those who see the manager as a leader and who may even equate managership and leadership, thus, in effect, treating all "led" activities as "managed." Others have concentrated on motivations and on leadership and have cast important light on these subjects.

That the study of human interactions, whether in the context of managing or elsewhere, is useful and important cannot be denied. But it can hardly be said that the field of interpersonal behavior encompasses all there is to management. It is entirely possible for all the managers of a company to understand psychology and its nuances and yet not be effective in managing. Both research and practice are finding that we must go far beyond interpersonal relations to develop a useful science of management.

The Group Behavior Approach. This approach is closely related to the interpersonal behavior approach and may be confused with it. But it is concerned primarily with behavior of people in groups rather than with interpersonal behavior. It thus tends to rely on sociology, anthropology, and social psychology rather than on individual psychology. Its emphasis is on group behavior patterns. This approach varies all the way from the study of small groups with their cultural and behavioral patterns to the behavioral characteristics of large groups. It is often called a study of "organization behavior," and the term "organization" may be taken to mean the system, or pattern, or any set of group relationships in a company, a government agency, a hospital, or any other kind of undertaking. Sometimes the term is used as Chester Barnard employed it, to mean "the cooperation of two or more persons," and "formal organization" is used to mean an organization with conscious, deliberate, joint purpose.[5] Chris Argyris has even used the term "organization" to include *all* the behavior of *all* the participants in a group undertaking.[6]

It is not difficult to see that practicing managers would not be likely to recognize that "organizations" cover such a broad area of group behavior patterns. At the same time, many of the problems of managers do arise from group behavior patterns, attitudes, desires, and prejudices, some of which arise from the groups within an enterprise, but many come from the cultural environment of people outside a given company, department, or agency. What is perhaps most disturbing about this school of thought is the tendency of its members to draw an artificial and inaccurate line between "organization behavior" and "managing." Group behavior is an important aspect of management, but it is not all there is to management.

The Cooperative Social System Approach. A modification of the interpersonal and group behavior approaches has been the focus of behavioral scientists on the study of human relationships as cooperative social systems. The idea of human relationships as social systems was early perceived by the great Italian sociologist Vilfredo Pareto. His work apparently affected modern adherents to this school through the influence of Chester Barnard. In seeking to explain the work of executives, Barnard saw them operating in, and maintaining, cooperative social systems which he referred to as "organizations."[7] He perceived social systems as the cooperative interaction of ideas, forces, desires, and thinking of two or more persons. An increasing number of writers have expanded this concept to apply to any system of cooperative and purposeful group interrelationships or behavior and have given it the rather general title of "organization theory."

The cooperative social systems approach does have pertinence to the study and analysis of management. All managers do operate in a cooperative social system. But we do not find what is generally referred to as managers in *all* kinds of cooperative social systems. We would hardly think of a cooperative group of shoppers in a department store as being managed. We would not regard the leaders of an unorganized mob as managers. Nor would we think of a family group gathering to celebrate a birthday as being managed. Therefore, we can conclude that this approach is broader than management and, at the same time, overlooks many concepts, principles, and techniques that are important to managers.

The Sociotechnical Systems Approach. One of the newer schools of management identifies itself as the sociotechnical systems approach.

This development is generally credited to E. L. Trist and his associates at the Tavistock Institute in England. In studies made of production problems in long-wall coal mining, this group found that it was not enough merely to analyze social problems. Instead, in dealing with problems of mining productivity, it was found that the technical system (machines and methods) had a strong influence on the social system. In other words, it was discovered that personal attitudes and group behavior are influenced by the technical system in which people work. It is the position of this school of thought, therefore, that social and technical systems must be looked upon together and that the task of the manager is to make sure that these two systems are made harmonious.

Most of the work of this school has consequently been concentrated on production, office operations, and other areas where the technical systems have such a close connection to people and their work. It therefore tends to be heavily oriented to industrial engineering. As an approach to management, this school is fairly new. It has made some interesting contributions to managerial practice, even though it does not, as some of its proponents seem to believe, encompass all there is to management. Moreover, it is doubtful that any experienced manager would be surprised that the technology of the assembly line or the technology of transportation or oil companies affects individuals and their behavior patterns, the way operations are organized, or the techniques of managing employed. Furthermore, as promising and helpful as this approach is in certain aspects of enterprise operations, it is safe to observe that there is much more to pertinent management knowledge than can be found in it.

The Decision Theory Approach. This approach to management science and theory has been based on the belief that, since it is the task of managers to make decisions, we should concentrate on decision making. It is not surprising that there are many scholars and theorists who believe that, since managing is characterized by decision making, the central focus of management theory can be decision making and the rest of management thought can be built around it. This has a degree of reasonableness. However, it overlooks the fact that there is much more to managing than making decisions and that, for most managers, the actual making of a decision is a fairly easy thing—if goals are clear, if the environment in which the decision will operate can be fairly accurately anticipated, if adequate information is available, if the organization structure provides a clear understanding of responsibility for decisions, if competent people are available to make decisions, and if many of the other prerequisites of effective managing are present.

The Mathematical, or "Management Science," Approach. There are some theorists who see managing as primarily an exercise in mathematical processes, concepts, symbols, and models. Perhaps the most widely known of these are the operations researchers who have called themselves "management scientists." The primary focus of this school is the mathematical model, since through this device, problems—whether managerial or other—can be expressed in basic relationships and, where a given goal is sought, the model can be expressed in terms which optimize that goal.

To be sure, the journal *Management Science*, published by the Institute of Management Sciences, carries on its cover the statement that the Institute has as its purpose to "identify, extend, and unify scientific knowledge pertaining to management." But, as judged by the articles published in this journal and the hundreds of papers presented by members of the Institute at its many meetings around the world, the school's almost complete preoccupation has been with mathematical models and elegance in developing mathematical solutions to certain kinds of problems. Consequently, as many critics, both inside and outside the ranks of the so-called management scientists have observed, the narrow mathematical focus can hardly be called an approach to a true management science.

No one interested in any scientific field can overlook the great usefulness of mathematical models and analyses. But it is difficult to see mathematics as a separate school of management any more than it is a separate school of physics, chemistry, or engineering.

The Systems Approach. During recent years, many scholars and writers in management have emphasized the systems approach to the study and analysis of management thought. They feel that this is the most effective means by which such thought can be organized, presented, and understood.

A system is essentially a set or assemblage of things interconnected, or interdependent, so as to form a complex unity. These things may be physical, as with the parts of an automobile engine; or they may be biological, as with the components of the human body; or they may be theoretical, as with a well-integrated assemblage of concepts, principles, theory, and techniques in an area such as managing. Because all systems, except perhaps the universe, interact with and are influenced by their environments, we define boundaries for them so that we can see them more clearly and analyze them.

The long use of systems theory and analyses in physical and biological sciences has given rise to a considerable body of systems knowledge. It comes as no surprise that systems theory has been found helpfully applicable to management theory and science. To make our subject "manageable," we set an arbitrary boundary of management thought—as in the definition of the managerial job in terms of what managers do—but this does not imply a closed systems approach to the subject. On the contrary, there are many interactions with the system environment. Thus, when managers plan, they must take into account such external variables as markets, technology, social forces, laws, and regulations. Moreover, when managers design an organization system to provide an environment for performance, they cannot help being influenced by the behavior patterns people bring to their jobs from environments external to an enterprise.

Systems also play an important part within the area of managing itself. There are such systems as planning systems, organizations systems, and control systems. And within these, we can perceive many subsystems, such as systems of delegation, network planning, and budgeting systems.

Intelligent and experienced practicing managers and many management writers with practical experience, accustomed as they are to seeing their problems and operations as a network of interrelated elements with daily interactions between environments inside or outside their companies or other enterprises, are often surprised to find that many writers regard the systems approach as something new. To be sure, conscious study of and emphasis on systems have forced many managers and scholars to consider more perceptively the various interacting elements affecting management theory and practice. But it can hardly be regarded as a new approach to management thought.

The Contingency, or Situational, Approach. Another approach to management thought and practice is the contingency, or situational, approach, which emphasizes the fact that what managers do in practice depends upon a given set of circumstances, or the "situation." Contingency management is akin to situational management and the two terms are often used synonymously. Some scholars, however, make the distinction that, while situational management merely implies that what managers do depends on a given situation, contingency management implies an active interrelationship between the variables in a situation and the managerial solution devised. Using a contingency approach, managers might look at an assembly line situation and readily conclude that a highly structured organization pattern would best fit and interact with it. According to some scholars, then, contingency theory takes into account not only given situations, but also the influence of given solutions on behavior patterns of an enterprise. Thus an organization structured along the lines of operating functions, such as finance, engineering, production, and marketing, might be most suitable for a given situation, but managers using it should take into account the behavior patterns of group loyalties to the function rather than to the company which often follow.

By its very nature, managerial practice requires that managers take into account the realities of a given situation when they apply theory or techniques. It has never been and never will be the task of science and theory to *prescribe* what should be done in a given situation. Science and theory in management do not advocate the "one best way" [8] to do things in every situation, any more than the sciences of astrophysics or mechanics tell an engineer how to design a single best instrument for all kinds of applications. How theory and science are applied in practice naturally depends upon the situation.

In other words, there is science and there is art, there is common knowledge and there is practice. These are matters that any experienced manager has long known. One does not need much experience to understand that a corner grocery store could hardly be organized like General Motors; or that the technical realities of petroleum exploration, production, and refining make autonomously organized product divisions for gasoline, jet fuel, or lubricating oils impracticable.

The Operational Approach. The operational approach to management theory and science attempts to draw together the pertinent knowledge of management by relating it to the managerial job—what managers do. Like other operational sciences, it endeavors to put together for the field of management the concepts, principles, theory, and techniques which underpin the actual practice of managing.

The operational approach recognizes that there is a central core of knowledge about managing which exists only in management; such matters as line and staff, departmentation, the limitations of the span of management, managerial appraisal, and various managerial control techniques involve concepts and theory found only where managers are involved. But in addition, this approach draws on pertinent knowledge derived from other fields, such as applications of systems theory, decision theory, motivation and leadership findings and theory, individual and group behavior theory, and the application of mathematical modeling and techniques.

The nature of the operational approach can perhaps best be appreciated by reference to Figure 1. As this diagram shows, the operational management school of thought has a central core of science and theory unique to management plus knowledge eclectically drawn from various other fields and approaches. The circle indicates

Figure 1. The scope of operation science and theory.

that the operational approach is not interested in all the important knowledge in these various fields, but only in that which is deemed to be most useful and relevant to managing.

Those who subscribe to the operational approach hope to develop and identify a field of science and theory which has practical application to the practice of managing and yet is not so broad as to encompass everything that might have any relationship, no matter how remote, to the managerial job. They realize that any field as complex as managing can never be isolated from its physical, technological, biological, or cultural environment. They realize, however, that some partitioning of knowledge is necessary and some boundaries to this knowledge must be set if meaningful progress in summarizing and classifying pertinent knowledge is ever to be made. Yet, as in the case of all systems analyses where we set system boundaries, we must realize that there is no such thing as a closed system and many environmental variables will intrude upon and influence any system proposed.

The Management Theory Jungle: Hopeful Tendencies Toward Convergence of Theories

As can be seen from the brief discussion above of the schools and approaches to management theory and science, there is evidence that the management theory jungle has flourished and become twice as dense as it was 18 years ago. It is no wonder that a useful operational management theory and science have been so tardy in arriving. It is no wonder that we still do not have a clear notion of the scientific underpinnings of managing nor have we been able clearly to identify what we mean by competent managers.

The varying approaches, each with its own gurus, each with its own semantics, and each with a fierce pride to protect the concepts and techniques of the approach from attack or change, make the theory and science of management extremely difficult for the intelligent practitioner to understand and utilize. If the continuing jungle were only an evidence of competing academic thought and research, it would not much matter. But when it retards the development of a useful operational theory and science and confuses practicing managers, the problem becomes serious. Effective managing at all levels and in all kinds of enterprises is too important to any society to allow it to fail through lack of available and understandable knowledge.

Realizing that these are only indications and signs along the road to a more unified and operational theory of management, and that there is much more of this road to map and travel, let us briefly examine some of the tendencies toward convergence.

Placing Greater Emphasis on Distillation of Basics Within the Empirical Approach. As we have looked at the many programs utilizing cases as a means of educating managers, we find that there appears to be much greater emphasis on distilling fundamentals than there was two decades ago. In the field of business policy, by which term these case approaches have tended to be known, there has been increased emphasis in teaching and research to go beyond recounting what happened in a given situation to analyzing the underlying causes and reasons for what happened. A major result of all this has been a new emphasis on and explanation of strategy and strategic planning. This has led the so-called empiricists to come up with distilled knowledge that fits neatly into the operational theorist's classification of planning.

Recognizing That Systems Theory Is Not a Separate Approach. When systems theory was introduced into the management field some two decades ago, it was hailed by many as being a new way of analyzing and classifying management knowledge. But in recent years, as people have come to understand systems theory *and* the job of managing better, it has become increasingly clear that, in its essentials, there is little new about systems theory and that practicing managers as well as the operational theorists had been utilizing its basics (although not always using the jargon) for a number of years. Nonetheless, as those in the field of operational theory have more consciously and clearly utilized the concepts and theory of systems, their attempts at developing a scientific field have been improved.

Recognizing That Situational and Contingency Approaches Are Not New or Separate Approaches. As perceptive managers and many management theorists have always known, it is now clear that the concept of situational or contingency management is merely a way of distinguishing between science and art—knowledge and practice—which, though different, are mutually complementary. To be sure, those writers and scholars who have emphasized situational or contingency approaches have done the field of management theory and practice a great service by stressing that what the intelligent manager actually does depends on the realities of a situation. But this has long been true of the *application* of any science.

That contingency theory is really application in the light of a situation has been increasingly recognized, as is evidenced by a recent statement of one of the founders of contingency theory. Professor Jay Lorsch recently admitted that the use of the term "contingency" was "misleading." [9] Even he appeared to recognize that an operational management theorist would necessarily become a situationalist when it came to applying management concepts, principles, and techniques.

Finding That "Organization Theory" Is Too Broad an Approach. Largely because of the influence of Chester Barnard and his broad concept of "organization" to refer to almost any kind of interpersonal relationships, it has become customary, particularly in academic circles, to use the term "organization theory" to refer to theory pertaining to almost any kind of interpersonal relationship. While many scholars attempted to make this field equal to management theory, it is now fairly well agreed that managing is a far narrower activity and management theory pertains only to theory related to managing. Management theory is often thought of as being a subset of organization theory and it is now fairly well agreed that the general concept of organization theory is too broad. This is a hopeful sign in clearing away some of the underbrush of the jungle.

Arriving at a New Understanding of Motivation. The more recent researches into motivation of people in organizational settings has tended to emphasize the importance of the organizational climate in curbing or arousing motives. The rather oversimplified explanations of motives by Maslow and Herzberg may identify human needs fairly well, but much more emphasis must be given to rewards and expectations of rewards. These, along with a climate which arouses and supports motivation, will depend to a very great extent on the nature of managing in an organization.

Litwin and Stringer found that the strength of such basic motives as needs for achievement, power, and affiliation were definitely affected by the organizational climate.[10] In a sample of 460 managers, they found a strong relationship between highly structured organizations and arousal of the need for power, and a negative relationship with the needs for achievement and affiliation. In a climate with high responsibility and clear standards, they observed a strong relationship of this climate to the achievement motivation, a moderate correlation to power motivation, and an unrelated to negatively related relationship with affiliation motivation.

The interaction between motivation and organizational climate not only underscores the systems aspects of motivation but also emphasizes how motivation depends on what managers do in setting and maintaining an environment for performance. These later researches, then, move the problem of motivation from a purely behavioral matter to one closely related to and dependent upon what managers do. The theory of motivation, then, fits nicely into the operational approach to management theory and science.

Melding Motivation and Leadership Theory. Another interesting sign that we may be moving toward a unified operational theory of management is the way that research and analysis have tended to meld motivation and leadership theory. Especially in recent years, leadership research and theory have tended to emphasize the rather elementary propositions that the job of leaders is to know and appeal to factors that motivate people and to recognize the simple fact that people tend to follow those in whom they see a means of satisfying their own desires. Thus, explanations of leadership have been increasingly related to motivation.

This melding of motivation and leadership theories has also tended to emphasize the importance of organization climate and styles of leaders. Whether the theory of leadership is based on situational, contingency, leader behavior and style, or path goal approaches, conclusions of scholars and researchers are tending in the same direction. Most recent studies and theories tend to underscore the importance of effective managing in making managers effective leaders. Implied by most recent research and theory is the clear message that effective leaders design a system that takes into account the expectancies of subordinates, the variability of motives between individuals and from time to time, situational factors, the need for clarity of role definition, interpersonal relations, and types of rewards.

As can be readily seen, knowledgeable and effective managers do these things when they design a climate for performance, when goals and means of achieving them are planned, when organizational roles are defined and well structured, when roles are intelligently staffed, and when control techniques and information are designed to make control by self-control possible. In other words, leadership theory and research are, like motivation, fitting nicely into the scheme of operational management theory, rather than going off as a separate branch of behavioral science.

Orienting "Organization Development" to Operational Management Theory. Both "organization development" and the field ordinarily referred to as "organization behavior" have grown out of the interpersonal and group behavior approaches to management. For a while, it seemed that these fields were far away and separate from operational management theory. But many researchers are now beginning to see that basic management theory and techniques, such as managing by objectives and clarifying organization structure, fit well into their programs of behavioral intervention.

There has been a disturbing tendency for members of this school of thought to draw an artificial and inaccurate line between "organization behavior" and "management." It does not appear to make sense to do this. In structuring and classifying management knowledge, all behavioral sciences related to managing should be interwoven with management concepts, theory, and techniques in an eclectic way.

Fortunately, a review of the latest books on organization behavior indicates that some authors in this field are beginning to understand that behavioral elements in group operations must be more closely integrated with organizational structure design, staffing, planning, and control. It is a hopeful sign that certain members of the behavioral schools of thought are beginning to see the deficiencies of the narrowness of their approach. It is a recognition that analysis of individual and group behavior, at least in managed situations, easily and logically falls into place in the scheme of operational management theory.

Incorporating the Impact of Technology: Researching an Old Problem. That technology has an important impact on organizational structure, behavior patterns, and other aspects of managing has been recognized by intelligent practitioners for many years. However, primarily among academic researchers, there has seemed to be in recent years a "discovery" that the impact of technology is important and real. To be sure, some of this research has been helpful to managers, especially that developed by the sociotechnical school of management. Also, while perceptive managers have known for many years that technology has important impacts, some of this research has tended to clarify and give special meaning to this impact.

The impact of technology is easily embraced by operational management theory and practice. And it should be. It is to be hoped that scholars and writers in the area of technological impacts will soon become familiar with operational management theory and incorporate their findings and ideas into that operational framework. At the very least, however, those of us who subscribe to the operational approach can incorporate the useful findings of those who emphasize the impact of technology.

Defecting from "Management Science." In the discussion of schools or approaches to management above, one of them is identified as the mathematical, or "management science," approach. "Management science" was put in quotation marks, since this group does not really deal with a total science of management but rather with mathematical models, symbols, and elegance.

There are clear signs among the so-called management scientists that there are defectors who realize that their interests go far beyond the use of mathematics, models, and the computer. These defectors are found especially in the ranks of operations researchers in industry and government where they are daily faced with practical management problems. A few academics are also increasingly coming to this realization. In fact, one of the leading and most respected academics who is widely regarded as a pioneer in operations research, Professor C. West Churchman (in conversations with the writer), has been highly critical of the excessive absorption with models and mathematics and, for this reason, has even resigned from the Operations Research Society.

There is no doubt that operations research and similar mathematical and modeling techniques fit nicely into the planning and controlling areas of operational management theory and science. Most operational management theorists recognize this. All that is really needed is for the few "management science" defectors to become a torrent moving their expertise and research more closely to a practical and useful management science.

Clarifying Semantics: Some Hopeful Signs. One of the greatest obstacles to the development of a more unified and useful theory and science of management has been the problem of semantics. Those writing and lecturing on management and related fields have tended to use common terms in different ways. This is exemplified by the variety of meanings given to such terms as "organization," "line and staff," "authority," "responsibility," and "policies," to mention a few. While this semantics swamp still exists and we are a long way from general acceptance of meanings of key terms and concepts, there are some hopeful signs on the horizon.

It has become rather common for the leading management texts to include a glossary of key terms and concepts, and an increasing number of them are beginning to show some commonality of meaning. Of interest also is the fact that the Fellows of the International Academy of Management, comprised of some 160 management leaders from 32 countries of the world, have responded to the demands of its members and have undertaken to develop a glossary of management concepts and terms, to be published in a number of languages and given wide circulation among many countries of the world.

Although it is too early even to hope, it does appear that we may be moving in the direction necessary for the development of a science—the acceptance of clear definitions for key terms and concepts.

TOWARD A USEFUL MANAGEMENT THEORY AND SCIENCE: QUO VADIS?

We have a great need for a unified, useful, and operational theory and science of management. There are some of us who believe that the operational theory approach is designed to meet that need and that managerially important and useful ideas, concepts, theory, and techniques from all the various approaches to management thought can eclectically be folded into this operational approach. There are also a number of intelligent and perceptive practitioners who have believed in and contributed to this operational approach. They include the person whom this book honors, Harold M. Smiddy, as well as such great practitioners as Henri Fayol, James Mooney, Oliver Sheldon, James O. McKinsey, Lord Wilfred Brown, Edward F. L. Brech, Luther Gulick, and Lyndall Urwick.

Unfortunately, the realities of the "management theory jungle" are still with us. But there are scattered and hopeful, even though limited, signs that movements are underway toward a useful operational theory and science of management. In the interests of a far better society through improved managerial practice in every type of enterprise, it is to be hoped that some means can be found to accelerate this movement.

NOTES AND REFERENCES

1. Book One of this study, entitled *General Electric's Growth*, was published in 1953; Book Two, entitled *General Electric's Organization*, was published in 1955; Book Three, entitled *The Work of a Professional Manager*, really a treatise on management, was published by the company in 1954. Book Four, *The Work of a Functional Individual Contributor*, was published in 1959.
2. For example, Peter Drucker informed me that the concept of "managing by objectives," for which he is so well known, was originally expressed to him by Harold Smiddy.
3. See my paper on "The Management Theory Jungle," *Journal of the Academy of Management*, December 1961, pp. 174–188, and "Making Sense of Management Theory," *Harvard Business Review*, July–August 1962, pp. 24ff.
4. George C. Homans, *The Human Group* (New York: Harcourt, Brace & World, 1958), pp. 7–9.
5. C. I. Barnard, *The Functions of the Executive* (Cambridge: Harvard University Press, 1938), pp. 65 and 4.
6. Chris Argyris, *Personality and Organization* (New York: Harper, 1957), p. 239.
7. Barnard, *The Functions of the Executive*, pp. 72–73.
8. Many writers who have not read the so-called classicists in management carefully have come up with the inaccurate shibboleth that classical writers were prescribing the "one best way." It is true that Gilbreth in his study of bricklaying was searching for the one best way, but that was bricklaying and not managing. Even Fayol recognized this clearly when he said, "Principles are flexible and capable of adaptation to every need; it is a matter of knowing how to make use of them, which is a difficult art requiring intelligence, experience, decision and proportion." See Fayol, *General and Industrial Management* (New York: Pitman, 1949), p. 19.
9. Jay Lorsch, "Organizational Design: A Situational Perspective," *Organizational Dynamics*, Autumn 1977, pp. 2–14.
10. G. H. Litwin and R. A. Stringer, Jr. *Motivation and Organizational Climate* (Boston: Harvard Graduate School of Business Administration, 1968).

George A. Steiner

21
Changing Managerial Ideologies

For two hundred years the classical business ideology has dominated the thinking of people in business about their responsibilities and the role of the business institution in society. While still widely accepted, especially in smaller organizations, this ideology is more and more being modified by a socioeconomic managerial ideology. This chapter explores the nature of these two ideologies and changes in the acceptance of each. Before discussing these ideologies it is useful to define the meaning of a business ideology and its purposes.

DEFINITION AND PURPOSES OF A BUSINESS IDEOLOGY

A business ideology is the content of the patterns of thought that are characteristic of the business classes. It is their system of beliefs, values, and objectives which concern, defend, and justify business behavior. In this respect, ideology is synonymous with business creed and philosophy. An ideology has several important characteristics. It is selective in subject matter, in that it does not seek to cover every facet of business interest. It is based on intuitive views, education, logical argument, and subjective values. More often than not, it is a reflection of self-interest. Business ideology, like other ideologies, is

This chapter is an updated version of Chapter 9 in George A. Steiner, *Business and Society*, 2nd ed. (New York: Random House, 1975).

348

often expressed in language designed to appeal to the emotions of the listeners. Usually the language is simple, if not oversimplified.

It is important to understand that not all managers subscribe to what we call a business ideology. Many important leaders have taken exception to the view that there is a prevailing ideology. As Kross and Gilbert note:

At no time has there been a content of thinking, a set of beliefs, or a body of opinion to which all businessmen subscribed. To be sure, there have always been some opinions which the majority of businessmen shared, and changed over time. . . . It must be evident . . . that . . . any conclusions about what businessmen believed should be cautiously stated and carefully qualified.[1]

About the purposes of the business ideology, Monsen said:

Generally speaking, ideologies may be designed to fill a number of purposes of the groups espousing them. So far as the business ideology is concerned, it might be said to fill such needs of the business group as these: to justify and rationalize the existence and the actions of business; to describe ideals to be sought; to establish standards for judging or appraising business organizations, their policies, and their leaders; and to provide an explanation of causal factors in the event of failure.[2]

The business ideology is certainly not passive. It has considerable emotional content if not passion. It links action with fundamental beliefs. It is designed not only to protect business from supposedly unwarranted outside forces, such as government controls, but also to convert ideas into social levers:

The business ideology is a source of logic and rationality by means of which business acts and can be judged. Votaw and Sethi make this point in these words: "A group without an ideology is likely to be a group without rationality to its behavior and, when confronted with a new problem for which it has no ideological reference, is likely to become immobilized."[3]

In addition to these general purposes of the business ideology there are some specific roles that it fills, which are discussed below.

In a masterful study of the business ideology, Sutton et al. advance the idea that the business ideology helps the business person to meet the strains faced as a business person. This is called the "strain" theory and they explain it in these words:

Briefly, our thesis is that the content of the business ideology can best be explained in terms of the strains to which men in the business role are almost inevitably subject. Businessmen adhere to their particular kind of ideology because of the emotional conflicts, the anxieties, and the doubts engendered by the actions which their roles as businessmen compel them to take, and by the conflicting demands of other social roles which they must play in family and community. Within the resources of the cultural tradition and within the limits of what is publicly acceptable, the content of the ideology is shaped so as to resolve these conflicts, alleviate these anxieties, overcome these doubts. For the individual businessman, the function of the ideology is to help him maintain his psychological ability to meet the demands of his occupation. It follows that the ideology has functional importance also for those on whom the actions of businessmen impinge and for the whole society.[4]

In taking this position these scholars reject the "interest" theory, that ideologies simply reflect narrow self-interest as conceived by their adherents. More specifically, they reject the idea that the business ideology is designed to persuade others to take action which will result in a profit advantage to businessmen. There is truth, but not the whole truth, in this theory. One cannot explain the determined resistance of many businessmen to an unbalanced federal budget, for instance, as one that has a direct beneficial influence on their profits. If this view governed public policy it would sooner or later reduce profits. On the other hand, according to the traditional capitalist theory people in business are expected to and do act in their own self-interest. One purpose of the business ideology is to protect those interests as business people see them.

People in business play many roles and often they find conflicts among the values associated with different roles. Business people are managers, owners, voters, members of society, competitors, husbands, wives, fathers, mothers, church members, and so on. Modes of behavior are culturally determined in these different roles. Their problems in deciding what to do as they assume these roles can become difficult and create major strains and stresses. For example, economic life demands that managers be competitive, but this may conflict with their roles as good neighbors to the competitor their action forces out of business. Business executives are faced with uncertainties of environment and they are responsible for outcomes of decisions over which they have limited control. Some of their roles place on them a responsibility—for community welfare, for instance—which they may think conflicts with other roles—protector of stockholder interests, for instance.

Another purpose of the creed is to slow down institutional changes and reforms. The established business order is thus given time to find ways of adapting to these modifications. In this view, the business executive who is an architect of change turns conservative and seeks more stability in the environment.

Finally, typical managers think of themselves and of business in general as being important to the progress of society. They believe that threats to the business system are threats to society in general and to their important roles in particular. Their ideology, therefore, is a shield against the erosion of their own group's role. They remember that the origin of the classical capitalist ideology rested in an effort to rescue business from government restrictions which were contrary to the business person's and society's interests. They do not want to see that suppression happen again.

THE CLASSICAL IDEOLOGY

The classical ideology finds its taproots in the exposition of capitalism as described by Adam Smith and his followers. Extracted from this body of literature have been particular ideas associated with what we call the classical ideology. Following are highly condensed highlights of this ideology.

Government. The classical view of government is one of hostility and distrust. Government is considered to be inherently evil, powerless to create, and negative in its relations to industry. There are many reasonable explanations of why business people hold this view. Government may be a scapegoat for those obscure forces which cause the outcomes of business decisions to differ from expectations. Business denigrates government because its administrators are not held to the same types of accountability imposed on people in business. Government is a regulator of business and is naturally resented. Government is a suitable target for resentments built up by a businessman. The hostile attitudes reflected in the American revolt against tyranny of a central government have probably carried over to this day.

Government Finance. Taxes are always too high, and ideology demands their reduction. The rationale is that taxes divert resources from business and consumers to be used by government in making unnecessary expenditures. Taxes, furthermore, stifle individual initiative and risk-taking, reduce the capital available to a firm, and inhibit business investment.

Government debt is regarded in the same way as the debt of an individual or a company; the mounting federal debt, to the classical creed, is a clear sign of impending bankruptcy if the trend continues. Correct budgetary practice is quite obvious—budgets must be balanced at all times, and when surpluses are generated the debt should be paid off. The general business view is that expenditures just about always are higher than they should be.

Profit. Prominent in the traditional philosophy, of course, is the importance of profit. Managers should seek to maximize profits for the benefit of the common stockholders. High profit levels indicate that managers are doing a good job and performing their proper role in society.

Competition. Competition is the touchstone of the economic system which, when allowed to operate freely without interference by government or by monopoly, will produce an overall harmony with many benefits to society. The ideology is filled with warnings of the evils attendant upon government and labor interference in the competitive processes. The people in business holding the classical ideology still talk as though they are always faced with a cold, impersonal market mechanism over which they have no control.

Consumers and Service. Consumers and service to them hold a supreme position in classical ideology. The consumer is pictured as having great and ultimate power over the fate of business managers. If managers meet consumer demands, they will succeed; if not, they will fail. Consumers are considered to be independent and fickle. Aggressive advertising is necessary and in the community interest because it stimulates consumers and business activity. Service likewise is emphasized as being in the interests both of consumers and society by "bringing a better life to all."

Labor. Many people in business insist that bargaining between employee and employer should be on an individual basis, free of compulsion or coercion by government or unions. This idea is captured in the slogan "right to work," which stands in opposition to the closed shop and other union security rules, including effective strikes. Large numbers of managers, however, today accept the right of employees to join unions, to bargain collectively, and to maintain job security irrespective of union membership. On the other hand, the creed insists that other rights must also be protected. This means, for instance, that violence, boycotts, organized picketing, and other such kinds of union activity should be prohibited. Furthermore, unions are considered to be monopolies and should therefore be subject to the antitrust laws. The traditionalist sees industrywide bargaining as a monopoly power, and resists it.

Management. Management, according to the creed, has a right to administer its property as it sees fit without union interference. Encroachment on what are considered to be managerial prerogatives by contract work rules is resisted. The ideology says that wage-rate increases should be correlated with rises in productivity. Union restrictions of output are deplored. Indeed, the ideology asserts that the true road to prosperity for all is increased productivity.

International Trade. Not unexpectedly, one finds a schism in attitudes toward trade. The classical theory, of course, is foursquare for free trade; but when free trade conflicts with self-interest, as it often does, protectionism is advocated. Today, therefore, industries threatened by cheaper foreign imports want to be protected. Others not so threatened and benefiting from foreign trade want continual reductions in trade barriers throughout the world.

Economic Growth. The creed places faith in the natural operation of the competitive system to recover from cyclical downswings and to ensure higher levels of economic output over time. Given freedom from interferences by government and labor unions, the system is held to be self-correcting.

Importance of the Business. One of the dominant themes in the classical ideology is praise for the achievements of the business system, such as rising output, higher standards of living, and "the conversion of the luxuries of yesterday's rich to the necessities of today's masses," as Sutton and his colleagues put it. Nonmaterial benefits are also praised, such as the creation in and by business of a spirit of service, the ability of those with talent to find personal achievement in the business world, and the great possibilities to find a type of freedom which this system alone makes possible. The importance of people in business and the justification for their relatively high salaries are not neglected.

Underlying Values. The values underlying traditional business ideology are well known. Central is individualism, which stresses responsibility and freedom. One aspect of this value is that individuals are enjoined to work hard. Another is that individuals must be able to make choices freely in pursuit of self-interests. To the traditionalist, these values lead to just distribution of income.

High praise for the material benefits resulting from the economic system is based upon materialistic values. The unabashed faith in the future finds support in a value of optimism. The virtues of hard work inherent in the Puritan ethic are considered of high importance. A certain universalism also underlies the creed, one expression of which is that "what is good for business is good for all." Finally, it should be mentioned that the tone of the traditional ideology is practical, assured, austere, and unbending in its assumption of rightness.

Reality vs. Ideology. It is fair and important to say that no matter how far removed from reality some of these views may seem to be, most of them are still held by a majority of business managers. Reality and ideology generally are not the same. The significance of the ideology is lost if it is not understood that, fundamentally, it is not meant to be a description of what is going on today but rather it is a prescription of what ought to be. For many people in business, especially in the larger companies, such events as the jolt of the depression of the 1930s, the Keynesian economic revolution, and the more recent concern about major social problems have resulted in significant disagreement with important parts of the classical ideology.

Small Business Ideology. The ideology of the small business person is but a minor variation of the classical creed. The traditional creed expounds the view that business generally is small, and larger companies maintain this tradition by decentralizing operations. Large corporations are accepted, however, and their social benefits extolled, but small business persons often find themselves in opposition to big business. Small business persons also unashamedly seek and accept government aid for their class. Other businesses seek government aid for themselves or their industry, but generally not for their class. The small business is not as well organized as other business groups in expounding beliefs.

THE MODERN SOCIOECONOMIC MANAGERIAL IDEOLOGY

More and more managers of large and small corporations have enunciated an ideology considerably different from the classical position. The new ideology is not as well articulated, complete, and specific as the classical one. It certainly has less consensus than did the classical position a few decades ago. Nevertheless, it seems to be much more widely accepted today than when it was first developed or even a few years ago. There seems little question about the fact that it will grow in general acceptance in the future.

Many ideas in the modern socioeconomic managerial ideology were expressed by business leaders over the past one hundred or more years. It has been only during the past two decades in the United States, however, that the ideology has begun to take a reasonably comprehensive form and acquire growing acceptance among business leaders. While many business leaders and others have participated in the articulation of the ideology, the main themes have been well set forth by executives who participated in the McKinsey lectures at Columbia University and business leaders associated with the Committee for Economic Development. The following description of the new ideology will, therefore, lean heavily on the expressions of these people.

The Committee for Economic Development (CED). The CED is a group of some 300 business executives and educators who conduct research on topics of their own choosing and prepare policy recommendations. Millions of copies of these documents have been distributed and discussed by CED-sponsored business groups throughout the nation. The CED does not presume to promote the special interests of business, nor does it assume it speaks for any other group. It is a body of men and women, most of whom are from large companies, who speak principally from a business point of view and only for themselves. Since its creation in 1942, the CED has published several hundred carefully prepared research monographs covering major issues of concern to both business and the nation.[5] In light of this huge compilation and scope of inquiry, the résumé presented here can no more than touch lightly upon a few highlights of the disseminated ideology.

The McKinsey Lecture Series. The McKinsey lectures, sponsored first in 1956 by the Graduate School of Business, Columbia University, were given by chief executives of the largest business organizations in the United States. Each lecture was on a topic chosen by the speaker and later published in book form. Lecturers included men like Ralph J. Cordiner, Theodore V. Houser, Roger Blough, Crawford H. Greenewalt, Frederick R. Kappel, Marion B. Folsom, Thomas Watson, Jr., David Rockefeller, Frederic G. Donner, and Myron A. Wright. Neither individually nor collectively was there an effort to present a complete ideology. Compared with the flamboyant confidence and arrogance of the business speeches of the late nineteenth and early twentieth centuries, the tone of the McKinsey lectures was calm, thoughtful, cautious, and perhaps at times a bit apologetic.

Business Seen in a New Setting. The CED was formed because its originators felt the old ideology was deficient in dealing with the anticipated economic problems following the end of World War II, particularly the role of government to reduce the disastrous effects of an expected economic depression. As its fields of inquiry have expanded, its questioning of older ideology has become more widespread.

The holder of the traditional view either sees little change in the economic system in the last 50 years, or ignores it. The new managerial ideology sees change and seeks to reflect it. The CED and McKinsey lecturers see a new economic system structurally different from the old and interrelated in new ways with society.

Professional Managerial Responsibilities. Cordiner's first lecture set the theme of a new managerial role, which was defined by David Rockefeller in the following passage:

The old concept that the owner of a business had a right to use his property as he pleased to maximize profits has evolved into the belief that ownership carries certain binding social obligations. Today's manager serves as trustee not only for the owners but for the workers and indeed for our entire society. . . . Corporations have developed a sensitive awareness of their responsibility for maintaining an equitable balance among the claims of stockholders, employees, customers, and the public at large.[6]

Professional managers, said Rockefeller, are obliged to plan ahead to ensure the survival and prosperity of their enterprises; they have deep responsibilities for the people of their organizations, and they have broad social responsibilities. This theme can be found throughout the lectures and the many publications of the CED.

Business Social Responsibilities. The CED in a milestone statement called the *Social Responsibilities of Business Corporations,* published in 1971, strongly accepted the idea that "business functions by public consent, and its basic purpose is to serve constructively the needs of society—to the satisfaction of society." Society today, said the report, has broadened its expectations of business into what may be described as

three concentric circles of responsibilities for the efficient execution of the economic function—products, jobs, and economic growth.

The intermediate circle encompasses responsibility to exercise this economic function with a sensitive awareness of changing social values and priorities: for example, with respect to environmental conservation; hiring and relations with employees; and more rigorous expectations of customers for information, fair treatment, and protection from injury.

The outer circle outlines newly emerging and still amorphous responsibilities that business should assume to become more broadly involved in actively improving the social environment.[7]

The report then went on to spell out in detail responsibilities in each of these circles.

Classical ideology focused solely on the first circle. It accepted the idea that a business person's responsibility was solely to utilize resources efficiently in producing goods and services that society wanted at prices people were willing to pay. Classical economic theory said that if this were done well then stockholder profits would be maximized. Classical theory also said that the individual's pursuit of selfish interest in this way would, as if guided by an unseen hand (to use Adam Smith's well-known phrase), promote the public good. The CED policy statement observed that this concept of self-interest should be considerably expanded: "It is in the 'enlightened self-interest' of corporations to promote the public welfare in a positive way. . . . Indeed, the corporate interest broadly defined by management can support involvement in helping to solve virtually any social problem, because people who have a good environment, education, and opportunity make better employees, customers, and neighbors for business than those who are poor, ignorant, and oppressed." [8]

The drafting committee of the CED had great difficulty in getting the report accepted by the CED policy committee but it eventually was approved. At the time of the report the average business manager did not accept the concepts in the report fully or with enthusiasm. In the years that followed, however, more and more managers, particularly of larger corporations, have embraced the basic ideas in the report.

Cooperation and Acceptance of the Power of Government. Quite contrary to the classical philosophy, the modern ideology accepts a certain partnership with government in society. James Roche expressed it this way: "Business and government can ill afford to be adversaries. So mutual are our interests, so formidable are our challenges, that our times demand our strengthened alliance. The success of each largely depends upon the other. Today, business and government are each becoming more involved in the affairs of the other." [9] While this view is generally accepted in many CED publications and among most McKinsey lecturers, there is not complete agreement. Cordiner and Blough, for instance, expressed fear of rapidly growing federal power. Comparable fears have been found in some dissents in CED policy recommendations. There is no doubt, however, that the way the managerial ideology sees government is a clear break with the traditional implacable business antipathy to government.

A paper prepared by the CED strongly supported the principles of the Employment Act of 1946 and was influential in getting this legislation passed. (The act was vigorously opposed by most business managers.) This meant, of course, that the CED accepted a strong government hand in economic life in fulfilling the purposes of the act. It meant, too, that the CED accepted the Keynesian idea that balancing the federal budget annually was less important than economic stability. While accepting budgetary deficits to promote economic activity, the prevailing managerial creed advocates that surpluses in prosperous years offset deficits in poor years so that the budget is in balance over the entire business cycle. There is not the same fear of debt as in the traditional view, but its size is bothersome, and managers would be happier to see it reduced in prosperous years. The CED was an advocate of rebuilding Europe and accelerating United States economic development programs in underdeveloped countries.

Business leaders advocate much more participation of their peers in government affairs, from advice to full-time jobs.[10] One of the reasons for the sympathetic view of the CED toward government lies in the fact that the CED is dominated by executives from large firms who understand the importance of government action in providing an environment in which business can prosper. Another is that many of these executives have held important positions in the federal government and understand its problems, its motivations, and the requirements placed upon it.

Need for Big Organizations. Justification of large organizations is not well articulated in traditional ideology, a shortcoming which the managerial ideology seeks to fill. In the McKinsey lectures, as one might expect, the emphasis is on large, not small, businesses, and the writers point with pride to the accomplishments of and the need for large organizations. Cordiner, for example, said, "Without . . . large-scale economic enterprises, a nation is today a second-rate power and its people suffer both lower standards of living and greater vulnerability to attack by aggressive nations." [11] The McKinsey lecturers also took pains to point out that competition among large companies was much different from that among small companies, but equally rigorous and demanding.[12] Kappel dwelt at length on a theme which would not be denied by others of this group—that large organizations can be imaginative, innovative, and satisfying places in which to work. A number of the lecturers pointed out that through decentralization the great advantages accruing to size can be achieved.

Stress on Human Values. Every one of the McKinsey lecturers dwelt at some length on the treatment of people in organizations. Indeed, it is the most dominant of all the themes in this series. The views of the managerial ideology are in stark contrast to the one-sided doctrine of self-interest in the classical creed.

Houser feels the most important tasks of managers concern people. He says:

It can no longer be taken for granted that ability will find its own level. In this age of the corporation, management must take specific steps to make sure that people have an opportunity to grow and develop; otherwise too many of them are likely to be lost in the labyrinthine processes of the organization. This is one of the major responsibilities of management today, a responsibility not only to its own people but to our free society.[13]

Kappel asks the question: "What makes a vital business?" and answers it: "Vital people make it." [14] He then elaborates at length on why and how. Watson says he believes IBM's most important philosophy is "our respect for the individual." [15]

There are many aspects of this increasing concern for individuals. For instance, several writers point out that some conformity is necessary, but that a large organization can stimulate innovation and creativity in people, can provide satisfying jobs, and can facilitate individual growth.

Labor. Despite the great importance of labor power, which business managers see as a formidable competitor, very few CED reports have been published on the subject; and, except for a discussion by Blough, the matter was almost completely ignored by the McKinsey lecturers. For many managers the classical ideology regarding labor is still fundamental. For more and more of them, however, the legitimacy of labor unions is accepted with relative equanimity.

International Trade. The CED takes a more liberal view of free trade than the classical ideology, which although equivocal, leans to protectionism. In a 1959 statement the CED saw advantages in some protection from free world markets, but in later statements it has put itself in the ranks of those seeking to reduce tariff barriers. For example, in 1964 the CED said: "Our principal recommendation is that the United States should seek in free world trade negotiations to obtain tariff reductions from its trade partners in return for reciprocal United States concessions, coming as close as possible to cutting free world tariffs by 50 percent, across the board."

Agriculture. The CED is in agreement with the traditional creed, as well as with many academic economists, in advocating for agriculture a return to a free market which will set price levels, rather than having the government do it.

Other Themes. The last McKinsey lecture was given in 1967. Since then business managers have substantially increased their public pronouncements about the new socioeconomic role of the large corporation in society. The CED continued to expand and clarify its views about business responsibilities beyond narrow economic pursuits as noted above. Individual corporations have taken strong measures to introduce the social point of view in the decision-making processes within their organizations and to account publicly for their social programs.

Many other business leaders have given much thought to the present and future needs of society and the roles of their organizations in meeting them. As one reads the reviews of these managers a number of major themes can be identified, such as the following, which the leaders of the CED and the McKinsey lecturers would find agreeable:

◇ A better world is possible, especially if we plan for it rather than only react to events.

◇ Business managers are in a position to influence the quality of our lives, for better or worse.

◇ Modern business leaders have far broader interests than short-range profit. They are socially and politically (civically) concerned and active. They take professional pride in their role and are continuously in the process of learning.

◇ Modern business leaders accept a responsibility to use the resources at their command to balance the many interests focused on their companies.

◇ It is important to discover new and better ways to improve public decision making.

◇ The better business managers are informed about factors that affect business and the full range of our social, economic, and political problems, the better they will be able to formulate positive programs for the protection and improvement of our society, and the more likely they will be to want to do so.

◇ As society becomes more affluent and enlightened, the greater is the responsibility of managers to consider more carefully human values both within and outside the firm.

◇ Business managers do have social responsibilities and must face up to discharging them.

◇ Corporation executives should strive to institutionalize the social point of view in the decision-making processes of their organizations.

◇ Corporations, especially the larger ones, are accountable for their social as well as economic programs and should report publicly about them in an appropriate fashion.

Precisely what all this means is not clear, but at these levels of abstraction a surprising number of executives and observers of the business scene would agree. There are many others than the CED and the McKinsey lecturers espousing the socioeconomic managerial ideology, both in the business world and elsewhere.[16]

Blending of the Traditional and New Ideologies. The reader must not conclude that the newer socioeconomic managerial ideology has replaced the classical ideology. That clearly is not the case. The business creed today is composed of an underlying traditional ideology upon which has been superimposed the new managerial ideology. The latter has both added important dimensions to the traditional ideology and significantly modified some older doctrine. As such, the newer ideology is a mix of some anachronistic debris of the past and enlightened adaptations to fit the needs of contemporary society.

Much of the newer ideology is vague and amorphous. Some of it is in stark contradiction to older ideology. This, of course, creates confusion about the ideology in and out of business. It can and does create ambiguities and frustrations in managers and their decision making. A clear example is the potential for social programs to reduce profits. A recent study of 439 executives showed clearly that many of them "want very much to serve society better (if only to avoid increased criticism and regulation). But they say they are severely constrained by the nature of their institutional mandate (they must, after all, generate profits regularly) and by an inability to determine who 'speaks for society' and therefore what society wants of them as business executives." [17]

A growing number of managers, however, see no inconsistency between the social demands of the newer philosophy and the pursuit of maximum profits in the classical ideology. More managers are accepting the following observation:

An appropriate blending of the social and economic performance of business will strengthen each and permit business to respond much better to the aspirations of people for a better life. . . . Corporations must pursue social goals as well as traditional economic objectives. Many see an inconsistency and conflict between these two roles, but corporations are demonstrating that the two roles can complement one another. The great challenge ahead for managers of corporations is to establish policies and programs which will pursue both economic and social goals which will be mutually supportive.[18]

No one knows how many executives agree with this statement nor with what intensity. I believe, however, that many managers agree with it. This is partially corroborated by a survey made among 164 executives of larger companies which asked them this question: "Social responsibility and wealth maximization are among many objectives that management must try to achieve." Eighty-seven percent said they agreed with the statement.[19]

It is altogether likely that in the future the newer views about business responsibilities will find greater acceptance and replace or downgrade some of the more obsolete classical formulations. Before taking too extreme a position against parts of the classical tradition, however, it is important to note that it contains some fundamental ideas and considerations of major significance to the workings of this society. Rigorous competition, the pursuit of self-interest, the importance of the individual, strong questioning of government use of power, the operation of laws of supply and demand in the marketplace, efficient utilization of economic resources, and so on—these are still relevant to the type of society we have and wish to keep. It is not so much the ideas and values that need modification as the often irrelevant way in which the business ideology formulates and uses them to resist change in specific cases. Reformulation of some old doctrines, together with greater attention to filling blanks and resolving inconsistencies, would strengthen the ideology.

GAPS IN THE IDEOLOGIES

The Classical Ideology. There are, of course, many other concepts included in the ideology, but rather than examine them, it seems more useful to consider some of the major blanks or inadequately covered issues. The ideology covers only part of the landscape and generally ignores things not easily explained, not agreeable, or not pleasant to consider. For instance, the old ideology is rather silent on business bearing any of the social costs of progress, such as unemployment, water pollution, or urbanization problems. In their evaluation of the creed, Sutton and his colleagues point out that it "rarely makes any claim on the esthetic quality of modern life, the superiority of the moral standards of our present society over those of earlier societies or of other countries, or the piety of life under the System. . . . Nowhere in the creed is there any suggestion that conflict exists between religion and capitalism, humanitarianism and money seeking. . . ."[20] Strangely enough, little space is given to the great improvements in such noneconomic values as health, span of life, or equal opportunity. The creed fails to point out that there are many reasons for the success of this society in improving the well-being of its people aside from business, as important as business is.

The Socioeconomic Managerial Ideology. This ideology, of course, fills a number of the gaps in the classical ideology but also has shortcomings. For instance, until Watergate and the payoff scandals of 1976–1977 very little was said about morality and ethical standards. It is true that many companies have had codes of ethics for many years but the subject was not a matter of discussion in the business community. The modern ideology still clings to the myth of stockholder control of large corporations. The ideology still clings to a laissez-faire tradition although in a less uncompromising fashion than the classical ideology.

The new ideology, like the classical one, treats relationships with government with ambiguity if not a certain element of hypocrisy. Today, as in the past, business people denounce government intervention in the economy in general terms but accept it, and often demand it, when their own interests are threatened. At any rate, there is a much better understanding and acceptance of government intervention in economic and social matters by today's business leaders than those of the past.

Heilbroner evaluated the McKinsey lectures and found a gap between statement and action. The pattern of the lectures, he asserts, is "more or less transparent defense of privilege masquerading as philosophy, the search for sanction cloaked as a search for truth. . . ." An even more serious indictment of the lectures, says Heilbroner, is the fact that they lack inspiration to deal with the tough problems ahead. He says:

At its core, the business ideology as a spiritual creed or as an historic beacon is vitiated by something that is missing—I cannot but think fatally missing—from its deepest conception. What it lacks is a grandiose image of society, a projection of human possibilities cast in a larger mold than is offered by today's institutions.[21]

Heilbroner's conclusions seem too harsh. There was and still is much rhetoric in business leaders' profession of social responsibility. Since these early McKinsey lectures, however, the record of institutionalizing the social point of view in the decision-making processes of larger corporations has improved tremendously. Both the McKinsey lecturers and early CED policy statements were forerunners in sensing that the time had arrived for larger corporations, especially, to continue productive efficiency and at the same time help society to improve the quality of life.

How rapidly the ideas in the new socioeconomic managerial ideology will spread through the business community in thought and action cannot be foretold. If these views become more generally accepted by business managers and replace elements of the traditional views with which they conflict, the business ideology will be more in tune with the changing expectations of society and more likely, therefore, to be a significant positive force in the achievement of the great society which is the dream of tomorrow.

The modern large corporation has still to win the prize of legitimacy. It is not likely to be won with an ideology that fails to respond appropriately to the aspirations of the American people. Many business leaders today understand and accept this idea. To institutionalize the ideology in the decision-making processes of the corporation will, however, necessitate changes in the way things are done.[22]

FROM THE CLASSICAL BUSINESS IDEOLOGY TO COMMUNITARIANISM

George Lodge believes that a major transformation is now taking place in which a new business ideology is replacing the old one.[23] He calls the new ideology "communitarianism," which will be described below. In an effort to measure attitudes of the business community with respect to the old and the new ideologies, William F. Martin and Lodge conducted a survey among the readers of the *Harvard Business Review*. A total of 1,844 readers participated in this survey. They were typically male American corporate executives in the upper ranks of companies manufacturing consumer or industrial products. Almost half were from the Middle Atlantic and Midwest states. About half were from large companies. The respondents were given descriptions of the classical ideology and of the new ideology and were asked to determine which one they (1) preferred, (2) found dominant in the United States at the time of the survey in 1975, (3) expected to dominate thinking in 1985, and (4) believed would be more effective in solving future problems.

A brief description of Ideology I, the classical philosophy, was given respondents as follows:

The community is no more than the sum of the individuals in it. Self-respect and fulfillment result from an essentially lonely struggle in which initiative and hard work pay off. The fit survive and if you don't survive, you are probably unfit. Property rights are a sacred guarantor of individual rights, and the uses of property are best controlled by competition to satisfy consumer desires in an open market. The least government is the best. Reality is perceived and understood through the specialized activities of experts who dissect and analyze in objective study." [24]

This is the essence of the classical tradition described above. It extolls the values of individualism, private property, free competition, and limited government.

Ideology II was described as follows:

Individual fulfillment and self-respect are the result of one's place in an organic social process; we "get our kicks" by being part of a group. A well-designed group makes full use of our individual capacities. Property rights are less important than the rights derived from membership in the community or a group—for example, rights to income, health, and education. The uses of property are best regulated according to the community's need, which often differs from individual consumer desires. Government must set the community's goals and coordinate their implementation. The perception of reality requires an awareness of whole systems and of the interrelationships between and among the wholes. This holistic process is the primary task of science.[25]

This is the essence of the communitarianism ideology, which views the individual as an inseparable part of the community "in which his rights and duties are determined by the needs of the common good. Government plays an important role as the planner and implementer of community needs."

Seventy percent of the respondents said they preferred Ideology I over Ideology II. About 62 percent of the readers believed Ideology I was the most dominant ideology in the United States at the time of the survey. However, 73 percent believed Ideology II will dominate in the year 1985. In response to the fourth question put to the United States respondents, 60 percent said they believed Ideology I would be the more effective one in dealing with future problems of this nation. About the same number of foreign respondents said they believed that Ideology II would be more effective in solving future problems.

Those preferring Ideology II seemed to have stronger convictions than those preferring Ideology I. Of those who preferred Ideology II, 95 percent thought this ideology would permit better solutions for future problems, while only 85 percent of those preferring Ideology I believed it would be best in dealing with future problems.

CONCLUDING COMMENT

It must not be thought, of course, that Lodge's concept of communitarianism, the socioeconomic managerial ideology, or the classical ideology are accepted by managers in their pure form or that any one of the ideologies is *the* business ideology. These major creeds are not complete, well-structured, or stable. Each is incomplete, has gaping holes in it, is continuously under attack, and is constantly changing.

For the great majority of business institutions, most of which are comparatively small companies, the classical ideology is accepted today by society and business people in those companies and probably will be for some time into the future. Most people do not expect a person whose business is desperately striving to break even to concentrate on much else than making a profit so long, of course, as that person abides by the law. For larger organizations, however, society expects much more and leaders of such corporations accept the challenges of the socioeconomic managerial ideology. However, it is altogether likely that many more managers in larger corporations will have a personal ideology which is a mixture of the classical and socioeconomic managerial ideologies than an ideology that is either pure classical or pure socioeconomic or pure communitarianism. This is the way it is likely to be for some time ahead.

REFERENCES

1. Herman E. Krooss and Charles Gilbert, *American Business History* (Englewood Cliffs, N.J.: Prentice-Hall, 1972), p. 326.
2. R. Joseph Monsen, Jr., *Modern American Capitalism: Ideologies and Issues* (Boston: Houghton Mifflin, 1963), pp. 9–10.
3. Dow Votaw and S. Prakash Sethi, *The Corporate Dilemma: Traditional Values Versus Contemporary Problems* (Englewood Cliffs, N.J.: Prentice-Hall, 1973), p. 50.
4. Francis X. Sutton, Seymour E. Harris, Carl Kaysen, and James Tobin, *The American Business Creed* (Cambridge: Harvard University Press, 1956), p. 11.
5. The reader is referred, in particular, to the following CED publications: *Toward More Production, More Jobs, and More Freedom* (1946); *Taxes and the Budget* (1947); *Economic Policy for American Agriculture* (1956); *Economic Development Assistance, A Long-term Policy for Assisting Economic Growth and Encouraging Independence in the Underdeveloped Nations of the Free World* (1957); *Toward a Realistic Farm Program* (1957); *Anti-Recession Policy for 1958* (1958); *The European Common Market and the Balance of Payments Problem* (1959); *Trade Negotiations for a Better Free World Economy* (1964); *Educating Tomorrow's Managers—The Business Schools and the Business Community* (1964); *Managing a Full Employment Economy* (1966); *Social Responsibilities of Business Corporations* (1971).
6. David Rockefeller, *Creative Management in Banking* (New York: McGraw-Hill, 1964), pp. 22–23.

7. Committee for Economic Development, *Social Responsibilities of Business Corporations* (New York: CED, 1971), p. 15.
8. CED, *Social Responsibilities*, pp. 27–28.
9. James M. Roche, "Understanding: The Key to Business-Government Cooperation," *Michigan Business Review*, March 1969, p. 6.
10. Marion B. Folsom, *Executive Decision Making* (New York: McGraw-Hill, 1962), pp. 134–137.
11. Ralph J. Cordiner, *New Frontiers for Professional Managers* (New York: McGraw-Hill, 1956), p. 3.
12. See, for example, Roger Blough, *Free Man and the Corporation* (New York: McGraw-Hill, 1959), pp. 10–11.
13. Theodore V. Houser, *Big Business and Human Values* (New York: McGraw-Hill, 1957), p. 4.
14. Frederick R. Kappel, *Vitality in a Business Enterprise* (New York: McGraw-Hill, 1960), p. 5.
15. Thomas Watson, Jr., *A Business and Its Beliefs* (New York: McGraw-Hill, 1963), p. 13, italics omitted.
16. For more comprehensive treatments of this ideology, the reader is referred to the following:
Daniel Bell, *The Coming of Post-Industrial Society* (New York: Basic Books, 1973); Gerald F. Cavanaugh, *American Business Values in Transition* (Englewood Cliffs, N.J.: Prentice-Hall, 1976); Lee E. Preston and James E. Post, *Private Management and Public Policy* (Englewood Cliffs, N.J.: Prentice-Hall, 1975); John J. Corson, *Business in the Humane Society* (New York: McGraw-Hill, 1971); Henry Ford, II, *The Human Environment and Business* (New York: Weybright and Talley, 1970); Neil Jacoby, *Corporate Power and Social Responsibility* (New York: Macmillan, 1973); George C. Lodge, *The New American Ideology* (New York: Knopf, 1975); David Rockefeller, *Creative Management in Banking* (New York: McGraw-Hill, 1964); George A. Steiner, "Institutionalizing Corporate Social Decisions," *Business Horizons*, December 1975; and Clarence C. Walton, *Corporate Social Responsibilities* (Belmont, Calif.: Wadsworth, 1967).
17. John L. Paluszek, *Business and Society: 1976–2000* (New York: AMACOM, 1976), pp. 2–3.
18. Steiner, "Institutionalizing Corporate Social Decisions," *Business Horizons*, December 1975, p. 12.
19. Charles P. Edmonds, III, and John H. Hand, "What Are The Real Long-run Objectives of Business?" *Business Horizons*, December 1976, p. 77.
20. Sutton et al., *The American Business Creed*, p. 49.
21. Robert Heilbroner, "The View from the Top," in Earl F. Cheit, ed., *The Business Establishment* (New York: Wiley, 1964), p. 35.
22. See, for example, Robert W. Ackerman, *The Social Challenge to Business* (Cambridge, Harvard University Press, 1975); Neil W. Chamberlain, *Remaking American Values* (New York: Basic Books, 1977); and George A. Steiner, *Business and Society*, 2nd ed. (New York: Random House, 1975).
23. George C. Lodge, *The New American Ideology* (New York: Knopf, 1975).
24. William F. Martin and George Cabot Lodge, "Our Society in 1985—Business May Not Like It," *Harvard Business Review*, November–December 1975, pp. 143–144.
25. Martin and Lodge, p. 144.

John F. Mee

22
Changing Values and Institutions

Tell me today what the philosopher thinks, the professor expounds, the schoolmaster teaches, the scholar publishes in his treatises and textbooks, and I shall prophesy the conduct of individuals, the ethics of businessmen, the schemes of political leaders, the plans of economists, the pleadings of lawyers, the decisions of judges, the legislation of lawmakers, the treaties of diplomats, and the decisions of state a generation hence.

—ANONYMOUS

"Every great movement of thought or practice materializes in some definite association of individuals organized to express its principles and follow its evolution." That was written in 1911 by Charles B. Going, editor of *Engineering Magazine* and author of the first book published under the title of *Principles of Industrial Engineering*. Those words from one of the early management educators could be used for a prologue to the evolution of the science of management, the management movement, scientific management, and the classical management literature that characterized the early twentieth century.

The "management movement" was generated by environmental forces, factors, and trends that emerged in the United States and Europe during the transition from an agricultural to an industrial economy and an economics-oriented society. Management as a subject for study, inquiry, research, and education is not very old. Its evolutionary process continues in a dynamic state into a post-industrial society and an impinging socially oriented society.

The science of management started its evolutionary process with the hope of separating waste and inefficiency from human effort to provide increased productivity and higher wages to decrease poverty. The general idea was greater prosperity for workers and owners. Prior to the management movement, the economy was suffering from low wages and low productivity. Results of the management movement after some 50 years include: (1) an average worker compensation increase of 5.4 percent and an average 3.4 percent increase in worker productivity per year during the decade of the 1970s; (2) a gross national product rate of a trillion dollars by 1970 and some 35 percent of the world's annual income; (3) a body of knowledge from experimentation and research that serves as the basis for management education in the nation's colleges, universities, and company management development programs; and (4) the cooperative efforts of the American Management Associations to advance the science and the practice of management worldwide.

During the twentieth century the business corporation developed into the dominant economic and social institution in a dynamic society characterized by upward mobility for the competent persons who embraced a work ethic. The corporation served as the institution that pooled land, labor, and capital to create wealth, reduce poverty, and distribute goods and services to an expanding population. The corporation served as the vehicle or transfer mechanism to create goods and services; management evolved as the governor of the corporations.

The ratification of the Constitution of the United States in 1789 provided the foundation for the private enterprise system. At the time of Thomas Jefferson, the United States was expected to develop into a nation of small farms and small businesses with owner managers as the backbone of the nation. Instead, there has developed a nation of employees working in national and multinational corporations. Managers have advanced in several stages, from the owner managers, who have been called captains of industry, to corporate speculators and exploiters, to professional managers, and finally to the emerging public-oriented managers. As business institutions progressed, and as the stages of management unfolded, the science and practice of management evolved from a concept of management as a system of authority based on the constitutional right of ownership to a concept of management as a resource based on the knowledge, skills, and values of the human workforce.

The history and development of the United States unfolded in response to changing values and institutions. Institutions and values originate with people, and in turn, those values and institutions influence the behavior and the purpose of people. Institutions are established by people to perpetuate practices and customs that become a persistent element in the life or the culture of organized social groups. The institutions become the foundation of what is termed the establishment, and the establishment prevails only as long as its sanctity or authority is upheld by the established institutions. Institutions can be shaken and rocked by changing values and priorities. Establishments are always modified or eroded in the long run. New establishments appear that are more in conformity with changing values and serving institutions.

Reciprocating forces between people and their prevailing values and existing institutions have been in motion in the New World since dissatisfied people began crossing the Atlantic in search of a better life. People have a long and successful record for using their intelligence and energy to shape institutions to satisfy their needs and reflect their values. Several major transitions or transformations have contributed to the development of our nation and the evolution of the science and the practice of management. There are some signals and indicators in society today that communicate to us that another major transformation is in progress. Society in the twenty-first century will be characterized by values and institutions that are now taking shape. The future is designed by the present.

PAST TRANSFORMATIONS

The history of the United States is a history of a series of transitions and transformations that have occurred because of discontent and dissatisfactions. Discernible trends indicate that another period of major transformation may be with us.

During the past century, the values and the practices of economic man have been dominant in our lifestyles, our institutions, and our managerial practices. Economic man flourished after the eras of religious man (circa 1660–1760) and political man (circa 1760–1860), and may now be in his zenith with a record of material achievement unsurpassed in the history of the world. But changing values and institutions are heralding the emergence of a so-called social man. If social man is successful in effecting a transformation in our Western civilization, we may expect some changes from the prevailing ethic of the individual with its economic institutions to a social ethic whose institutions are characterized by concern for the society as a whole.

At present there seems to be an atmosphere of doubt and concern that causes loss of confidence in our institutions and their leadership. Signs of lost confidence appear in the government, in the mass media, in the church, in the military, in the universities, and in business. Established ideas, beliefs, and assumptions that gave our institutions legitimacy, stability, and authority are being eroded by a flow of new concepts, values, and priorities. Business, government, and educational administrators find it difficult to operate in an environment of declining stability where old ideas, values, and institutions are no longer accepted.

Any period of transition is characterized by uncertainty and concern for the future until proper perspectives are formulated. Some confidence in the future can be generated if we relate the present turmoil to other transformations during the development of our nation. We can be optimistic if we remember that we have always achieved success after frustration and adversity. Let us quickly review the past periods of transformation since the 1607 founding of the Jamestown Colony.

Religious Man. Our first major institutions were religious and educational in nature. Since the landing of the Pilgrims in 1620 and the founding of Harvard College in 1636, people have been preoccupied and concerned with their personal objectives, values, and lifestyles. The century between 1660 and 1760 could be labeled the era of religious man. People were more concerned with their religious values and institutions than subsequent political, economic, and social ones. The objective of the faithful was survival and salvation. Their lifestyle was shaped by religious motivations and institutions so that they could be of greater service to the Lord. The early colleges were devoted to training ministers and an educated laity capable of understanding the scriptures. Satan was the enemy of the establishment under attack, and the establishment was the oppressive Church of England.

Religious man enjoyed success in establishing religious and educational institutions; he was guided by a prevailing set of religious and educational institutions and beliefs. He gave us the foundations of a religious philosophy and an educational philosophy, from which we are still operating.

Political Man. During the century between 1760 and 1860 new values and priorities started to shape a new lifestyle. Political man joined religious man in the New World. Political man struggled not only for survival but for democracy. The new enemy became the Crown of England, and the establishment under attack was the monarchy, labeled a tyrant. As political man worked for political freedom against tyranny, he was reinforced by religious man and the idea of religious freedom.

Political man achieved the objectives of democracy and the democratic process. The United States Constitution was ratified in 1789, after a Declaration of Independence in 1776. England was vanquished in 1815 after the close of the War of 1812. Mexico was set in place in 1848, and the Civil War was over by 1865.

With periods of transformation that established the values and the institutions of religious man and political man, the nation was developing with guidelines from both operating religious and political philosophies.

Economic Man. During the era of 1860 to 1960, a new set of environmental conditions evolved and the nation underwent another period of transformation. Economic man appeared to proclaim poverty and privation the enemy, and the objective was economic freedom for all willing to work and save to acquire property, income, and wealth to realize the American dream.

Wealth and power shifted from agriculture and rural areas to industry and urban areas. Private enterprise prevailed. Scientific management appeared and flourished. Communism and socialism were avowed enemies. Colleges expanded their programs to support the efforts of economic man. Following the Morrill Act of 1862, schools of engineering flourished. Schools of business flourished after the founding of the Wharton School in 1881.

Public policy furthered the influence of economic man through the Employment Act of 1946, which called for a national economic policy "to promote maximum employment, production, and purchasing power." It was believed that full employment would prevent depressions and enable the greatest number of people to prosper. During the decade of the 1960s the operation of the Employment Act may have boosted economic man to his pinnacle and concurrently initiated forces for social change.

It is difficult to criticize the achievement record of economic man. Property, wealth, and income have been generated in a magnitude unequaled in the history of the world. Economic man has equaled the accomplishments of religious man and political man. Less than 5 percent of the people produce food for the other 95 percent with a surplus to export to other nations. Colleges and universities now have enrollments of over 11 million students compared to about 238,000 in 1900. The corporation and the multinational corporation have become dominant economic institutions of economic man. Unions have become powerful labor institutions to represent employees. Managers have become more public-oriented and socially responsible.

The values and the institutions of economic man enabled the United States to become the world's first trillion-dollar economy, that is, the first nation to exceed a trillion dollars in both gross national product and personal income. To equal that achievement, the combined product of four leading nations is required: Russia, Japan, West Germany, and the United Kingdom. Those nations have double the population of the United States with more land area. The citizens of the United States can claim only 6 percent of the population and 7 percent of the land of the world. Yet those relatively few people have created half of the wealth of the world and they realize about 35 percent of the world's annual income. There is no historical precedent for so much wealth being created by so few people.

During the recent 1960s when everything was going so well for economic man, it appears that he now may have enjoyed his greatest moment prior to facing another major transformation in our continuum of civilization. Never have so few people created so much wealth and income in one decade and at the same time experienced so much dissatisfaction and opposition. Before the close of the decade of the 1960s, it appeared that many people, especially young people, were rejecting the institutions and values of economic man. They voiced their aversion to the materialistic culture; they called for a blending of socially oriented objectives with the economic objectives of economic man. The new enemy became the system, and the establishment under attack became the corporate structure. Young people resisted putting on the organizational harness of corporate structures and being housebroken to competitive and dehumanizing situations with emphasis on science and technology at the expense of social and human values.

Social Man. The objectives of so-called social man are not as sharp and vivid as those of religious, political, or economic man in retrospect. So-called social man seems to be rejecting the values of an industrial society and the acquisitive pursuits of people for wealth, property, and income. Social man seems to be struggling for liberation from many of the beliefs and values that provided the materialistic lifestyle of economic man as well as relief from many of the norms that guided the behavior of religious man and political man. During previous periods of transformation, people sought liberation from sin, oppression, and poverty. Their objectives were focused on salvation, political democracy, and economic security.

Stable and influential institutions were fostered and developed during the eras of religious man, political man, and economic man. Religious, political, and economic philosophies were formulated and followed by succeeding generations. The United States became the most wealthy and powerful nation in the world. Then the citizens began to lose faith in their institutions and develop a critical attitude toward religious, political, business, and educational leaders and organizations. Economic man and the so-called system that is providng 218 million Americans with the highest standards of living, health, and education in the world are under attack from members of a developing new culture or counterculture.

The Need for a Social Philosophy

Our institutions, and especially our educational institutions, seem to be operating without a unifying social philosophy. Consequently, we are hampered by pluralism and diversity. A special report from the Conference Board in 1970 announced that the number one problem facing Americans is that of the divisions in our society. Such divisions—white-black, rich-poor, elite-nonelite, young-old, urban-rural—are weakening our national unity and purpose. Reunification will be a long and costly process.

Many business leaders are accepting the concept of corporate social responsibility. However, such social responsibilities are neither clearly understood nor stated. The belief that business is both an economic and a social institution is generally accepted. Social man is trying to change and modify our values and beliefs. Unfortunately, social man and the movement he is trying to develop lacks the unifying philosophies of the Judeo-Christian ethic and tradition, natural rights, the Constitution, and Social Darwinism. Social man is calling for a new system with a base of humane values—love, peace, cooperation, and consideration for the environment.

Dissatisfactions and the Turning Point

Why should concern about our institutions and a general malaise have appeared in the United States at a time when employment, income, production, spending, education enrollments—most of the economic indicators—were at historical high points? Instead of appreciation for such a state of prosperity, our managers of business and governmental institutions were confronted with an array of social problems, such as:

◇ Disruption in our best educational institutions and alleged educational irrelevance.
◇ Divisiveness in our society between black and white, young and old, rich and poor, urban and rural.
◇ Deterioration of the physical environment and mounting environmental concern.
◇ Inflation and monetary devaluation.
◇ Undesirable urban spread.
◇ Dissatisfaction with work assignments.
◇ Disregard for law, order, and authority.
◇ Rise of a youth culture and a questioning of the traditional values of society.
◇ Concern with equal employment opportunities for women and minorities.
◇ Concern about poor quality of products and poor quality of work.
◇ Dissatisfaction with distribution of income.
◇ Criticism of business institutions and business leadership.
◇ Human rights movement vs. property rights.

Greater abundance of wealth, income, production, employment, and spending in the decade of the 1960s did not result in greater satisfactions and approvals of the producing and the consuming public in the 1970s.

THE TURNING POINT

During the past century, owner managers and professional managers have oriented their activities and interests toward economic growth, operating on the assumption that the infusion of any economy with capital and technology would result in progress and betterment. Evaluated by the criteria of economic growth, the records of managers of business and industrial enterprise during the past century must be given honor grades. How will the future managers in society be evaluated and judged? For what virtues will future managers be rewarded?

One of the reports from The Club of Rome, *Mankind at the Turning Point,* concludes that "growth for growth's sake in the sense of ever increasing numbers and larger size simply cannot continue forever." If an economy grows at a 5 percent annual rate, by the end of the next century it would become 500 times greater or 50,000 percent higher. Irreplaceable resources are being used at a rate that cannot be sustained even if the use of materials declines in relation to the rise in economic output. The lifestyle achieved by the upper fifth of people in the Western world cannot be enjoyed by the rest of a rapidly increasing humanity. Economic man has striven for economic growth in physical and biological terms; emerging social man will work for growth in social and psychological dimensions.

Sometime between now and the end of the twenty-first century, there will be a turning point or a recognition point for the managers of business and industry. At that point the values and priorities introduced by social man will dominate and meld with the values and priorities of economic man. The emerging public-oriented manager, a descendant of the owner managers through the present professional managers, will be required to use fewer materials and less capital while making a better and greater utilization of human talents and resources. Increasing numbers of people will attain higher levels of formal education and will become more quality oriented with fewer quantitative needs for material playthings for prestige.

Our nation has become a nation of employees (manager employees, worker employees, professional employees, scientific employees, and so on). The employees have developed into a dependent population, dependent upon a paycheck for survival and satisfactions from institutions in the economic system. All classes of employees have raised their educational preparation for careers; they have thereby raised their expectations and aspirations for interesting, challenging, and inspiring work. They expect social and psychological satisfactions in addition to basic economic rewards from work. The charge is made that present professional managers, oriented to the assumptions of economic man, have not provided the so-called knowledge workers, as compared with manual workers, with work that brings self-esteem and self-realization. Consequently, increasing numbers of knowledge workers are disillusioned, dissatisfied, and disappointed. As a result, absenteeism, lackadaisical work, and poor quality output give the consumer inferior and poor products at inflated prices. Thus, dissatisfaction becomes rampant, and more sectors of society look to the managers for leadership toward a state of improved worker satisfactions in a stable economy in a more humane society.

PRESENT TRANSFORMATIONS

The future economy will be favorable for public-oriented managers with the skill, the knowledge, and the values to design employment that can utilize the talents of higher-educated employees. Material resources will be husbanded and more limited in use. (Perhaps energy and new raw material reserves will be stored for future space exploration and travel for new homes on other planets for the survival of *Homo sapiens.*) Human resources will claim first priority among managers, who will be expected to structure work and organizations that will give employees work objectives to inspire them instead of job procedures that bore them.

After economic man has merged with social, humane, or intellectual man, some managers will suffer rapid obsolescence and disutility. Other managers will ascend to positions of prominence and leadership in the maintenance of a private enterprise economy that will be stimulated by the values and priorities of social man.

Individualism. The values and priorities that guided economic man for more than a century are being changed and eroded by the pressures of social man. In our traditional set of beliefs, the individual plays the major role in the world of economic man. The individual accepts a life of hard work, thrift, obedience to a recognized authority, and delayed gratifications caused by preparation, thrift, and saving. Economic man engages in a struggle to survive and acquire property, wealth, and income. In the changing beliefs, social man seeks satisfaction, not from heroic individual efforts, but from participation in a social process. He seeks a place in his community to satisfy his desire for belonging and affiliating with a social organization. He is guided by a social ethic rather than the individual ethic of economic man.

Property. Economic man considered property as an extension of an owner's person. An owner possesses authority over the use of property, and authority flows from the ownership of property. The right of private ownership for the individual is provided in the Constitution. Property rights give the individual freedom from sovereign encroachments. For social man, property rights give way to the rights of membership in the community. Social man tends to use property without the rights of ownership by renting, leasing, or contracting. He prefers to enjoy property, health, and income as well as other rights by virtue of his membership in the community. Social man fosters programs for equal economic opportunity, civil rights, and affirmative actions for all members of the community. He seeks the benefits and enjoyment that property offers without the struggle and responsibility for ownership. He prefers to use rather than to own.

Competition. For economic man, competition in the marketplace controlled the use of property. Individuals competed with each other during the process of acquiring or losing property, wealth, and income. A belief in the survival of the most fit was accepted generally. Social man, however, prefers to use community need to satisfy the desires of the consumer. Competition is being replaced by need for the purpose of controlling the use of property. The philosophy of Social Darwinism is suffering erosion. Attempts are being made to use administered prices and wages in place of the market supply and demand.

Role of Government. Economic man considered the best government to be the least government. The government should provide the climate for economic man to acquire property in competition with other individuals. Social man with his social ethic, however, looks to the government as the monitor for his activities. The role of the government in economic and social affairs has been expanding. Almost 20 percent of the workforce is employed by some government agency or political subdivision. The government gives subsidies, allowances, and contracts to universities, business firms, and farmers. The government tends to move more and more into the economic activities of the nation to regulate or control the employment, safety, health, conditions of employment, hours, and wages of members of the workforce. The government is attempting to move into the control of the use of land as well as regulate the money market. Thus, economic man is under government control in his use of labor, land, and capital for his economic pursuits. His authority based on property rights is being displaced by government authority.

Specialization. Economic man believed in the advantages of specialization. He believed that if he attended to the parts, somehow the whole enterprise would work all right. He believed that if every individual followed his self-interest and did what was best for him, the result would be in the best interests of the whole society. Somehow a greater interdependency of the parts has developed, and social man advocates a perception of the total system composed of the parts. Economic man started with a confidence in the independence of individuals. As business grew into complex organizations, individuals became dependent upon the organization. The trend is now toward greater interdependency of both individuals and organizations.

Stages of Management. During the centuries of religious man, political man, and the first portion of economic man, the owner manager prevailed. Ownership provided the right to manage a business or an enterprise. Some owner managers, motivated by the values set by the Puritan ethic, the Rerum Novarum of Pope Leo XIII, Social Darwinism, and the natural laws, built large-scale organizations. Although they were still owner managers, they became known as captains of industry. They started and developed our basic industries in steel, transportation, petroleum, iron, communications, and banking. At the turn of the century, the captains of industry gave way to the financial managers who had control of the businesses but not ownership. The joint stock companies and the corporations evolved from the growth of the firms managed by the captains of industry. Ownership and management of businesses became separated when the financial managers, also known as corporate speculators and exploiters, gained control of large-scale enterprises after World War I. Through reciprocal agreements and stock pool manipulations, they worked at creating wealth and acquiring property for themselves. They failed to operate successfully. Much unemployment resulted and a great depression occurred in the 1930s.

Professional managers appeared in the depression period to join forces with the government to operate the business firms and recover from the economic depression and social distress. Professional managers professed to have the knowledge, the skills, and the values to manage the business firms of the nation and provide employment for the labor force, and they achieved world records in creating wealth, property, and income.

A new stage of management, that of the public manager or the public-oriented executive, seems to be emerging. The professional manager will advance from the status of a hired man for the shareholders to that of a public-oriented manager who will manage in the best balanced interests of the shareholders, the employees, the customers, the vendors, and the public in general.

The professional manager served the interests of economic man. The public-oriented manager will attempt to serve the interests of social man. Professional managers had an accepted set of beliefs and a philosophy to guide their efforts. Public-oriented managers are lacking a social philosophy or an accepted set of beliefs from social man.

Institutional Imperatives. If another transformation is indeed in progress we can expect the impact of discernible trends on society in the twenty-first century.

1. Social man with his social ethic will impose his values and priorities on those of religious man, political man, and economic man. Business and educational institutions will add the mission of social institutions to their objectives and priorities. How fast social man makes an impact in the twenty-first century will depend upon the viability of his not yet formulated social philosophy.

2. The developing social man will modify our powerful

economic philosophy of private enterprise with its emphasis on individualism, property, competition, limited government, and specialization. Whereas economic man touted the rights of the individual, social man announces equality and egalitarianism in using the product of society regardless of one's contributions. At present, one can speculate on the differences that characterize the two types as follows:

Competitive man	vs.	Humane man
Acquisitive man	vs.	Sharing man
Material man	vs.	Intellectual man
Wrecker man	vs.	Builder man

In speculating about society in the twenty-first century, we can wonder whether people will shape the institutions of the century or whether the prevailing institutions will shape the philosophies and values of people at work to introduce another transformation.

3. Future managers and leaders in society will be influenced by the values and institutions of social man. Certainly, future managers will be influenced by a melding of our guiding economic philosophy with a social philosophy that will evolve.

Guideposts to the Future

The future begins now; it is not a state or a condition that arrives with a sudden noise or a great awakening light. Satisfactions or dissatisfactions with the present state of society cause actions that start trends to shape the future situation. Future managers will have knowledge, skills, and values for the performance of the management function in society. The best preparation for maintaining managerial excellence is the acquisition of knowledge and skills and the development of a viable, open-ended value system that is sensitive to signals of change in society.

The present is the time for those performing the management function in society and for those who are preparing and aspiring to enter or continue careers in management to assess the total societal situation. What are the forces and trends already in motion that will influence the knowledge, the skills, and the values essential for the survival and success of the managers in society who shape our lifestyles through shaping the nature of our institutions.

Prudent managers will anticipate the future, make intelligent assumptions about the future, and evaluate the alternatives for survival and progress. Their choices of alternatives for decisions about the future will be based upon knowledge about the past.

Maintaining the excellence of future management requires the identification of signals of opportunities or disasters that managers may receive from the reports of the neo-wagon scouts, or the scanner on the future-o-scope. Management excellence in the future depends upon the capacity of present managers for some opportunity thinking for "pro-active" management to avoid later "crisis reactive" management. Present problems must not obscure the vision of desired future results and the actions needed to realize those results.

Somehow future managers will bring about a symbiotic or synergistic effect from the environmental elements of religious, political, economic, and social institutions and the philosophies that enable their survivals. Consequently, future managers will operate as public managers or public-oriented managers as they manage in the best balanced interests of religious, political, economic, and social claimants. They will be promoted to institutional leaders from hired men for shareholders.

For all practical purposes, the twenty-first century will be shaped by the millions of students now enrolled in universities and colleges, with some inputs from faculty, administrators, parents, clergy, politicians, and businessmen. Hopefully, the students will keep in mind that people of little success, usually poor, plan for Saturday night. Successful people, usually rich, plan for two generations ahead. What should our potentially successful and rich students consider while contemplating their future careers of leadership and influence? From what experience and knowledge can they receive guidance and inspiration? Some observations and suggestions follow:

◆ The United States has generated the greatest wealth and income of any nation in history. Yet there is rampant dissatisfaction with economic man resulting from his rape of the environment, reckless use of irreplaceable materials, and inability to distribute national income more equitably.

◆ Social man demands improvement over the creation and distribution of property, wealth, and income of economic man. However, he depends upon the fruit of the labor of economic man. The people who talk most about social benefits seem to have the least means to produce the benefits.

◆ Social man will seek to erode the rights of the individual for establishing the equality of individuals. Signals indicating equality stem from:

Employment rights—affirmative actions.

Health delivery rights.

Pension fund rights and liabilities.

Social security and welfare rights.
Educational rights.
Housing rights.
Environmental rights.
Land use rights.
Capital formation rights.
Population rights for consumption.

Future managers will have a more complex managerial situation in which to operate because of the transformation to the many claimants of social man as contrasted to the narrow economic objective of economic man.

◆ Future managers will need to seek relevant motivations for the workers that hold the values and priorities of social man. Our nation has become a nation of employees. What motivations can management provide for social man to replace the financial motivation of economic man?

◆ If economic growth is going to slow down in future years, then managers and politicians will have to change their ideas of products and policies. For the past twenty-five years, our economy and our society have thrived on growth. A low growth economy will reward wisdom and effective management rather than aggressiveness. Corporations will be forced to consider quality of product or service rather than quantitative manipulations. Durability and cost will be important and scarce materials and environmental conditions will get greater attention. For the first time, managers will be thinking about a stationary economy and the building of models to survive in one.

Legitimacy of Management

The evolving science of management will be shaped by the changing criteria for the legitimacy of management. Concepts of economic justice are being melded with concepts of social justice. A new ideology for the management of business institutions may be developing.

In colonial times merchants and businessmen were considered legitimate if they operated under the political charter of a monarch or a sovereign authority. After the U.S. Constitution was ratified, the managers of businesses operated under a government by law rather than a government by men. The constitutional right of private ownership of the factors of production gave legitimacy to the managers of businesses who had ownership of land and capital. They had legitimacy of management by right of ownership rather than by a political right or a birthright.

At present there is a trend toward such concepts as a psychology of entitlement or an equality of results instead of an equality of opportunity. Considerations of social justice, which places the legitimacy of community need on an equal basis with the right of economic justice based on ownership, are generating values that may make the use of property more important than ownership of property.

Through the opportunity for upward mobility of all segments and members of society, the U.S. became the number one economic nation in the world with the highest standards of per capita income, health, and education of any major nation in the world. During this period of transformation, a big question is whether or not public-oriented managers of private enterprises can continue to provide the upward mobility of opportunity for the many with overtones of egalitarianism and entitlement to equal results. Will our economic system of capitalism shade into a system of communitarianism, as identified by Professor George C. Lodge of the Harvard Business School?

Some early warning signals that will influence the evolution of management science are:

◇ The rejection of capitalism by some segments of society.
◇ The attacks on the practices of multinational firms.
◇ The increasing concern for the environment.
◇ The increasing pressure of consumerism.
◇ The demands for participation of all organizational members and codeterminism.
◇ The criticism of faulty lines of communication among segments of society.
◇ The predictions of the twilight of authority based on capitalism.

During the present transformation in Western civilization from an economically oriented to a socially oriented society, practicing managers have two main choices for shaping the future philosophy of management.

1. Present professional managers can be indifferent to the social responsibilities of their firms and acquiesce to the belief that government should tax their companies to finance the growing social programs for human rights to entitlement and equality of results. They can maintain the position that professional nonowner managers are hired only to enrich the owners of private enterprises and perhaps overlook the fact that the power to tax is the power to confiscate.

2. Present professional managers can begin to advance and develop into public-oriented managers who enrich the lives of owners

and also employees, customers, vendors, and the general public. Such managers can become institutional leaders who can preserve and maintain the private enterprise system. They can be promoted to a higher calling than that of hired managers for shareholders. They can advance the concepts and practices of management science by formulating an operating philosophy of management by results in the best balanced interests of society, and they can show their commitment to those results through the full use of human talents rather than by merely managing in compliance with laws and regulations with disregard for human abilities and expectations.

Andrew F. Morlion, O.P.

23
The Economic, Social, Civic, and Cultural Dimensions of Management

The future of our industrial civilization depends upon the government of the business enterprise, an art about which there is now an organized body of knowledge based on fundamental disciplines to be practiced in the scientific temper and spirit, an art not inferior to that of the government of the state. For more than a hundred thousand years, that is since the earliest ages of primitive mankind, the government of the enterprise has been a function of the government of the family. Within the last hundred years the basic, organic cell of our economy has ceased to be the paternal artisan shop. It has become the factory or office governed by men who in their community and in their nation are sometimes more powerful than the political authorities themselves.

This fact brings us face to face with the gravest problem of our age—the training of business leaders for the government of the enterprise. We must face this problem with full knowledge of its deeper causes—the effects of the Industrial Revolution, which resulted in the birth of a new kind of society. We must have a clear idea of the means necessary to the establishment of the economic-social democracy of the future, and a firm will to use them both efficiently and effectively.

I propose that we should first examine the basic facts, then the basic difficulties, and finally the basic solutions.

The First Phase of the Industrial Revolution

The basic effect of the Industrial Revolution has been a division of the world's economy into two independent yet interdependent natural societies, both necessary for the life and progress of mankind: the family, which continues to be the main consumers' unit, and the enterprise, which has become the main producers' unit.

The invention and gradual application all over the world of the machine based on natural sources of power has relegated to the past the primacy of a production based on manual effort. The father of the family, for a thousand centuries, had been able to produce with the help of his children and a few mates and apprentices the goods necessary for life. Suddenly he lost his customers, his property, his independence. He found himself just one unit of manpower, obliged to sell his physical energy at a meager price to the owner of machines developing thousands of horsepower. He became a number in the accounts of the enterprise, an unimportant item in the mass labor market.

He became a proletarian, a man without a father in the working community and, in a sense, without a fatherland. His wife and his children were, however, his enterprise. In his family he was still a man who wielded authority. But the factory or the office were not his enterprise. They were the property of a man who bought the labor of individuals and who did not create a working community of men who consent to authority for their common good. Economy, *oikos nomos,* in the Greek, Roman, medieval, Renaissance periods meant "the science of the government of the house," a house animated by the stream of family life. Economy now came to signify a soulless mass of bricks and iron, around which were clustered "hands," adjuncts to and less important than the machines.

This was reality only 100 years ago, and still seems real in the minds of millions. The echoes of Marx are still powerful: "Proletarians of all lands, unite; you have nothing to lose but your chains."

We cannot face this first great difficulty: "the revolt of the masses," without examining the other phases of the industrial era. The superiority of the entrepreneurs, owners of the machines, over the proletarians, owners of the hands, represented only the initial phase. The Industrial Revolution naturally progresses into successive phases; the basic error of the Marxists is that they do not follow progress, but continue to fight an evil capitalism which died a natural death long ago.

THE SECOND PHASE: PROFITS FOR THE COMMON GOOD

The capitalism of the Manchester school was the government of the enterprise for the entrepreneur, by the entrepreneur. The capitalism of today has become the government of the enterprise for the people, by the people.

The dialectics of history have proved again to be stronger than a theory, stronger even than the theory of dialectical materialism, which has been applied in practice to historical materialism.

First, the government of the enterprise for the entrepreneur has become impossible. The striking power of the trade unions has proved to the entrepreneur that the united willpower of the workers brings the machines to a standstill if just demands for wages and other human rights are not met. The voting power of the citizen-workers in democracy has imposed on all enterprises social legislation, channeling part of the profits to social security, assistance, or public works, for the common good.

Second, the government of the entrepreneur has become impossible in the enterprise. The machines themselves, having been made more complicated for mass production, have become more expensive. To buy the necessary machines the entrepreneur has been obliged to call in associates, stockholders, banks, and, as in Italy and in other countries, state participation. So on the one hand, the entrepreneur had to relinquish the major part of his legal, financial, and economic authority to partners: to the board, to depositors in the banks, and to the citizens in the state. Mass production, mass factories, and mass offices have developed, which cannot be governed by one man. On the other hand, the capitalist had to relinquish his social authority to the managers, from the chief director down to the shop steward.

Property has ceased to be the source of authority in the enterprise. The government of the enterprise has become government by consent of the people. Just as one source of authority is now practically the fruit of the labor of the people, the savings invested, so the second is the free will of the people working in the enterprise.

Third, government by the entrepreneur without participation of the people is becoming nearly impossible in the enterprise. The entrepreneur, with his managers and production, distribution and finance, has to listen to the suggestions of the customer. The customer votes by buying or not buying the products or services of the enterprise.

This active participation by the people in the decisions of authority is the first aspect of government by the people in the enterprise. But the modern personnel manager has had to introduce two-way and three-way communications, so that the order given from above may be followed by comments, proposals, requests from below, for the sake of more efficient production methods and better human relations. There is an incipient participation in government inside the enterprise by the people who work there.

All this is happening even in the totalitarian empires created by the followers of Marx. The belated concession in Communist countries of more production for consumption, which will make disarmament policies ever more inevitable, is a first, half-smothered victory of the masses who want government of the enterprise for the people. The accelerating rise of the managerial class, an acceleration faster even than that of the Sputniks, is a first sign that government in the enterprise and in the nation must be based on raising the quality of the life of people rather than on older political considerations. Government by the people will start also, silent and unrelenting, in those countries where, for the last time, it was possible to put back for a few centuries the clock of history.

WHO WILL GOVERN?

History itself is now moving at an accelerated speed. In less than 100 years, economic progress has brought forth more social progress than the sum total of thousands of years. In the next 50 years atomic energy, electronic "brains," and automation will have created the material conditions for the full development of man all over the world.

The question is now: who will govern the enterprise which can create a higher standard of living, spiritual as well as material, for every man and woman on earth? The answer is obvious: not the political organizer but the economic-social manager. This is the great message of the writings of Harold Smiddy. Political democracy is not rich enough in energies and incentives to face what Henry Luce once called "The Fabulous Future." Economic-social democracy is the new organic texture described by Peter Drucker in his classic book *The New Society.* It makes democracy grow in every community.

Stephen Dubrul in his introduction to the International University translation of James Mooney's comparison of the *Principles of Organization* (*Principi di Organizzazione,* published by Angeli in Milan) in state, army, church, enterprise, gave the principle of the connection between economic-social and political democracy. "Management," he writes, "must assume an active interest in all phases of the community's progress, going further than the immediate interest of the enterprise."

This is the basic solution of the difficulties which the Industrial Revolution created (although, at the same time it brought immense advantages). Managers must be trained to be not only good economic-social managers of the enterprise in which they wield official authority, but also to be leaders of the community for which they are in fact also co-responsible. Although our wars, revolutions, and devaluations have made us lose step with economic-social history in some parts of the world, our European managers are already well over the first phase of the Industrial Revolution—government for the people by good labor relations. We have seen many managers boldly undertake the second step: government by consent of the people through good human relations with shareholders and with central government.

We must train future leaders for the third phase also. This third phase is the specific phase of industrial democracy: government by the people through civic and public relations which in the highest sense express the public philosophy of the enterprise.

The government of the enterprise is called upon by history to furnish leaders for the government of the community, of the nation, and, earlier than we can dream, of the world. The government of the enterprise requires more than inventive energy and driving power. It requires knowledge of all the other organs of a living and growing democracy and the will to reject all action in the pursuit of private profit which cannot be harmonized with the achievements of public good.

THE CULTURAL DIMENSION

Industrial training requires university education. It is not by chance that this message is launched by the modern International University of Rome with the motto "Pro Deo," or as paraphrased in English "for democracy under God."

Let us state the deeper universal requirements for the full education as well as for the training of industrial leaders, and the universities will understand their responsibilities. Let us make known, to all, and especially to the leaders of the state and of the universities, the fruits of experience, which show that the development of managers for the future can no longer be an internal process of trial and error nor a result of empiricisms, improvisation, or good luck, but is a responsibility of the universities.

Let us reaffirm our conviction that humanism, which is the basis of our culture, must be harmonized with modern teaching methods; that academic education is incomplete unless it includes professional training in the new academic and social responsibilities that face business leaders.

Let us stress three concrete possibilities in conversations with university leaders:

◇ That, at the least, a course of management and of industrial relations (personnel–labor–public relations) be inserted in all university curricula.

◇ That at least some special courses on the principles and practice of organization (which are essential to the state, to all organizations, including schools themselves) be inserted in the university curriculums of law, political science, economics, education, philosophy, and humanities.

◇ That, in the schools of economics, at least a department of management provide an adequate preparation for the future leaders of modern industry, commerce, and banking.

We had to resort in Rome to the creation of a private International University, to be able to introduce in 1948 the first European, full-curriculum application of the schools of business management and industrial relations which were already traditional in the United States. The postgraduate schools for management cannot forever continue to call out of the enterprise young managers who should have received a minimum of professional preparation in the universities that gave them their undergraduate degrees.

An exciting new economic-social chapter of history is dawning, when management and industrial relations can be seen as modern applications of the age-old study of social philosophy, and more specifically as an integral part of the philosophy of democracy. It is our duty to bring home to the universities their full responsibility for providing ever newer curriculums to meet the needs of those called to the government of the business enterprise for the people, of the people, by the people.

Stanley C. Vance

24
Business Heroes from Homer to Horatio to Hawley

Literature is a mirror to a nation's soul. The early poet Homer, in his *Odyssey* and *Iliad,* not only depicted the epic doings of the Greeks and their gods, but also gave excellent insights into successful leadership. For example, Odysseus (or Ulysses in Latin) was extolled for his cunning, strategy, and wise counsel; yet in post-Homeric legend this same hero was pictured as a wily, lying, evil man whose greatest feats were invariably tainted with treachery, blood, and death.

An earlier mythological character, Hercules, son of Zeus, was depicted as the paragon of strength, integrity, and perseverance. According to legend, when he was given 12 impossible labors, this precursor of the modern superchief executive officer completed each of the 12 impossibles with speed and dispatch and finesse. In an allegorical sense, Hercules also had a business connection in that he finagled the golden apples away from the Hesperides and their dragon, Ladon. As a meticulous manager, he cleaned the filth and stench from the Augean stables, captured the Cretan bull, and outsmarted the Amazons by filching the golden girdle of Ares from the Amazon queen, Hippolyte.

Hercules' adventures with Jason and the Argonauts, likewise, had business or commercial implications. These ancient merchant adventurers had to contend with obstacles which can even today destroy many a successful executive; for instance, they were seduced by beautiful women, attacked by unfriendly warriors, buffeted by storms, and haunted by all sorts of demons and monsters.

Even though Jason and his Argonauts overcame all perils and recovered the golden fleece, the gods, nevertheless, had short memory spans. Subsequently, Jason transgressed and the gods condemned him to endless wandering. In his old age he dared to return to Corinth to see once again the Argo, his beloved ship. Resting in the ship's shadow, Jason was killed when the Argo's prow toppled upon him. Is this not reminiscent of corporate prows toppling on so many contemporary corporate Jasons—RCA's Robert Sarnoff; Georgia-Pacific's Robert B. Pamplin; Becton-Dickinson's Farleigh S. Dickinson, Jr.; Genesco's Maxey and Franklin Jarman, and many others?

Although this capsule commentary on mythological heroes with tenuous business connections appears to be somewhat far-fetched, it is commerce that has and continues to put action into civilization. Pre-Hellenic Phoenician, Babylonian, Minoan, and Egyptian empires all flourished with the rise of industry, trade, transportation, and finance.

Many archeological findings also have indirect industrial connections. For example, there is a theory that the great Egyptian pyramids were more a make-work matter, creating jobs for unemployed Egyptians, than they were mausoleums for the Pharaohs. And much of the ancient hieroglyphic and cuneiform writing deals with prosaic, rudimentary bookkeeping of commercial transactions. This is quite obvious in the Babylonian code of Hammurabi and the Minoan tablets of ancient Crete, which translate into trade accounts, shopping lists, and all sorts of rules and prescriptions regulating industry, comparable to the edicts of our own FTC, SEC, FCC and OSHA and ERISA. And, as archeology so plainly shows, a decline in commerce invariably leads to the decline of nations and empires.

Despite its omnipresence, business in ancient times never produced leaders, much less heroes, comparable to those emanating from government, religion, the military, or the arts. Actually, both ancient Greeks and Romans despised work and delegated management to lower-level overseers. In Rome, a wealthy class of businessmen, the Equestrian Order, did come into being but it generated few equites or knights who made the pages of history.

And even the book of books, the Bible, while it seems to glorify the work ethic, also puts moneychangers (businessmen) and tax collectors (managers) in a very bad light. The fishermen apostles and Joseph, the carpenter, are remembered not for their industrial competence but for their religious zeal.

The reawakening of Europe, after the Crusaders brought unbelievable booty back from the Mideast, led to Marco Polo's travels eastward in search of trade and new industrial ideas. Columbus's remarkable voyage with spices, silks, and other goodies in mind, propelled Europe into the Age of Discovery, both geographically and industrially. The victorious Venetians in the mid-sixteenth century gave further impetus to the coming new look of business and its leaders. The Fuggers and other merchant bankers of Central Europe helped transform the sin of usury into the virtues of saving and lending. Nevertheless, there existed an intellectual disdain for the mundane in business and it was expressed in Shakespeare's characterization of Shylock as a despicable moneylender in the *Merchant of Venice*.

Moving ahead two centuries, here in the United States, the first meaningful literary characterization of business acumen and industry was the image of Poor Richard, portraying a homespun Benjamin Franklin trundling a wheelbarrow to his printer's shop. This familiar picture conveyed a feeling for workmanship and perseverance. It meshed perfectly with the spirit of individualism which sprouted in the eighteenth century to counter the statism of the mercantilists. Franklin, a truly "self-made man," worked hard at a variety of lowly tasks, established a foothold in business, and at age forty-two was sufficiently wealthy to retire. He then interested himself in civic affairs, found time to invent bifocal glasses, lightning rods, and the first practical heating stove. He also established the University of Pennsylvania, the Philadelphia Free Library, a workable postal system, and the *Saturday Evening Post*. He was the prototype of today's many-faceted business leader who dedicates innumerable hours to cultural and philanthropic causes.

Although Benjamin Franklin's *Poor Richard's Almanac* (begun in 1732) was not considered to be a business novel, neither was Poor Richard, by any stretch of the imagination, a businessman. The *Almanac*, which continued in popularity for more than a quarter of a century, contributed much in the way of "wise saws," many of which still are quoted: "If you would know the value of money, go and try to borrow some." "He that goes a-borrowing, goes a-sorrowing." "Creditors have better memories than borrowers." "A plowman on his legs is higher than a gentleman on his knees."

Many of Poor Richard's maxims were borrowed from the wisdom of the ages, and they gave a shrewd insight into human nature. Some of these wise saws were combined into a kind of essay, "The Way to Wealth," in which a sage old man, Father Abraham, admonishes a group of complaining citizens. Franklin, with his feet always planted squarely on the ground, set a positive and realistic, cultural and moral base for the tremendous American dynamism in industry, and the ingenuity and productivity that was still to come.

Poor Richard's admonitions to be honest, industrious, thrifty, self-reliant, upright, curious for knowledge, and always ready to help your government and fellowman, stimulated the spirit of individualism that was essential for the War of Independence. His advice was well received by most leading Revolutionary War heroes, who, in addition to being patriots, law makers, or dedicated soldiers, virtually all had bases in business. The Boston Tea Party, Bunker Hill, and all that followed was the consequence of the colonies seeking commercial freedom even more than political freedom. Boston patriots were either well connected merchants or, like New England's leading silversmith, Paul Revere, they were competent artisans, frustrated by Britain's repressive laws.

In the immediate post-Revolutionary War era, with British imports shut out, American industry boomed and commercial success was equated with moral success. Risk-taking, innovation, and 24-hour-workdays constituted the American dream, and the work ethic was pre-eminent. In a sense this was a ripple effect of the philosophical realism preached by Adam Smith and his contemporaries, with value systems stressing "the invisible hand" and "economic man" ideals.

Cultural changes come even slower than economic changes. It was not until the end of the eighteenth century that any meaningful novels were published in the United States. The first professional novelist, Charles Brockden Brown, published several works advocating social reform. Since American commerce and industry were then on such a minuscule scale, there seemed little for Brown to condemn in this sector. Moreover, it would have been strange for Brown to write in an anti-business vein particularly since after 1800, as a penurious author-publisher, he turned merchant in order to support himself.

James Fenimore Cooper was the first major American novelist; yet of his more than 50 publications, none dealt with a strictly business theme. Even a generation after Charles Brockden Brown, American industry and business were still in gestation, and Cooper's imagination was not stirred along this vein. Instead, the critical issues during the first half-century of American independence dealt largely with the clash between the frontier wilderness and the encroaching civilization. Consequently, Cooper's classic *Leatherstocking Tales* (1823–1841) are a saga of the expanding American frontier and of the trials and tribulations of both the aggressive settler and the dispossessed native American. In his later works Cooper expressed disillusionment with what he saw of the abuses of America's infant democracy and he became a critic of such abuses. Perhaps if industry and commerce had flourished in his time, Cooper would have become a forerunner to Upton Sinclair and the antibusiness school of novelists.

A Canadian contemporary of Cooper's, Thomas Haliburton, also had a historical predilection and was intrigued by the dynamism of the expanding American frontier. His focus, however, was less on the clash between native- and frontier-American mores and more on the rapidly developing postcolonial values. In particular, he viewed the rudimentary commercial practices of early rural America, where bartering (including horse-trading) provided a vital civilizing link. Among the early rural traveling salesmen were the walkers, the hawkers, and, of course, the peddlers.

Haliburton, both jurist and author, used the pseudonym Sam Slick. One of his earlier novels, *The Clockmaker: or the Sayings and Doings of Samuel Slick* (1836), depicts a cunning Yankee peddler, Sam Slick, clockmaker and salesman, who "could sell a $6.00 clock to a tight-fisted New England farmer's wife for $40.00 when she didn't even want one." In almost 20 editions of this series, including *Sam Slick's Wise Saws and Modern Instances* (1853), Haliburton set the "slicker" prototype of the early American businessman: canny, cagey, and opportunistic, balanced with homespun philosophy, bad grammar, horse sense, and a general likableness. Slick, who stood a few notches below Poor Richard, was portrayed in a fairly favorable light as the enterpriser not to be quite trusted.

In the decade prior to the Civil War, Herman Melville wrote a series of stories. One of his characters, Israel Potter (1854), is a kind of folk hero, an American frontier Yankee peddler who goes to France and meets Ben Franklin. Poor Potter, the rustic unpolished sharpy, meets more than his match in the master bargainer who "does Israel out of something at every turn and then reads him a moral lesson. 'Every time he comes in he robs me,' Israel complains, 'with an air all the time, too, as if he were making me presents.' " [1]

In *The Confidence Man: His Masquerade* (1857), a pessimistic satire on materialism, Melville's hero combines contradictory traits; he is both a canny trickster and a preacher of faith in one's fellow man. Melville, however, was more a moralist than a business novelist—his prime focus, particularly as expressed in *Moby Dick,* is on symbolism, the power of philosophical dualism with the tragic implications of man's quest for eternal truth.

There appeared at the same time, on another continent, a flood of literature depicting the eccentricities of British early industrial urban life. Unlike Melville, who wandered into the symbolic and metaphysical, Charles Dickens attacked the very real injustices of the law and the social system of his times. His own experience as a youthful laborer in a blacking warehouse, when his father was cast into a debtor's prison, colored his thinking. His remarkable depictions of the character, aspirations, ordeals, and eccentricities of British third-generation Industrial Revolution citizenry have become classics. But, as with Melville, Charles Dickens did not really focus on business and industry. In his novels, for every Scrooge there appeared several dozen equally strange characters, with no direct connection to business. Dickens, however, was probably the greatest social-reform novelist (antedating Upton Sinclair and Sinclair Lewis by almost a century), and his use of sentimental pathos conditioned a whole school of muckraker and Depression era writers whose singular objective was to change the face of the world and the mores of mankind.

Between the harsh realism of Dickens and the American Jeremiahs of the early twentieth century emerged a pleasant interlude of Horatio Alger stories which influenced several generations of Americans. Several million copies of the approximately 100 Alger books were sold between 1867 and 1910. Horatio Alger's works had a common theme implicit in titles such as: *Strive and Succeed: Julius or the Street Boy out West; Jed, the Poorhouse Boy; Phil the Fiddler, or the Story of a Young Street Musician;* and *Struggling Upward: or Luke Larkin's Luck.*

By dint of hard work and unbending morality the hero born in poverty climbs the business ladder to eminence. Pluck plus luck, clean living, and uncounted hours of overtime work were vital ingredients in the Horatio Alger success stories, which began with *Ragged Dick,* a bootblack, who earns his way to riches and respect. An entire Alger school capitalized on this formula, and even in our own era of supreme cynicism, an increasing number of "doers" in business seem to validate Alger's hypothesis. As summarized in *Business Week,* there seems to be a rapidly increasing band of dedicated young executives in their early and middle thirties who almost religiously follow the Alger formula for success.[2]

As growing pains from rapid economic expansion in the late 1800s became more pronounced, novelists began to see possibilities for interesting fiction. The influence of the westward movement created sharp contrasts between the new businessmen and the rock-rooted, old-line New Englanders. In order to survive and succeed, the new businessmen had to adapt to the rugged ways of the Wild West. For this reason, many leaders of American life, groomed in the Ivy

League schools, looked upon them with contempt and considered these boorish upstarts a threat to their orderly way of life.

This sentiment became the basic theme of a school of novelists in the late nineteenth century. In *A Daughter of the Philistines* (1883), H. H. Boysen depicts the era's businessman, Zedekiah Hampton, as a shrewd speculator, a force for change and momentum, but lacking in manners, education, and culture. Hampton's son-in-law, with a Ph.D. from prestigious Freiberg, is portrayed as a white knight preserving old-fashioned morality and the solid traditions of the "fine families."

Again a similar theme is presented by Charles Dudley Warner in *A Little Journey in the World* (1889), and once again a sharp line is drawn between the calloused "Uncle" Jerry Hollowell and his polished Ivy League younger partner, Rodney Henderson. Both partners specialize in "wrecking," that is, capturing control of thriving railroads and then raping them of their assets. However, while the partners equally benefit from wrecking, the young Ivy Leaguer presumably participates with reluctance and is swayed into these reprehensible actions by the older, uncouth partner. The reader is led to believe that the evil in wrecking a railroad is less heinous if the wrecker happens to be a scion of gentility.

Another writer whose protagonists were old-school businessmen is William Dean Howells. In *A Hazard of New Fortunes* (1890) he dwells on the conventional contrasts between Jacob Dryfoos and his son, who is determined to become a minister. Jacob will tolerate none of this nonsense and insists that his son follow in his economic and ethical footsteps. The struggle between these two antithetical forces gives Howells the rationale for expounding his mildly socialistic leanings. It also portends violent reactions toward businessmen yet to come.

Although Henry Blake Fuller was born in Chicago, the city symbolizing the vigor and brazenness of new industry, he nevertheless adhered to the opinions of his contemporaries. In *The Cliff Dwellers* (1893) his central character, Erastus Brainard, is portrayed not only as the crudest of banker types, but also as ugly to behold.

In *The Gospel of Freedom* (1898) Robert Herrick presents a self-made, successful midwestern industrialist and his antithesis, a refined art critic. When the heroine leaves her industrialist husband, "she does so not primarily in protest against his immoral business practices, but because she has grown bored with him and with Chicago. . . . She perceives that Wilder [the industrialist] is the American peasant." [3]

Another of Herrick's eight business novels, *The Memoirs of an American Citizen* (1905), deals with the rise of a midwestern farm boy to wealth and position, first as a meat-packing industrialist and ultimately as a United States senator.

Frank Norris, in *The Pit* (1903), has his hero, Curtis Jadwin, a wheat speculator, operating in the seemingly chaotic Chicago grain market. The hero displays many strong traits as he contends not so much for money as for the excitement, the challenge, and the exhilaration of winning. And even when this strong business hero suffers defeat, he gains respect and stature because of the way he faces up to defeat.

Another early realist, Theodore Dreiser, viewed not only the business scene but also the panorama of American life. His first successful novel, *Sister Carrie* (1900), is a story of a country girl who attains material success via the oldest profession. The stark realism of this success story moved the publisher into suppressing its distribution. Dreiser's second novel, *Jennie Gerhardt* (1911), likewise, was considered to be immorally frank. However, after two successful sex stories, Dreiser then turned to business themes and produced a trilogy: *The Financier* (1912), *The Titan* (1914), and *The Stoic* (1947). The first of these, *The Financier,* deals with an unscrupulous industrialist, Frank Cowperwood, and his rise to economic power. However, since Dreiser also gave Cowperwood an admirable side, it is difficult to type him entirely as a villain. He describes the business leader in a realistic setting, and although he does not condone the new industrialist's breaches of ethics, he does point an accusing finger at those segments of society that are equally guilty of low morals.

But even as Norris and Dreiser were preoccupied with and writing about the split character of the good and bad of the rising American industrialist, other novelists described the industrial leaders as rapacious despoilers. At this end of the spectrum the denigration of the American businessman is best epitomized in Upton Sinclair's *The Jungle* (1905), a gory tale of anguish and exploitation in Chicago's meat-packing industry. From this point, business literature began to swing dramatically to the left, focusing on the doctrinaire and proletariat. Characterization and fiction, for storytelling's sake, gave way to ideology and the socialist creed. Sinclair's views did not stay riveted to what he saw as the evils of free enterprise—he used his sharp pen to jab other assorted culprits: journalism, in *The Brass Check* (1919), and education, in *The Goose Step* (1928). In the latter, moreover, he attempted to show the harmful and unrelenting pressure of corrupt capitalism on institutions of learning and culture. Sinclair's major claim to fame is his one-sided portrayal of industrial evil, as evidenced in *King Coal* (1917), *Little Steel* (1938), and a dozen other of his 80 books.

Sinclair was the leftist spiritual head of an entire generation of single-minded novelists, who used their literary talent to try to turn society away from crass materialism and unbridled competition and toward what they believed to be the order and equity of socialism. The many collisions and frictions of rapid industrialization in the first quarter of this century gave these reformers ample themes and ammunition. And, of course, the Great Depression accentuated the sorry situation. John Steinbeck, in works such as *Tortilla Flat* (1935), *The Grapes of Wrath* (1939), and *Cannery Row* (1944), tells about the nation's disinherited poor. Implicitly, it is the system that is evil and the system's managers who are at fault.

Of the score or more other vehement social reformers, John Dos Passos warrants special attention. His outstanding trilogy, *U.S.A.* (1937), which includes *The 42nd Parallel* (1930), *Nineteen-Nineteen* (1932), and *The Big Money* (1936), has a central character, Charley Anderson, a technological and manufacturing whiz, who gradually degenerates with age and success. Presumably, Dos Passos was trying to show the enervating and contaminating evils of free enterprise. The remarkable feature about Dos Passos is that he ultimately reversed his views, and his subsequent works lauded the conventional and conservative. In his second trilogy, *District of Columbia* (1952), Dos Passos came to the defense of many of the principles he previously had attacked.

But even as a majority of writers were deprecating the businessman, some took a less virulent approach. Sinclair Lewis, for example, while ridiculing the Midwest small-business types, may have even helped to reverse the swing of the pendulum away from the muckraking extreme. His *Babbitt* (1922) portrayed the businessman as prosaic, banal, petty, and lacking ideals and integrity, but Babbitt is far removed from the muckrakers' Mephistos. "George F. Babbitt had seemed rather pathetic but a good egg at bottom. As for Babbitt being *the* U.S. businessman, however, . . . he may have been typical of a time and a place, provided that you remembered he was not in manufacturing or banking or any of the more solid businesses. The time and place, however, have long since vanished." [4]

The businessman was not Lewis's sole target. His earlier *Main Street* (1920) was a satire on small-town life, *Arrowsmith* (1925) tarnished the medical scientist, and *Elmer Gantry* (1927) blasted religious revivalism. And although his *Dodsworth* (1929) put the business executive in a less ridiculous light, his hero nevertheless remained a philistine. It was *Babbitt*, however, that seemingly left an indelible mark, and George Babbitt is remembered as a dullard but not a dunce, a cad but not a crook, a simpleton but one with a soul. Even today, while

Babbitt connotes a cultural and educational void in business leaders, virtually every university in the United States welcomes businessmen as guest lecturers, confers honorary degrees on them, names buildings after them, and invariably includes business leaders as trustees, governors, and overseers.

While certainly not remembered as a business novelist, Booth Tarkington did make one major contribution in this sphere—his *Plutocrat* (1927) is one of the very few novels of that period which gives the businessman his due (in the good sense of the term). Despite his crudeness and vulgarity, Tarkington's hero, the business leader Tinker, is shown as being far more admirable than his hyper-intellectual but effete son-in-law, Ogle, whose phantasmagoric social reform ideals are discredited. Tinker is called a "new Roman, virile, triumphant, riding a white camel in barbaric pomp toward long-conquered Carthage. He is a great barbarian with great power." [5]

Although Tarkington attempted to inject realism and balance, he was a lone voice in praise of business endeavor. The era of muckrakers and the steady stream of reformers, bent on converting American enterprise to European socialism, focused on the doctrinaire and the utopian. In the period between the two world wars, the American businessman, despite his phenomenal contributions, still failed to get a favorable literary review. In the social reform era, from Upton Sinclair through the Depression, most business novels were, according to Robert Falk, a lopsided mixture—"In the 30s it was 75 percent Marx and 25 percent Freud."

The period after World War II saw a perceptible shift away from Marx to Freud, and a sizable injection of realism, with focus on a "how to succeed in business and like it" philosophy. John Phillips Marquand's *Point of No Return* (1949) tells about the aspirations of Charley Gray, who strives to be promoted to a bank vice-presidency. The hero's flaw is that he is an organization man. He sees himself as a crewmember of a corporate boat and he pulls his oar with the rest. He has no desire to rock the boat, much less to rebuild it. He wants status, a healthy family life, and above all, stability and security. In *B.F.'s Daughter* (1946) Marquand tends to belittle success in business, but his slap is gentle and his criticism is more like chiding.

Before Cameron Hawley came on the scene, business novelists had not really had any meaningful contact with industry, commerce, or finance. In fact, a reverse relationship seemed to exist; the further removed from the realities of business, the more critical and cynical were the authors. Cameron Hawley, by contrast, had a distinguished 24-year career at Armstrong Cork Company, where he had served in a variety of capacities, retiring as director of advertising and promotion. During his years at Armstrong Cork he contributed regularly to a number of leading periodicals such as *Saturday Evening Post, McCall's, Good Housekeeping,* and *Woman's Home Companion*. As a seasoned writer and a knowledgeable businessman he was able to produce four outstanding business novels: *Executive Suite, Cash McCall, Lincoln Lords,* and *Hurricane Years*.

Executive Suite (1952) has sold well over one million copies and has been translated into more than 20 languages. Its appeal is its timeliness and realism. Hawley reveals that all business motivation is not crude greed and exploitation. Indeed, great business leaders are also superb artists who shape their organizations in the way that Rembrandt, with paint and canvas, and Michelangelo, with blocks of marble, shaped their masterpieces.

Cash McCall (1955) is described as "a twentieth-century buccaneer, a man who buys and sells and merges companies. . . . But behind the deals and dollars is a human being, an intriguing man not yet forty. A man who is hero to some, a villain to many, and a lover to one." [6]

The hero in *Lincoln Lords* (1960) is a middle-aged executive who suddenly finds himself unemployed through no fault of his own, and then, phoenix-like, rises to a new and greater career. At a climactic point, when he could have remained silent and saved himself and his organization considerable ordeal, he proves himself to be both honorable and courageous.

Hurricane Years (1968) reflects on the strains and stresses of modern society that cause anguish for all, but especially for strivers and achievers in all facets of life. Judd Wilder, a successful executive in his mid-forties, is struck down by a heart attack, and is impelled to scrutinize his life and his goals.

In the decade since Cameron Hawley's death in 1968, there has been no one to replace him. Vartanig Vartan in *50 Wall Street* (1968) combines the practitioner's experience with the writer's competency. Vartan, a financial writer for *The New York Times,* portrays Wall Street as a magnificent edifice, yet having some nasty cracks visible only to one who has had a long and intimate contact with the Street. Despite its authenticity, *50 Wall Street* fails to reach the Hawley heights. Perhaps its overemphasis on sex diminishes its credibility. It is hard to believe that those who run the American money machine spend all their time and energy going from bedroom to bedroom, to the neglect of the corporate boardroom.

Close to the Hawley style is Wilma Dykeman's *Return the Innocent*

Earth (1973). It is the saga of the Clayburn family, three generations of southern farmers turned entrepreneurs in a fabulously successful canning company. Although Dykeman injects sufficient sex and unethical episodes, there is never any doubt that the Clayburn heritage was one of hard work and stern morality. Hardship, struggle, and sacrifice, even of love, ultimately are crowned by success. Dykeman, even surpassing Hawley's realism at points, weaves into this excellent novel the hard clash of traditional values and the inexorable push for dynamism and change.

Louis Auchincloss, who has written over 20 novels in 20 years, occasionally ventures onto the business scene. In *The Embezzler* (1966) he focuses upon Guy Prime, a legend in his lifetime and also a betrayer and infamous scoundrel who causes havoc on the Stock Exchange.

Typical of one whose knowledge of the business world is near zilch, William Gaddis has turned *JR* (1975) into fantasy rather than fiction. JR, an eleven-year-old boy, supposedly parlays a bid to supply the Army with 9,000 gross of wooden picnic forks into a multinational conglomerate. This wheeler-dealer whiz-kid operates out of a phone booth and gets his leads by reading dozens of assorted business periodicals. Without doubt *JR* would make an interesting modern-day Alice in Wonderland, but it cannot be recommended as a meaningful looking glass for business.

To date, as business novels continue to appear unabated, and uninspired, one recent contribution to the business scene, yet to be tested, is *Aria* (1978), by Brown Meggs. Its setting is a modern leisure-oriented conglomerate wherein the hero, Harry Chapin, strives to make the chronically money-losing, classical-music segment profitable. In typical Cameron Hawley style, Meggs describes the business setting realistically and precisely. Also, while his hero has his sexual diversions, he plays the business game with zest. Like Hawley, *Aria*'s author is one of the handful of business novelists with authenticity; he spent 18 years as an executive of a major record company.

If the foregoing commentary on the business novel seems rather sketchy and brief, even inadequate, it is because business has never been a major literary theme. Of the thousands of works of fiction that are published annually, only a fraction take place on the business stage. In some respects this is disappointing. Proportionally more business-theme novels were written 50 years ago, when the businessman was barely represented in the prestigious *Who's Who in America;* less than 1 percent of *Who's Who* listings at that time were from the business sector, while today over 30 percent of *Who's Who* biographies are business executives.

America's great political leaders have received more literary attention than America's great business leaders. A spot check at the University of Tennessee Graduate Library reveals: 397 catalog cards on Abraham Lincoln, 283 on Thomas Jefferson, and 142 on Andrew Jackson; about one-fifth of these refer to fiction. By contrast, Henry Ford, who places first on virtually every list of great businessmen, has only 31 cards, of which nearly half are fiction. Andrew Carnegie merits 21 cards; Thomas A. Edison, 20; John D. Rockefeller, 15; Alexander Graham Bell, 13; Harvey S. Firestone, 6; and Cornelius Vanderbilt a scant 3 (Amy Vanderbilt, the arbiter of good manners, rates better than the Commodore, with 5 references).

One wonders whether our leading businessmen are perhaps too moral or too goody-goody to write about since the public prefers to read off-color, sensational scripts. Yet our leading business villains, Samuel Insull and Jay Cooke, have only four catalog cards each, and Jay Gould, James Fisk, and the infamous butcher-trader, John Jacob Astor, have only three cards each.

If moral or ethical aberration is the vital ingredient in successful fiction, then today's writers have ignored the fact that about 350 major American corporations have admitted to unethical activities such as bribery of foreign officials and illegal political contributions. As a result, Congress has placed heavy penalties on these wrongdoers. Yet despite condemnations from Congress, the courts, and the press, scandals of the Gulf Oil and Lockheed magnitude have not produced a single novel that could electrify the public as did Upton Sinclair's book *The Jungle*.

Even such colorful swashbucklers as Bernie Kornfeld and Robert Vesco have failed to stir writers' imaginations. Bernie Kornfeld, however, received some biographical attention from three top editors of the *Sunday Times* of London—C. Raw, B. Page, and G. Hodgson. Their book, *Do You Sincerely Want to Be Rich?*, is not a business novel but it does give a graphic portrayal of the nondescript Brooklyn-bred social worker who became a glamorous international financial finagler. Robert L. Vesco, who picked up the pieces from Bernie Kornfeld's Investors Overseas Services (and picked them clean to the bone), is another overlooked figure for a business novel. Also overlooked is the master-keeper of the bunny hutch, Hugh Hefner of *Playboy* fame, who could stir and titillate the imaginations of many.

Perhaps the paucity of business novels attests to the intelligence of the American reading public. It no longer sees business leaders as rough-and-tumble Argonauts, prissy Poor Richards, naive Horatio Algers, muckraker villains, or ambidextrous bedroom-boardroom rascals. On the contrary, it views its business leaders as a highly motivated, highly competent, supremely dedicated group of citizens, beset with all the frailties of ordinary human beings. Their dealings and doings are just too prosaic for prose.

REFERENCES

1. Robert Falk, "From Poor Richard to the Man in the Gray Flannel Suit," *California Management Review*, Vol. 1, No. 2 (1959), p. 4.
2. "Young Top Management: The New Goals, Rewards, Lifestyles," *Business Week*, Oct. 6, 1975, p. 56.
3. Henry Nash Smith, "The Search for a Capitalist Hero," in Earl F. Cheit, ed., *The Business Establishment* (New York: Wiley, 1964), p. 92.
4. John Chamberlain, "The Businessman in Fiction," *Fortune* (November 1948), p. 135.
5. Falk, "From Poor Richard to the Man in the Gray Flannel Suit," p. 9.
6. Cameron Hawley, *Cash McCall* (New York: Pocket Books, 1956).

James C. Worthy

25
The Behavioral Dimensions of "Span of Management" Theory

A span of management is not simply a mechanical arrangement for a certain number of people to report to a particular superior; it is a dynamic system of human and organizational relationships. Some of these relationships are specific and subject to precise definition. Others are in varying degrees imprecise, intangible, and elusive but highly important as they exemplify the ways people behave within organizations and the effectiveness with which organizations function.

In this chapter we shall see that in any particular set of organizational circumstances a variety of factors combine to determine the workable span of management, that some of these factors are to some degree subject to deliberate managerial control, and that there are important advantages in so shaping these factors as to establish as wide a span of management as circumstances can be arranged to allow.

FACTORS THAT DETERMINE THE SPAN OF MANAGEMENT

It has long been recognized that there is no universally applicable span of management.[1] Urwick's dictum that an individual superior cannot direct effectively the work of more than five or six subordi-

405

nates whose work interlocks [2] has been superseded by recognition that a variety of factors, in addition to interdependence of tasks, goes into the determination of the optimum span of control. Factors which have been identified include:

◇ Limits on the range of permissible discretion on the part of subordinates (government functionaries cannot be permitted the range of individual judgment expected of management consultants).

◇ Limits on the acceptable range of variation in product (components of space vehicles must be built to far closer tolerances than components for furniture and hence require closer and stricter supervision and control in their manufacture).

◇ Character of work (manufacturing generally requires closer supervision and shorter spans of management than retailing; patient care is largely the professional responsibility of individual practitioners subject to only the most general overseeing).

◇ Stability of operations (a work process that is well established and routinized requires less supervision than a new process or one susceptible to frequent and drastic change).

◇ Competence of superiors (other things being equal, the more competent superior can direct the work of more subordinates than one who is less competent).

◇ Character of supervision imposed on superiors (superiors subject to detailed supervision from above are likely to set up shorter spans of management in order that, in the interests of their own survival, they can exercise detailed supervision on those below them).

◇ Skills of subordinates (a bimodal distribution probably exists here: unskilled work and highly skilled work tend to require less supervision than semiskilled work).

◇ Availability of information for decision making at various levels in the organization structure (effective decisions cannot be made at levels below which pertinent information is reasonably accessible).

These are some of the variables which influence the span of management. Other variables might be identified, but those named are sufficient to demonstrate the necessity for a contingency approach to determining the optimum span in any particular organizational situation. Depending on the directions in which these variables lean—and we must recognize that some may lean in one direction, others in another—a feasible span may be quite narrow in one case and very wide in another, and both may work equally well.

Furthermore, the optimum is a range, not a point. Even if all variables could be identified and quantified, it is most unlikely that means will ever be found to determine precisely the *one* best span for any given set of conditions; rather, in any particular situation there is a range of feasible spans. This range will be somewhere in a broader continuum from very narrow to very wide, and there probably will always be a lower and an upper limit to the workable range in a given set of circumstances.

CONTROLLING THE VARIABLES OF THE SPAN OF MANAGEMENT

Some, though not all, of the variables significant to the span of management are susceptible in some degree to conscious managerial control. Some of the possibilities along this line will be suggested in this section. In general, there are great advantages to be realized in finding ways to operate effectively at the broadest feasible range.

The span of management is obviously related to the extent to which an organization is centralized or decentralized. Broad spans require greater decentralization of authority and responsibility than narrow spans. Herein lies the root advantage of broader spans of management: they tend to develop better human organizations.

If substantial delegations of authority and responsibility are to be made, there is a premium on having highly qualified subordinates; if delegations are limited, the importance of quality in subordinates is correspondingly reduced.

In studies made some years ago at Sears Roebuck and Co.,[3] it was found that division and department managers in "flat" organizations tended to be more competent than those in otherwise similar but "tall" structures.

The flat Sears structures had very broad spans of management: thirty-odd division managers in medium-size retail stores reported to a single management team consisting of a store manager and an assistant; forty-odd heads of major buying departments reported to a single merchandising vice-president. In both the retail store and the parent buying organization, the key executives were spread very thin. The amount of time they could give to any of their large number of subordinates, or the amount of individual surveillance or support they could provide, was very limited. The only way a store manager could build a satisfactory hardware business was to find or develop a highly qualified hardware merchant; the merchandising vice-president was under similar compulsion in his efforts to build sales and profits in the forty-odd buying departments for which he was responsible. Neither the store manager nor the vice-president had the time to involve himself in divisional or departmental details; in each instance, the key to successful performance lay in the competence of division and department manager personnel.

In retail stores of similar size but with "tall" organization structures (that is, with an intervening level of supervision and correspondingly shorter spans of management), the store manager was less dependent on high competence at the division manager level because of the closer direction, control, and support made possible by the additional supervision.

Not only were executives who were operating in structures with broad spans of management under strong compulsion to recruit top quality personnel for key positions, but that personnel, once in place, was exposed to an especially rich learning and development experience. To function effectively in such a structure, division and department managers had to learn to accept and handle relatively more autonomy than their counterparts working under closer supervision. They had to make more decisions on their own; they could not run constantly to higher authority to help; they had to take greater personal responsibility for the performance of their units. If they made mistakes, they could not blame someone else and had to rely more on their own devices to work their way out. If they were successful, the success was their own and not someone else's. In both events, learning and growth were enhanced.

Most emphatically, in neither the parent merchandising organization nor the flat store organization were authority and responsibility delegated carelessly. In both instances, the senior executives displayed a keen ability to evaluate people. They had good people judgment. They could select personnel with development potential, they could follow their progress, and they could sense with accuracy when individuals were ready to assume more responsibility. They were able to bring people along as fast as individuals were ready, but not so fast as to exceed their still-growing capacities; and because the executives knew which of their key subordinates could move ahead largely on their own and because they were not burdened by the details of many departments, they were able to give help to those subordinates who needed it and stay as close as necessary to them as long as circumstances required.

Altogether, the structures with broad spans of management tended to recruit more competent personnel for key positions and to provide them with a richer, more stimulating learning environment in which individual growth was enhanced.

These structures were not, however, altogether comfortable or easy ones in which to work. They made great demands on people. They required that men and women take personal responsibility for themselves and their work. They provided support, but not nearly as much as that provided by spans of management where there was more structure on which to lean. Not everyone could be successful, much less happy, in such an organization, and those who could not adapt to it were likely to be weeded out fairly quickly.

This process of selectivity points to another characteristic of this kind of organization structure: in it, problems are more likely to be seen as problems of people rather than as problems of things. If improvement is needed in a department, the situation is likely to be defined as one requiring working with the department manager, not just to correct the problem at hand but to strengthen the department manager's capacity to deal with this and with future problems as well.

In fact, under these flat structures the greater part of the process of management tended to be seen as developing people: setting goals for them, holding them to high standards of performance, encouraging them to assume larger measures of autonomy and responsibility, and giving them help as needed for their own individual growth. There is much to be said for a philosophy and practice that sees a large part of management as a task of developing people rather than refining procedures.

DESIGNING MANAGERIAL JOBS

Other things being equal, shorter spans of management may well be more effective than longer for accomplishing a given set of results, economic or otherwise, within a short period of time. It may be more expeditious for higher authority to intervene directly to correct a departmental problem than to work with the department manager to improve his problem-solving ability. Unfortunately, such a course is likely to require continuing intervention, whereas strengthening capacity to handle problems at the departmental level is more likely to enable higher management to stay freer of operating details and to concentrate on the kinds of problems with which only higher management can deal. This is an important advantage and well worth additional thought and effort to find means for broadening the span of management to the highest level of the workable range in particular sets of circumstances.

Not all variables influencing placement of the range are susceptible of deliberate modification and control, but some of them are. Among these, pre-eminently, are the interrelatedness of organizational tasks and the selection of key personnel.

Urwick's definitive wording of the span-of-control concept reads: "No superior can supervise directly the work of more than five, or at most six subordinates *whose work interlocks*" [4] (Urwick's italics). Quite clearly, this implies that broader spans of management are possible if the work of subordinates can be made *less* interlocking, *less* interdependent. In many organizations, the work of constituent units is more interlocked and interdependent than it needs to be. Classical organization theory encourages the grouping of similar tasks together on the theory that this makes supervision easier, improves worker skills, and increases overall productivity. But it also greatly increases the interdependence of units organized in this fashion because none of them can operate except in close synchronization with the other specialized units; in other words, their work is closely interlocked and the viable span of management for their direction is correspondingly shortened.

Rather than bringing like work together chiefly because it is like work, it often makes better sense to group specialized activities around the purposes they are intended to serve.[5]

The effort should be made to organize work into units that are as nearly autonomous as possible, so that those heading each unit have control over the maximum feasible number of elements that go into the accomplishment of complete tasks or significant components of complete tasks. Considerable thought and experimentation have gone into job design for workers. Managers' work, no less than workers', needs to be meaningful, needs to be structured in holistic fashion. Managerial work needs to be designed not only with technical elements in mind; insofar as possible, technical elements should be clustered in meaningful configurations. Managers, like workers, need a sense of *accomplishing* something, not just *doing* something; their results need to be comprehensible and measurable in real units, not abstract processes. And they need the maximum feasible degree of control over the factors which enter into the accomplishment of meaningfully identifiable tasks.

This approach to organization can greatly enlarge the extent to which practical delegations of authority and responsibility can be made. Authority over and responsibility for more elements of a total task provide a richer learning and growing experience. By this means, managers do not merely become increasingly expert at particular specializations but gain more and more experience in managing, to their own benefit and that of the organization.

Study of the best ways to design jobs for managers is a singularly promising field of endeavor that should be explored more imaginatively and more aggressively than it has to date. Broader spans of management are likely to be a by-product of the effort to develop more human organizations.

Personality in Relation to Organization

Reference has been made to the Sears Roebuck studies of flat and tall organizations, the one with very broad and the other with much narrower spans of management. One of the interesting findings of these studies was that managers of the two types of structures tended to be somewhat different in terms of personality. For our purposes, stores with the flat structure are designated "X" and those with the tall structure, "Y."

Although store managers in both the X and Y groups were individuals with personal characteristics very much their own, they could be classified roughly into two fairly distinct personality types. The differences between them were particularly apparent in their general attitudes toward the people in their organizations. These attitudes revealed themselves in the way they talked about their people and in their face-to-face relationships.

Managers of the X type stores tended to take pride in their employees. Walking through the store with a visitor, they were likely to pause frequently to introduce the visitor to division managers, salespeople, and others, each time making some complimentary comment about their performance or the condition of their division, or relating some recent incident of merit. These managers took special pride in their promotable younger people. They would recount their history, their special qualifications, what was being done to further their training, and how soon they would be ready for more responsibility. These managers were not indiscriminate in their pride or praise. They held their people to high standards and they were critical of those who failed to measure up. They were generally good judges of people, able to evaluate their strengths and weaknesses and to deal with them accordingly. In part because of these skills, they usually *did* have people in whom they could take pride.

Managers of the Y type stores tended to be much less warm and out-going. They were likely to be distrustful of people, and at some time during the store visit many of them made such remarks as: "It's hard to get good people these days; they've been spoiled by the unions (government)." Or, "There's something wrong with the educational system—people just don't believe in doing a fair day's work anymore. They're out for all they can get and give as little as they can get away with." Or, "Young people have lost their ambition. You don't see many of them these days who are willing to *work* to get ahead the way we used to have to do." These managers often seemed to expect the worst of their people, and not infrequently found their fears justified. They felt that people had to be watched, that their work had to be checked closely—otherwise, no telling what might happen.

This sketch of the two types of managers was deliberately over-drawn to emphasize their different personality types. But there was a definite difference in their general outlook on life and in their general attitudes toward people, and *this difference reflected itself in the kinds of organizations they set up and the ways they related themselves to the people in them.*

At the time of these studies, Sears as a company was administered with a high degree of decentralization. The individual store manager was vested with considerable latitude in the way he ran his store, and this extended, within limits, to the manner in which he set up his own organization. It was clear that the two types of managers had tended to set up the kind of organizations with which they could work comfortably.

The Y managers had little confidence in their people; they felt their employees had to be closely supervised, that someone (themselves or their key staffs) had to do the "real thinking," and that detailed controls had to be set up to make sure that those further down the line followed through. These managers had sought to create the kinds of organizations that would accomplish this.

The X managers, on the contrary, had considerably more confidence in the capacities of their people, and they had enough skill in evaluating people to have a feeling of sureness in their judgment as to whom they could place their confidence in and how far. They relinquished none of their responsibility for guidance and direction or for final results, but they sought to capitalize on the initiative and good sense of their subordinates rather than trying to do all the "real thinking" for them. Their primary method of solving problems was to work with the people involved, not only to solve the immediate problems but to strengthen the ability of their subordinates to deal with other problems in the future. To this end, they liked to work directly with their division managers rather than through an intermediate staff, which they were likely to feel would only get in the way. The X managers, like the Y managers, had tended to set up the kind of organization with which they could work comfortably.

These observations on the relationships between personality and structure raised questions as to how well the Y type personality could work in the X type structure. Doubts on this score were reinforced by following what often happened in store manager changes. It was not uncommon for a manager transferred from a Y type store to one already set up on an X basis to begin reconstituting the organization along lines more nearly approximating the structure to which he was accustomed. These changes were usually not begun immediately nor, once begun, accomplished quickly; the movement was gradual but its direction clear. Always, of course, the changes were presented as quite "logical": inventory problems, the need for building up, say, the soft line divisions, a shortage of sufficiently high-caliber people for division manager jobs, and so on. Whatever the series of steps by which it occurred the organization structure of the manager's new store tended to be reshaped into a form not too different from the one he had left (assuming there was no significant difference in the size of the two stores).

The reverse process was also observed. An X type manager transferred to a Y type store (again assuming approximately equal size) was likely before too long to report to his zone office that he had become familiar with his new store and felt that he no longer needed two merchandise managers and one was available for transfer. Sometime later he might report that as soon as he could make certain moves he had in mind to strengthen some of his division managers, he would probably have a second merchandise manager who could be moved elsewhere. Here, too, the result was likely to be conversion of the organization of the manager's new store to correspond more closely with that of his old.

The task of changing organization structures thus appeared as considerably more involved than merely issuing directions and redrawing organization charts. Given some leeway for individual discretion, the way any organization is set up is likely to reflect the personality and temperament of its key people—above all, the person at the top.

Thus, the critical factors in building effective organizations are the design of managerial jobs and the selection of key people. Both these factors involve considerations of structure, of which span of management is a particular case.

REFERENCES

1. For a concise history and a comprehensive bibliography of the span-of-management theory, see David D. Van Fleet and Arthur G. Bedeian, "A History of the Span of Management," *The Academy of Management Review,* July 1977.
2. Lyndall Urwick, "Executive Decentralization with Functional Coordination," *The Management Review*, December 1935, p. 356.
3. See J. C. Worthy, "Factors Influencing Employee Morale," *Harvard Business Review,* January 1950; "Organizational Structure and Employee Morale," *American Sociological Review,* April 1950; *Big Business and Free Men* (New York: Harper, 1959), esp. chaps. 6 and 7.
4. Lyndall Urwick, "The Manager's Span of Control," *Harvard Business Review,* May–June 1956, p. 41.
5. A theoretical framework for this train of thought and several concrete examples are presented in Worthy, *Big Business and Free Men* (New York: Harper, 1959), chap. 6. See also Worthy, "Some Aspects of Organization Structure in Relation to Pressures on Company Decision-Making," *Industrial Relations Research Association Proceedings 1952.*

Preston P. Le Breton

26
Management
Awareness
Strategies

The manager's role in large organizations—business firms, government agencies, educational institutions—continues to increase in complexity and difficulty, because of the accelerated pace and magnitude of change taking place in our society and the ever-widening zone of responsibility thrust upon the manager by society. As in the past, business managers need to be alert to changing consumer-customer needs and expectations; to introduce new production technology as inventions and discoveries make existing systems obsolete; to add to, relocate, or shut down distribution outlets in response to shifting population patterns and buying habits; and to bring in and develop new management talents to replenish and add to the ranks. One new element in management assignments is the dramatic shrinking of the lifespan of each assignment.

The total management task can be viewed as made up of a series of individual, at times interrelated assignments. Top-level managers in large organizations, during a typical work week, may find themselves involved in executive actions relating to organization design, management assessment, product design, major equipment acquisition, long-range planning, advertising-marketing strategy determinations, site selection, and price-setting policy. Regardless of its nature, each assignment begins with an awareness that a problem or opportunity exists and continues through the development and implementation of a response. The time lag between becoming aware of the possible desirability of, let us say, changing a product's style or adver-

415

tising strategy, the introduction of change, and the obsolescence of the new strategy has been considerably reduced. A strategy which may once have had a life expectancy of one, two, or three years may now have a shortened life of six, twelve, or eighteen months. Because of the shortened time frame, there is an increase in the frequency with which management assignments occur for given subject areas.

The manager's task is further complicated because of the addition of new assignments without a parallel reduction of past assignments. Current examples would include social responsibility issues (such as affirmative action programs) and ecological demands with special attention focused on air, water, noise, and visual pollution.

These two developments—accelerated pace of change and new areas of management responsibility—place a heavy, almost impossible burden on a manager's awareness system. All managers can reflect with a certain degree of uneasiness upon recent assignments in which their response to a problem or opportunity was less than ideal simply because they did not become aware of developments until the problem was fairly advanced or actually acute or the opportunity had vanished or was made significantly less attractive by alert action on the part of competitors.

It is not an exaggeration to state that the awareness function is the most crucial part of the management task. Why does it play such a central, commanding role? Because no conscious human act is ever initiated until someone becomes aware that a condition may warrant attention. Managers do not examine a price policy, consider a new venture, a likely morale problem, or an inventory condition until they become or are made aware that these situations should command their attention.

The condition of a problem or opportunity situation when managers become aware usually influences the quality of the response. The very nature of the problem or opportunity usually undergoes considerable change over time. A management grievance which might have been resolved through consultation, a modest salary increase, or job redesign may result in a replacement problem if adequate attention is not given during early stages of development. Obviously, if a manager does not know about a problem until it becomes advanced, there is no way the problem can be solved at an early stage of development.

Of course, awareness of an opportunity or problem situation does not necessarily lead to a quality response or any response at all. It is quite clear, however, that there will be no response until there is awareness, and the quality of the response is tied directly to the level of the awareness.

PROBLEM-OPPORTUNITY AWARENESS ORIENTATION

The best way to get an operational feel for the awareness concept, and thus to take the first step in developing an awareness strategy, is to reflect upon fairly typical management activities over a designated, recent period. Two things are required: first, identification of actual and potential problem and opportunity situations, and second, examination of how the responsible manager became aware of the need or opportunity for possible management action. For illustrative purposes we will view the awareness activities of a hypothetical corporate president after he has completed a week of intense interaction with subordinate managers. Through a series of questions, insights can be obtained about awareness strategies in use:

◆ Did your marketing manager rush into your office with an emergency message that the new product line introduced one month before is meeting heavy consumer resistance? That first month sales are 20 percent below target?

◆ Did your production manager inform you through daily or weekly reports that the output of all product lines but one is right on schedule and within quality and cost standards? Were you told that the delay in the one product line results from unanticipated breakdowns and the lack of adequately trained workers? Did he convey the fact that the affected product line sales manager has been badgering him about the loss in sales resulting from the slowdown, but that at least no poor quality items are delivered?

◆ And what of your conversation with your finance manager? Did he report that the cash flow situation is still precarious and that conditions are likely to get worse before they improve? Did he pass on to you the call he received from the Securities and Exchange Commission which was directed toward the accuracy, specificity, and completeness of the prospectus which has been filed?

◆ What was the major thrust of your extended discussions with your internal security chief? Has he reported progress in reducing the high level of pilfering of the new pocket-size calculators and selected tools and spare parts from the maintenance shed? Was he able to guarantee you that there would be no recurrence of hiring scientists and engineers who are serious security risks?

◆ Was your research and development director able to present encouraging news regarding the status of the complete redesign of the company's major product? Or did he request an additional six-month delay? And what about the status of the experimental production line for product line "A"? Will the new system obtain the desired 12 percent cost reduction, thus putting the company in a favorable competitive position?

◆ Has the difficulty with the women's task force for equality been resolved? Is the affirmative action program that was prepared by the director of industrial relations and approved by the executive committee and board of directors achieving its goals and objectives? What is the likelihood that the company will suffer another two-day walkout by its women office employees?

◆ How did the consultation go between you and your chief economist? Was his forecast of the economy which was used as the basis for the current and the three- and five-year plan found to be reasonably accurate at the end of the first quarter? Is there a need for significant change in company plans as a result of actual and projected conditions?

◆ Were you in touch with your legal counsel during this period as you had been the previous quarter regarding the class action suit filed by homeowners residing in the area where the company has initiated large-scale expansion of facilities? Did the company settle the patent infringement suit filed by a leading competitor?

◆ Were you able to obtain additional, specific information relating to the hot rumor floating around the industry that a Japanese manufacturer is likely to enter into direct competition in your market with an advanced product design and a relatively cheap price? And what about the consolidation-merger talks between the third and tenth ranked competitors in the industry? Is this prospective merger likely to come off?

◆ Are the monthly executive committee meetings still productive from a problem-opportunity identification standpoint? Does each manager talk in terms of future opportunity-problem areas or are agenda items concerned mainly with present problems?

Obviously, readers will identify with some of these situations more readily than with others. The purpose of these hypothetical situations is to demonstrate that all decision-making activities are preceded by an awareness episode.

With an awareness inventory in hand, we can now move one phase forward.

Classification of Awareness Experiences

Managers may never know about many opportunities which were missed or not considered because of lack of awareness. As for problems, managers are only too painfully aware of them because lack of awareness at an early stage has usually allowed the problems to grow as a result of neglect. Before an awareness strategy can be developed, it is helpful to examine three possible awareness levels, classified by the time and the stage of development of the opportunity-problem situation.

1. Awareness in anticipation of events and awareness as a result of organization members being the agents of change.
2. Awareness while event is at an early stage of development.
3. Awareness significantly after the fact. That is, problem is well advanced or opportunity has passed or is almost lost.

Of course, there are other gradations of awareness between the polar positions. By placing these three categories on a continuum, all management awareness experiences can be placed at some point on the continuum. At least two purposes can be served by performing this exercise. First, at a given point in time, managers can assess their awareness strategies in terms of the three categories—are they getting on top of their management assignments significantly in advance of events, after the fact, or during initial stages of development? Second, managers can have a chance to consider the awareness strategy alternatives beyond the one chosen or used. But first a few definitions.

Anticipatory Stance. There are two components to this stance. One is a conscious looking ahead in an effort to anticipate developments even before an idea or concept has been formulated or an event or program planned. A forecast of political, economic, social, and technological developments and conditions three or five years in advance is an example of how this kind of strategy could be implemented. A conscious looking ahead strategy covers more than a forecast of general developments within society. Particular attention should be given to likely future actions of competitors, consumers, customers, suppliers, distributors, legislators, and other significant individuals, groups, and organizations.

The second component is related to the efforts undertaken by an organization through invention and discovery to be an agent of change, thus, in a sense, forcing others to respond to its initiative, innovation, and creativity, rather than responding to events and conditions created by others. The great emphasis on research and development is an example of this type of anticipatory stance. In a real way, a company becomes aware of an opportunity to introduce a new product or service or marketing strategy by developing an approach superior to its own current offerings as well as the offerings of its competitors.

Concurrent Stance. Awareness during the initial stages falls between the other two awareness levels—it is neither in advance of critical events nor is it significantly delayed after the fact. The desire is to know about problems as soon as there are indications that a situation is deteriorating or to be alert to opportunities when they first appear. Most control systems in use today fall within this category, although some of the more advanced models attempt to anticipate events and some of the less advanced ones tend to give a delayed reading.

Reactive Stance. At this level of awareness, significantly after the fact, the organization prepares itself to respond to a situation or condition only after the problem is quite advanced or the opportunity well established. Examples of situations and conditions at this awareness level are easy to come by because even when companies use the other two strategies, there are always some events which are identified after the fact. Examples are an open revolt by senior managers, a wildcat strike, a machine or production line breaking down unexpectedly, an end-of-the-year audit disclosing failure on the part of several managers to comply with a variety of company guidelines.

Awareness Continuum and Its Use. The three awareness levels— anticipatory-generating, concurrent, and reactive—can be placed on a continuum, as shown in Figure 1. Let us see how our hypothetical president might use the continuum to get a quick, tentative reading of the awareness strategies applied to his experiences. The president's experiences covered the following topics: product research and development, sales, production, cash flow, company prospectus, pilferage, internal security risks, experimental production system, affirmative action, possible strikes of women office employees, accuracy of previous economic forecast, status of class action suit, and patent infringement suit, new competition from Japanese businesses, possible merger of competitors, quality of management.

Among the awareness methods and techniques used were face-to-face contact with initiative taken by either the president or his subordinates, monitoring and controlling systems, research and development and possibly industrial engineering, forecasting, direct observation, formal and informal analysis and assessment.

The president used all three awareness strategies. The

Figure 1. The awareness continuum.

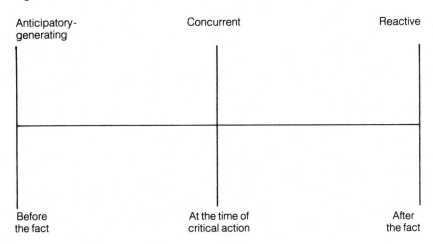

anticipatory-generating stance is illustrated best by the use of economic forecasting, product and production system research and development, and analysis of likely future competition from a Japanese company and stronger competition resulting from the possible merger of two competitors.

The concurrent strategy could apply to a sensitive monitoring of production and sales results, daily analysis of the cash flow position, and frequent review of the affirmative action program. A reactive strategy reflecting a significant deficiency before awareness took place is illustrated by the high level of pilfering of supplies and spare parts, the two-day walkout, and the class action suit.

From these examples we can see that a sensitive awareness system is not defined simply and solely in terms of how quickly after a given incident managers are informed of the situation. Rather, the quality of the system is measured best in terms of the stage of the problem or opportunity when awareness takes place.

Usually if managers know well in advance that workers may engage in a walkout, that disgruntled customers may file a class action suit, or that specific, new forms of competition may emerge, they are in a better position to take corrective, even preventive, action than they could if their awareness follows the completed act or event. To develop new products in advance of present product obsolescence or to introduce an advanced production system before it is generally available within the industry may be preferred strategies. But it would be a mistake to conclude that an anticipatory-generating awareness strategy is always preferable or that there is no place in an effective efficient management system for a concurrent or response awareness strategy.

SOURCES OF INFLUENCE AND STAGES OF AWARENESS

Before one can determine which of the three broad awareness strategies is most appropriate, it is necessary to identify the variety of sources of significant influences and to understand how ideas, concepts, and plans progress from inception to completion. Awareness strategies need to relate to the situation and environment in which they are to be used. It is necessary, therefore, to identify those individuals and formal and informal groups and organizations, including governments, whose behavior exerts a significant influence on unit efficiency and effectiveness. A task for each manager is to identify all significant sources of influence and then to itemize what each source does that is of importance. Such sources might include competitors, suppliers, distributors, employees, government agencies, customers-clients, financial institutions, and management. Figure 2 illustrates the kind of influence that these sources may exert.

Progression of Significant Behavior

Once a manager has a feel for the sources of significant influence and the activities they may engage in, it is helpful to examine the logical progression of an idea, thought, or concept from its inception through the decision-making, planning, implementation, and post-implementation stages. This insight is important because it indicates to a manager the options available when an awareness strategy is being developed.

For a simple example, let us see how a consumer might approach a purchasing situation. There is usually a prior condition that makes a consumer become aware of a possible need or desire to replace an item he owns, add another item of the same kind, or purchase a given item for the first time. Initial awareness may take place as a result of increased income, the introduction of a new model, advertisements, or because of the destruction, breakdown, obsolescence, or loss of an item presently in use. For nonimpulse items a consumer may wish to analyze his need or want partly in terms of the severity of the need or intensity of the desire, the availability and price of the item under consideration, his access to available financial resources, and alternative uses of financial resources.

Figure 2. Sources of influence.

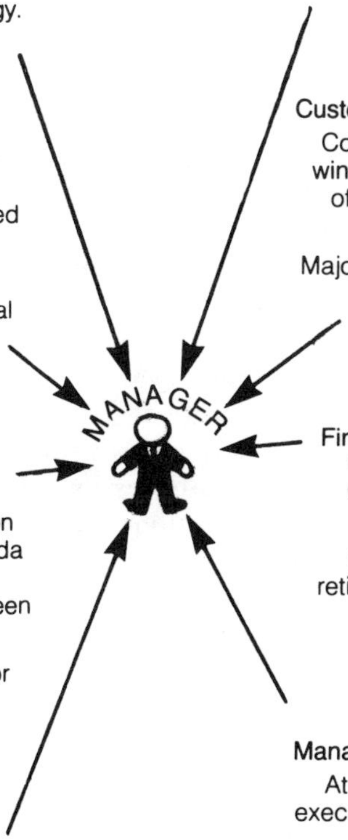

Competitors

Major competitor has increased its research and development budget by 10% over previous year.

Conglomerate recently bought out two small competitors.

Strong competitor announced a major new marketing strategy.

Government Agencies

Received notice that the Environmental Protection Agency will visit one of your facilities to check on citizen complaints regarding air and noise pollution.

Suppliers

Second shipment in a week from major supplier contained significant shortages.

Important supplier is experiencing critical financial problems.

Customers-Clients

Competitors working hard to win over a major customer by offering attractive price and customer is interested.

Major customer is faced with a likely strike or slowdown.

MANAGER

Distributors

At recent national convention of distributors a major agenda item dealt with the need to improve relationships between producers and distributors.

Rumor suggests that a major distributor is considering shifting its primary supply source.

Financial Institutions

Several banks have or are contemplating increasing their prime rate.

Bank handling company's retirement funds recently lost its top trust officer.

Management

At annual review, two senior executives were again rated as average.

The controller indicated receipt of an attractive offer from leading competitor.

Task force working on cost reduction in packaging department has failed to report progress.

Director of Research and Development is optimistic that new product will be ready for test run three weeks in advance of schedule.

Employees

Recent employee attitude survey indicates that women and members of minority races are still extremely disturbed over perceived inequities in promotion opportunities.

Employment manager reports that absenteeism and tardiness are likely to increase in foundry until ventilating system is fully installed.

After an initial analysis, he may decide to do nothing or delay his purchase, or he may make a tentative decision to purchase the item under review after further research including shopping around. His investigation may include a comparative analysis of price, terms of sale, quality, service, and delivery dates. After the analysis of alternative products the consumer may decide not to buy or to delay purchase, or he may decide to purchase the item, and he then enters into negotiation which if successful results in his acquisition of the product. Upon receipt, item may be inspected and, if found deficient, returned for repair or a replacement. When the item is in use, both initially and after an extended period, performance is likely to be assessed. If significant deficiencies occur, the item may be returned for a replacement, repair, or a cash payment. If the item is returned after repair or if a replacement is given, the cycle which was followed after the initial receipt of the purchased item begins anew. If performance throughout the use period, from the initial receipt of the product, is viewed as satisfactory the consumer-purchaser-user may be said to be beginning a new cycle. He is at the "before need-want is fully developed" stage moving toward the "new initial awareness" stage. This behavioral cycle, illustrated in Figure 3, can be viewed as continuous for certain products and consumers.

Using this outline of the progression of consumer behavior, a manager concerned with the selection of an awareness strategy can set forth the options open to him. The manager of a company selling a product under review by a consumer may seek to become aware of the consumer's attitude and behavior at one or more of the following points:

> Before a need or want is present.
> After a need or want is present, but before consumer awareness.
> At the initial stage of consumer awareness.
> During the decision-making process.
> At the time a tentative decision is made.
> At the time a final purchasing decision is made.
> At the time of purchase.
> At the time of consumer's receipt of the product.
> During the initial test stage.
> During the use stage.
> At the complaint stage, if any.

For purposes of simplicity and to illustrate the applicability of this outline to other awareness situations, the points of awareness can be grouped under four broad headings:

Figure 3. Cycle of consumer need–purchase–use.

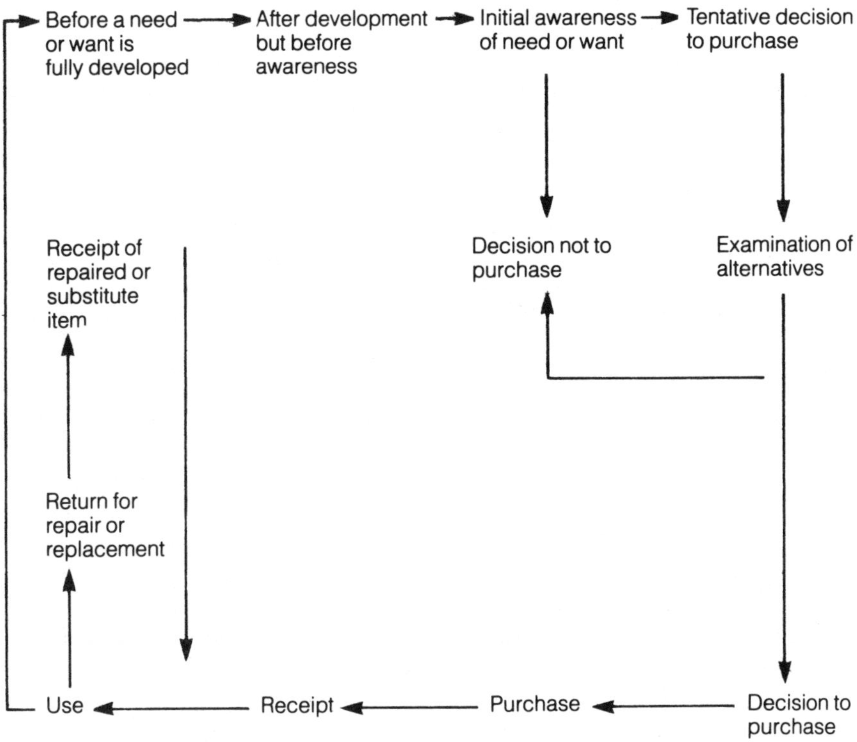

Before a need or want is fully developed → After development but before awareness → Initial awareness of need or want → Tentative decision to purchase

Decision not to purchase

Examination of alternatives

Receipt of repaired or substitute item

Return for repair or replacement

Use ← Receipt ← Purchase ← Decision to purchase

1. *Before Decision Making and Planning*

Prior to development of situation which will result in problem or opportunity and after development but prior to awareness.

2. *Decision Making and Planning*

During the decision-making and planning phases, including initial awareness and final decision.

3. *Implementation*

At initiation of implementation effort and while the new plan or decision is being made operational.

4. *Postimplementation*

After the plan, program, or strategy has been made operational.

Let us see how a manager's awareness strategy relative to possible actions of competitors could be examined by using the four awareness designations. Actions of competitors likely to be of interest and concern to a manager include the introduction of a radical new product design or production technology or significant changes in price policy, advertising strategy, or channels of distribution. For consumer goods, the introduction of such changes can be identified rather easily at the time of introduction (implementation stage) or some time thereafter. The results obtained by the initiator while the marketing strategies are in use (postimplementation stage) are likely to be highly important, but the acquisition of the data by an interested competitor may be difficult in the short run. In the longer run, the desired information is likely to be easily available but of less use.

A more sensitive awareness strategy could be designed to keep a manager informed of likely changes in product or marketing strategies of competitors while discussions and studies are underway (the planning, decision-making stage). The most advanced and successful awareness strategy attempts to uncover subjects likely to be examined by competitors before competitors are aware of the need or opportunity (before decision making and planning). To acquire the desired information at this stage, a manager must attempt to forecast internal and external conditions likely to be faced by competitors. Decisions by a company to introduce new marketing strategies are based on their assessment of their past, present, and likely future situations. The challenge faced by a competitor is to do a similar analysis before or at least concurrent with the actions of their competitors.

It is not difficult to relate the behavior of most significant individuals, groups, and organizations to the four awareness stages. The activities of legislators, consumers, customers, distributors, suppliers, citizens, employees, government officials, bankers, stockholders, judges, and others are in response to or in anticipation of events. Decisions are made as to appropriate courses of action. Plans are drawn. Approval is obtained. Implementation is initiated and is continued until there is a new need or opportunity to change. For an awareness strategy to be appropriate for each significant source of influence, it is helpful to describe and examine the steps taken by each source throughout the four awareness stages across all critical areas of influence. Figure 4 illustrates the interrelationship of awareness points, stages, and strategies.

CRITERIA FOR CHOOSING A STRATEGY

For the manager who wants to be an agent of change, an innovator, a creative force, there is no substitute for the generating awareness strategy. A manager who wishes to be aware of potential problems or opportunities or of likely actions of significant sources of influence needs an anticipatory strategy. Managers who wish to be informed

Figure 4. Interrelationship of awareness strategies, stages, and points.

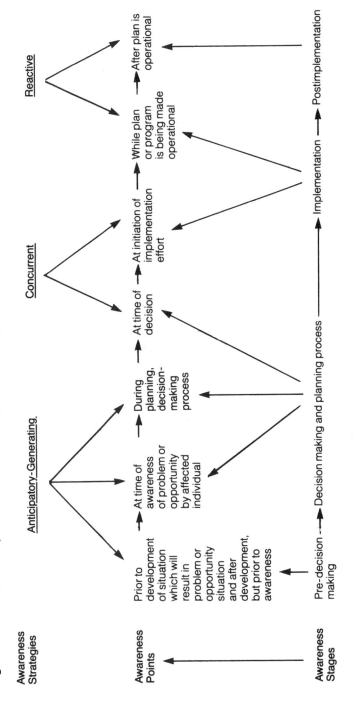

while sources of influence are deliberating issues or at the time a tentative decision is made also need an anticipatory stance.

There are situations where it would be sufficient for a manager to be informed of actions taken by others at the time a new plan, program, policy, or strategy has been decided upon or is being introduced. A concurrent awareness strategy would be appropriate under these conditions. At times for certain subjects it may be satisfactory for a manager to become aware of actions by others after full implementation has taken place, after programs have been made operational. Under these conditions a reactive awareness strategy may be adequate.

The range of actions in two or three of these strategies may overlap for given issues. In a sense, a concurrent strategy can be a backup for an anticipatory strategy; it can serve to confirm or disprove conclusions drawn from the initial awareness effort and can supply additional information about actual developments. A reactive strategy can be a backup for both strategies as well as provide up-to-date information relating to the issues under review. A manager might express the need for all three strategies across a logical time sequence: I wish to know what significant sources of influences are likely to do before they become aware of the need to contemplate action. I wish to know of their discussions and debates before they arrive at a decision. I wish to know of their decisions as soon as they are made. I wish to know of their implementation action at the time of initiation and during the introductory stages. I wish to be kept informed of the progress throughout the life cycle of the program under review.

It might appear that an anticipatory strategy is the most logical awareness strategy because it places a manager in a control and command position, but there are several good reasons why other strategies may be more realistic and appropriate. In fact, because of the variety of complex tasks carried out by a chief executive, it is likely that different strategies will be found appropriate for different assignments.

Several criteria need to be considered when examining alternative awareness strategies: the costs and benefits associated with the requisite awareness system; legal, moral, and ethical constraints; the state of the science and art of intelligence gathering and processing; the leadership role assumed by the organization; the personality, management style, and competence of the executive who is developing the strategy; and organization capability.

To apply the above criteria, it is helpful to recognize that the

Figure 5. Awareness units.

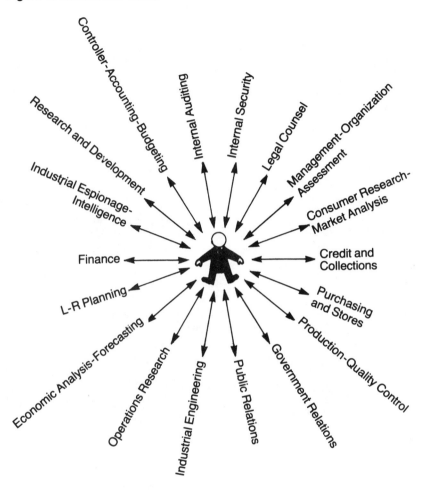

implementation of an awareness strategy requires the design and introduction of a support awareness system. Three of the critical components of an awareness system are (1) participants, (2) methods and techniques, and (3) tools and items of equipment for the generation, collection, processing, transmission, storage, use, retrieval, and disposal of the required information. Figure 5 indicates the variety of specialized units within a large organization, operating independently and in cooperation with one another, which may have a primary role in carrying out a viable awareness strategy.

Each unit is likely to contain a variety of individuals—economists, engineers, accountants, mathematicians, psychologists, political scientists—who possess specialized training, education, and experience which equips them to carry out one or more phases of the awareness process. Increasingly such specialists use sophisticated methods and techniques requiring extremely complex tools and items of equipment.

Cost-Benefit Analysis. An experienced manager knows that an incremental improvement in an awareness system may necessitate an added cost above the expense required to maintain a less sensitive or timely system. The key to cost-benefit analysis is to compare the incremental costs and benefits associated with a change in the awareness system under review. A good working philosophy is to downplay absolute cost, recognizing that a high or low cost determination itself has little meaning.

When viewing the benefit side of the cost-benefit equation a manager needs to determine the incremental gain or loss which is likely to result from a more advanced or delayed awareness of a significant opportunity or problem. For example, what are the financial advantages of knowing about a competitor's plans before implementation is undertaken rather than after full implementation has been achieved? What are the financial advantages of uncovering a likely acquisition opportunity before the affected organization even contemplates such a development? What are the financial advantages of identifying emerging discontent among employees before production is affected or before there is significant change in absenteeism, tardiness, or turnover?

For an orderly and systematic approach, a manager should identify all sources of influence which are of major importance. For each source it is then necessary to determine the kinds of decisions and actions they initiate which are likely to be of concern. Each significant action needs to be examined across all segments of the overall progression of behavior. The separation we have been using should provide a sense of direction and a starting point. Figure 6 can be used as a guide for cost-benefit analysis across all awareness points and strategies for each source of influence. When viewing benefit, a manager can determine the likely advantage to be gained at each awareness point.

All benefits, direct and indirect, should be translated into dollar amounts to facilitate comparison with related costs. This includes such benefits as improvement in morale, motivation, government and community relations, and planning and decision making.

The basic costs to consider are those required to carry out the

Figure 6. Awareness strategy selection criteria for significant sources of influence (competitors, suppliers, distributors, government agencies, employees, customers, stockholders, legislators).

Awareness Strategies → Awareness Points → Decision Criteria	Anticipatory		Concurrent		Reactive	
	Before condition indicates need for response — At Time of Awareness	During planning decision-making process	At time of decision	At initiation of implementation efforts	While plan is being made operational	After plan is operational
Cost Benefit						
Behavioral Guidelines						
State of Relevant Science and Art						
Organization's Leadership Role						
Characteristics and Qualifications of Managers						
Organization's Capability						

intent of the awareness strategy. As indicated above, the three primary cost elements are participants, methods and techniques, and tools and items of equipment required for the generation, collection, processing, transmission, storage, retrieval, use, and disposal of the desired information. The cost analysis should extend across all awareness points.

In computing costs it is necessary to prorate or allocate costs across two groups of users of the services of specialized individuals and their methods and equipment. An awareness system will be used to inform managers of the behavior of a variety of individuals, groups, and organizations. Some specialists such as economists, operations researchers, and psychologists are likely to conduct studies across two or more influence groups, say, competitors, regulatory agencies, and employees. The cost of their services should be allocated to each significant influence group if an accurate cost-benefit analysis is to be determined.

A second cost allocation may be desirable when personnel, techniques, or equipment are used for dual purposes. Costs associated with their use for nonawareness assignments need to be separated out and assigned to other projects, programs, or activities.

The results of the cost-benefit analysis will indicate to a manager the relative advantage (benefit over cost) or disadvantage (cost over benefit) likely to result from the use of each awareness strategy for each significant source of influence. With the results available, a manager is likely to discover that different awareness strategies may be appropriate for different competitors, different government agencies, different suppliers, and different customers.

Behavioral Guidelines and Constraints. Major constraints on the acceptance and use of a given awareness strategy are found in the innumerable guidelines which are meant to direct the activities of managers. Among these are laws at all governmental levels, moral and ethical codes, customs of the trade, and standards of professional etiquette. Some of these guidelines have an independent influence while others are incorporated in organization policies, codes, rules, and regulations and procedures.

These guidelines are of significance because they may affect the selection and use of participants throughout the awareness system, the way in which they carry out their assignments, and the methods, techniques, tools, and items of equipment used. For example, an anticipatory awareness strategy to be implemented successfully may require the acquisition of information which is held confidential and secured by the possessor or owner. The only way the information may be obtainable is by an undercover agent using subterfuge, stealth, bribery, or force.

Because of the complexity and importance of this exercise, it may be desirable to use the same approach here as for the cost-benefit analysis of alternative awareness strategies. For each awareness point, all the participants and activities which would be required to make the awareness strategies operational would be identified. The applicable guidelines would then be determined and examined. For example, to implement an anticipatory awareness strategy for one influence group, say competitors, it might be determined that the required participants, methods, or equipment are demonstrably illegal, unethical, immoral, or contradictory to the prevailing code of conduct and contrary to organization policies. For a concurrent strategy, it might be determined that no unacceptable behavior would be required.

It should be emphasized that the behavioral guidelines are being examined solely in terms of their applicability to alternative awareness strategies. The appropriateness of the prevailing guidelines is not under review. Nor is consideration given at this time to the state of compliance by given managers or other organization participants. It is interesting and useful to note, however, that a manager viewing both criteria cost-benefit analysis and behavioral guidelines might begin to question those guidelines which impose a costly restriction.

State of the Relevant Science and Art. A preferred awareness strategy which is affordable may not be possible because the requisite methods and techniques or tools and items of equipment needed to implement the strategy are not available or are totally inadequate. Managers of multinational conglomerates would be very interested in knowing in advance, with a high degree of certainty, likely political, economic, and social changes in third-world host countries. Domestic managers are interested in determining or being informed of employee unrest, consumer dissatisfaction, actions of competitors, or mental or moral breakdown of subordinate managers before these events or conditions occur. To what extent is anyone able to forecast or anticipate such developments well in advance of their occurrence so that preventive action can be initiated?

The point to emphasize is that an awareness strategy needs to meet the reality test. This is important because managers may engage in wishful thinking and even convince themselves that they will be kept adequately informed of potential or pending actions of others. In practice, a manager might be encouraged to expect such unlikely advanced warning by a specialized staff which is eager to please or overly optimistic about their capability. With realistic expectations, contingency plans can be formulated for the unknown or uncertain. There are no false expectations or needless recriminations when expected results are not forthcoming. When an early warning could result in a significant advantage but is precluded because of gaps in theory, methods, techniques, or equipment in use, it might be appropriate for the affected manager to consider initiating a research and development program to correct such deficiencies.

Organization's Leadership Role. Some organizations are known for their creativity and innovation in marketing, finance, and engineering, and in employee, government, and consumer relations. Other organizations, because of their nature, such as certain government agencies, school systems, small businesses, are purposely nonleaders. Still others may be nonleaders because of a well-thought-out strategy. They have found a niche for themselves and are content to let others initiate change and explore new approaches. Other organizations may be highly innovative in product or package design or advertising. They may follow the custom of the trade in using distributors, in organization design, or employee incentives. They may be highly conservative in financing new facilities or granting credit. In other words, there is not just one prevailing ideology, style, or strategy.

It is important to determine the degree and extent of innovation and creativity within an organization so that an appropriate awareness strategy can be chosen. For those areas, for example, product design, packaging, distribution, or advertising, where a company as a matter of market strategy chooses to follow the custom of the trade or to be even more conservative than the general practice, an anticipatory or generating awareness strategy would seem to be inappropriate. On the other hand, a concurrent or response awareness strategy is likely to be unsatisfactory for an organization seeking to expand its market share through innovative styling and creative advertising. This is not to say that the predominant posture of an organization—creative and innovative, custom of the trade, conservative—should determine the selection of a single overriding awareness strategy. It is more likely that different awareness strategies will be found appropriate when applied to the variety of activities and programs normally found in large, complex organizations. The key is to fit the awareness strategy to the leadership strategy in use for each subject under review.

Characteristics and Qualifications of Managers. The choice of awareness strategies by managers is influenced by their personality, style of management, personal values, and competence. Managers vary as to their interest in and ability to handle sketchy, ill-defined, speculative, ambiguous data relating to actual, likely, or possible behavior of competitors, regulatory agencies, or customers. Some managers have a higher level of tolerance than others regarding the use throughout the awareness system of questionable individuals, methods, and items of equipment. Managers differ also in their willingness to take risks, to experiment and innovate, to act before all the facts are available. One measure of the correctness and appropriateness of an awareness strategy is the extent to which the contemplated strategy is congruent with the values, attitudes, and capability of the affected manager.

Organization Resources and Capability. An awareness strategy is useful only when it can be applied operationally. What is appropriate or desirable in theory may not be practical because of limitations within the organization where it would be used. An organization may not have the required technical or specialized manpower or equipment. Furthermore, it may not have or be able to obtain adequate financial, physical, and human resources available at the time of analysis. However, a different result may be possible if a longer time frame is used. The results of a cost-benefit analysis might indicate that a given awareness strategy is demonstrably superior to other strategies. Present limitations may make it impossible to implement the strategy. A reallocation of resources across programs and activities during a subsequent fiscal year might make existing funds, personnel, or equipment available to support a desired awareness strategy. The justification for such a reallocation is found in the improvement in organization effectiveness and efficiency beyond what would be achieved through some other allocation of resources.

The human resource constraint goes beyond the manager who is contemplating an awareness strategy and the specialists who have a primary role in the collection, processing, and transmission of the desired information. It is necessary to include all significant individuals within and outside the organization who will participate in the response activities. Some individuals will participate at various stages of the planning and decision-making process. Others will implement the new or modified program. It is important to include such participants in the analysis of awareness strategies because awareness is not an end in itself. Early awareness may indicate that if quick, decisive action is taken a significant advantage might be gained or a potential problem prevented. Decisions have to be made, plans formulated and carried out. Without these support and follow-through actions, an early awareness is of little practical use. The personality, work style, value system, and competence of each significant participant needs to be congruent with the contemplated awareness strategy.

It should be clear after this brief review of criteria that it is very difficult to treat each criterion separate from and independent of all other criteria. As each criterion was discussed, an attempt was made to isolate and examine those factors which exert a major independent influence. What is of greater importance is the need for a careful assessment of alternative awareness strategies before a selection is made. What one wants may not be possible or feasible. What is possible may not be appropriate.

SUMMARY AND CONCLUSION

The lack of a well-developed theory of management awareness is a crucial gap in management science. This subject needs further attention because no planning or decision-making efforts are initiated until a manager becomes aware or is made aware of an opportunity or problem situation. The quality of the response is tied in directly with the timeliness of the awareness. A delayed awareness may result in the loss of a promising opportunity or an increase in the severity of a problem. An early awareness may allow a manager to capitalize on an opportunity before others become aware or initiate action or allow him to prevent problems or respond to problems while they are in a developing stage.

Intuitively, experienced managers create formal and informal awareness systems. What is needed is a formal, systematic approach for the determination of awareness strategies which are appropriate to the tasks at hand. Three broad awareness strategies are available. They are anticipatory-generating, concurrent, and reactive.

A four-step approach can be used to facilitate the selection process:

◇ Each significant source of influence needs to be identified. Competitors, distributors, suppliers, government agencies, employees, customers, citizens, stockholders, legislators are a few sources likely to be of concern to managers of large corporations.
◇ The areas of impact or subjects covered by each source have to be determined. For competitors, for example, product style, package design, channels of distribution, pricing, credit policies, and production technology are some likely subjects of interest.
◇ An approach is needed for identifying and examining how each source of influence becomes aware of and responds to opportunities and problems. One useful approach is to divide the management process into four stages: pre-decision making and plan-

ning, decision making and planning, implementation, and post-implementation.

◇ A basis for examining and evaluating alternative strategies across all sources of influence and significant subjects or topics has to be developed. Several criteria which have been found to be useful are: the costs and benefits associated with the requisite awareness system which will make the strategy operational; legal, moral, and ethical constraints; the state of the science and art of intelligence gathering and processing; the leadership role assumed by the organization; the personality, management style, and competence of the executive who is developing the strategy; and organization capability.

Using this approach, managers are more likely to develop awareness strategies which meet their unique needs. The acid test of an awareness strategy is its contribution to unit effectiveness and efficiency.

William H. Newman

27
External
Integration of
the Firm

One of the central pillars of management as conceived by Harold Smiddy and his General Electric colleagues is *integrating*. Along with planning, organizing, and measuring, integrating is a vital task of every manager.

The concept of integrating has yet to receive widespread use by scholars and practitioners of management. Such reluctance may stem from two inherent features of Smiddy's integrating proposition. First, as set forth in the General Electric doctrine, integrating embraces a wide variety of activities—such as coordinating, motivating, building continuing relationships, taking corrective action—and it applies to both internal and external actions. This is too big a bite for many people; they prefer to deal separately with several of the components. Second, integrating implies synthesis rather than analysis, and we Westerners have difficulty thinking in terms of a total con-figuration—a *gestalt*—especially when that gestalt is as ambiguous as a dynamic social structure.

For these reasons I shall deal in this chapter with only one part of the total integrating process—the integration of a company with its resource contributors. The underlying issue is a simple and funda-mental one: How must a firm conduct its affairs so as to assure a continuing flow of such necessary resources as men, materials, machinery, money, market demand, government aid, and public tol-eration? How will the firm integrate its actions with the demands of these key cooperating groups in its environment?

438

Where Is External Integration Vital?

A whole array of resource inputs are necessary for a company to survive. Government cooperation, risk capital, able workers, satisfied customers—to cite obvious examples—are all essential. Unfortunately, the business and economic literature is oversupplied with silly arguments about which input is *most* essential. Each specialist sees the entire world revolving around his particular contribution. One can read in any economics text about the central role of profits or discover in the beginning book on marketing that all business activities are really concerned with satisfying customers.

The obvious fact is that capital must be attracted, customers found, and a whole lot of other resources obtained all at the same time. Just as life in the human body depends on proper functioning of the heart, lungs, liver, nerves, and other vital parts of the total system, so too does an enterprise require a variety of inputs. This means, of course, that the managers of an enterprise must deal simultaneously with external integration on several fronts.

As a practical matter, company managers cannot spend large amounts of their time on each necessary resource input. Some sorting out must be done. Fortunately, many necessary inputs can be obtained on known, reliable, and acceptable terms; and as long as these circumstances prevail these inputs require little attention. For most, though not all, businesses, mail and telephone service, equipment repair, legal counsel, and the supply of paper fall into this category. Other inputs are surrounded by uncertainty as to quality, availability, price or other terms; union labor, energy, markets, and capital for expansion are typical examples. Such uncertainty demands attention. Often a company merely tries to predict what will happen and make appropriate internal adjustments. But in some arenas the company tries to influence the uncertainties through advertising, negotiation, concessions, external coalitions, and so on. Clearly, such attempts at restructuring the external relationship require even more attention. Each company must decide for itself which of its resource inputs warrant prime attention.

Theoretically, an identification of which resource contributors are key ones for a specific company can be determined by "risk analysis." For each uncertain resource the array of possible conditions, the consequences for the company if those conditions prevail, the value attached to such consequences, and the odds of the event occurring are estimated. Then a comparison of the estimated results will reveal where the greatest vulnerability lies. A further refinement is to estimate what the company might do to reduce unfavorable uncertainties or increase the odds for favorable ones, and also to predict the cost of such manipulation. The more *net* improvement that a company might make in the estimated risk associated with particular resources, the greater attention that resource warrants.

Through such an analysis, done either formally or informally and subjectively, a company can classify its resources into, say, three groups: key ones which will be watched and "managed" continuously, potential trouble/opportunity resources which need to be monitored and treated with care, and resources which will be dealt with on a routine basis. External integration is concerned predominantly with the first group.

Two implications are inherent in this approach. First, no one or two resources are necessarily key for all companies. We can prepare lists of likely candidates,[1] but each enterprise should determine its own key resource contributors. Second, the classification of a resource may change, perhaps dramatically, with the passage of time. Recent shifts in the importance attached to energy and to political contributions are examples.[2]

Each resource contributor, of course, attaches his own independent value to his relationship with the company. From his viewpoint, ties with the company may be key, potentially key, or routine—and this categorization is not necessarily the same as the company's. Whatever the category, he probably feels that he is a stakeholder in the company.

CONTINUING, DYNAMIC TWO-WAY RELATIONSHIPS

The nature of an integrated relationship with a key resource contributor is usually more complex and subtle than is often realized. A two-way exchange must prevail if cooperation is to continue. The company receives goods or services with particular characteristics which it wants, and the supplier receives benefits which he finds attractive.

Much more than money is involved. Employees, for instance, are concerned about meaningful work, stability of employment, reasonable supervision, future opportunities, and a whole array of fringe benefits in addition to their paychecks. Suppliers of materials want a continuing market, sure and prompt payment, convenient delivery times, quality standards suited to their facilities, minimum returns, and the like. Investors are concerned about uncertainty of repayment, security, negotiability of their claims, veto of major changes, and perhaps some share in the management.

Note that a continuing relationship is typical. Both a company and its banker expect their ties to continue for years. The same is true of employees. We think in terms of regular suppliers of raw materials and, on the other side of that coin, of repeat customers. In other words, the relationship normally covers a flow of services, not a single transaction. Mutual trust and expectations are established, implied obligations build up. Today's exchange is strongly conditioned by its effect on many tomorrows. Effective integration assumes at least some degree of continuing mutual support, mutual benefits, and mutual dependence.

Nevertheless, most external relationships do change over time. As a company grows, modifies its technology or its services, and adjusts to new demands from other resource contributors, the characteristics of its needs from a specific supplier will change. Similarly, the needs and the alternative options available to that supplier shift with time. Consequently, a recurring adjustment in the terms of the exchange takes place. At some point a relationship may be terminated; new ones will be established. (The process by which these adjustments are negotiated is discussed below.) [3]

These two features—the importance of relationships with key resource contributors noted above, and the complicated and dynamic two-way exchange just sketched—help explain why external integration warrants careful managerial action.

VIABILITY OF TOTAL COMMITMENTS TO RESOURCE CONTRIBUTORS

Winning continuing cooperation of each resource contributor has its price. In addition to money payments on products/services distributed, various guarantees, timing of actions, veto rights, alternative actions rejected, and similar limitations may be granted. Now, if the concessions made to one resource group place too heavy a burden on the company, it may become impossible to grant the *quid pro quo* desired by other contributors. The simple example of this problem appears in cash flows; a drastic jump in energy costs or wage rates (or drop in selling prices) may absorb so much cash that other demands for payment cannot be met.

Again, the problem is not simply a matter of cash. Pollution controls on plant operations, seniority "rights," delivery commitments, bond indenture restrictions on sale of assets, and a host of other constraints may be inserted in one or another agreement with a resource contributor. And under some circumstances these constraints may upset the viability of the entire enterprise. For instance, promises of stable employment may be incompatible with protections promised to suppliers of capital.

The trade-offs between accommodating to one resource contributor and hurting another contributor can rarely be reduced to a simple dollar calculation. Instead, company managers are working with *diverse systems of cooperation.* For example, in obtaining local community support for a new building (to treat drug addicts or to fabricate asbestos) the values involved, the institutions concerned, and the usual mechanisms for reaching agreement form one kind of system. In contrast, the values, institutions, and agreement mechanisms for floating a bond issue are quite different. Because the systems for reaching cooperative agreements are so different, rational comparisons of incremental costs and benefits are difficult even to formulate.[4]

In a sense, managers of the company serve as mediators between the various claimants. But since the various resource contributors rarely meet face to face, it is the central managers who must consider the impact of demands of one group upon ability of the company to comply with other demands. This is the overall or consolidated integrating task.

The ability of a company to reconcile diverse desires of resource contributors depends to a large extent on its *conversion technology.* The way resources are converted into outputs affects the nature and quantity of outputs available.

Every enterprise has its technology for converting resources into outputs. For example, a school has its teaching technology, an insurance company has its technology for policy risks, and a beauty shop has its technology for shaping unruly hair. This internal conversion technology involves much more than mechanical efficiency. The desired outputs include interesting jobs, low capital risks, minimum pollution of the environment, improved job opportunities for women and minorities, and a host of other features.

The overall integrating task, then, involves a combination of (a) negotiating cooperation agreements with key resource contributors, and (b) designing a conversion technology, such that the array of outputs at least meets the diverse commitments made to resource contributors.[5]

STRATEGY—A CHOICE IN EMPHASIS

The integrating task sketched in the preceding section is inherently complex. Even when we give primary attention to key resource contributors and a compatible conversion technology, we are faced with a maze of relationships. One practical way to deal positively with this network is to adopt a company strategy.

A cardinal feature of each strategy is the selection of a few relationships by which the company seeks to distinguish itself. These selected relationships become the basis for differential advantage over other competitors for scarce resources (including customers).

A few examples will highlight this feature of strategy. IBM has always stressed customer service, customer orientation in product design, and liberal treatment of its employees.[6] Humble Oil rose to prominence because it gave high priority to acquiring an advantageous crude oil supply. Merck and Boeing stressed building better mousetraps—ethical pharmaceuticals and aircraft, respectively. Conglomerates derive their differential advantage predominantly by the way they raise capital.

Each company singles out perhaps one, but more likely a few areas having synergistic ties. In these areas it tries to develop an unusually favorable resource relation compared to that of competitors; typically, a new form of relationship with a key contributor group is coupled with an internal technology in a symbiotic interaction. If the company is wise (or lucky), it selects for emphasis relationships which will become especially important strengths in the future competition within its industry.

In the numerous external relationships not selected as a source of differential advantage, a company "satisfices." Often a company is too small to attempt any more than following general industry practice; its location, history, personal preferences of key executives, or existing resource base may not provide a good springboard; or management may deliberately decide that effort applied in other directions will be more rewarding. These secondary relationships cannot be neglected; they must be adequately maintained, like Herzberg's hygiene factors. Moreover, the secondary relationships should be designed so that they support or are at least compatible with the primary thrusts of the selected strategy.

Of course, over time a company may shift its choice of areas in which it seeks differential advantage. Critical factors for success change; the company changes; new opportunities for distinctiveness emerge. Adapting to these opportunities by adjusting the emphasis placed on various external relationships is a crucial aspect of successful strategy.

DUALITY IN RELATIONSHIPS—THE PIE-MAKER'S PREDICAMENT

Recognizing the importance and variety of relationships with resource contributors still leaves unanswered the question of how desired relationships can be developed. A comprehensive review of this process is far beyond the scope of this paper; however, a few comments will add another dimension to the concept of external integration.

Every relationship with a resource contributor has two sides. First, how can the input that is made available be fused and blended into company operations so as to most improve the quantity and quality of company output? Second, there is bargaining over the terms of the exchange—just what resources are to be provided under what conditions, and what inducements will the provider receive as a result? This is the familiar pie-maker's predicament—how to increase the total size and quality of the pie while seeking acceptance by each helper of the size of his particular piece. When contributors become primarily concerned with size and shape of their respective pieces, the total pie may suffer.

This duality of both bargaining and collaborating is a common feature of cooperative relationships. Auto manufacturers and dealers have much to gain from their concerted action, but at the same time they may be bickering over how each will fare as a result of their merged efforts. Joint authors provide mutual help and yet are concerned with who is gaining what from the collaboration. Even allies in war are bargaining while collaborating—witness the relations between the United States and Russia during World War II.

We have already noted that resource inputs vary in attractiveness because of their timing, adaptability, reliability, and other characteristics. Sometimes the resource contributor is quite willing to adjust a characteristic to suit the needs of the company. For instance, a particular worker may be willing to take different jobs and even to live in various locations; or, if the company is robust a banker may not care how the funds he advances are used. To paraphrase Chester Barnard, contributors may have at least some "zone of indifference." However, with respect to other input characteristics a contributor may be willing to cooperate only if he receives an offsetting inducement, and under still other conditions he may refuse to play ball at all.

As with inputs, some benefits to contributors will be easy for the company to provide, others inconvenient and costly but possible, and some ruinous. Each contributor will want his own set of benefits, so company managers have to weigh compatibility between different demands (clean air, low price, assured supply for an electric utility company, for instance) as well as the consolidated total.[7]

As a practical matter, there can be no pie to divide unless some stability and predictability of resource supply is achieved. Modern production—of education as well as shoes—requires an established social and technological system. And haggling about conditions of exchange seriously interferes with cooperative effort to overcome tough problems. Consequently, all those interested in making the system produce find it advantageous to separate negotiating the terms of cooperation from the subsequent joint activity. Normally, once a bargain is set then teamwork is expected. For example, union contracts, the law of the land, or the price of a product must have some stability for complex and long-cycle activities to proceed.

Several things contribute to this necessary stability, or at least predictability. Many relationships between resource contributors and companies are shaped by firmly established institutions and traditions; they are parts of the appropriate system of cooperation. Stocks and bonds are sold through well-worn channels in financial markets; labor negotiations are surrounded by a host of laws, boards, regulations, and rituals; patents and licensing guide new plant construction; customers are increasingly protected by labeling requirements, outright bans, price restraints, and the like; government subsidies are obtained via elaborate procedures. External integrating always takes place within these contexts.

Also, wise management tries to anticipate the need for modifying a relationship with a resource contributor and to arrange an orderly transition. Except for tactical reasons noted below, new conditions of input or output are negotiated in advance so that plans can be adjusted. Of course, there are many surprises, and lead times may be uncomfortably short. But part of the art of integrating is to anticipate environmental pressures and opportunities.

BARGAINING MODE

The bargaining phase of integrating can be carried on in many ways. A brief review of four different modes found in union relations will suggest the array of options.

Horse-Trading Approach. Here the union is assumed to be unreliable and conniving; consequently, bargaining is conducted in an air of suspicion, and sharp bargains are quite in order. In keeping with this approach are deals that resolve current difficulties but that are untenable in the longer run. As one advocate of this mode said, "It is just a question of whether you can outsmart the other guy."

Follow the Leader. Smaller companies may try to establish an understanding with the union that they will grant any wage increase or fringe benefits that have been agreed to by leading companies of the industry. These firms feel that they are too small and weak to bargain aggressively with the union. The most they hope for is to be no worse off than their large competitors. This is an illustration of "satisficing," mentioned above. Low labor costs cannot be one of the bases for strategic differentiation. We should note, however, that by minimizing the hard feelings which often arise during tough bargaining, the company may be in a better position to negotiate adjustments in conditions of work which will aid its internal operations.

Straight Business Relationship. When both company executives and union leaders take a mature view of their relations, a company may approach union negotiations as a straight business proposition. This can occur only after union recognition has been accepted and the bitterness so often associated with such activities has receded into the background. There is mutual confidence, respect, and trust. Company executives must recognize that union leaders hold elected offices and that at times they must press grievances simply in response to pressure from some of their constituents. In the straight business mode, this pressure does not create a strong emotional reaction but is regarded simply as a normal part of the relationship.

Union-Management Cooperation. Another mode is to enlist the union as an ally in improving the efficiency of the business. There have been outstanding examples in the clothing industry and occasionally in the steel industry of joint study of ways to increase output, improve quality, and the like; in fact, at one stage in the ladies' garment industry union professionals took the initiative in improving management practice. (It is not uncommon for a large customer such as the federal government to initiate management practices in its suppliers; likewise, banks on occasion provide management counsel to their customers.)

In such situations bargaining takes a secondary place. Normally the company and union have a prior agreement about the way wages and related benefits will be related to company performance; if the pie is bigger a commitment already exists on how it will be divided.

Although the preceding paragraphs have dealt with union relations, it is easy to project how horse-trading, follow the leader, open business negotiation, and sharing in devising improvements can also be ways of dealing with material suppliers, regulatory bodies, or customers. Obviously, the choice of the bargaining mode is determined by the resource contributor as well as the company, but the company by its actions can encourage one type of relationship.

EXTERNAL COALITIONS

One additional dimension of external integration should be mentioned. The interaction of a company with its environment is not confined to exchanges at its boundary. A company may pursue a strategy that extends well beyond an exchange of dollars for goods or services at the factory gate.

The eagerness of a resource contributor to cooperate with a specific company, and the terms on which that cooperation is conducted, depend substantially on *other* opportunities and threats which the contributor faces. So one way a company can build satisfactory relationships for itself is to engage in a bit of active empathy with its resource suppliers. Basically, the company tries to create external environmental conditions—through forming coalitions or otherwise—which make cooperating with it more attractive.

Well-recognized examples include working with a local community to develop schools and other amenities which will help attract competent employees, or using a trade association as a coalition to pressure Congress to provide a subsidy. The feasibility of opening a new coal mine in Kentucky may depend upon inducing a railroad to install service between the mine and a utility customer. An equipment dealer arranges with a local bank to provide his customers with credit. In each of these illustrations action of the company extends to third parties with whom the company has no direct transaction.

All sorts of indirect help, reciprocity, coalitions, roundabout pressure may be involved. Some types of coalitions will be frowned upon by the Federal Trade Commission, whereas other joint action may be encouraged. As companies find themselves increasingly the targets of boycotts, environmental protection groups, or consumer advocates, the arena and the jousting tools change.

The point here is not to flag a new set of inputs and outputs of sufficient importance to a company to warrant inclusion in its strategy. Rather, the way by which a company makes itself attractive to important contributors is extended. As the examples noted above suggest, the company enlists allies. Frequently these allies perform activities that are quite distinct from company operations but are functions which are important to the resource contributor.

Forming external coalitions is a dimension of integration which often receives too little systematic attention.[8]

Conclusion

To achieve external integration managers must operate in at least these ways: (1) Distinguish between relationships with resource contributors that should be actively managed, monitored, or handled routinely. (2) Especially with the first group, develop continuing, two-way relationships. (3) At the same time, keep *total* commitments to all resource contributors achievable with the company's conversion technology. (4) Use company strategy to guide emphasis to be placed on selected relationships which will give the company a differential advantage. (5) Provide for the pie-maker's predicament—the need for both bargaining and collaborating with each resource contributor. (6) Select a bargaining mode with an eye on subsequent collaboration. (7) Participate in external coalitions to reinforce desired relationships.

This framework, rather than listing specific external groups with which a company must "integrate," offers a generalized approach. This basic approach to external integration has several advantages. It encourages flexibility in deciding which resources are key at any particular moment. It urges empathetic, dynamic treatment of key resource contributors. It relates the concept of integration to company strategy and to external coalitions. And it has the distinct advantage of fitting all sorts of enterprises—nonprofit organizations such as hospitals and schools as well as business firms ranging from manufacturing to retail and diverse service companies.

NOTES AND REFERENCES

1. See, for example, Part Two of W. H. Newman and J. P. Logan, *Strategy, Policy, and Central Management,* 7th ed. (Cincinnati: South-Western Publishing Co., 1976).
2. A technique for identifying vital sectors for a specific company is outlined in H. E. Klein and W. H. Newman, "SPIRE: Systematic Probing and Identification of the Relevant Environment," unpublished working paper, 1978.

3. For an illustration of dynamic, two-way relationships in a single industry, see J. E. Post, *Risk and Response: Management and Social Change in the American Insurance Industry* (Lexington, Mass.: D. C. Heath, 1976).
4. Organization theorists explore various systems of interaction between a firm and key elements in its environment. See D. Katz and R. L. Kahn, *The Social Psychology of Organizations* (New York: Wiley, 1966), chap. 2; W. H. Starbuck, "Organizations and Their Environments," in M. D. Dunnette, ed., *Handbook of Industrial and Organizational Psychology* (New York: Rand McNally, 1976); J. D. Thompson, *Organizations in Action* (New York: McGraw-Hill, 1967); A. H. Van de Ven, "On the Nature, Formation, and Maintenance of Relations Among Organizations," *Academy of Management Review* (October 1976); B. E. Williamson, *Markets and Hierarchies* (New York: Free Press, 1975).
5. In abstract symbols, the technology should meet the following conditions: With each resource contributor designated by subscripts $l, i, e, s, c, \ldots , n$ and where S = satisfactions required by a resource contributor

C = contributions by a resource contributor

CT = conversion technology

O = total output of satisfactions

then:

$$O \geq (S_l + S_i + S_e + S_s + S_c \ldots S_n)$$
$$O = f\,CT\,(C_l + C_i + C_e + C_s + C_c \ldots C_n)$$

and as viewed by each resource contributor:

$$S_x \geq C_x$$

6. See T. J. Watson, Jr., *A Business and Its Beliefs* (New York: McGraw-Hill, 1963).
7. Economic theory assumes that *price* based on incremental contributions and outputs will take care of external integration. In practice, the presence of many noncash considerations, along with difficulties in measuring the value of incremental contributions, make integration a much more intangible, multifaceted task.
8. The best discussion of this area in print is I. C. MacMillan, "Business Strategies for Political Action," *Journal of General Management,* Autumn 1974. See also MacMillan's forthcoming book, *Strategy Formulation: Political Concepts* (St. Paul, Minn.: West Publishing Co., 1978).

Billy E. Goetz and Dennis J. Gaffney

28
Management and Accounting

It is appropriate to begin with two axioms, or perhaps two versions of the same axiom:

◇ Enterprises and managements do *not* exist to provide something about which records can be kept and reports rendered.
◇ Accounting *does* exist to provide information to assist managements to plan and control the operations of enterprises.

The relationship between the enterprise and its environment imposes a bifurcated set of imperatives on accounting. There is a set of external institutions which have the power both to *dictate* what, when, and whether data should be reported and to *impose* sanctions which are sufficiently disagreeable to assure an attempt to comply with the established rules and regulations. From a management perspective, two principles govern mandatory external reporting:

◇ Determine what the requirements are and comply.
◇ Where the requirements allow a choice, investigate the consequences of each alternative and choose the one most advantageous to the enterprise.

The alternative most "advantageous" to the enterprise is defined as the one which yields the most favorable discounted net cash flow.[1]

The requirements imposed by the external institutions and the regulations interpreting the requirements are often technical, complex, and arbitrary. Different institutions can and do impose different requirements. As a result, virtually all enterprises of any consequence employ in-house specialists—for example, tax experts and

450

appraisers—to research and interpret the maze of statutes and regulations, and to design information systems to produce the mandated reports.

So much for conventional financial accounting. It is important. At the minimum, it is necessary to keep the enterprise out of legal difficulties and managers free from financial penalty, if not incarceration. Insofar as it helps predict certain cash flows, it even provides data which are useful in managerial planning. But managers must recognize that, by and large, reports mandated by outsiders are inappropriate as input data for managerial use.

The major functions of management are planning and controlling enterprise operations. As a basis for planning, management requires three classes of information:

◇ Information concerning available resources and the current commitments (legally enforceable obligations) concerning these resources.
◇ Information regarding probable future cash flows.
◇ Information about the past performances of individuals and/or groups of individuals on the basis of their assigned tasks and responsibilities.

An ideal position statement, with supporting detail, would supply the first type of information. An ideal cash budget, again with supporting detail, would supply the second type of information. And an ideal operating statement, with supporting detail classified according to responsibilities, would provide the third type of information.

IDEAL POSITION STATEMENTS

Existing position statements are sadly incomplete and inadequate, often flawed by omissions and obsolete valuations. An ideal position statement would report *all* resources available (including those represented by executory contracts—future purchase) to management, and *all* the obligations the enterprise must meet.

There are numerous resources available to the enterprise which are usually omitted from its position statement, such as accounts that will be receivable on enforceable sales contracts where delivery or shipment has not been made, materials purchased but not received or paid for, the value of the enterprise's organization and staff, the value of accumulated customer goodwill, the goodwill related to the sources of materials and funds (that is, the enterprise's credit rating), the value of research and development completed and in progress, the value of occupancy during the tenure of a valid lease, and a number of lesser items.

Among the obligations usually omitted from the conventional position statement are obligations involving sales not yet shipped or paid for (ask Westinghouse about its sales commitments for uranium to fuel nuclear reactors that it sold), accounts to be payable on purchase commitments neither received nor paid for, rental liability under a valid lease for future periods, salary and fringe commitments under binding employment contracts,[2] and possibly others.

Most position statements still value assets (resources) at original historical cost without regard to age, obsolescence, and inflation. Such data can only mislead users of position statements. Managers *need* current market values as a basis for decision making. Either entry or exit market values or both may be relevant. If any alternative considered envisages replacement of currently held assets, either now or in the foreseeable future, replacement market value discounted to present value is relevant. If any contemplated alternative includes disposing of an asset, exit market value is relevant or, more precisely, opportunity cost, since there may be alternative uses other than resale. These are the valuations implied, or explicitly cited, as the appropriate input data for the mathematical models which are becoming increasingly popular as decision-making tools.

The liability (obligation) side of the traditional position statement also exhibits obsolete valuations in many cases. As interest rates vary, the present value of liabilities changes. A twenty-year bond issued when interest rates were 4 percent can usually be bought-in far below face value when interest rates have accelerated to 8 percent—and the latter value is far more significant in decision making than the misleading figure (par adjusted for premium or discount) displayed in the traditional position statement.

IDEAL CASH BUDGETS

The present worth of future cash flows is becoming the accepted approach to making decisions involving capital expenditures. It is also appropriate in choosing among alternative possibilities in formulating long-term policies.

Most cash budgets are projected month by month for a year. Enlightened managers will continuously tack another month on the far end of the projection as each month passes from future to past. A growing number of enterprises prepare five- or ten-year projections. Theoretically, cash budgets should extend as far into the future as the time horizon of the longest-term alternative considered. This normally involves forecasting cash receipts from sales as some smoothed function of time, for example, as a function of population growth or of projections of GNP. Of course, other factors should be considered, particularly for the near-term future. Some managers balk, claiming that such long-range forecasts cannot be accurate enough to be taken seriously. Yet those same managers will plan a new factory building which they expect to occupy for 40 years or more. If the manager were asked why he needed the new factory building, he could reply, "To accommodate our growing sales volume." Ask the manager, "Why not 20 percent larger?" and he would reply, "We don't expect our sales to grow that fast or that much." The point is that the manager has, in fact, formulated a budget, albeit in an intuitive and unscientific manner.

Cash flow estimates are at least as essential for short-term planning. When will bank credit be needed? How much credit will be needed? On what schedule can interest and principal payments be made? If a manager plans to borrow, he had best be prepared to answer such questions since the bank will probably ask them. But even if the bank were not to ask these questions, a prudent management must know the answers to protect the solvency of its enterprise and to maintain sufficient flexibility—liquidity—to be able to seize attractive opportunities as they are discovered.

The naive proprietor who conducts his business and makes decisions on the basis of what is in his cash register is on the right track, only outrageously short-sighted. He should predict the balance of his cash drawer month after month for years to come, and day by day if near insolvency. Accrual accounting is a vastly inferior substitute. Many elementary accounting texts suggest the looming emergency of major asset replacements if provisions are not made by retaining assets via depreciation allowances (which reduce the apparent earnings—as indicated by the swelling contents of the cash register—and discourage overly liberal distributions of "earnings"). These same texts may mention that accrual-depreciation accounting doesn't make such provision for replacements: that depreciation is, in fact, merely an amortization of original historical cost and often bears little relationship to replacement cost. With generally rising prices, the naive proprietor may find replacing major assets almost as much of a problem with depreciation accounting as with cash drawer accounting.

The solution is to prepare cash budgets extending well into the future. If such estimates generate a queasy feeling because of the uncertainty associated with the future, so much the better. Long-range planning is desirable; the fact is that it warrants a queasy feeling and will make managers more prudent and less apt to make major commitments on whimsical, optimistic hunches.

Ideal Operating Statements

An ideal operating statement would reveal how much better (worse) off the enterprise was at the end of a period than at the beginning, how the improvement (decline) came about, and who was responsible for how much of the change in position. Admittedly, this is a big order.

For an overall indication of how an enterprise is better or worse off, we return to the ideal position statement. Recall that the ideal position statement at the end of each period exhibited current market value (entrance market at replacement cost and/or exit market at salvage value) of each item. However, the succession of such statements are not comparable because the value of the measuring rod—money—has changed. So all position statements at the end of previous periods should be adjusted for changes in price levels. This is accomplished by dividing each item on each position statement by the price-level index of its date and multiplying by the price-level index of the date of the current position statement. No doubt there is some question as to what the appropriate index is—the consumer price index, the implicit GNP deflator, or some other index. Since computers are able to cope with the mathematical conversions quickly and economically, several price-level adjustments could be made until one proved to be clearly superior. It is possible that different indices would be preferable for different items. The difference between total enterprise value at the beginning and end of a period not only measures the enterprise's worth in the Hicksian sense, but it also provides a measure of the enterprise's ability to continue making profits at the end of the period compared to its ability to produce profits at the beginning of the period.

The total adjusted profit (loss) should be subdivided into components with supporting detail to reflect the responsibility of organizational subdivisions and their managers. Note that there is no compulsion to make the whole equal to the arithmetic sum of its parts. If two or more subdivisions or managers have substantial control of some profit segment, each can be held responsible for the entire segment, with notice that they are jointly responsible and they had best cooperate or all will suffer.

On the other hand, some components may be fixed, sunk, or committed beyond anyone's control and these *should not be arbitrarily allocated* among organizational units or managers. At best, these allocations dilute responsibility and distort comparisons; at worst, they can mislead managers into serious mistakes. For example, suppose the occupancy costs of a building are allocated among departments in proportion to space occupied by the respective departments. First, different locations (in square feet) have different values, a fact commonly neglected in allocating "rent" to departments. Second, different hours (of the day) have different values, another fact commonly neglected in allocating "rent" to jobs or products. Third, if managers were "charged" for the space they use, they could be motivated to use less space. But saving space may have no effect on the total cost of occupancy, and department heads may waste time working up proposals to double-tier storage or otherwise save space. The result might be additional costs (for example, in racks) in order to add to existing unused space.

In addition to this comparison of price-level adjusted, current-market-based position statements, it is desirable to determine how the enterprise got from one financial position to the next. The present approach is akin to the navigator's use of dead reckoning from compass direction, RPM of a ship's screws, and winds and currents as compared to periodic fixes by celestial observation or loran directional radio beacons. No doubt price-level adjusted, current-market-based operating statements are difficult to formulate if the accounting axiom of an arithmetic link between position statements and operating statements is slavishly followed. A statistical approach is probably better, with comparisons of revenue and cost items with one another and from period to period.

In preparing operating statements, the criteria should be utility of the information to managers in making decisions, and ease of communication in implementing the decisions, in motivating people (those outside the enterprise as well as those within), and in making judgments about promotions and severances.

Conclusion

All these suggestions envisage a heroic shift in objectives and accounting methods and a jettisoning, for managerial purposes, of many traditional accounting postulates and conventions based on objectivity, verifiability, and convenience. If necessary, however, the traditional approaches could be retained for external reporting purposes when mandated by powerful institutions.

The proposed suggestions are needed to further management science; the approach is to inquire consistently as to the nature of managerial problems and to arrange all classifications, evaluations, and comparisons to produce information which is of the greatest *utility* to managers. For example, mathematical managerial models would be investigated to ascertain the characteristics of appropriate inputs, and a system (accounting and/or statistical) would be devised to monitor operations and environment and to report these data inputs at appropriate times. Finally, such inputs would include a great deal of physical and/or exogenous data. It would by no means be restricted to internal, financial matters.

NOTES

1. The choice between or among accounting principles may not affect real profits, but it can have a substantial effect on reported profits and hence on taxes. To the extent that the choice (e.g., depreciation methods or inventory pricing procedures) postpones taxes, it will increase cash flows.
2. We would even discount future wages where an employment contract provides for automatic increases. This would involve discounting future dollars to present dollars and incorporating a probability factor for separations by quits, discharges, and death.

Herbert G. Hicks

29
Codetermination: West Germany's Concept of Industrial Democracy

Three decades after the end of the [Second World War], an uneasy posture of penance has been altered, transformed now into something more comfortable and familiar to the German character: pride. The pride is readily understandable. Only seven years after surrender, German factories rebuilt with U.S. Marshall Plan aid were churning out a trade surplus; by the end of the sixties the surplus had grown twenty-fold. The now-famous *Wirtschafswunder*—the "economic miracle"—propelled the Federal Republic into the role of Western Europe's most powerful economic force. . . . How did the West Germans manage to avoid the plagues—spiraling inflation, labor strife, a weakening currency—that have afflicted other nations? And can Germany remain Western Europe's most substantial monetary and military bulwark? [1]

Full answers to these questions are not possible here. But it is possible to examine one aspect of the West German miracle, one aspect which makes labor relations in West Germany uniquely different from any other in the world. The West Germans practice a concept called *Mitbestimmung*—codetermination—a concept that has caught fire in several European nations, but is nowhere practiced as extensively as in West Germany.

What is codetermination? Basically, codetermination is the sharing of management by persons representing the workforce with persons representing the ownership, or executive managerial force, in an industry.

This chapter examines West German codetermination, looking at several aspects of this theory of labor's co-responsibility with management in decisions affecting the operations of industry. First of all, what is the historical background of codetermination? How does it work in practice? What are some attitudes toward codetermination? Has codetermination had any influence on the Common Market? And finally, what are some problems with codetermination?

HISTORICAL DEVELOPMENT OF CODETERMINATION

The idea of joint responsibility between labor and management is not a new one in Germany. Looking back over the years, we see that in 1920 the Weimar Republic inaugurated a form of codetermination. A law was passed which put "works councils" into business and industry. These works councils were primarily concerned with matters of social welfare for the workers, though in a few companies, they did have some economic control. However, the works councils had little to say on the boards of directors. Insofar as the daily management of the plant was concerned, these works councils had no authority at all. At this time, the Social Democratic Party (SDP) was demanding a full-scale economic democracy in its political program. The SDP was not impressed with the works councils—they felt that economic comanagement was the first step toward thorough-going Socialism, and began to push for just such a state of affairs. However, the rise of Hitler, with his National Socialism, ended their move, and both workers and owners found themselves marching to Hitler's tune.[2]

Condition of West Germany After World War II. In 1945, the Third Reich was dead. Paramount among the tasks facing Germany was the rebuilding and reorganizing of the industrial complex. The Zonal Military Governments were asked by a number of German state governments for permission to make comanagement compulsory in industry. Some permissions were granted, and the new system began in 1950.

These new councils were not like the works councils of the Weimar Republic. They had more economic control, and were, of course, still interested in matters of social welfare. Far from a stopgap attack on the chaos German industry was in, these new councils were the foundation of a progressive labor system that would soon be popularized and utilized nationwide.

What were the conditions in West Germany at the close of World War II? Most of the owners of the iron and steel plants in the Ruhr Valley had been associated with the Nazis. They were now either dead, in prison, or were out of the country in hiding. But the workers were available, and were eager to have a voice in the reconstruction that was about to take place.

The particular system of corporate structure in Germany was especially suited to comanagement. Unlike the familiar American structure, German joint stock and limited liability companies were by law divided into two governing bodies, the *Aufsichtsrat* and the *Vorstand*. The *Aufsichtsrat*, the lower tier, is a supervisory board of directors elected by the shareholders. The *Vorstand* is the board of management, whose members are appointed by the supervisory board. A member cannot belong to both boards. Thus, the management of companies was already effectively divided into two entities, and this made the introduction of joint management with the workers fairly simple from a structural viewpoint.

Role of the British in Establishing Codetermination. The climate in Germany after World War II was one of change—and as interested in change as anyone were the Allied powers, who realized that it was Germany's heavy industry—notably iron, coal, and steel—that had made Germany strong enough to initiate and fight two world wars. It was a matter of historical coincidence that much of the heavy industry was concentrated in the British Zone of Occupation. For when the labor unions were reorganized, and demanded that the firms be taken over by government, or, failing that, that labor have an equal voice in operating them with the owners, the Labor government of Britain agreed with the proposal. And so in the Ruhr Valley, labor came into the fore, with British concurrence, in the management of the heavy industry that was so vital to Germany's recovery.[3]

Some Influences of the German Culture. Why should the concept of employee representation be so strong in Germany? "Many societies have found other answers to this problem [of industrial democracy] than the solution practiced in Germany, and some have not felt any strong need to establish employee representation at all. What are the forces, then, conceptual and pragmatic, which created this peculiarly advanced system of participatory democracy in industry?"[4]

The first argument was that industry, which helped put Hitler in the saddle, must be watched, but as time went on and there seemed to be no danger of another Hitler coming into power, the need to watch the politics of industry diminished. However, the trade unions began to argue that large enterprises have a social relevance, and the public they so much affect should have some say in their control. There are certain social responsibilities that automatically go with the ownership of private property, the trade unions insisted. These unions saw in codetermination a way of seeing to it that industry and business lived up to social responsibilities.

Another argument put forth in favor of codetermination was that the individual worker needed more concern for his relationship to the company authorities, and even to society at large. German authority patterns before the Second World War were almost military in their severity. Some of the largest of the steel companies had been controlled by employers who cared little for the individual worker's self-esteem and welfare, and whose dictatorial methods set the style for lower echelons of management. The labor unions felt that democratization of industry would show a certain regard for employees. Further, codetermination would allow workers the opportunity to question decisions of management, and to have influence in the final judgments. According to this view the industrial firm is considered similar to a structured political system. Under codetermination, employees are representing other workers as they sit on the boards with the other directors.

A final argument for codetermination was that industry and the society in which it flourished should reinforce each other in terms of both being democratic. Democracy at work would be translated into political democracy, and vice versa. Codetermination was, in effect, seen as a kind of social revolution.

The 1951 Codetermination Law. The first codetermination law in West Germany was the 1951 Codetermination Act, which was based on the law, "On the Reorganization of German Coal Mining and the Iron and Steel Industry," published by the Allies in 1950.[5] Essentially, this act provided for parity representation on supervisory boards in the coal, iron, and steel industries. "Parity" means equal representation.

The 1951 statute accomplished two goals. It first established an 11-member supervisory board which would have five representatives of the shareholders, five members to represent the employees, and a chairman of "neutral" position. The employees chose their five representatives in the following manner: two were elected by the works council, two were appointed by the trade union, and there was one independent representative who might be a scholar, a lawyer, or a businessman, who was nominated by the trade union.

The second goal was the inclusion of a labor director on the managing board. (This labor director is the equivalent of a personnel director or industrial relations officer in the United States.) The employees' representatives on the supervisory board recommend the labor director for election. This law applied only to the coal, steel, and iron industries.

The 1952 Act. The Works Constitution Act of 1952 extended workers' representation on supervisory boards to most other companies in West Germany employing 500 or more. The act has been noted by some as laying the foundation for workers to participate in management at the lowest possible level. The 1952 act was updated and reissued in 1972. It further provided for the election of works councillors to help each industry realize that there are social consequences to market decisions, and also to give the workers a means for making known their feelings about the workplace and their work.

This law allowed for only one-third participation by employee representatives, and this was one of the reasons why it was opposed by the trade unions. Another law, passed in 1956, provided for the election of a labor director in managing boards of firms with one-third codetermination.

The 1976 Act. The most recent law is the New Codetermination Act of 1976, which went into effect on July 1, 1976. West German companies were allowed a period of two years during which they would come into compliance with the new law. The new law applies to shareholding companies with 2,000 or more workers. The coal, iron, and steel industries still operated under the old system. The 1976 law was expected to affect 600 to 650 businesses, and the employees in these businesses total 7 million. Further, approximately 23 percent of the labor force and 50 percent of the gross national product were affected under the terms of the 1976 law.

Supervisory boards depend upon the size of the firm for their numerical composition. They may have 12, 16, or 20 members. Half of the board memberships belong to the workers, half to the shareholders. The principal trade union holding collective bargaining privileges in the business has the right to name two representatives to the boards with 12 and 16 members. It may name three representatives on the 20-member boards.

The composition of the rest of the employees' delegation to the supervisory board, elected by delegates in a very complex procedure, discloses the lack of real "parity" under the new law. In all firms there are considered to be three categories of employees: wage earners, salaried employees, and senior executives. Based on proportional representation, each of the three groups must be represented on the employee side. Regardless of size, they are guaranteed at least one position in the workers' delegation. Admittedly, it is difficult to imagine a situation where the "senior executive" member of the workers' side would fail to support the shareholders' side. But if he does, there is another safeguard to insure that the shareholders will have their way.

A two-thirds majority vote of the supervisory board elects the chairman and vice-chairman. If a two-thirds majority is not achieved, the shareholders' representatives nominate the chairman, and the employees' representatives nominate the vice-chairman. The boards are composed of an even number; therefore, it is possible that an evenly split vote might occur. If that happens, the chairman may cast a second vote, which decides the issue.

The Role of Works Councils. Local unions, in the American sense, do not exist in Germany. There, unions engage in collective bargaining at the state or national level. What local unions do in the United States is more commonly performed by the works councils in German industry. Actually, these works councils were a kind of forerunner to full determination, for certain management decisions must be codetermined by management and the works councils. In other words, the works councils must give their approval. This approval is required in matters pertaining to allocation of work, transfers, policies on dismissals, and other aspects of the workers' relationship to their workplace. Besides this right, the works councils also have the right to consult with management about certain other decisions. The employer can do anything he pleases, but he must keep the works councils informed. Such matters as wage structure, training, job evaluation, discipline at the workplace, promotions, holidays, pensions, and plant health and safety beyond existing regulations are areas in which consultation is held.

CODETERMINATION IN PRACTICE

To appreciate the West German system of codetermination, let us look at codetermination in practice.

Procedure. The precise procedure under which managerial codetermination is practiced in West Germany begins with the election of the boards of directors in firms employing over 2,000 workers. The stockholders' assembly chooses one half, the other half is selected by the workers; these candidates must be nominated by one-fifth, or at least 100, of the blue collar or white collar employees, by the entire group of management employees, and by the labor union, or unions, represented in the firm.

Board Elections. In firms with more than 2,000 workers, management employees, defined as those who exercise "true entrepreneurial functions," are allowed to nominate two candidates; the one receiving the most votes from all white collar and management employees together is automatically elected to the board. The unions, too, are guaranteed the election of three of their candidates; the remaining six labor representatives are chosen by the blue and white collar employees from among their ranks in separate or joint elections, as they wish. The boards of smaller firms have fewer members, but the ratios remain the same. In firms with more than 8,000 employees, the model envisions, as a rule, election of the board members by workers' delegates, one delegate for every 60 workers, chosen either jointly or separately by the three groups according to their total number in the firm. Direct elections are also possible if desired.

Selecting the Chairman. After the complete board has been elected, the chairman and deputy chairman are then chosen. As mentioned above, the shareholders' representatives nominate the chairman, and the deputy chairman is nominated by the employees' side. If the two-thirds majority is not achieved to elect the two positions, the shareholders' representatives choose the chairman, and the employees' side chooses the deputy chairman. Then the chief executive officers are elected.[6]

The 1976 law did not change the parity system in the coal, steel, and iron industries, where deadlocks are resolved by a "neutral member" rather than by the board chairman. Further, the 1976 law does not change the two thirds/one-third capital/labor ratio in companies with less than 2,000 employees, as provided in the 1952 and 1972 laws.

EXAMPLES OF CODETERMINATION

We now examine some examples of codetermination in practice. The first example is that of an industry which has had codetermination the longest.

Codetermination in the West German Steel Industry. The West German steel industry has had experience with codetermination since World War II's aftermath. What have been the results there?

A study of ten German steel companies was conducted by W. Michael Blumenthal for the Industrial Relations Section of the Department of Economics and Sociology of Princeton University. Among his findings are the following points:

1. The labor representatives often initially lacked proper training and qualifications.

2. As a rule, labor and management were able to maintain and improve the overall operation of the enterprise and avoided serious disagreements.

3. Mutual agreement was usually achieved. The ownership representatives never chose to overrule their labor colleagues. Where voting splits did occur, they were commonly among the five members of the labor side.

4. Labor and management representatives usually engaged in a kind of "horse-trading" so that each side dealt with those areas it was the most familiar with. Equal participation by both sides in *all* decisions was replaced by a careful allocation of special rights for each of the two groups over different issues.

5. Absence of conflict is also explained by the limits on the board's functions, the fact that many issues represented earlier compromises reached elsewhere in the company, and the use of techniques to limit controversy, such as behind-the-scenes consultation, postponing and tabling important issues, and so on.

6. The labor director on the board of management was usually a well-qualified individual.

7. The labor director was given major control over labor and personnel matters and merely retained a varying measure of "questioning" rights over most other phases of management.

8. The labor director had the power to force concessions from his two colleagues because the latter were anxious to retain freedom of operation in their own areas. (The board of management in these steel companies is generally composed of three directors—a technical director, like a vice-president in charge of production in an American firm; a commercial director, in charge of the firm's sales, purchasing, accounting, and advertising activities; and the labor director.)

9. The level of labor earnings rose more in the steel companies than in comparable German noncodetermination industries, even more than in certain other industries represented by the same union and facing similar market conditions.

10. Greater labor earnings in iron and steel were not apparently attributable to higher productivity or greatly increased output. Most executives thought that the role of the labor director and labor representatives had been instrumental in bringing about higher labor earnings.

11. The expenditures on voluntary social benefits increased substantially under codetermination.

12. The company's ability to make layoffs, necessitated by cutbacks in production schedules, was not appreciably affected by codetermination in the long run. However, the period necessary to do so was apparently drawn out. More careful and just procedures (to the workers) were probably used to carry out these adjustments.

13. The labor director was often successful in bringing about a substantial improvement in employee-management communication in the plant.

14. Codetermination does not seem to have had any other important effects on the prevailing personnel administration practices.

15. There was a convincing body of direct and indirect evidence that the incidence of strikes and work stoppage declined under codetermination.

16. Other indices of the industrial climate showed no sign of dissatisfaction with codetermination. Few plant grievances could not be settled at relatively low levels in the companies and had to be taken to the labor courts for adjudication.

In his conclusion, Blumenthal states: "It is clear that codetermination is a peculiarly German phenomenon which developed only because of a particular historical and environmental setting. Perhaps it provided a means of overcoming the traditional intransigence of many German employers in their dealings with workers. . . . Codetermination may have been a good means of accomplishing for German labor what American workers . . . have long since achieved by other means." [7]

The Porst Group. For another example in codetermination, let's look at the Porst group, which has extended the managerial concept of codetermination into a profit-sharing plan as well.

This group is formed of three companies. They are united under a general holding company, Porst Verwaltungs GmbH. Cameras are sold and distributed by Photo Porst KG, which obtains the cameras, made to its own specifications, from a variety of other countries. The photographic processing workshop that serves Photo Porst is Eurocop KG. Finally, the third company is Deutscher Supplement Verlag, a publishing venture which sells a television program guide to approximately 200 German newspapers. The legal management board of the holding company is made up of Porst, president of Photo Porst; the president of Eurocop; and the group personnel and finance directors. This board is extended to take in three other functional directors, however (the three directors of codetermination—technical, commercial, and labor).

A nine-member supervisory board oversees the managing board.

This supervisory board is loaded in favor of the employees' representatives. Five of the board members are elected by the workers, with two being chosen by Mitarbeiter Beteiligungs GmbH (MAB), a company which has been set up to take care of the employees' 50 percent monetary share in the Porst group.

MAB's two boards, management and supervisory, are chosen by the employees. Two other directors come from the outside, and are nominated by the Porst family's foundation, which controls the remaining shares.

At year's end, the Porst family foundation receives a share of the profits that equate to a return on its investment of 3 percent above the current bank rate. They receive a minimum return of 7.5 percent. The remaining money is put back into the business for the workers. It is not unusual for the workers' share of the profits to amount to 8 percent of their investment.[8]

Another interesting aspect of the Porst group's venture into codetermination is that the managers are all carefully examined by the employees every two years. The manager actually has to step down if a majority of the workers under him decide they no longer approve of him as boss. The company does try to find another job for such managers, and they usually suffer no pay loss. Even Porst goes through the examining procedure.

A happy result of the experiment, according to Porst, is that labor turnover has gone down by two-thirds over the past three years, during the time that the worker participation scheme was being implemented. The Porst group is therefore a good example of how codetermination in management can lead to a sharing of profits with workers and to even greater worker participation in management.

The Volkswagen Experience. In early 1974, Volkswagen plunged into the red and had losses close to a billion marks by the following year. A new chairman was called in—and his first proposal was to cut the workforce by one-fifth—23,000 employees. The supervisory board which had to vote on this proposal was composed of two-thirds capital, one-third labor. For the first time in the supervisory board's history, the vote was not unanimous. The workers' side naturally voted against the layoff. However, the owners' majority prevailed. Once the layoff was a reality, the unions and workers were in full cooperation. They called neither for a strike, nor for violence. The workers, each of whom received $4,000 in severance pay, just left. Much of the layoff was achieved by older men retiring, working wives leaving, and by foreign workers going home.

A second proposal voted for by the workers' representatives was that VW build an assembly plant "in the U.S. to make Volkswagens more competitive there. . . . To safeguard German jobs, the workers had won agreement that cars from the American plant would not be sold outside the U.S. or Canada, and that additions to the plant would have to be approved by the supervisory board. The episode illustrates the power of *Mitbestimmung:* To force a company to take the interest of its workers into consideration before making a major decision, and to provide a mechanism for finding peaceful solutions." [9]

ATTITUDES TOWARD CODETERMINATION

Whenever such a sweeping change is made in the economic life of a country, strong opinions will be voiced and definite attitudes revealed. What, then, are some of the attitudes toward codetermination in West Germany?

Poll Results. Not all West German industrialists are sold on codetermination. A poll taken early in 1976, before the new act was passed, showed that 25 percent of the businessmen asked were for the new proposal (passed later in 1976), while 46 percent of those asked in the population as a whole were in favor of it.[10]

Government Opinion of Codetermination. Spokesmen for the West German government see codetermination as a major force in helping the Federal Republic of Germany achieve social peace since the end of World War II. Chancellor Helmut Schmidt believes that workers, by sharing in the industrial decision-making process, come from a position of opposing management to one of sharing responsibility with management. He further believes that codetermination held the incidence of strikes down to 26 days per year per 1,000 workers in 1973, and that it also is responsible for the fact that labor settlements have been termed reasonable and justified by independent experts.

Of course, the experience with codetermination by the iron, coal, and steel industries is a telling point for the government side. More than 400,000 mining jobs had to be eliminated between 1957 and 1973, and it was codetermination, so the government maintains, that helped achieve these layoffs more painlessly. There was a kind of teamwork between labor and management on such difficult problems as mine closings, reemployment and retraining programs, and early retirement. This teamwork accomplished the layoff without the usual conflicts and stalemates that might be expected.

The Politics of Codetermination. Codetermination was a political football prior to the passage of the 1976 act. Chief opponents were the Social Democratic Party (SDP), which is heavily union-supported, and the Free Democratic Party (FDP), which has the support of businessmen and professionals. "The FDP . . . agreed to support a compromise law . . . at the urging of the SDP. . . . Since then, the Free Democrats have suffered severe election losses in Hesse and Bavaria, as well as a slump in monetary contributions. To head off further losses, FDP chairman Hans-Dietrich Genscher wants to recast the codetermination bill to reduce the power of organized labor." [11]

As we saw when we studied the 1976 law, the act finally passed does not give labor the true "parity" that it so badly wanted.

Businessmen's Fears. What exactly are West German businessmen afraid of under codetermination, as reflected in the poll taken among them? After all, the government has praised codetermination as a "peace-keeping" device. Specifically, the new law strengthens the works councils. They have more real power in the day-to-day affairs of the firm, including a voice in decisions about such things as hours, holidays, rates of pay, and hirings and firings. They even have the power to require that any new jobs be offered first to present employees.

Further, works councils are now backed up by a conciliation board. Employers and employees are equally represented on this board, and there is a neutral chairman with a casting vote. If labor and management cannot come to terms about a problem, this conciliation board would have the final say. Therefore, management could find itself overruled on such vital matters as plant closures or mergers—even though, technically, the conciliation board is supposed to take the industry's economic interest into account. [12]

CODETERMINATION AND THE COMMON MARKET

Another effect of codetermination is seen in the Common Market. Since 1972, the EEC Commission's efforts have been directed toward giving workers seats on the boards of all EEC public companies. Countries outside of codetermination's West German bailiwick have become interested in the new experiment, even though the EEC is now admitting that the two-tier board might not be everyone's cup of tea. However, the EEC plan still wants to see directors chosen from the workers having seats on supervisory boards. Also, the EEC plan calls for a great degree of flexibility as nations try to incorporate codetermination into their socioeconomic structures. It does not prescribe any particular form of participation, but does suggest that the

German-style or the Dutch-style boards be tried. The Dutch boards give one-third of the seats to the shareholders, one-third to the workers, and one-third is co-opted by both sides.[13]

There are several examples of codetermination in Common Market countries. The first, of course, is West Germany, which began the whole thing, and whose influence has made codetermination an issue of some importance within the Common Market.

Dutch trade unions unfortunately are putting pressure on the Dutch law of 1971. It is unfortunate because the Dutch method in some ways is more attractive than the German. The supervisory boards in Holland do have extensive powers, and their memberships are equally divided between worker and shareholder representatives. However, either the shareholders or the executive committee of the works councils may nominate members to the board, and may also object to a nominee because of unsuitability, or "because it would mean that the supervisory board was not 'properly composed.' "[14]

France has had the most discussion on codetermination. President Giscard d'Estaing appointed a 12-man committee with Pierre Sudreau as leader in 1974 to look into the reform of France's antiquated company laws. It was hoped that part of the committee's work would be to come up with a reasonable structure for worker participation in the governing of industry.

The Sudreau report comprised 90 proposals. Important among these was the proposal for "co-surveillance" boards, which would give French employees the right to elect a third of the directors. Actually, these boards would be a form of cosupervision rather than the German model of codetermination. However, the two most important French union federations are not in favor of workers participating in management. They see management and labor as having different functions, and do not want to mix the two.

The winds of change that have blown across Germany since after World War II seem to be sweeping across the Continent, challenging other industrial democracies to bring the democracy of the political systems into the productions systems as well.

SOME PROBLEMS OF CODETERMINATION

No system of economic change can be effected without concomitant problems. I have touched on problems to a degree, pointing out the fear of German businessmen that the 50/50 codetermination that is the result of the 1976 law could impede the progress of industries and work to the economic detriment of Germany. There are other specific problems, as well as certain conceptual ones.

Problems of Multinationals (MNCs). One specific problem is the effect of the German codetermination law on multinational companies, more particularly, on American multinationals. Statistics show that 70 of our biggest 200 companies and 260 of the top 500 either have German subsidiaries or affiliates. Of these, 6 rank among the top 50 companies in Germany, 18 are found in the top 200—and these together account for more than 10 percent of West Germany's total capitalization. In the last five years, our American direct investment in West Germany has grown at about 10 percent a year.

What do these figures mean in terms of the vulnerability of American multinationals to the mechanics of codetermination? Consider some views of George S. McIsaac and Herbert Henzler. Writing before passage of the 1976 law, they pointed out that if the 1976 law passed, codetermination would likely be extended to all major industries and firms—and that scores of U.S. and other foreign-based multinationals would be included in this expansion. Becoming subjects of a new kind of industrial learning experience could be painful for these companies. First of all, they might be getting a foretaste of a new kind of labor-management partnership that would soon be across German borders. Second, the peaceful transactions between MNCs and the sovereign host nation might come to a halt. Already, the American Chamber of Commerce in Germany has protested to Federal Chancellor Helmut Schmidt and to the leaders of the parties in the Bonn parliament, as well as to the U.S. State Department. The chamber hired a noted law professor, Wilhelm Wengler, to prepare the brief upon which the protest is based. This brief denies in no uncertain terms that the new law can legally be applied to foreign-owned companies that already exist in West Germany. To do so would be to breach the German-American trade treaty of 1954. This treaty laid out the rights of American companies operating in West Germany once that country was again a sovereign power.

German labor and government leaders were not pleased with what they saw as interference by U.S. business with West Germany's own affairs. And it is hardly to be expected that the West German government will exempt U.S. subsidiaries and affiliates from the requirements of its own domestic law. The multinationals are right to be anxious. The new law makes it entirely possible that workforce representatives on the supervisory board will be able to call the tune on such important issues as investments or divestments, the repatriation of dividends, the appointment or replacement of key managers, and other critical matters.

For foreign-based companies, of course, these decision areas are especially vulnerable to possible interference on nationalistic grounds. German labor, like labor all over the world, has always tended to give very high priority to national self-interest, and it takes no great amount of imagination to detect a strain of economic nationalism in the current German mood. Depending on the aggressiveness of labor representation on the supervisory board, it could be but a short step from the decisions mentioned above to such delicate matters for multinationals as transfer pricing and financing policy. This could be the hidden noose of codetermination.[15]

Because of the ever-increasing interdependence of nations, it is hardly possible for one link in the chain to change its shape or size without affecting the other links. German codetermination is of interest, not only to that country, but to all who deal with it or work in it.

Conceptual Problems. Besides specific problems of codetermination, there are five general conceptual problems, as stated by Dr. Klaus Fassler, Siemens AG, Munich:[16]

The following five essential sets of problems can be distinguished:

1. The motives of those who demand codetermination within a firm (codetermination, why?)
2. The form in which industrial codetermination is carried out (codetermination, through whom?)
3. The scope of industrial codetermination (codetermination, which decisions?)
4. The intensity of industrial codetermination (codetermination, how strong?)
5. The bases for legitimatizing codetermination (codetermination, on what power base?)

To answer the first question—*"codetermination, why"*—Fassler says that workers' motivation may be understood by the concept of business as a social order—as a group of people, and a group of groups of people. When all interest groups in the enterprise cooperate, a potential value or profit is created. This value, which may be income, or chances of promotion, or employment security, should be distributed in such a way as to answer the needs or demands of the members of the groups. Ordinarily, the needs of the group are boundless, while the value has definite limits. Therefore, there will be tension and conflict among the members of the groups. "In this connection, codetermination can be on the one hand a means to an end if it is the medium for realizing personal aims (that is, workers hope codetermination will bring improved incomes). On the other hand, codetermination can appear as an end in itself, for codetermination in the sense of self-determination as against determination by others. Codetermination now stands in addition to the need to obtain a certain income, for example."

The question of *codetermination, through whom* is answered in two ways—either direct participation with every member of the group having a say, or indirectly, with delegates or representatives of the groups having the say. Most groups use delegates, as in a common response to what is rather a law of nature; social organizations of a certain size seem to form power structures of an oligarchic type. But when indirect codetermination is used, this leads to the problems associated with management selection and management legitimization.

The *scope of codetermination* by workers or workers' representatives can be limited by the things with which the group deals—codetermination, which decisions? Codetermination can be used for decisions about the aims of a business, and also for decisions about how these aims will be reached. When any group is trying to determine which decisions will be discussed and made, that group must remember that interdependence of aims and means must be considered. Any decisions which have to do with the budget of the enterprise are tightly bound up with each other. It is not possible to make a decision about wages, say, without also considering dividends and salaries. The common interests dictate a compromise solution.

"The question of *the intensity of industrial codetermination* opens up a much wider set of problems. The organizational decision-making process can be seen as a process of obtaining and processing information which goes through the stages of stimulation, looking for alternatives, optimizing the decision-making problem and control." Each member of the group may take part in this process differently. If a member has the authority to bring about a particular decision, he obviously has the greatest influence in information processing. But if a member is involved only in acquiring and processing preparatory information, the influence of that member is smaller.

When examining *the power base behind codetermination,* the discussion, according to Fassler,

must move into political dispute. The cornerstone of any new arrangement is the distribution of the power bases of the interest groups organized within the enterprise. This new arrangement must be made under consideration of the possible consequences for individual sectors and for the economy as a whole. . . . Undoubtedly, extension of qualified codetermination leads to redistribution of power from the group of capital owners to that of workers.

It must be considered, and also asked, whether an altered decision-making and governing power does not have a negative effect on the extent of the "value volume" which is to be distributed.

These five conceptual questions would pertain to any group considering codetermination. Because of the experience of West Germany with codetermination in the years since World War II, an educated guess as to the answers to these questions can probably be made by any nation considering the same socioeconomic system.

SUMMARY

This chapter has tried to give an overview of the nature of codetermination and some of the problems, both conceptual and specific, that arise from this particular type of industrial democracy. We have discussed codetermination in the Common Market, some attitudes to codetermination, looked at codetermination in practice, and seen its historical development from the 1920s in the Weimar Republic to the most recent law.

The opening statement concerned the miraculous growth of West Germany from the chaos of defeat at the end of World War II to its present enviable economic condition. Questions about West Germany were asked—how it has avoided the economic problems that beset its competitors, whether or not it can remain an example of stability—and codetermination was explored as a partial answer to these questions. When a new method of doing business is introduced into an economy, and when business improves, it behooves us to look closely at the innovation. Whether or not codetermination as practiced by West Germany is a signpost to the road ahead for other countries as we move toward the last decades of this century is a matter for conjecture. But there is no question that this movement has sparked the fire of change, and has stilled some cries for participatory management very effectively.

In conclusion, the West German use of codetermination offers a profound experience that appears to deserve the close attention of government leaders and managers throughout the world.

REFERENCES

1. John J. Putnam, "West Germany: Continuing Miracle," *National Geographic*, August 1977, p. 149.
2. Jeremiah Newman, *Co-responsibility in Industry* (Westminster: The Newman Press, 1955), pp. 20–22.
3. *Columbia Journal of World Business*, January–February 1970, p. 50.
4. Heinz Hartmann, "Codetermination in West Germany," *Industrial Relations*, February 1970, p. 140.
5. The following discussion of the background and history of this law is drawn from *American Federationist*, October 1977, pp. 10–13.
6. Ann M. Dreyer, *Challenge*, March–April 1976, p. 55.
7. W. Michael Blumenthal, *Codetermination in the German Steel Industry*, Industrial Relations Section of the Department of Economics and Sociology of Princeton University, 1956, pp. 107–110, 114.
8. David Clutterback, "Porst Focuses on Company Democracy," *International Management*, August 1976, pp. 37, 38.
9. Putnam, "West Germany: Continuing Miracle," p. 162.
10. Dreyer, p. 56.
11. *Business Week*, January 27, 1975, p. 64.
12. *Economist*, November 13, 1971, p. 95.
13. *Economist*, November 15, 1975, p. 20.
14. Trevor Owens, *Personnel Management*, February 1976, pp. 16–18.
15. George S. McIsaac and Herbert Henzler, "Codetermination: A Hidden Noose for MNCs," *Columbia Journal of World Business*, Winter 1974, p. 68.
16. The following discussion is drawn from Klaus Fassler, *Management International Review*, Vol. 10, 1970/2–3, pp. 105–114.

Peter F. Drucker

30
Why Management Consultants?

The management consultant has come to be taken for granted. But the management consultant is an extraordinary and indeed a truly unique phenomenon. There is no precedent for him and no parallel. The management consultant is not only a major part of the practice of management. He has been, above all, central to the development of the theory, the discipline, and the profession of management.

There is "management science" and there is "art" in management. But management itself is a "practice," just as is law and medicine. In every practice, it is the practitioner rather than the scholar who develops the discipline, who synthesizes experience into testable concepts, that is into theory, who codifies, who finds and tests new knowledge, and who teaches and sets the example. In every practice, it is the practitioner who leads the profession and who has responsibility, both for the advancement of its capacity to perform and for its ethics.

It should thus not be much of a surprise that among the great men of management there are only two pure scholars, Max Weber and Elton Mayo. In this respect, management is indeed no different from medicine or from law, where the pure scholars are commentators and codifiers rather than major originators. But management is very different in respect to the kind of practitioner who has been a leader and a founding father.

To be sure, there are among management's great names quite a few pure practitioners, that is, people who made major contribution in and through their own work and leadership: a Towne, for instance, a Pierre DuPont or an Alfred Sloan, to name some of the Americans; a Georg Siemens in Germany, or a Hans Renold in Great Britain. Management also has its practitioner-scholars. In the early years there was Shibusawa Eichii in Meiji Japan; Seebohm Rowntree, Henri Fayol, and Walter Rathenau in Europe before World War I; and Chester Barnard in the interwar years. These men, like medicine's William Osler or Chief Justice Coke in the law, were eminent practitioners who then distilled a lifetime of experience and performance into pioneering theory and management philosophy.

But what is unique to management is that from the very beginning the consultant played a key role in the development of the practice, the knowledge and the profession of management. There were Frederick W. Taylor, Gantt and the Gilbreths; Eugen Schmalenbach and Mary Parker Follett; Lyndall Urwick and Harold Smiddy. There are counselors and advisors in other areas, too. But only in management is there the professional consultant. And only in management has the consultant become a central figure as a practitioner, but also as the fountainhead of knowledge, as the leader in thought, in conceptualization, and in establishing a profession. Surely, this is a remarkable phenomenon. But even more remarkable is that apparently no one has yet asked, "Why management consultants?"

One reason for the role of the consultant in management is precisely that management is a practice rather than a science or an art. In a practice, one gains insight through practice. One learns by synthesizing experience into knowledge. One advances by testing concepts on cases. To be sure, exposure by itself is not enough, for it may only mean busyness. But in a practice, one cannot learn without exposure. There are no "thought experiments" in a practice, but also there is no laboratory. There are only cases. Without exposure to cases, a practice can develop neither a body of knowledge nor the practitioner's own diagnostic capacity and professional character. In medicine, the exposure is built into both training and practice. The cases are in the hospital or come into the physician's office. In the law, exposure is built into the practice and can be simulated in the classroom. In management, however, if the practitioner is a practicing executive, he lacks exposure. He has enough practice, but it is mostly, if not always, with the same "patient." He works with the same organization—or at most, with very few. He lacks exposure and cannot gain it. Nor can he simulate it.

And this, clearly, is the first reason why the management consultant emerged, both in the practice and in the discipline of management. The consultant is a practitioner and, in this respect, like any other executive. But unlike the executive in the organization, the consultant has exposure. He sees and treats, as it were, a great many patients and studies a great many cases. He has exposure in depth, but also in breadth and variety. Even the most conceited consultant would not claim that he knows more than his clients, the executives in organizations. Indeed, every consultant knows that his clients are his teachers and that he lives off their knowledge. The consultant does not know more. But he has seen more.

But there is a subtler and perhaps even more important reason for the emergence and the importance of the consultant in the practice, the discipline, and the profession of management. "It is a fool who has himself for a client," says an old legal proverb. And physicians learned long ago not to treat their own families, let alone themselves. The professional needs commitment to the client's cause or to the patient's recovery. But he must stay free of involvement. He must not himself be a part of the problem. And the practitioner-executive is always a part of the problem, is, indeed, as Chester Barnard first pointed out, always the main problem. The practitioner-executive cannot treat his organization without treating himself. That his own interests are at stake is probably quite irrelevant; the present-day belief that a responsible professional cannot rise above his own self-interest is little but vulgar superstition. But the executive in an organization is also always a member of the organization, shares its traditions, its beliefs, its joys and its sorrows, its greatness and its pettinesses. He is like the physician who treats his own family—he diagnoses with the heart and always takes his own pulse rather than that of the patient.

And thus, the management consultant brings to the practice of management what being professional requires: detachment. He makes it possible to have a professional diagnostician in management, a professional therapist and a true scholar. In other words, he makes it possible for management to be a practice and yet be a profession and a discipline.

But this also raises a serious dilemma, the dilemma of the large, diversified, and complex organization. For to practice management successfully for such an organization, a great deal of specific knowledge and information is needed, which is difficult to acquire in casual contact. It requires the insider. But to be effective as a professional requires the outsider.

It is this dilemma to which Harold Smiddy addressed himself when he first created in a large company, General Electric, the inside management consulting staff, which is both truly professional and detached, and an insider. Lyndall Urwick, the Englishman, can be said to have created the profession of management consultancy. There were management consultants before Urwick—Taylor, Gantt, the Gilbreths, and that remarkable pioneer, Mary Parker Follett. It was Urwick, however, who first established a professional consulting practice, worked out the concepts for it, the rules, the standards, and the relationships. It was then Harold Smiddy in America—25 years later—who took the professional consulting practice into the large, diversified, and complex business enterprise.

And the practice of management, precisely because it is a practice, needs both the outside management consultant who practices on his own, and the inside management consultant who is not only a professional, but also a conscience within the large, complex, and diversified enterprise.

Lyndall F. Urwick

31
Epilogue

When at the beginning of the twentieth century, the American mechanical engineer Frederick Winslow Taylor first suggested that the processes of managing in business and in other forms of human collaboration might be analyzed and applied scientifically, he put a match to the train of what he himself described as "a mental revolution." [1] Yet within a dozen years of Taylor's early death at the age of fifty-nine in 1915, the World Economic Congress of 1927 was recommending those ideas to the nations as a means of correcting the economic confusion which was the aftermath of World War I. [2]

This was a remarkable acceptance of a group of ideas which their own author had described as "revolutionary." Insofar as Taylor's ideas really were accepted by business leaders, generally that result can be traced to the vigor and energy with which they were applied both educationally and also practically by certain progressive corporations in his own country, the United States. In 1884, the year in which Taylor was, more or less informally, appointed Chief Engineer of the Midvale Steel Company, there was one university in the United States teaching management formally. By 1927 there were 108, and, by 1947, 158. It was a remarkable development of educational faculties in a new field of study. [3]

It could not have taken place without the energy and enthusiasm with which certain leading corporations in the United States, and in other countries, adopted Taylor's general philosophy. And this again could not have taken place without the skill and dedication with which certain leading executives in those great corporations devoted themselves to introducing the idea of a more scientific approach to problems of management.

Among such corporations, the General Electric Company from 1940 onwards was outstanding. Its president was Ralph Cordiner and his principal assistant in the task was Harold Smiddy.

Harold Smiddy did not write very much. He probably felt, and rightly, that in the very large and practical task which faced him, too much penmanship would be offering hostages to fortune. It is virtually impossible in any book to record fully and accurately *all* the human complications involved in any reorganization of a large and ongoing human undertaking. Statements in print necessarily oversimplify the human factors involved. And the writer's words are quoted back at him in situations which, while they may appear similar, in fact, do not remotely resemble the "model" about which he has written.

In this writer's personal library of management literature, collected since 1915, there are, however, three volumes published by the General Electric Company in 1956. The set, which owes its existence to Harold Smiddy, is entitled *Some Classic Contributions to Professional Managing.*[4]

Yet, even here, his self-imposed modesty about penmanship holds good. The three volumes contain in all 782 pages. Of these, only 42 pages, or less than 6 percent, are from Smiddy's own pen. And of this modest contribution, 31 pages, or more than 75 percent, are a joint article written with Lionel Naum and reprinted from *Management Science*, Volume I, October 1954, under the title, "Evolution of a 'Science of Managing' in America." Could self-restraint from excessive penmanship go further?

It was because his contemporaries felt this self-restraint in Harold Smiddy, this absolute dedication to the job in hand, this indifference to personal reputation as advertisement, that he has won the respect of students of management all over the world.

NOTES AND REFERENCES

1. "Scientific management cannot be said to exist, then, in any establishment until after this change has taken place in the mental attitude of both the management and the men, both as to their duty to cooperation in producing the largest possible surplus and as to the necessity for substituting exact scientific knowledge for opinion or the old rule-of-thumb or individual knowledge." F. W. Taylor, Testimony before the Special Committee appointed by the House of Representatives, Jan. 25, 1912, reprinted in *Scientific Management* (New York: Harper, 1947), p. 31.
2. See Urwick, *The Meaning of Rationalization* (London: Nisbet, 1929), for a

discussion of the relation between Taylor's ideas and the resolutions of the World Economic Conference of 1927.

3. "Education for Management"—Report of a Visit to the U.S.A. in 1951 of a Specialist Team concerned with Education for Management, Anglo-American Council on Productivity, November 1951, Appendix VII, p. 48.

4. The three volumes are: *Selected Papers* (Vol. I); *Historical Perspectives* (Vol. II); *New Perspectives in Management* (Vol. III), by Henry Arthur Hopf.

About the Contributing Authors

PETER F. DRUCKER
Clarke Professor of Social Sciences at the Claremont University Graduate School

DENNIS J. GAFFNEY
Associate Professor of Accounting, Michigan State University Graduate School of Business Administration

BILLY E. GOETZ
Professor of Accounting, Florida Atlantic University

RONALD G. GREENWOOD
Professor of Management and Marketing, University of Wisconsin

HERBERT G. HICKS
Professor of Management, Louisiana State University College of Business Administration

REGINALD H. JONES
Chairman and Chief Executive Officer, General Electric Company

482

HAROLD KOONTZ
Mead Johnson Professor of Management, Graduate School of Management, University of California Los Angeles, and Chancellor of the International Academy of Management

PRESTON P. LE BRETON
Professor of Management, University of Washington Graduate School of Business Administration

JOHN F. MEE
Mead Johnson Professor of Management, Indiana University School of Business

ANDREW F. MORLION, O.P.
Chancellor, International University of Social Studies "Pro Deo," Rome

LIONEL NAUM
Assistant to the President, Division Director for Life Sciences and for Social Sciences, Syracuse Research Corporation

WILLIAM H. NEWMAN
Samuel Bronfman Professor of Democratic Business Enterprise, Columbia University Graduate School of Business

GEORGE A. STEINER
Director, Center for Research and Dialogue on Business and Society and Professor of Management and Public Policy, University of California Los Angeles Graduate School of Management

STANLEY C. VANCE
William B. Stokely Professor of Management, University of Tennessee College of Business Administration

JAMES C. WORTHY
Professor of Management, Northwestern University Graduate School of Management

LYNDALL F. URWICK
Director of the former International Management Institute and subsequently founder and Chairman of Directors of Urwick, Orr and Partners Limited, Management Consultants

MELVIN ZIMET
Associate Professor of Management, Manhattan College

Index

484